W9-BKX-634

W9-BKX-634

DISCOVERY OF

LOST WORLDS

Edited by JOSEPH J. THORNDIKE, Jr.

Published by AMERICAN HERITAGE PUBLISHING CO., INC., New York
Book Trade Distribution by SIMON AND SCHUSTER, New York

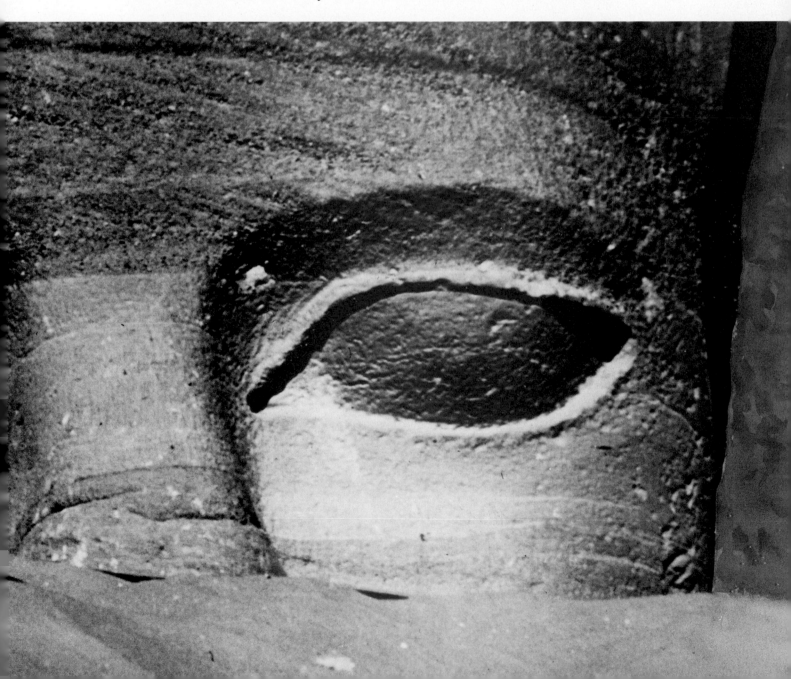

AMERICAN HERITAGE BOOKS
DIRECTOR
Beverley Hilowitz

Staff for This Book
EDITOR
Joseph J. Thorndike, Jr.
ART DIRECTOR
Murray Belsky
ASSOCIATE EDITOR
Constance R. Roosevelt
MANAGING EDITOR
Brenda Niemand
PICTURE EDITOR
Gail Nussbaum
ANTHOLOGY EDITOR
Henry Wiencek
ASSISTANT EDITORS
Kate Delano Condax, Donna Whiteman
FOREIGN PICTURE RESEARCHERS
Rosemary L. Klein, *London*
Maria Terese Hirschkoff, *Paris*

AMERICAN HERITAGE PUBLISHING CO., INC.
CHAIRMAN OF THE BOARD
Samuel P. Reed
PUBLISHER
Beverley Hilowitz

HALF-TITLE PAGE: *An Etruscan warrior head*
VILLA GIULIA
TITLE PAGE: *The eyes of the pharaoh Ramses II gaze over the sands at Abu Simbel.*
PIERRE BOULAT

Library of Congress Cataloging in Publication Data
Main entry under title:
Discovery of lost worlds.
    Includes index.
    1. Civilization, Ancient—Addresses, essays, lectures. 2. Antiquities—Addresses, essays, lectures. I. Thorndike, Joseph J., 1913—
CB311.D516   930   79-15881
ISBN 0-8281-0308-9
ISBN 0-8281-0309-7 deluxe

CONTENTS

INTRODUCTION

Before the Renaissance, man's knowledge was equally restricted in time and in space. Geographers knew as little about distant places as historians knew about the remote past. In the great burst of oceanic exploration that began with Prince Henry the Navigator, the world was rounded and the shores of the continents mapped with what seems in retrospect amazing speed. In our own time the last mountain top and jungle valley have been laid bare to men's eyes. Geographically speaking, there is no mystery left on the planet.

Discoveries in time did not come so fast. During the Renaissance, scholars burrowing into long-neglected libraries rediscovered the classical world of Greece and Rome. But there their knowledge stopped. The ancients themselves, it was quite apparent, had scant knowledge of what had happened before their own times. Vaguely it was known that other civilizations had existed before the classical age, especially in Egypt. But they had left few records and most of those were written in languages that could not be read. Much of what they had built lay buried under the earth.

In the eighteenth century the excavation of the buried cities of Pompeii and Herculaneum kindled Europe's fascination with its past, but still that past was limited to the Greco-Roman world. For the first great breakthrough in the rediscovery of the preclassical world, archaeology owes a debt to Napoleon. Along with the army that he led into Egypt in 1798 he took a corps of savants. To Europe they brought back an eye-opening record of a civilization more than three thousand years old.

In other areas there had been not one continuing civilization but many successive ones, and their traces were buried deep. The difficulty of finding them and sorting them out is exemplified by the long history of mistaken notions about Troy.

The site of Troy was known to the Greeks of the classical age, but its history was known only from Homer's *Iliad*, an epic tale of events that had supposedly happened some eight centuries before. The early Greek heroes who had conquered Troy were held in reverence. When Alexander came to the site on his way to the conquest of Persia, he stripped and oiled his body, according to ancient custom, and raced naked around what passed for the tomb of Achilles. Five centuries later the emperor Caracalla, who hero-worshiped both Achilles and Alexander, did the same thing, drawing some laughter from his cynical Roman legionaries. During the next thousand years or so the very site of Troy was lost to memory.

So matters stood when a German businessman named Heinrich Schliemann arrived in 1868 to search for the real Troy. From close comparison of the *Iliad* with the geography of the area, he concluded that the ancient city must lie beneath a hill known as Hissarlik. Four summers of digging laid bare layer upon layer of ancient construction but little in the way of treasure. What happened next is the classic rainbow's end of archaeology. On the very last day before he planned to end the dig, a glint in the bottom of a trench caught his eye. Within a few hours on a hot June morning he dug out a princely cache of gold rings, bracelets, necklaces, and diadems, together with objects of silver and ivory. As he brought them forth he deposited them in his wife's red shawl. Schliemann had no doubt about what he had found. "Priam's treasure!" he proclaimed—the king's hoard that must have been packed in Troy's last hours but lost in the destruction of the city.

It was not Priam's treasure. The archaeologists who followed Schliemann have identified no fewer than forty-six layers of settlement at the site of Troy; the hoard that Schliemann found was buried in a layer that dates from a thousand years before Homeric Troy. They have identified the level that must have been a living city in the thirteenth century B.C., when Troy supposedly fell to the Greeks. But still they have found no clear evidence that the Trojan War was fought there.

Elsewhere archaeologists have had more luck in linking their discoveries to names and places familiar from the ancient writings. Paul Emile Botta unearthed the palace of the Assyrian king Sargon II at Khorsabad. Robert Koldewey identified the Tower of Babel as a Sumerian ziggurat. Leonard Woolley found evidence at Ur of the Biblical Flood (or at least of a severe flood in the Mesopotamian Valley around Noah's legendary time). In the ancient lands between the eastern Mediterranean and India, archaeologists have made historic sense of a whole parade of civilizations including some—Hittite, Minoan, Mitannian, Indus River Valley—that were hardly more than names, if that, to scholars of a hundred years ago.

By modern standards some of the nineteenth-century archaeologists were scandalously careless of what they found. It comes as a shock to find John Lloyd Stephens, the respected discoverer of Mayan cities, telling how he shot the sculptured face off a goddess on an Egyptian temple (see page 280). Or Lady Hester Stanhope ordering the deliberate destruction of a fine statue her crew dug up in Syria. Any museum curator today would gasp at the methods of Giovanni Belzoni, an Italian of huge size who had made his living as a strong man before he began searching out Egyptian antiquities. Recounting his exploits at the necropolis of Thebes, he wrote: "When my weight bore on the body of an Egyptian, it crushed like a band-box. I sunk altogether among the broken mummies with a crash, of bones, rags, and wooden cases." Yet Belzoni performed great feats of archaeology in partially clearing the sand from the great temple of Abu Simbel, discovering the sepulcher of the pharaoh Seti I, and opening the pyramid of Chephren at Giza. At least he got to some of these places ahead of the grave robbers.

The common purpose of most of the early archaeologists was to find some splendid treasure, grab it, and bear it back in triumph to their own country. The same impulse that led Lord Elgin to wrench the marble sculptures from the Parthenon led Austen Henry Layard to ship the man-headed beasts of Nimrud back to London.

Whether society has gained or lost from such plundering is a question. The Elgin marbles are carefully protected in the British Museum, whereas the sculpture that remains on the Acropolis is being eaten away by the acids in the air of Athens. On the other hand, the carvings on the Egyptian obelisk called Cleopatra's Needle are disintegrating just as fast in the New York smog.

In any event, the freebooting period of archaeology began to peter out after the First World War. The early archaeologists had much in common with the Gold Rush pioneers, who found nuggets lying in stream beds and ore in veins close to the surface. The treasures of the past are hidden now, and deeper, if they are there at all. And the laws of most nations now forbid their export.

Some modern archaeologists are looking further back, beyond the time of palaces and golden diadems, to the simple societies that preceded the rise of civilization. They have the benefit of new technology such as radiocarbon dating and microscopic pollen analysis. With such tools they have pushed the beginnings of agriculture back to some time around the eighth milennium B.C. Art is much older, stretching into the past beyond the splendors of the Lascaux and Altamira caves to images sculpted in stone or clay some thirty thousand years ago. That takes us two thirds of the way back to the crucial time (between forty and forty-five thousand years ago) when modern man—Cro-Magnon man or *Homo sapiens sapiens*—got the upper hand over Neanderthal man. From there it is a long and generally unmarked journey back down the evolutionary trail for three million years to the first manlike creatures in Olduvai Gorge.

The findings of the new, scientific archaeology do not generally contradict the conclusions of the pioneers, although they may refine the dating. It is still true that the first civilizations, marked by cities, governments, armies, laws, religion, and writing, arose in the Mesopotamian Valley between three and four thousand B.C. and at the same time or almost as soon (though without cities) in Egypt. It is during that magic millennium that the comprehensible record of civilized man begins. The discovery of selected chapters of that record is the subject of this book.

1: The Earliest Cities

by LIONEL CASSON

This fond Sumerian couple, depicted in a clay votive offering, lived about 2700 B.C. The background picture shows the ruins of the Sumerian city of Ur, with the partially reconstructed ziggurat in the distance.

It was all so clear twenty-five years ago. Archaeologists and anthropologists were sure that they knew quite clearly how and when mankind took that crucial step that brought them to the threshold of civilization, the creation of cities.

This headdress of gold, silver, and lapis lazuli was found in one of the royal tombs at Ur.

ministrative or religious headquarters were established, and these gradually grew up into towns and finally cities. This ultimate status was achieved about the middle of the fourth millennium B.C. in Lower Mesopotamia at Uruk, Ur, and other similar urban complexes founded by the gifted Sumerians.

They started from the premise that the earliest form of social unit was the hunting band. Such groups had no fixed home but were forever in motion, following in the tracks of the flocks they preyed on. The first break out of this way of life came with the introduction of primitive herding. Stone Age hunters, the speculation went, would every now and then catch alive the young of the hunted and raise them; eventually the idea dawned that having animals available for slaughtering was a surer way of getting one's daily meat than chasing after it.

Next it was the turn of wild plants to be domesticated. Hunters had all along eked out their diet of flesh with wild fruits, berries, nuts. In the course of time they added wild grains. The decisive moment came when, instead of collecting these, they learned to grow them—decisive because agriculture, even in its most rudimentary form, promotes a tendency to settle down. The nomadic bands, slowed down by herding, came to a full stop with farming, and the earliest villages sprang into existence, occupied at first only for part of the year, when plant food was ripening. Now, grain requires more care than meat off the hoof or fruit off the tree before it becomes food. It has to be collected, stored, carried, cooked. And so receptacles were created for these purposes, of wood, basketry, leather, eventually of that material so dear to archaeologists, clay. Pottery, of the highest use to housewives and of none whatsoever to hunters, was hailed as the hallmark of embryonic urbanization. As time passed, some of the tiny farming villages gradually became centers where specialized crafts were carried on and ad-

It was a seductive scenario. The only trouble is that, as the results of a quarter of a century of archaeological discovery have shown, it is mostly wrong. There was no concerted progress from hunting to herding to farming. There was no concerted rise from nomadic tribe to settled village, marked by the presence of the householder's essential tool, pottery, and then on to town and city. There were developments, to be sure, striking developments as it turned out, but they were sporadic, occurring at different times in different places. What is more, some of the most significant went back thousands of years before the fourth millennium B.C. In fact, the earliest that we know about took place as long ago as 8000 B.C. at Jericho, just east of Jerusalem.

From 1930 on, John Garstang, the noted British archaeologist, carried out a series of excavations at ancient Jericho. Digging down through the Bronze Age level, he arrived at the Neolithic level. In it he found, as he expected, plenty of pottery. But in 1935, as he probed even further, he found what he did not at all expect: here were levels of occupation that clearly represented a long period of time—they were no less than forty-four feet deep—yet there was not a trace of pottery in them. Before he could explore the mystery further, World War II broke out and stopped all work.

After the war another able British excavator, Kathleen Kenyon, picked up where Garstang had left off. In the 1950's she made a discovery that took her and the whole archaeological community by surprise: far down in the levels underneath the

Neolithic, she came upon a massive series of defense structures. There was a ditch fully twenty-seven feet wide and eight feet deep hacked out of solid rock. Rising from its inner edge was a wall, nine feet thick and twelve high, of rough blocks of stone that had originally been faced with mud plaster; the stones had been carried to the site from half a mile away. And rearing up behind this was a tower, more than thirty feet in diameter and twenty-five high—at least that was the height that survived; the original may have been even taller. It was of waterworn round stones set in hard clay. Inside, access from the top to bottom was provided by a circular staircase of twenty steps, each a slab of stone three feet across, roughly dressed by means of hammers. These discoveries were made on the west side of town; later other parts of the wall were picked up to the north and south. Carbon-14 tests revealed that it had all been done at varying times between about 8000 and 7350 B.C.

Here, then, at this incredibly early period, three thousand years before pottery was used in the place, there was a people with the unity, the administration, and the need to build a series of fortifications as impressive as those belonging to far later days of unquestioned civilization. Excavation has shown that the occupied area stretched over eight acres, within which dwelled a population of some three thousand people. The total circuit of the wall must have been not much less than one-half mile, and towers like the one discovered presumably stood at fixed intervals all around. It was a mighty wall, a fitting ancestor of the one that frowned upon Joshua's trumpeters and was overcome only by virtue of divine aid.

The town behind these fortifications was by no means unimpressive. The inhabitants lived in rectangular houses that contained well-proportioned rooms communicating by means of doors. The walls were of mud brick; the floors were of plaster in two layers, a coarse layer of gypsum plaster topped by a fine layer of highly burnished plaster, pinkish or creamy in color. At least one building, it could be deduced, was dedicated to religion. In its center was a large chamber twenty feet by thirteen, and in the middle of this sat a small rectangular basin, plastered and strongly scorched. Surely it served some ritual observance, though exactly what we have no idea.

One religious practice of the people of Jericho we do know: they had a form of skull cult. They buried their dead under the floors of houses, but first removed the skulls. These they turned over to artists who restored the features in plaster—our very earliest sculptured portraits, and exceedingly well done. The skulls were found together under the floor of one house, no doubt a specially consecrated area.

Why this precocious leap forward at Jericho? For once there is a satisfactory answer: Jericho lies in an oasis with an abundant supply of water from a gushing spring that produces a thousand gallons of water a minute. This is a rare blessing in the parched Near East. Archaeologists have found traces of wheat, barley, lentils, figs. The figs were wild but the other three were cultivated, the wheat and barley, moreover, being domesticated varieties, improvements over the wild strains.

The climatologists are of the opinion that during the time when Jericho's massive defenses were going up, the area was suffering from an increasing aridity. Jericho, then, spared the country-wide dearth, would have attracted people from all around. This would explain how the ditch, wall, and tower got built and also why: an influx of the hungry provided the hands to carry out the work, and it was work they went at with a will, since when completed it would guarantee that they could keep Jericho's largess for themselves.

No one has ever questioned that the earliest developed civilizations we know of, those of Egypt and Mesopotamia, grew up on the banks of great rivers. One of the favored notions of recent years has been that this was connected with the origins of agriculture. Jericho clears the record. Agriculture did not arise along the Nile or Euphrates, and for good reason: to quote Sir Mortimer Wheeler, excavator of the great civilization found in the valley of the Indus River,

To anyone who has seen a river of this category [i.e., the Indus or Nile or Euphrates] in ill-controlled annual flood, mercilessly destroying the landscape which it fertilizes, the thought of primitive, unengineered and unorganized farming in such an environment is inconceivable. Wherever agriculture in fact first emerged, it was assuredly in some kindlier and more restricted setting.

Jericho was as kindly a setting as the Near East could provide.

Yet Jericho, early as its farming was, cannot claim to be the birthplace. That distinction, on the present evidence, goes to Mureybet, a site in northern Syria on the eastern side of the Euphrates some fifty miles southeast of Aleppo. The first settlers here were a group of simple fishers and hunters living in flimsy wooden huts. Around 8500 B.C. their primitive settlement was destroyed by fire and on its ashes rose a new one, created by a more sophisticated people who supplemented their diet of fish and game with a number of wild plants—lentils, vetch, possibly peas, grain, and barley. Now, neither grain nor barley was native to the area; the nearest natural habitat would have been some sixty to ninety miles away to the northwest. It is, of course, conceivable that the inhabitants foraged that far afield to collect food, but it is not likely. A much more plausible hypothesis is that they took wild specimens from there and successfully transplanted them locally. Their stage of agriculture was clearly very early, since the remains of grain and barley that the archaeologists have found are all of wild varieties that have not yet undergone even the first changes into the domestic strains that later become common. For the moment, then, Mureybet is the earliest known farming village.

Its inhabitants were precocious in other ways too. By about 7500 B.C. they were living in rectangular as well as round houses built of slabs of local limestone—which, as it happens, was so soft it could be cut with flint tools—set in clay mortar. And they decorated the insides with murals, rows of horizontal zigzags in black on a buff ground— hardly an aesthetic triumph, but the first example to date of painting on a man-made wall.

A decade or so after the discoveries at Jericho, still more dramatic proof of human precocity came to light, this time in Asia Minor, over eight hundred miles away to the northwest, as the crow flies. In the early 1960's James Mellaart, a British excavator, probed a large mound at Çatal Hüyük in the wide plain of Konya. He had to leave off after four years, long before getting down to virgin soil, but, as at Jericho, what he found was enough to upset many a fondly held idea about man's earliest steps toward civilization.

The most astonishing aspect of Çatal Hüyük was its size. Here, from about 6200 to 5400 B.C., there was a thriving community that spread over thirty-two acres—more than three times the size of Jericho. In its heyday it boasted some one thousand dwellings housing a population of five to six thousand at a minimum. Enough skeletons have come to light to give us some idea of what the people looked like. They were by no means homogeneous: some sixty per cent were a long-headed Eurafrican type, fifteen per cent a long-headed proto-Mediterranean type, twenty-five per cent a short-headed type.

The houses the inhabitants of Çatal Hüyük lived in were so alike in size, shape, and layout that they almost seem to have been built to some rough standard. They were rectangular (eighteen feet by twelve) or square (fifteen by fifteen), consisting of one large living room flanked by a small storeroom. The latter was entered by either a low doorway or porthole, but the living room by a hole in the roof; ladders kept against an outside wall enabled people to get up and down. The houses snuggled one against the other like the cells of a beehive (see page 19). Since they climbed a hillside, each level was higher than the next; light came through windows in the part of the wall that overtopped the structure below, as well as through

This finely carved gypsum figure stood at a temple altar in the Sumerian city of Nippur about 2700 B.C. Her golden mask with painted eyes was originally backed by a wooden head. She is more than twice as old as the Greek Venus de Milo but not much more than half the age of the plastered skull on page 16.

the hole in the roof. There were no streets or even lanes, just a solid mass of adjoining houses; one got from place to place by walking across the roofs. Living was, no question about it, intimate. The excavator, noting that the skeletons show an abnormal number of head wounds, suggests that these may have been the result of too close neighbors getting on each other's nerves.

Amid the houses were shrines. Some forty have been found, easily identified by an elaborate scheme of decoration that is striking witness to the imagination and skill of Çatal Hüyük's artists. Wall painting, for example, had advanced far beyond the first primitive steps visible at Mureybet. Done with brush and mineral or vegetal colors on white plaster, it runs the gamut from simple monochrome panels through panels with textilelike patterns to complicated scenes—a landscape with a settlement flanked by an erupting volcano, vultures at work on human corpses, men and animals in games (including a form of bull-baiting in which one man pulls on the tail and another on the tongue; the artists had a strong sense of fantasy). The paintings all had a religious function; they were done to celebrate some event or occasion, and when that had passed, they were covered up with white plaster.

The shrine walls were decked as well with reliefs of painted plaster, often of monumental size, over six feet high. We see a goddess giving birth to a bull's head or a ram's head, we see leopards face to face, their bodies richly decorated with spots. The painters do not repeat themselves—no two shrines are alike in décor—and there is a mingling of media: wall paintings, plaster

The ancient city of Jericho lies beneath the great mound that stretches across the top half of the picture on the opposite page. In the foreground is the modern city and at top left the oasis that made the site a natural crossroads. Jericho is the oldest city yet discovered. At right, a vertical cut through the mound reveals more than ten thousand years of settlement. The man at top stands on the present surface; the man at bottom stands in a ditch that was cut out of rock, without metal tools, in the eighth millennium B.C.

This portrait head was photographed where excavators found it in the rubble of Jericho. It was made by applying plaster to a skull, molding the features, and placing shells in the eye sockets. Dating from the seventh millennium B.C., the plastered skulls of Jericho are the oldest three-dimensional portraits known. They are thought to represent ancestors or, possibly, enemies killed in battle.

relief, intagliolike figures in sunken relief, and the cementing in of actual objects, such as bull's horns, animal skulls, animal jaws.

Many statuettes have been found, carved out of limestone, grey schist, marble, or other stones, or modeled in clay and then baked. A favorite subject was what was obviously the chief local deity, a goddess who is represented sometimes as a young woman, sometimes as a mother with child, sometimes as an old woman. The sculptors often turned out groups: a goddess embracing her child, a goddess flanked by a pair of felines, a boy riding a leopard, and so on.

Çatal Hüyük, as we mentioned above, flourished between approximately 6200 and 5400 B.C., in other words, a millennium or more after Jericho. By this time pottery was known, and the local housewives cooked and served in homely clay utensils. The potters were but one of a number of specialized craftsmen. We have already described the impressive products of the painters and sculptors. The stonesmiths, if not as creative, were equally skilled: excavation has uncovered multitudinous specimens of fine tools and utensils (hammers,

axes, mortars, pestles, etc.), weapons (arrowheads, spearheads, daggers), and beads with holes so fine that a modern steel needle is too thick to pass through. They were even able to make mirrors of obsidian, burnishing this stubborn material by some laborious technique. (The mirrors, like the wall paintings, were religious, meant for the grave and not the toilette: they were found along with jewelry decorating women's corpses). There were woodworkers who fashioned bowls and boxes of elegant design and excellent workmanship. There were weavers who produced woolens of fine yarn in tighter or looser weaves, decorated with fringes and dyed red, blue, or yellow with vegetal dyes. There were bonesmiths, basketmakers, even metalsmiths who hammered out pendants and beads, not only from native copper but from copper smelted from ore, as we deduce from the traces of slag that have been found.

Why did they gather here and not someplace else? The answer is not as easy as in the case of Jericho. The nature of the soil and a nearby river, which supplied water for irrigation, ensured abundant crops, and there must have been good pastures, since cattle herding was actively carried on. Moreover, hunters were able to add to the supply of meat from the flocks of aurochs that roamed the Konya plain. But all this simply means that, once Çatal Hüyük's population began to burgeon, there was enough locally available to feed it, indeed to feed it well. What caused the influx in the first place? Was it trade? The excavators have uncovered sacks containing as many as twenty-three spearheads in prime condition made from local obsidian; were these exchanged on a large scale for the seashells from the Mediterranean that have been found, or the cowries from the Red Sea? The expensively decorated shrines that were so numerous are indisputable evidence that cult played a large part in the life of the people. Is this what drew them there? Was the cause of Çatal Hüyük's growth religious rather than economic?

Çatal Hüyük, as we have observed, had pottery, but it was by no means the only settlement of the times that did. In fact, pottery had come into being well-nigh a thousand years before this. The earliest has been found neither in Asia Minor nor Palestine but in Iran, at Ganjdareh, not far from Kermanshah. Here, between 7300 and 7000 B.C., was a village that boasted not only precocious potters but precocious house builders as well. For the inhabitants lived in rectangular structures built of mud brick that in some cases were two stories high. As at Çatal Hüyük, the dwellings formed one solid mass without streets or alleys. The ground floor was usually a rabbit warren of cubicles, often no more than a yard square. These were probably for storage; at any rate, it was here that the pottery, either unbaked or very lightly fired, was found. Above this ground level in a number of structures there was a second floor, resting on beams overly-ing the cubicles, where the living quarters were. The bones that have been found show that the villagers were herders of goats. Mortars, pestles, clay bins, and other indications make it very likely that they also did farming, but, despite the archaeologists' careful searching, no traces of any actual grains have been found.

From the point of view of advances in architecture and town planning, one of the most significant sites is again neither in Asia Minor nor in Palestine, not even Iran, but off on the island of Cyprus. On the south coast, at Khirokitia, excavators found a settlement of the sixth millennium B.C., in other words, more or less contemporary with Çatal Hüyük. Çatal Hüyük already had pottery, Khirokitia, not yet. On the other hand, Khirokitia was ahead in domestic architecture and town planning.

These mud-brick domes on stone foundations were the homes of the people who lived at Khirokitia on the island of Cyprus in the sixth millennium B.C. The large hut, whose side is cut away in this reconstruction painting, had a center hearth of baked clay and a partial upper floor supported by wooden beams. Residents are shown grinding corn, spinning wool, and carving stone receptacles with the use of stone tools, sand, and water.

The inhabitants went in for beehive-shaped houses set well apart from one another; in size they ran from nine to as much as eighteen feet in diameter. They were strongly built, the lower portions of the walls being of limestone blocks, the upper portions and the domed roofs, of mud brick. The largest houses had stone pillars inside which supported a semicircular loft, reached by a ladder, where the inhabitants slept. The floors were paved with stones. Some houses had courtyards outside, also paved; domestic activities must have been carried on here. Most interesting of all, the settlement was cut in two by a stone-paved boulevard that ran straight through; nearby houses had stone-paved ramps connecting with it. The excavators cleared only about fifty of the dwellings, but they estimate that there must have been a thousand in all.

"What strikes one about these . . . sites is the diversity of economy and craftsmanship rather than a uniform pattern of development," wrote Mellaart. He was referring to those he had dug in Anatolia, but his remarks apply to the whole of the Near East: massive fortifications at Jericho but nowhere else; copper smelting at Çatal Hüyük but not at Jericho; pottery at Çatal Hüyük but not at contemporary Khirokitia; paved streets at Khirokitia but not at Çatal Hüyük, and so on.

The key question is: do any of these settlements, incomplete as their progress was in one way or another, qualify for the distinction of being called, if not a city, more than a village? Mellaart has no doubts:

Sites with shrines, temples, workshops, residential quarters, etc., do not fit into "village life"; on the contrary, they represent something more, and closer to the classical concept of a town or city, the centre of authority, the nucleus of a state, however petty.

Mortimer Wheeler and Kathleen Kenyon and a number of other noted excavators agree. But theirs is by no means the general opinion. Anthropologists and sociologists in particular have strong reservations and prefer to regard what has been found as villages, well-developed to be sure, but still just villages. The social scientist Paul Wheatley, for example, says rather sniffily of Kenyon's claim for Jericho on the basis of its wall, "Needless to say, reliance on a single morphological feature of this character would, if pushed to its logical extreme, make most of the world urban for most of its history."

If not one morphological feature, then how many? And which? V. Gordon Childe, whose books on prehistory were standard a quarter of a century ago, suggested that in order to be called a civilization, a society should have

primary producers (fishers, farmers, etc.), full-time specialist artizans, merchants, officials, priests, and rulers; an effective concentration of economic and political power; the use of conventional symbols for recording and transmitting information (writing), and equally conventional standards of weights and measures of time and space leading to some mathematical and calendrical science.

The inclusion of writing goes too far: the Incas had no writing, yet they achieved what we must surely acknowledge was a civilization. But most students of the question more or less approve the other features: specialization of crafts (artisans), presence of trade (merchants), service as a religious and administrative center (priests, rulers, officials). Some like to add monumental architecture, but this is simply to substitute effect for cause: it takes priests or rulers or officials plus gangs of specialist craftsmen to produce such architecture—a point Wheatley overlooked in his critical remark quoted above.

But there is something else, much harder to define, which makes a city, i.e., distinguishes a mere settlement from that which is the basic building block of that greatest of all human achievements we call civilization. It is not size of population; some famous medieval cities were far smaller than, say, East European villages of the last century. It is not density of population; rural China runs in places to one thousand heads per square mile, a figure sociologists tend to use as a yardstick for urban living. It is not the presence of specialist craftsmen; one could find the gamut of them on large country estates. It is not the presence of such

The Neolithic city of Çatal Hüyük in Anatolia, as it looked in the seventh millennium B.C., is shown in this drawing by its discoverer, James Mellaart. The mud-brick houses were built in a block, probably to give the walls added support but perhaps also as a defense against enemies or floods. A resident reached his house by walking across his neighbors' roofs and entering a second-story door.

The earliest known city view is the painting at right, found on a wall at Çatal Hüyük. Above is a copy which shows more clearly the rows of houses and, above them, the twin peaks of the Hasan Dag volcano rising from the Konya plain some eighty miles away.

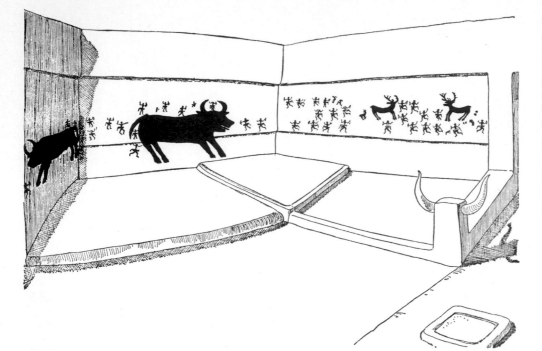

The people of Çatal Hüyük adorned one of their shrines with wall paintings of huge animals and small human figures. At left is a reconstruction drawing of the shrine and, below, a section of standing wall with a painting of a great red bull. The people in the paintings are not hunting the animals but teasing them, perhaps as part of a religious ritual. In the redrawn scene on the facing page, one man is pulling a deer's tail while another pulls its tongue.

Mesopotamia, arose because of nothing more than an increase in the birthrate:

As more labour becomes available through natural population growth, agricultural systems are intensified. This intensification eventually demands a still larger labour supply, and the birth rate . . . increases accordingly. . . . In time and in certain circumstances the amount of land available [in southern Mesopotamia] for cultivation actually began to decline. Conflict became more common. Both factors accelerated the need for intensification. When and where the pressures were greatest urbanism appeared on the scene as a means of organizing and controlling the increased population, the intensified economic structure which supported that population, and the labour force which made that intensification possible.

A reviewer of the book, an anthropologist, was heartened by the results:

We have seen [in it] the potentiality of making determinative factor cross-references on such situations as minimal and maximal community size under specified cultural-ecological conditions; the adaptive and fundamentally regularizing value of the village-type settlement has been forcibly argued; and we have much better insights than we had a dozen years ago on the interactive or systemic relationships of various factors involved in the rise of civilizations.

An archaeologist, chosen to sum up the results of the conference, rather thought otherwise; the conference reminded him, he said, "of what a friend of mine once wrote about the later novels of Henry James. 'James,' he said, 'takes us into a rich and varied world where no sound is heard save the sound of splitting hairs.'"

craftsmen along with religious and administrative figures; one could find all that on a feudal estate. It is somehow all of these raised to a certain power, mixed in a certain way, and it is the height of the power and the nature of the mix that is so hard to establish. In 1970 a conference was held in London in which archaeologists, anthropologists, sociologists, urban planners, etc., met to exchange their ideas on Settlement Patterns and Urbanization. It spawned a book, *Man, Settlement and Urbanism*, containing over eighty contributions that totaled just under a thousand pages. The authors grappled manfully with the problem of defining a city. The answers ran from such a minimal definition as "a relatively large, dense, and permanent settlement of socially heterogeneous individuals" or "a unit of settlement which performs specialized functions in relationship to a broader hinterland" to long and intricate formulations. A second question that exercised the contributors just as much was: What brought urban complexes into being? What caused people to flock together at a given place? Defense, argued one; trade, a second; religion, a third. A fourth held that the earliest acknowledged cities, those of southern

Who inhabited Jericho, Çatal Hüyük, Khirokitia, or any of the other sites discussed above is a mystery. The first people of whom we have identifiable records are the Sumerians—who at the same time are the greatest figures in the development of civilization. The Sumerians made their appearance about 5000 B.C. in Lower Mesopotamia. They were responsible for two momentous achievements: the invention of writing and the founding of what were, beyond all cavil, cities.

In its heyday Sumer boasted a number of cities—Uruk, Ur, Eridu, to cite just a few. The first to merit the name city was Uruk—or Erech as the Bible calls it—situated on the east bank of the Euphrates. During the fourth millennium B.C. Uruk grew until it encompassed an area of some two hundred acres with a population of around twenty-five thousand. By 3000 B.C. or a little later its inhabitants had surrounded themselves by a defense wall no less than six miles long. Like the other Sumerian cities, Uruk was first and foremost a religious center, and its outstanding feature was its temple. Sumerian temples stood on terraces—areas so consecrated that when the first structures raised upon them were ready for replacement, these were filled in and the new built on top. On the temple terrace of Uruk over the centuries there rose a succession of impressive buildings, the largest of which reached the dimensions of 250 feet by 100 (the Parthenon is 228 feet by 101). Some had foundations of stone and floors of stone slabs overlaid by a paving of gypsum blocks. Some were decorated with mosaics made by embedding hundreds of thousands of clay cones with heads painted black or red or white in clay mortar to form brilliant and glistening patterns. One temple had a portico of eight free-standing columns—the earliest example of the monumental use of columns in the history of architecture.

Behind the erection of these structures lay a directing power that issued orders, an administration that organized and co-ordinated, and a labor force, including gangs of specialists, that executed. And all the personnel, working full time on God's behalf, were fed through the efforts of farmers charged with the raising of crops (mostly barley) on the lands that lay about and of herdsmen charged with the tending of flocks (mostly sheep) pastured roundabout. To provide the quantities of grain that Uruk's inhabitants consumed, irrigation was necessary; the area came to be crisscrossed with a network of dikes and canals. And that, too, required its own organization of effort on the grand scale, an effort that went on forever. The building of a temple, no matter how long it may take, eventually comes to an end; the maintaining of an irrigation system, never.

We assume that initially the moving spirit in all this activity was the temple, that it served as the political and economic focal point as well as the religious. The earliest documents we have from Sumer, dating about 3500 B.C. and written in primitive pictographs that only centuries later would be stylized into cuneiform signs, are inventories or lists that have to do with the temple. Writing, it would seem, arose as a way for the priestly administration to keep track of its holdings and activities.

Archaeology has brought to light evidence of the wide range of specialized skills that existed at Uruk and elsewhere, and the level of ability achieved by those practicing them, not merely the architects and bricklayers and masons who erected the temples but workers in all crafts. Sculptors by the end of the fourth millennium B.C. were producing remarkable results; one head fashioned of white marble found at Uruk and dating about 3000 B.C. displays the modeling of a master, a level not to be reached again for hundreds of years (see page 27). Carvers turned out those delicately fashioned cylinder seals bearing imaginative, often

Sir Leonard Woolley, shown above unearthing a statuette, spent thirteen years excavating at Ur. One of his most intriguing finds is this board game (opposite page) with its buttonlike men and triangular dice. The squares are of shell, inlaid with lapis lazuli and red sandstone. The game had not been used since 2500 B.C., and, unhappily, no rules came with it.

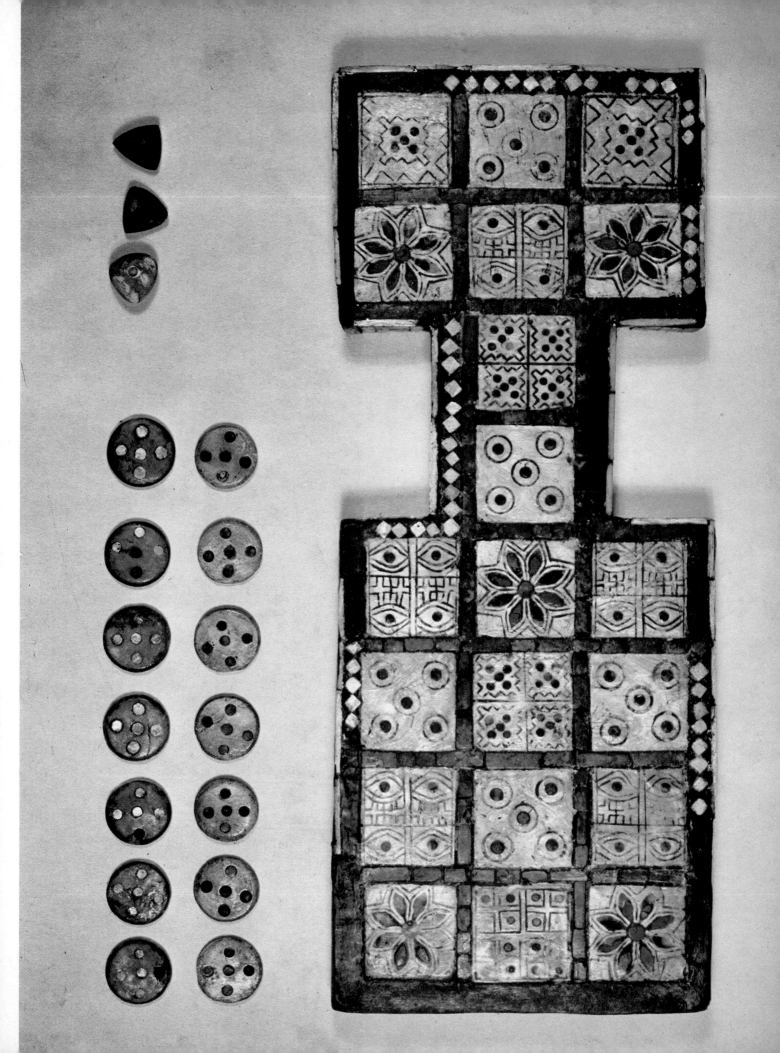

fantastic, animals and scenes that are the hallmark of Mesopotamian civilization; like the seals used by later ages for impressing on wax, they were used to indicate ownership, to identify the user. They were rolled in wet clay, and the sealing was attached to sacks, jars, and the like. Potters now shaped their dishes and bowls on the wheel and no longer by hand. The greatest advance was registered by the workers in metal. Uruk and other Sumerian centers, notably Ur, were wealthy, and the smiths now had gold and silver at their disposal as well as copper. They had learned how to extract silver from lead, to alloy copper with tin to produce bronze, to cast in bronze by the lost-wax process, a technique that is still in use today. They had learned the arts of chasing, engraving, filigree, repoussé, cloisonné. They could join by soldering, sweating, or riveting.

Shortly after 3000 B.C. the lordly temple had to share its dominance with a rival, the king's palace. A particularly good example has been excavated at Eridu, some forty miles southeast of Uruk. It was a rectangular complex, 213 feet by 148, with the corners oriented toward the cardinal points of the compass. Two walls surrounded it, the outer of which was eight feet thick. But the most striking evidence for the increasing power and riches of the rulers of the Sumerian centers is the Royal Cemetery at Ur, excavated by Leonard Woolley. He gave this name to a number of royal burials there, some of which date back to 2500 B.C., a time when the practice of sending a king's retainers to death along with him was still carried on. Two chambers contained the corpses of the king and queen; on the ground around them were fifty-nine bodies, most of them of women. A spacious shaft grave nearby held another seventy-four, sixty-eight of which were of women. The treasures accompanying the burials were beyond price. Here is a description by Max Mallowan, one of the

Among the spectacular treasures found by Woolley in the Royal Cemetery at Ur was this statue of a goat with its front hoofs resting on the branches of a golden tree. Standing twenty inches tall, the figure is made of gold foil, shell, and lapis over a wood core. Another splendid find was the harp on the opposite page, bearing the head of a golden bull with beard of lapis. The original wooden parts of both objects, crumbled to dust, have been replaced.

25

great British excavators of the Near East:

Woolley believed that all the persons and the animals immolated at the time of the funeral had descended into the pits alive. The animals were probably slaughtered by their attendants and the men and women took poison from little bowls which were ready for them in the shafts. To the last they may have played the funeral dirge on the gorgeous musical instruments, golden harps and bull-headed lyres, which were provided for them.

No one who was present at the time of that discovery is likely to forget the ghastly scene of human sacrifice, a crowd of skeletons so gorgeously bedecked that they seemed to be lying on a golden carpet upon which gold and silver vessels, headdresses, jewellery and a multitude of other treasures rested undisturbed, a dream of a cave far richer than Aladdin's come to life. [See also Woolley's account on page 134.]

The treasures are now the glory of the British Museum in London: the renowned Standard of Ur, which bears, inlaid in shell and lapis lazuli, scenes of the Sumerians at peace and at war; a lyre adorned with a bull's head of gold leaf on a wooden core; a statuette of a goat of gold and lapis lazuli hobbled to a golden tree; headdresses and necklaces and other jewelry rich with gold; solid vessels of hammered gold, and so on. Some of the materials which went into these objects came from Arabia, Iran, Afghanistan, even India.

The flight of people from country to city began in ancient Sumer. That is how their urban complexes grew, at the expense of the rural surroundings. Archaeologists have figures to offer that prove this beyond a shadow of doubt. The excavation of Lower Mesopotamia indicates that around 3200 B.C. there were in all some 146 settlements, of which only two were greater in extent than fifty hectares (125 acres). By about 2800 B.C. the total was down to seventy-six, but the number of those covering at least fifty hectares had doubled. A few centuries later, the total had dropped to twenty-four, but there were now eight of the larger centers, each set amid farmland extending for one-half to two miles all around.

As temple and royal wealth increased, so did the need for workers, for more laborers and artisans, more secretaries and bookkeepers, more department heads, bailiffs, inspectors, and so on. Not only did the priests and the kings require such office personnel but so did the private merchants who now appeared on the scene, carrying on trade with all the lands of the Persian Gulf and beyond. Clerks were in demand, too, for loftier purposes— to inscribe on clay tablets the works of Sumerian literature, the tales of their gods and mythological heroes, the epic of Gilgamesh and others, which would eventually be translated into many of the languages of the Near East and Asia Minor and would profoundly affect the literature of the peoples living there.

Clearly, by the end of the fourth millennium B.C. and the beginning of the third, the Sumerians were living in cities.

But were they the very first? Is there no case to be made for, say, Jericho, or Çatal Hüyük? Admittedly these were far smaller, far less sophisticated, than Sumer's centers and, of course, had no writing. Yet the defenses of the one or the shrines of the other could not have come into being without a directing agency, an administrative staff, and gangs of specialized workers, all supported by the produce of lands roundabout— which in turn required their own administration and organization. A case certainly can be made, assert the archaeologists who excavated them. In the words of Mellaart:

The difference between Çatal Hüyük and Protoliterate Uruk is one of degree, but basically the pattern remains the same. . . . Urbanization as a development was not confined to late fourth millennium Lower Mesopotamia or early third millennium Egypt—it happened there, but it had precocious predecessors no less entitled to the rank of civilization. In archaeology as in human life, it is achievement which counts, not the arbitrary and often prejudiced bestowal of titles.

This head of a Sumerian woman, almost life size and beautifully sculptured in white marble, was found in the ruins of Uruk. Originally it had inlaid eyes and brows and probably a headpiece of gold or copper. Dated to the early part of the third millennium B.C., it is a masterpiece of ancient Mesopotamian art.

The first sight of Petra: the Pharaoh's Treasury, seen through the walls of the Siq

IN SEARCH OF . . .
Petra, the Rose-Red City

Approaching Petra from the east, across the barren waste of southwest Jordan, the traveler comes first to a deep, narrow cleft in a wall of rock. This is the entrance to the Siq, a gorge cut by an ancient river but now made into a passage for men and horses. The pathway leads for more than a mile, twisting and turning, through a chasm that seems almost a tunnel, so high and close are the overhanging cliffs. At last the traveler rounds the last turn of the dark passage and sees before him, shining pale red across a gulf of sunlight, the façade of a classical temple carved out of the facing cliff.

If this first sight of Petra seems today like a vision from some land of fable, think how it must have looked to ancient traders who came by this same route after months of travel by camel caravan across the harsh Arabian desert. Petra lies in a dry river valley called the Wadi Musa, at a point where passes intersect the surrounding mountain chains. Blessed with plentiful water, it became the crossroads of the trade routes that ran east and west between Egypt and Mesopotamia, north and south between the Mediterranean and the Indian Ocean.

The first inhabitants of this land— or at any rate the first known to history—were the Edomites, whose wars against the neighboring Israelites are chronicled in the Old Testament. Shortly before the second century B.C. the Edomites moved away, and Petra was occupied by the Nabataeans, a nomadic desert people who settled down, built the city of Petra, and grew rich from the caravan trade. The city itself, with its houses and markets, occupied a stretch of valley enclosed by rocky walls. Out of the soft sandstone the Nabataeans cut temples for the worship of their gods and tombs for the burial of their dead. The city itself has long since crumbled into ruin, but the façades of the temples and tombs are still intact, though eroded by sand and rain.

The style of these façades reflects the artistic currents that flowed through Petra from the corners of the

John Burckhardt dressed as an Arab

Hellenistic world. In the earlier temples there are traces of Persian, Assyrian, and Egyptian design within a predominant Greek style. The later ones bear witness to the arrival of Roman power and Roman architectural influence.

Petra was too rich a prize to be left independent by the expanding Roman Empire. In the second century A.D. it was conquered by an army of the emperor Trajan and shortly afterward visited by his successor Hadrian; the new rulers adorned the city with a theater, fountains, and a street of columns. For a century or more Petra continued to prosper under Roman rule, but it went into decline when trade shifted to more convenient routes through Palmyra and Aleppo. In A.D. 350, when a severe earthquake shook down most of the city, there were few Nabataeans left to mourn the loss.

During the next 1,450 years Petra faded from the memory of the outside world. Then in 1812 a young Swiss named John Burckhardt, with the backing of an English exploration society, set out on a journey through the Middle East. Because most of the Islamic world had been closed to infidel visitors since the seventh century, Burckhardt prepared for his trip by learning fluent Arabic, studying the Koran, and accustoming himself to the costume of a Bedouin. As soon as he passed behind the Moslem iron curtain of that time he began to hear reports of a lost city in the hills of ancient Edom. Telling his suspicious company of guides and servants that he was making a pilgrimage to the tomb of Aaron on a nearby mountain peak, he pressed forward until he stood among the carved stone temples and tombs of the lost city. On August 22, 1812, he was able to write in his journal: ". . . it appears very probable that the ruins in the Wadi Mousa are those of ancient Petra."

To the Bedouins who kept their flocks of goats in the hills around

Petra the dead city was a place of unlikely legend and vague menace. The rock-cut temple that faces the Siq they called the Khasneh al Faroun—"Pharaoh's Treasury"—in accord with the local belief that anything old and wonderful must have been built by Egypt's pharaoh. One of their pastimes was taking pot shots at the urn that stands in a niche above the temple entrance, in hopes that it would burst open and disgorge some royal treasure.

But to European travelers of the Romantic Age, Petra was the most satisfying of the ruined cities of the

A stone head found at Petra

Middle East. Unlike Babylon and Nineveh, which were hardly more than mounds of rubble, Petra offered the grandeur of solid carved rock to inspire the brushes of artists and the pens of poets. In Burckhardt's footsteps the pilgrims came by horse and camel, usually got up in Arab turbans and caftans to fool the locals or at least to heighten the thrill of adventure. Others did not even need to leave England to feel Petra's magic. It was one such armchair traveler, John William Burgon, later dean of Chichester, who gave the city its enduring tag: "the rose-red city, half as old as time."

Rock tombs cut into the sandstone cliffs at Petra, photographed from a cave on the opposite cliff

2: The Realm of the Mother Goddess

by ALEXANDER ELIOT

The island of Crete, whose northwest coast around Suda Bay appears in the background picture, was one of the homes of the Mother Goddess. Above is an early figurine of a fertility goddess, the Venus of Willendorf, found in Austria and dated about 30,000 B.C.

Try this blessing—"In the name of the Mother, the Daughter, and the Holy Spirit." It's not a bit easy at first, is it? Most religious gospels that we possess, together with a large majority of the myths and legends that have come down to us from remote antiquity, would seem to emphasize the male principle as opposed to the female. The Judeo-Christian tradition, for example, plainly centers upon a male-gendered God. The pagan religions of Greece and Rome, similarly, revolved around the All-Father Zeus or Jupiter. For these reasons most scholars naturally assumed, until well into the nineteenth century, that the eastern Mediterranean birthplace of our civilization must have been dominated by male gods from the beginning.

In fact the opposite is true. We know this now, thanks to the discoveries of modern archaeology. New evidence from beneath the earth overwhelmingly contradicts the written record. The oldest cult statuary found, dating from as early as 30,000 B.C., is invariably female. Among the Neolithic farming peoples of southwest Asia and the eastern Mediterranean basin, the Mother Goddess reigned supreme as the spirit of fertility and the life-creating force. She was worshiped as the Earth Mother and sometimes as the Queen of Heaven as well, from Neolithic times down almost to the dawn of history.

Poetic justice calls for some adventurous female archaeologist to have made this discovery. However, women did not begin to lead archaeological expeditions until recently. And so the honor fell to a Victorian gentleman, a rather deliberate although brilliant Britisher, who carried a walking stick familiarly known as Prodger. The first hero of this tale, then, was Sir Arthur Evans.

Born in 1849, Evans attended Harrow, Oxford, and Göttingen. An interest in the origins of writing was what led him to Crete, the large Greek island

Snakes figured in the worship of this Minoan goddess, found at Knossos. Her waist, arms, neck, and head-dress are festooned with reptiles.

in the eastern Mediterranean. There he studied whatever ancient inscriptions he could find above ground, and also pottered about a bit, poking likely heaps of rubble with Prodger. At that time Crete was under Turkish domination, but the expansive eye of Evans's mind saw the island as it had been before the Greeks themselves were there.

The odd configurations of ground underlying an olive grove at Knossos by the sea intrigued Evans. Under the olive roots, he half-guessed, might lie the remains of a lost civilization. Being independently wealthy, he negotiated to purchase the property. The owner of the grove chose to exaggerate the number of trees it contained. This business maneuver so incensed the proper Britisher that the whole deal nearly fell through, and many years passed. Fortunately, Evans swallowed his outrage at last, and by 1900 the grove was his. The trees themselves meant nothing to him in any case. Imperiously pointing with Prodger, he put a digging crew to work. Within hours they found the tops of some very ancient masonry walls. Within weeks 8,400 square feet lay exposed, and by 1901 Evans had uncovered a five-and-a-half-acre palace complex.

One more year's work, he thought, would suffice to complete his excavation. A quarter-century later he was still at it, and Knossos had meanwhile become the partly reconstructed capital of a totally new area of ancient history. The civilization which Evans had uncovered, and which he named Minoan, had flourished for sixteen centuries, from around 3000 to 1450 B.C.. It was a thalassocracy, or peaceful sea empire, with trading posts in the Cycladic islands, mainland Greece, Rhodes, Cyprus, Sicily, Ischia, Naples, and Marseilles. The Minoans built paved roads and aqueducts, ports and palaces galore, but no fortifications until almost the end of their span. Also no monuments; they appear not to have cared for the spurious "immortality" that inscriptions convey. In dress they were not quite bizarre, but children of playful fashion. The males wore wide belts, embroidered loincloths, and sometimes calf-high boots. The women, in contrast, adorned themselves in the most elaborate and teasing-yet-regal manner imaginable. They affected peaked caps, slit gowns tailored to show off every motion of their buttocks, and shirtwaists so designed as to both frame and thrust forward their naked breasts. Some women shaved their heads in order to accommodate ringleted wigs or, occasionally, dress helmets. Not only the surviving frescoes and figurines but a quantity of engraved gems show these things. Released from underground, unlocked by Evans, the treasures at the great Archaeological Museum of Heraklion, for example, speak more eloquently than any words of a rich, joyous, free-and-easy culture with a feminine cast.

Among the most striking objects unearthed at Knossos were figurines of a bare-breasted, snake-wielding deity. She was evidently worshiped in public temples and in shrines within each household. "Clearly," Evans concluded, "the goddess was supreme."

The name Minoan refers to Greek myths concerning King Minos of Crete, the vicious husband of lustful Queen Pasiphaë. The myths in question are the opposite of edifying, yet they cast an odd raking light on what really went on at the palace that Evans found. Here is the gist of them, baldly and briefly given:

Poseidon the sea god sent a glorious white bull out of the waves to King Minos. The king should have sacrificed it, but instead he turned it loose among his cattle. Queen Pasiphaë fell in love with the animal. She prevailed upon Daedalus, the great artificer at court, to build a cow in which she might conceal herself and receive the bull. Thus, Pasiphaë conceived the monstrous Minotaur, a bull-headed man. King Minos had Daedalus construct a most elaborate maze, the Labyrinth, in which to keep the Minotaur imprisoned without chains or bars. Then Minos levied a heavy tribute upon the city-state of Athens to the north. Every ninth year Athens had to send him fourteen noble young men and women to be ritually devoured by the Minotaur. Theseus, an Athenian prince, volunteered when he came of age to join the sacrificial band. Princess Ariadne, daughter of Minos and Pasiphaë, enabled him to slay the Minotaur and escape the Labyrinth. Then she eloped with him, but Theseus abandoned her to the favors of the wine-god Dionysus.

Is there a kernel of truth in all this? Evans thought yes. The palace which he had uncovered was about the same size as Buckingham Palace today, but far less regular in form. Architecturally it sprawled and coiled in upon itself in a most erratic manner. Any contemporary visitor to the building would soon have been hopelessly lost inside it, Evans reasoned. The palace itself, he concluded, was what gave rise to the Greek legend of the Labyrinth.

Doubtless a culture capable of creating such a structure, with its sophisticated plumbing and ventilating systems, its tapered columns and magnificent wall paintings, would easily have dominated the relatively primitive Greeks of the pre-Homeric age. And it would have been natural for the later Greeks to take belated revenge upon their erstwhile Minoan masters by denigrating Minos and Pasiphaë in myth. The unpleasant business of the unsacrificed bull and the unchained Minotaur also pointed to something real. A series of "bull-dance" frescoes which Evans found reasonably intact upon the palace walls proved that bulls must indeed have served as the splendidly awesome protagonists in many a Minoan ritual. In *The Palace of Minos*, Volume III (1930), Evans himself had cogent things to say regarding this most important piece of evidence:

That the painted reliefs of bull-grappling scenes . . . may have left their impress on later traditions of the Minotaur and of the captive boys and girls is . . . by no means improbable. But there is no reason to go further than this

Arthur Evans (in white suit) stands with his staff assistants and crew members on the grand staircase of the palace of Knossos during its excavation and restoration in 1901. Evans spent thirty-five years and more than $1,000,000 of his own money in bringing to light the Cretan civilization which he named Minoan after its legendary King Minos. The Labyrinth, in which Minos confined the Minotaur, was, Evans thought, the many-roomed palace itself.

and to suppose that the acrobatic figures of either sex engaged in these dangerous feats actually represent captives, trained like Roman gladiators to "make sport" for the Minoan holidays. . . . They are, as we have seen, elegantly tired, and . . . often of noble mien. In these champions of either sex we must recognize the flower of the Minoan race, executing, in many cases under a direct religious sanction, feats of bravery and skill in which the whole population took passionate delight. . . . So, too, the participation of women in the Minoan bull-grappling scenes can by no means be regarded as a symptom of bondage or of a perverse tyrant's whim. It was rather . . . the outcome of the religious organization in which the female ministers of the Goddess took the foremost place in her service.

The most complete and compelling representation that Evans found represents a lithe young lady seizing the horns of a charging bull. She seems about to lift herself up and over the animal in a front somersault. At the picture's center a ruddy-skinned youth in the process of just such a maneuver alights momentarily, head-down, on the bull's back. At right, meanwhile, a second girl awaits with arms upraised to catch and steady each partner as he catapults over the bull's tail.

Bullfighters and rodeo performers insist that what the picture shows is quite impossible; it never happened. Like an oncoming train, they say, a charging bull is not to be played with that way. Then, does the picture lie? This would seem unlikely. In the first place, many similar representations have since been discovered. In the second place, the artist's rendering appears keenly observed. Unquestionably, however, the artist did exaggerate the dimensions of the charging bull. Perhaps the violence of its motion was unduly dramatized also. Like circus horses, the bulls used may have been specially bred and trained for exhibitions of this sort. If Spanish fighting bulls are raised to be fierce and brave, the Minoan variety may conversely have learned gentle grace. But even if that was the case, bull-dancing must have been extremely dangerous.

Too dangerous, in fact, to be called a sport; yet seeming aristocrats of both sexes took part. Was its purpose religious? The Greek myth, in its backward way, would seem to support that assumption. Queen Pasiphaë's name connects her with the moon. She must have been a moon goddess, it would seem, or else an earthly representative of the moon. The white bull from the sea, with its crescent horns, also possessed lunar overtones. By their meeting, these two part-supernatural beings brought to birth a son whom King Minos dared not destroy. The creature was contained, without violence, in the Labyrinth or else the palace itself. Princes and princesses played with the Minotaur,

perilously, and thus augmented the fertility of the Minoan realm. Theseus's conquest of the Minotaur would seem, in this context, to represent invasion from the north, an overturning of the ancient fertility rites, and effective destruction of the Minoan bull cult. That did happen historically, in fact, during the fifteenth century B.C..

At that time Crete was invaded by the ancient Greeks whom we know as Mycenaeans from their city of Mycenae on the Greek mainland. The Mycenaeans were descendants of relatively barbarous Indo-European tribes who had come down into Greece early in the second millennium B.C.. Theirs was a nomadic warrior-culture, hard-edged, gloomy, self-consciously masculine. They worshiped not the Earth Mother but fierce, fiery, and thunder-loud sky gods. Zeus, the All-Father, was their special patron.

With the arrival of the Mycenaeans in Crete sixteen centuries of independent Minoan civilization came to an end. In the Greek world, the older Minoan religion was absorbed into the worship of the new Indo-European deities. The familiar Greek pantheon of gods and goddesses, with Zeus at their head, reigned supreme. The Mother Goddess was reduced to a swirl of lesser deities bearing such names as Rhea, Leto, Demeter, Hera, and Aphrodite.

To return to the myth, it will be recalled that Princess Ariadne was abandoned by Theseus, who left her stranded on the island of Naxos. But there the wine-god Dionysus found and actually married her. Translation: the Minoan mystery-religion was not quite lost. It entered the underground cult of the wine god, for example, at Eleusis, not far from Athens itself. We will have occasion to touch on such mystery cults again. They generally centered upon a deathlike "initiation" beyond which stood the Mother Goddess promising immortality.

It was Evans's privilege to uncover a fully developed civilization in which the Mother Goddess had reigned supreme. Under different names she was worshiped throughout the eastern Mediterranean world. Her counterpart in Egypt was Isis. In

Syria she was called Astarte, in Anatolia, Cybele. Often the goddess had a male companion, but he was never her equal. He might be her son, lover, husband, or all three. Such in Greek mythology was Adonis, the youth beloved of Aphrodite, who spent half the year with the goddess and half beneath the earth with Persephone. As Aphrodite was the goddess of fertility, Adonis represented the cycle of the seasons.

How was the Mother Goddess worshiped? In the absence of written records, who can say for sure? In Crete the bull-dancing must have been in her honor. Doubtless flowers, and beasts too, were sacrificed in her name now and again. Was that all, or did the Mother ask for human sacrifice as well? Most students of the subject now surmise that this was so. Their argument derives from a great weight of anthropological and also legendary evidence, drawn from around the world. This was first pulled together by the indefatigable Sir James G. Frazer, who published his epochal book *The Golden Bough* in 1890. Frazer was not an archaeol-

ogist, though he had familiarized himself with the classic sites of Greece and Italy. He did his excavating mainly in the library of Cambridge University. But, nonetheless, what Frazer had to say still plays an important role in the new understanding of prehistory. Like Sir Arthur Evans, his compatriate, Frazer too must be reckoned a hero of the present tale.

If one may summarize millions of words in a paragraph or two, Frazer's main understanding was this: our remote ancestors, and primitive people down to the present day, tend to see the world as being under the governance of some special maternal deity. Call her Nature, if you will. Her children personify vegetation, among other things. And it is plain that most vegetation must "die" seasonally, in order to be born again. Human society can help this process along, or so our ancestors were taught, by regularly sacrificing human representatives of gods to the Mother Goddess. Frazer gives hundreds of examples of this from all over the world. His eastern Mediter-

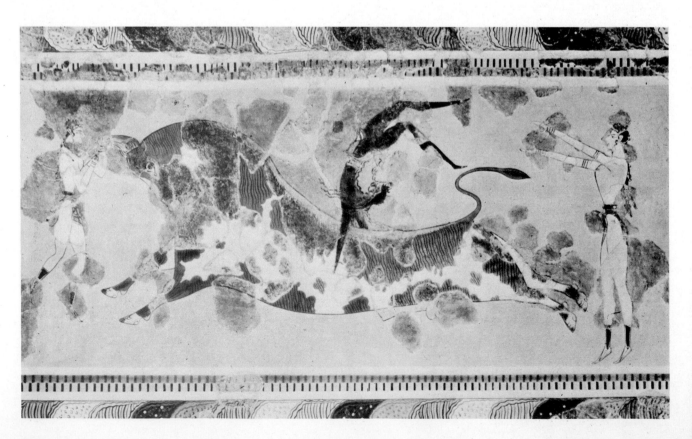

ranean cast of sacrifices includes representatives of Adonis in Syria and on Cyprus, Attis in Asia Minor, Dionysus Zagreus (represented as a bull, intriguingly enough) in Crete, and Virbius at Nemi in Italy. Concerning this last instance he has the following to say:

We may conclude that the worship of Diana in her sacred grove at Nemi was of great importance and immemorial antiquity; that she was revered as the goddess of woodlands and of wild creatures, probably also of domestic cattle and the fruits of the earth; that she was believed to bless men and women with offspring and to aid mothers in childbed . . . further, that Diana of the Wood herself had a male companion, Virbius by name, who was to her what Adonis was to Venus, or Attis to Cybele; and, lastly, that this mythical Virbius was represented in historic times by a line of priests known as Kings of the Wood, who regularly perished by the swords of their successors.

In veiled language Frazer presumes to hint, at the very end of his book, that Christian religion, with its Virgin birth and Crucifixion, also partakes of the immemorial pattern. Nemi, he reports,

has changed but little since Diana received the homage of her worshippers in the sacred grove. The temple of the sylvan goddess, indeed, has vanished and the King of the Wood no longer stands sentinel over the Golden Bough. But Nemi's woods are still green, and as the sunset fades above them in the west, there comes to us, borne on the swell of the wind, the sound of the churchbells of Rome ringing the Angelus. *Ave Maria!* Sweet and solemn they chime out from the distant city and die lingeringly away across the wide Campagnan marshes. *Le roi est mort, vive le roi! Ave Maria!*

Coming from a science-minded scholar, Frazer's conclusion is surprisingly pretty, if not sentimental. In fact it must have been a wretched day for man, a blood-red streak across the dawn of human consciousness, when our ancestors came to feel that the mysterious organizing force that continually recreates the world in the teeth of entropy had to be renewed, ritually, by human sacrifice. From that moment in prehistory the Mother Goddess grew to be a three-dimensional object of love and terror equally in the human psyche. Thereafter, unquestionably, she did often preside over the

The famous mural on the opposite page, found in the palace of Knossos, depicts the Minoan sport—or rite—of bull-leaping. One female athlete grasps the bull's horns, at left, while a male athlete catapults over the animal's back and another female holds out her arms to catch him. The myth of the Minotaur—half man and half bull—has long been a favorite theme of artists. In 1937 Picasso portrayed the dying Minotaur, below. In 1958 Matisse drew Queen Pasiphaë, mother of the Minotaur, wearing a bull's horns.

39

Iran, second millennium B.C.

Motya, first millennium B.C.

Sar Dheri, third century B.C.

In time as well as space, the worship of the mother goddess extended over a vast span. These images were made in periods as remote from each other as the Ice Age and the Roman Empire. They were found in places as far east as India and as far west as central Europe. At far left on the opposite page is a Phoenician terra-cotta figurine of a fertility goddess from the island of Motya, west of Sicily. Before a religious rite it was filled with liquid through an opening in the head; during the ceremony wax plugs in the breasts were discreetly melted, allowing the liquid to flow forth as if by magic. The other figures, from left, are: an Iranian goddess from Turang Tepe; a deity from Sar Dheri, India; a Paleolithic Venus found in Czechoslovakia; the many-breasted Diana of the Ephesians.

Czechoslovakia, 20,000 B.C.

Ephesus, first century A.D.

sacrifice of young priests for the renewal of harvests, and of young kings for the rebirth of kingdoms.

This was the pattern, especially in the Mediterranean region. It held good among the agricultural and trading tribes for thousands of years, in most cases, before their written histories began. Even after the Mother Goddess was supplanted in Greece by the Indo-European sky gods, her worship continued in the religious underground.

The most renowned "mystery religion" of the prehistoric sort which lived on into late pagan times was celebrated, as has been said, at Eleusis. There, according to the poet Pindar, Dionysus "the god of the flowing locks" was enthroned beside Demeter the corn goddess and her daughter Persephone, queen of the dead. The rites themselves were not to be revealed to the uninitiated, on pain of death; and strangely enough that prohibition held good. We still don't know what happened there; which is a loss to us. For, Pindar exulted: "Happy is he who having seen these rites goes below the hollow earth; for he knows the end of life and he knows its god-sent beginning."

Eleusis and the Eleusinian Mysteries, a classic study by George E. Mylonas published in 1961, makes very plain that whatever the central "mystery" may have been it did not entail human sacrifice except in a symbolic sense. Each initiate apparently suffered a sort of death and rebirth in the course of the rite, and came away filled with courage, feeling himself to be at one with nature and, at the same time, somehow immortal. Professor Mylonas concludes:

We read in Cicero that Athens has given nothing to the world more excellent or divine than the Eleusinian Mysteries. Let us recall again that the rites of Eleusis were held for some two thousand years; that for two thousand years civilized humanity was sustained and ennobled by those rites. . . . When Christianity conquered the Mediterranean world, the rites of Demeter, having perhaps fulfilled their mission to humanity, came to an end. The "bubbling spring" of hope and inspiration that once existed by the Kallichoron well became dry and the world turned to other living sources

for sustenance. The cult that inspired the world for so long was gradually forgotten, and its secrets were buried with its last Hierophant.

That reverential approach to the matter comes as a pleasant antidote to the popular view, derived from Frazer's generation of research scholars, that the mysteries of the Mother Goddess must in general have been savage, superstitious, cruel, and bad. But the man who has done the most to combat such apparent prejudice is Robert Graves, whose beautiful although very largely unproved flight of intuitive scholarship, *The White Goddess*, was first published in 1946. The poet in Graves worshiped the Mother; he made no bones about this. But he was no prophet, as he confessed, and "would never presume to say: 'Thus saith the Goddess.'" Nonetheless, Graves concluded, "A simple loving declaration: 'None greater in the universe than the Triple Goddess!' has been made implicitly or explicitly by all true Muse-poets since poetry began."

To try dispensing with the Mother is willfully to violate nature and lose eternity. The father, Cronus, time itself, then does devour one. Better to run back and find the Mother if one can. She also devours, it's true, but she gives birth anew. Hence, Graves's argument goes, all poets in particular, and all who strive for reconciliation with nature, really belong at the Great Mother's court. What if her palace-temple proves to be a Labyrinth from which there is no escape? Graves zestfully leads the way in, and in again, until his brain-weary reader longs for some Princess Ariadne to come and show the way out of the maze once more.

There is perhaps no way out. But the best hints we have concerning the whole nature and extent of the continuing Mother Goddess worship in Mediterranean lands during historic times come from a risqué novel, written in Latin about the middle of the second century A.D. The author, Lucius Apuleius of Carthage, was an aristocrat, a lawyer, and a widely traveled sometime profligate who became a priest of the Egyptian Isis cult. Wherever *The Golden Bough* is required reading, Apuleius's book should be read at the same time in

This marble statue of Demeter, goddess of fertility in classical Greece, was found in a temple at Cnidus. In the Greek pantheon that succeeded the prehistoric Mother Goddess, Demeter took her place as protector of the corn harvest and guardian of fruitfulness in humans and animals as well as crops. She and her daughter Persephone, queen of the underworld, were central figures in the Eleusinian mysteries, which perpetuated the worship of the Mother Goddess into later Greek and Roman times.

order to restore one's faith in human nature. We are, on the whole, gentler folk then Frazer's towering volume of savageries indicates. Apuleius's book shows this to be true; it leads us to laugh at ourselves, and also reverence the Mother of our dreams. Conveniently, it also has the word "golden" in its title: *The Golden Ass.*

Apuleius purports to give a first-person account of what it was like to suffer magical transformation into a donkey and, after many sufferings, to regain human shape at last, thanks to the Mother Goddess. His climactic chapter is so packed with important references as to merit extended quotation (the translation, appropriately enough, is by Robert Graves):

A dazzling full moon was rising from the sea. It is at this secret hour that the Moon-goddess, sole sovereign of mankind, is possessed of her greatest power and majesty. She is the shining deity by whose divine influence not only all beasts, both wild and tame, but all inanimate things as well, are invigorated; whose ebbs and flows control the rhythm of all bodies whatsoever, whether in the air, or on the earth, or below the sea. Of this I was well aware, and therefore resolved to address the visible image of the goddess, imploring her help. . . . Seven times I dipped my head under the waves . . . and with joyful eagerness, though tears were running down my hairy face, I offered this soundless prayer to the supreme Goddess: "Blessed Queen of Heaven, whether you are pleased to be known as Ceres, the original harvest mother who in joy at the finding of your lost daughter Proserpine [Persephone] abolished the rude acorn diet of our forefathers and gave them bread raised from the fertile soil of Eleusis; or whether as celestial Venus, now adored at sea-girt Paphos, who at the time of the first Creation coupled the sexes in mutual love and so contrived that man should continue to propagate his kind forever; or whether, as Artemis, the physician sister of Phoebus Apollo, reliever of the birth-pangs of women, and now adored in the ancient shrine at Ephesus; or whether as dread Proserpine to whom the owl cries at night, whose triple face is potent against the malice of ghosts, keeping them imprisoned below earth; you who wander through many sacred groves and are propitiated with many different rites—you, whose

The walls of a stone temple, built about 4,500 years ago, stand on the island of Malta. Statuettes found in the temple and in nearby tombs suggest that the Mother Goddess may have been worshiped there.

A MONUMENT TO THE MOTHER GODDESS?

Silbury Hill (opposite page) in Wiltshire, England, is the tallest manmade prehistoric thing in Europe. It is an earthen mound, 130 feet high, conical in shape, with a circular setback near the summit and a ditch around most of the base. But what is it and why was it built? Some observers have thought it was a Stone Age fortress, but it has no defensive ramparts or signs of human occupation like the hill forts of southern England. Others, believing it to be a tomb, have tunneled through it but found nothing. The

womanly light illuminates the walls of every city, whose misty radiance nurses the happy seeds under the soil, you who control the wandering course of the sun and the very power of its rays—I beseech you, by whatever name, in whatever aspect, have mercy on me in my extreme distress. . . ."

All the perfumes of Arabia floated to my nostrils as the Goddess deigned to address me: "You see me here, Lucius, in answer to your prayer. I am Nature, the universal Mother, mistress of all the elements, primordial child of time, sovereign of all things spiritual, queen of the dead, queen also of the immortals, the single manifestation of all gods and goddesses that are."

Having regained his human shape with help from the goddess, the former ass was secretly initiated into the mysteries of Isis. Apuleius is at pains to explain that they, like the sacred rites practiced at Eleusis, cannot be revealed directly. However, he goes on to say, "not wishing to leave you, if you are religiously inclined, in a state of tortured suspense, I will record as much as I may lawfully record for the uninitiated, but only on condition that you believe it. *I approached the very gates of death and set one foot on Proser-*

pine's threshold, yet was permitted to return, rapt through all the elements. At midnight I saw the sun shining as if it were noon; I entered the presence of the gods of the underworld and the gods of the upper-world, stood near, and worshiped them."

And that final quotation is about as close as anyone has come, so far, to the innermost core of Mother Goddess worship. Scholars do keep poring over the teasing and yet solemn statement of Apuleius, and a good many are now convinced that there, at least, he did not lie. Apuleius spoke from experience. Subjective experience? Yes, of course. There was an objective correlation to this, but it has since been irrevocably lost. The archaeological discoveries made in this field of late have been marvelous and mind-boggling, it's true, but not even they can restore the ancient rituals.

In fact, examination of the archaeological record can be rather unsettling because it covers so much so sparsely. One feels a certain agoraphobia. It is as if one were to catch a syllable here and there from one single, interminable chant of praise to latest theory, advanced by Michael Dames, a lecturer in the history of art at Birmingham Polytechnic, is that Silbury Hill is a monument to the Mother Goddess. The body of the goddess, he proposes, is formed by the irregular surrounding depression, which in rainy periods (and perhaps always in prehistoric times) is filled with water. The goddess is lying on her side (in the same position as the Sleeping Lady from Malta, opposite page), and the great mound is her womb. At the same time, says Dames, the monument represents the eye, a familiar symbol of the Mother Goddess. In this aspect the hill is the iris and the circular formation at the top is the pupil.

the Great Mother. Let us look first at what may be her earliest temples, and the paintings that adorn them. These are the deep caverns in the Basque region of southern France and Northern Spain, where Cro-Magnon man hunted the hairy mammoth, bison, and wild horse, along with reindeer and smaller beasts down to the hare, some fifteen thousand years ago, with delicate weapons of chipped stone. Many prehistorians now believe that these caverns afforded our remote ancestors access to the inmost recesses of the goddess herself. Moreover, the Cro-Magnons would seem to have conceived of the Earth or Mountain Mother as giving birth, continually, to the animals upon whose flesh they lived. Accordingly, these people invented wall painting, it would appear, in order to plant magical images of game animals in the Mother's womb and thus make her yet more fruitful than before. This was truly an awesome triumph of human creative imagination, and the most amazing thing about it is that the art sprang full-blown, immediately genius-filled. Nobody who has gone down into Altamira or Lascaux can

doubt that the fur-clad mammoth-chasers of those infinitely far-off times included in their ranks artists—whether male or female—on a level with Michelangelo. Yes, as an aesthetic experience these caverns do rival the Sistine Chapel.

The painted record breaks off, unaccountably as yet, during the eleventh millennium B.C., but the sculptural record (which began much earlier) remains continuous down to the present day. It starts in the Paleolithic period of more than thirty thousand years ago, with stone figurines of a melon-breasted, pumpkin-bellied woman: surely the fertile Mountain Mother in little. The so-called Venus of Willendorf and Venus of Menton (both named for the sites from which they were exhumed) are prime examples of this type. More equivocal is the swan-necked and, as it were, half-spiritualized—down to the waist—wide-bottomed Venus of Lespugue, a carved ivory found in France.

Intriguingly enough, the Lespugue type proved to be the wave of the future. The Neolithic ceramic Sleeping Woman found at Malta is also mountainous in her posterior and relatively etherealized above. The same goes for the Neolithic images of the goddess that have been located throughout the Baltic peninsula. Her image in the Aegean islands, Anatolia, Cypress, Syria, and Mesopotamia down through the third millennium B.C. tends to be birdlike above and hippy below, with a strikingly emphasized pubic triangle. Why so? The Jungian anthropologist Erich Neumann has surmised that this development points in the direction, suprisingly enough, of thrones.

Motherliness [Neumann explains] resides not only in the womb but also in the seated woman's broad expanse of thigh, her lap on which the newborn child sits enthroned . . . It is no accident that the greatest Mother Goddess of the early cults was named Isis, "the seat" . . . The original throne was the mountain . . . the immobile, sedentary symbol that visibly rules over the land. First it was the Mountain Mother, a numinous godhead; later it became the seat and the throne of the visible or invisible numen; still later the "empty" throne upon which the godhead "descends."

That insight helps to illuminate later representations of Isis, the Egyptian counterpart of the Mother Goddess, holding the pharaoh in her lap, as well as the ubiquitous Christian statues of the Madonna and Child, from medieval Catalonia to Henry Moore. It also gives a most important clue, I think, to the character of the megalithic shrines that were Stone Age man's original venture into monumental architecture. New Grange in Ireland, Stonehenge and Avebury in England, Carnac in Brittany, and more than a thousand lesser sites of the same kind scattered from Norway all the way down to Spain and Malta, may each be seen as representing, in greater or less degree, the lap of the Mother Goddess. Some of these places served astronomical purposes, and others became burial chambers, but these facts only reinforce the conclusion that their primal dedication may have been to the Mother herself. Astronomy connects Mother Earth to the sky. Burial in her temple gives hope that one may be reborn.

"Hold on!" the reader may exclaim. "Is it really permissible to extrapolate so much of a religious nature from archaeological evidence which is in itself totally wordless?" Perhaps not, after all. But ethnological study of the most ancient forms of faith that still survive provide a reassuring double-check on what the dumb signs put together by our Stone Age ancestors appear to be saying. Navajo Indian religion, for example, carries over from before the coming of the white man—that is, from Stone Age America. And this is what Washington Matthews, the pioneer penetrator of Navajo culture, reported in his brilliant (although to this day largely unsung) *Navajo Legends* of 1897:

It is generally acknowledged by the Navahoes that their most revered deity is *Estsanatlehi*, the Woman Who Changes (or rejuvenates herself). Much is said of her in the legends, but something more is to be obtained by conversation with the shamans. The name *Estsanatlehi* is derived by syncopation from *estsan*, woman, and *natlehi*, to change or transform. She is so called because, it is supposed, she never remains in one condition, but . . . grows to be an old woman, and in the course of time becomes a young girl again, and so passes through an endless course of lives, changing but never dying. It is probable that she is an apotheosis of Nature, or of the changing year. The deity of fruitful nature is properly a female and a beneficent goddess. She is properly too, as the legends tell us, the wife of the Sun, to whom nature owes her fertility.

This gentle nature worship had a bloody counterpart in the celebration of the Phrygian Mother Goddess Cybele, which Emperor Claudius brought to Rome itself in the first century A.D. In Phrygian myth, Cybele took a mortal lover named Attis, who castrated himself in a frenzy of passion, and was then transformed into a pine tree. Cybele's priests suffered ritual castration in remembrance of Attis; or, what is more likely, the myth itself serves merely to explain the savage rite. As enacted annually at Rome, the seedtime ceremonies honoring Attis were very popular. In outline, this is what happened:

On March 22 a pine tree would be cut down and brought into Cybele's Roman sanctuary. The trunk of the pine was swathed like a corpse in woolen bands, and decked with violets—for violets were thought to have first sprung from the blood of Attis. On the twenty-third of March trumpets were sounded, and the pine was revered. Then, on the twenty-fourth, the archigallus or high priest slashed his own arms in order to spatter the pine with blood. Flutes shrilled, cymbals clashed, drums dryly rumbled, and horns ominously droned as the priest's cohorts followed his lead. Whirling with streaming hair, the eunuch devotees danced wildly about the pine, crimsoning it from head to foot. Their purpose, on this ghastly "Day of Blood," was to "strengthen Attis"; that is, to help his resurrection in the fields of Campania, celebrated for their fertility.

In his book entitled *Ugarit and Minoan Crete* (1966) Professor Cyrus Gordon points out how popular religion tends to preserve reverence for the Mother Goddess and to propagate images of her, long after her eclipse by "God the Father." In Crete, he writes, the popular religion

was geared to fertility and venerated the goddess of fertility. In Israel we find much the same situation. We know from the Bible that the official deity was male and imageless, but the common people persisted in worshipping pagan deities such as the goddesses Ashera and Astarte. In Judean houses down to the destruction of the Temple in 586 B.C., we find Astarte images of the nude fertility goddess but no representations of God. . . . If we had no Bible but only the information provided by Palestinian archaeology, we would think that Israelite religion was mainly the worship of Astarte.

The most controversial archaeological find, in this respect, occurred in the 1930's on the right bank of the Euphrates in northern Syria. There, in the course of excavating what was once the Roman frontier town of Dura-Europos, a Hebrew synagogue dating from the year 245 A.D. was laid bare. Astonishingly enough, it proved to be covered with

Isis, the great goddess and universal mother of Egypt, spreads her protective wings about the smaller figure of her brother and husband, Osiris. This green schist statue, thirty-two inches tall, taken from her temple at Thebes, is now in the British Museum. The worship of Isis spread throughout the Roman Empire.

49

mural representations of a sacred sort. To say that this find caused a stir among historians of religion would be putting it mildly.

The anthropologist Raphael Patai gave the reasons for this in a seminal little book published in 1967 called *The Hebrew Goddess.*

Here were pictures illustrating Biblical stories, executed according to a master plan that utilized all the vertical wall surfaces of the synagogue, including its western wall in whose center was a scallop-capped niche that originally must have contained the Ark. And, what is more, one of the largest and most elaborate murals flanking the Ark from the left and having the rescue of the infant Moses from the Nile as its subject, is centered upon the naked figure of a woman! The Dura discoveries thus occasioned not only a correction in the traditional view of the Jewish historical attitude on representational art, but also a revision of the equally traditional idea concerning Jewish modesty and bashfulness.

But just whom did the nude figure, standing up to her thighs in the Nile and holding the infant Moses, represent? A pagan goddess, doubtless, experts agreed. Anahita, the Persian version of

Aphrodite, was considered most likely. Patai, however, argues otherwise: "The admittance of a pagan goddess in the form of her painted image on a synagogue wall would be totally impossible. . . . The artist . . . would have been guilty of gross idolatry, and also the congregation which tolerated the mural in the synagogue would have been guilty of the same sin."

The Old Testament prophets were wont to inveigh against what appears to have been persistent native worship of "heathen idols." Moreover, Hebrew religion had a strong bias toward the male. The God of the Jews, like the Christian God, was and is traditionally "He." Yet Patai daringly suggests that the nude figure in the synagogue represented God, the One God, as feminine!

Profound and prolonged research, much of it against the grain of Orthodox scholarship, convinced Patai that in the bedrock of Hebrew tradition the Father God and the Mother Goddess merge into one. This truly startling thought lifts consideration of the present chapter's theme from

the academic realm, to plant it squarely in present religious consciousness. Devout heirs of the Judeo-Christian tradition must ask themselves whether or not the notion of an all-encompassing male-female deity is possible, or if it simply contradicts their faith.

Remember Frazer's evocation of the Angelus, the *Ave Maria* wafted from Rome over the lake of Nemi. It seemed a far-fetched leap for him to make, from pagan Diana with her cruel rites to the gentle mother of Jesus. Yet Saint Bonaventura went so far as to call Mary "the Spouse of the Eternal Father." And Saint Peter Damian, in the eleventh century, described her as the golden couch upon which God lay down to rest.

As for Dr. Patai, he designates the feminine aspect of God as being the Shekhina, and goes on to establish a close connection between this figure and the prophet Moses. Referring to the Kabbala, a body of traditional Judaic wisdom dealing with the mysteries of the universe, he writes:

In the Kabbala, this relationship was to culminate in the statement that Moses, and he alone of all men, not only became the husband of the Matronit (= Shekhina), but copulated with her while still in the flesh. In the earlier Talmudic and Midrashic sources this idea is adumbrated in the assertion that, of all men, Moses was the only one to whom the Shekhina spoke "every hour without setting a time in advance," and that therefore, in order to be always in a state of ritual purity and readiness to receive a communication from the Shekhina, Moses separated himself completely from his wife. When Moses died, the Shekhina, we are told, took him on her wings and carried him from Mount Nebo to his unknown burial place four miles away. The Shekhina's function at his death is paralleled by her administration to him at his birth. When the daughter of the Pharaoh, we read in the Babylonian Talmud, found the ark of bulrushes into which his mother had placed Moses, and opened it, "she saw the Shekhina with him."

By the same token, modern archaeology and scholarship, in opening up the earth and ransacking the past for hidden wisdom, keep lighting upon the figure of the Mother Goddess. She is there, and forever here as well.

"So God created man in his own image, in the image of God created he him; male and female created he them." The twenty-seventh verse of the Book of Genesis, in the standard King James Version, supports our overriding assumption. For if God made male and female in his own image, then God himself (or herself) will have been both male and female in the act of creation. So, too, is the creative aspect of humanity itself.

Put it this way: The discovery of the Mother Goddess through modern archaeology is really a rediscovery of something never altogether forgotten, something which has to do with the very nature of the human soul.

This strange mural painting was found on the wall of a Hebrew synagogue in the ancient town of Dura-Europos in Syria. It evidently depicts a version of the Biblical story of the rescue of the infant Moses. The baby has been taken from his little ark and is held by a nude female figure who stands thigh-deep in the Nile. Who could she be? Some scholars identify her as a princess or as the pagan goddess Anahita, but the anthropologist Raphael Patai believes she represents the female aspect of the Hebrew God.

51

The Sacred Well of the Maya

When Edward Herbert Thompson was a college student in 1879, his imagination was aroused by the theory that refugees from the "lost continent" of Atlantis had founded the Mayan civilization of Central America. During his long career as an archaeologist he never quite gave up that fanciful notion, but in his study of Mayan records he came upon a mystery of much more substance: the sacred well at Chichén Itzá.

Bishop Diego de Landa, one of the early missionaries to New Spain in the sixteenth century, was the first to record Mayan tales of the *cenote* or well of sacrifice in the Yucatán jungle. "Into this well," he wrote, "they have had . . . the custom of throwing men alive as a sacrifice to their gods in time of drought. . . . They also threw into it a great many other things, like precious stones."

Thompson entered the diplomatic service and got an appointment in 1885 as United States consul in Yucatán. When he made his first journey to the ruins of the Mayan ceremonial center at Chichén Itzá, the site was almost hidden by dense jungle growth. Standing on top of the great stone temple pyramid that was built about A.D. 900, he could barely make out the Sacred Way that led some 325 yards to an oval limestone

A reconstruction drawing of Chichén Itzá as it looked in Mayan times, with the sacred well at bottom left

sinkhole where the rain god Chac was thought to live. To find out what lay at the bottom of the well became the goal of Thompson's life.

Taking a leaf from John Lloyd Stephens, who had bought the Mayan site of Copán (see page 78), Thompson acquired the ruins of Chichen Itzá as his personal property. Next he won the backing of the American Antiquarian Society and the Peabody Museum at Harvard. In 1904, after training himself as a deep-sea diver, he returned to Chichén Itzá with a derrick, boom, and bucket dredge.

Since the well was 187 feet across at its widest point, the first problem was to decide where to lower the bucket. Ingeniously, he had models of heavy wood carved in the rough shape and weight of Yucatán Indians and tossed them from the high banks of the well. Where they landed, he calculated, was about where the human sacrifices would have sunk to the bottom. At that spot he began dredging.

On its first scoop the bucket brought up nothing but sludge. Thereafter for many days it retrieved only rocks, tree trunks, the bones of deer and jaguar—and a few broken pieces of pottery. The potsherds might mean something or nothing. As Thompson noted, "boys are boys, whether in Yucatán or Massachusetts, and have been for some thousands of years. The instinct of a boy is to 'skitter' any smooth hard object, stone or potsherd, across smooth waters like those of the deep water pit and then it rests amid the mud and rocks at the bottom until brought up by the dredge."

One day when he was almost ready to give up hope, the dredge brought up two yellow-white globular masses which turned out, upon tasting, to be resin. Thompson recalled the words of H'Men, a Mayan wise man: "In ancient times our fathers burned the sacred resin—*pom*—and by the fragrant smoke

A photograph of the sacred well today, taken from the edge looking down into the pool

their prayers were wafted to their God whose home was in the Sun."

From that day on, the well began to yield all manner of objects: pots and temple vases, incense burners, arrowheads and lance points, obsidian knives, flint axes and hammers, statuettes of Mayan deities, beads, disks and pendants of gold and copper, fragments of jade. There were numerous tiny bells, each with its tongue removed as a token that the bell had been "killed" and its spirit released to plead for the suppliant.

While watching the dredge at work from a scow floating in the well, Thompson divined the explanation of a puzzling passage written in 1579 by the Spanish *alcalde* of Valladolid, Don Diego Sarmiento de Figueroa. Don Diego had written:

"The lords and principal personages of the land had the custom, after sixty days of abstinence and fasting, of arriving by daybreak at the mouth of the *Cenote* and throwing into it Indian women belonging to each of these lords and personages, at the same time telling these women to ask for their masters a year favorable to his particular needs and desires.

"The women, being thrown in unbound, fell into the water with great force and noise. At high noon those that could cried out loudly and ropes were let down to them. After the women came up, half dead, fires were built around them and copal incense was burned before them. When they recovered their senses, they said that below there were many people of their nation, men and women, and that they received them. When they tried to raise their heads to look at them, heavy blows were given them on the head, and when their heads were inclined downward beneath the water they seemed to see many deeps and hollows, and they, the people, responded to their queries concerning the good or the bad year that was in store for their masters."

Looking over the edge of his scow, Thompson saw in the turbid water what did indeed look like "many deeps and hollows" but were in fact the reflections of cavities in the surrounding limestone walls above him. He saw also "many people of their nation"—the reflected faces of his workmen, leaning over the edge of the well. The sound of their voices "struck the water surface and was deflected upwards to my ears in words softly sounding in native accent, but intelligible." Thus Thompson explained the sights and sounds reported by the women who were thrown into the well and hauled out to tell of mysterious beings who dwelt in the sacred waters.

When the yield of the dredge began to thin out, Thompson donned his waterproof canvas suit and heavy copper diving helmet. "As I stepped on the first rung of the ladder," he recorded, "each of the pumping gang, my faithful native boys, left his place in turn and with a very solemn face shook hands with me and then went back again to wait for the signal. It was not hard to read their thoughts. They were bidding me a last farewell, never expecting to see me again." As he sank slowly to the bottom, some sixty-five feet below the surface, Thompson felt "a strange thrill when I realized that I was the only living being who had ever reached this place alive and expected to leave it again still living."

On the bottom Thompson was presently joined by a Greek sponge diver whom he had hired. Together they groped their way through a thick mixture of water and silt, which no light could penetrate. Around them were the walls of the

A dredge at work, photographed by Edward Thompson

Treasures from the well: parts of a gold mask (left); an inscribed gold disk (above); a jade carving (below)

cavity made by the dredge. Every once in a while a large stone would break loose and plunge to the bottom, but slowly enough through the muddy gruel so that a pressure wave in the water gave the divers enough warning to get out of the way. Despite native belief, there were no strange reptiles in the depths, although for a moment Thompson feared there were. He reported:

"Suddenly I felt something over me, an enormous something that with a stealthy, gliding movement was pressing down on me. Something smooth and slimy was pushing me irresistibly into the mud. For a moment my blood ran cold. Then I felt the Greek beside me pushing at the object and I aided him until we had worked ourselves free. It was the decaying trunk of a tree that had drifted off the bank of mud and in sinking had encountered my stooping body."

The objects that Thompson recovered from the sacred well, including human skeletons and sacrificial offerings, were not of great intrinsic value. The Maya had no gold except what they imported from far away, and their sacred objects were generally made of a rather poor copper-gold alloy. But the well yielded plentiful proof of the ancient legends. Thompson's treasure was shipped back to the Peabody Museum at Harvard, which in later years voluntarily returned part of it to the Mexican government.

To the end, Thompson clung to his early theory that the Maya had come originally from Atlantis. Concluding his account of his work at the sacred well, he wrote: "It is conceivable that some of these objects have graved upon their surfaces, embodied in symbols, ideas and beliefs that reach back through the ages to the primal homes of these peoples in that land beyond the seas. To help prove that is worth the labor of a lifetime."

3: The Horse in History

by LIONEL CASSON

The Iranian mountain valley in the background picture is one of the places where horses may first have been raised for the chariot corps of ancient armies. The rider above is a Scythian of the fourth century B.C.

In this tr[...]
prehistoric [...]
rock painti[...]
are being [...]
foot traps,
use as foo[...]
nor in the
nium B.C. as [...]
horses, we [...]
use as draf[...]

One day in 1879 a group of Kirghiz, a Mongolian people specializing in the hunting down of wild camels, came back with the skin of a curious kind of horse they had happened upon and killed. They gave it to the chief magistrate of Zaizan, the administrative center of their area, who in turn presented it to Nikolai Przhevalski, the celebrated Russian explorer of central Asia.

The animal, though unquestionably a horse, differed in a number of distinctive ways from the familiar *Equus caballus*. It had a short erect mane, no forelock, and a tail like a donkey's, i.e., with the long hairs beginning two thirds down rather than right at the root. In honor of the recipient of the gift—and for lack of a better name—it was called Przhevalski's horse.

Ten years later hunters discovered a whole herd of these creatures and managed to shoot down three stallions and a mare. A decade or so after that, Karl Hagenbeck, founder of Hamburg's zoo and an important figure in the development of modern zoos, launched a full-scale effort to capture some alive. He sent forth a team of no fewer than two thousand Kirghiz. They were eminently successful, returning with thirty-two foals of both sexes.

Zoologists for a while had entertained the idea that the Przhevalski was not a true horse. But study of the living specimens proved otherwise. It was a horse, all right, the one surviving type that had forever remained wild: it could trace its lineage back to ancestors who ranged the plains of central Asia in prehistoric times. It was, to be sure, no equine beauty. It was small—twelve hands, or four feet, tall—and heavily built; it carried its head low,

and it had in general a rather coars[...]
But what it lacked in looks it ma[...]
muscle: it was powerful. Its discov[...]
cleared up what had always puzzl[...]
where the ancients got the sturdy ho[...]
they rode into battle.

All horses alive today go back to a [...]
Eohippus, as the geologists have dub[...]
pus lived in the Eocene Epoch, som[...]
years ago. It was no bigger than a c[...]
cat, walked on pads, four-toed on th[...]
three-toed on the hind. Over a [...]
geologic time it increased in size,
became a hoof when several toes [...]
leaving, as it were, a single one. Eo[...]
into a number of horselike creature[...]
by early Pleistocene days, a millio[...]
had developed into *Equus caballus*, t[...]
the horse we know today.

Stone Age man hunted *Equus*
related species, such as the wild a[...]
eat, not to ride on or get pulled by. [...]
have been found are mingled with [...]
game, and the long bones are often [...]
that the hunters had gone after the [...]
caballus was still too small to be ridd[...]
load of any size. And of course t[...]
wheeled vehicles to pull.

The wheeled vehicle was invente[...]
East shortly before 3000 B.C. The ear[...]
appear in pictures done by the [...]
Sumerians, that gifted people of nort[...]
tamia who share with the Egyptians t[...]
many pioneering contributions to ci[...]
Sumerian cart was at first a most po[...]

3: The Horse in History

by LIONEL CASSON

The Iranian mountain valley in the background picture is one of the places where horses may first have been raised for the chariot corps of ancient armies. The rider above is a Scythian of the fourth century B.C.

One day in 1879 a group of Kirghiz, a Mongolian people specializing in the hunting down of wild camels, came back with the skin of a curious kind of horse they had happened upon and killed. They gave it to the chief magistrate of Zaizan, the administrative center of their area, who in turn presented it to Nikolai Przhevalski, the celebrated Russian explorer of central Asia.

The animal, though unquestionably a horse, differed in a number of distinctive ways from the familiar *Equus caballus*. It had a short erect mane, no forelock, and a tail like a donkey's, i.e., with the long hairs beginning two thirds down rather than right at the root. In honor of the recipient of the gift—and for lack of a better name—it was called Przhevalski's horse.

Ten years later hunters discovered a whole herd of these creatures and managed to shoot down three stallions and a mare. A decade or so after that, Karl Hagenbeck, founder of Hamburg's zoo and an important figure in the development of modern zoos, launched a full-scale effort to capture some alive. He sent forth a team of no fewer than two thousand Kirghiz. They were eminently successful, returning with thirty-two foals of both sexes.

Zoologists for a while had entertained the idea that the Przhevalski was not a true horse. But study of the living specimens proved otherwise. It was a horse, all right, the one surviving type that had forever remained wild: it could trace its lineage back to ancestors who ranged the plains of central Asia in prehistoric times. It was, to be sure, no equine beauty. It was small—twelve hands, or four feet, tall—and heavily built; it carried its head low,

and it had in general a rather coarse
But what it lacked in looks it mad...
muscle: it was powerful. Its discove...
cleared up what had always puzzle...
where the ancients got the sturdy hors...
they rode into battle.

All horses alive today go back to a si...
Eohippus, as the geologists have dubb...
pus lived in the Eocene Epoch, some...
years ago. It was no bigger than a ca...
cat, walked on pads, four-toed on the
three-toed on the hind. Over a v...
geologic time it increased in size,...
became a hoof when several toes...
leaving, as it were, a single one. Eoh...
into a number of horselike creatures
by early Pleistocene days, a million...
had developed into *Equus caballus*, th...
the horse we know today.

Stone Age man hunted *Equus*...
related species, such as the wild ass...
eat, not to ride on or get pulled by. T...
have been found are mingled with t...
game, and the long bones are often s...
that the hunters had gone after the m...
caballus was still too small to be ridde...
load of any size. And of course th...
wheeled vehicles to pull.

The wheeled vehicle was invented...
East shortly before 3000 B.C. The earli...
appear in pictures done by the a...
Sumerians, that gifted people of north...
tamia who share with the Egyptians th...
many pioneering contributions to civi...
Sumerian cart was at first a most pon...

3: The Horse in History

by LIONEL CASSON

The Iranian mountain valley in the background picture is one of the places where horses may first have been raised for the chariot corps of ancient armies. The rider above is a Scythian of the fourth century B.C.

In this tra... prehistoric ... rock painti... are being ... foot traps, ... use as food... nor in the ... nium B.C. as... horses, wer... use as draft

One day in 1879 a group of Kirghiz, a Mongolian people specializing in the hunting down of wild camels, came back with the skin of a curious kind of horse they had happened upon and killed. They gave it to the chief magistrate of Zaizan, the administrative center of their area, who in turn presented it to Nikolai Przhevalski, the celebrated Russian explorer of central Asia.

The animal, though unquestionably a horse, differed in a number of distinctive ways from the familiar *Equus caballus*. It had a short erect mane, no forelock, and a tail like a donkey's, i.e., with the long hairs beginning two thirds down rather than right at the root. In honor of the recipient of the gift—and for lack of a better name—it was called Przhevalski's horse.

Ten years later hunters discovered a whole herd of these creatures and managed to shoot down three stallions and a mare. A decade or so after that, Karl Hagenbeck, founder of Hamburg's zoo and an important figure in the development of modern zoos, launched a full-scale effort to capture some alive. He sent forth a team of no fewer than two thousand Kirghiz. They were eminently successful, returning with thirty-two foals of both sexes.

Zoologists for a while had entertained the idea that the Przhevalski was not a true horse. But study of the living specimens proved otherwise. It was a horse, all right, the one surviving type that had forever remained wild: it could trace its lineage back to ancestors who ranged the plains of central Asia in prehistoric times. It was, to be sure, no equine beauty. It was small—twelve hands, or four feet, tall—and heavily built; it carried its head low,

and it had in general a rather coarse But what it lacked in looks it ma... muscle: it was powerful. Its discov... cleared up what had always puzzle... where the ancients got the sturdy hor... they rode into battle.

All horses alive today go back to a s... *Eohippus*, as the geologists have dub... pus lived in the Eocene Epoch, som... years ago. It was no bigger than a ca... cat, walked on pads, four-toed on the three-toed on the hind. Over a ... geologic time it increased in size, ... became a hoof when several toes ... leaving, as it were, a single one. Eoh... into a number of horselike creatures by early Pleistocene days, a million had developed into *Equus caballus*, th... the horse we know today.

Stone Age man hunted *Equus* ... related species, such as the wild ass... eat, not to ride on or get pulled by. Th... have been found are mingled with t... game, and the long bones are often s... that the hunters had gone after the m... *caballus* was still too small to be ridde... load of any size. And of course th... wheeled vehicles to pull.

The wheeled vehicle was invente... East shortly before 3000 B.C. The earli... appear in pictures done by the a... Sumerians, that gifted people of north... tamia who share with the Egyptians t... many pioneering contributions to civi... Sumerian cart was at first a most po...

In 1778 an Italian merchant while traveling near Cairo bought from a group of Arabs a document written on—to him—an unusual form of paper, a kind made from the fibers of the papyrus plant. His purchase was a roll three and a half feet long covered with indecipherable writing. The Arabs had forty to fifty others; they were using them for fuel, since the stuff gave off a rather pleasant smell, in any event an improvement over such alternatives as camel dung. On his return to Italy he presented his acquisition to Cardinal Stefano Borgia. The language was identified as Greek, written, however, not in the careful printed fashion familiar from medieval manuscripts but in a cursive handwriting such as people use for letters. The cardinal entrusted his new possession to a professor of Greek from the University of Copenhagen, Niels Iversen Schow, who happened to be in Rome at the time. To everybody's disappointment it turned out to be no great piece of literature, no lost play of Sophocles or the like, but merely a list, drawn up in A.D. 192, of names of men from a little village in what is today the Fayum, who were being called up for compulsory labor on the local dikes.

Today we know that this was not the first example of Greek writing on papyrus paper to come out of Egypt. One, for instance, had somehow fallen into the hands of the erudite sixteenth-century scholar Giovanni Giacomo Grineo; unacquainted with the cursive script, he had concluded, for some reason known only to himself, that the language was Turkish. A few others had turned up as well, but all, because of the unfamiliar writing, had gone unrecognized. The Charta Borgiana, to use the title with which scholars subsequently dignified this list of lowly workmen, was the first to be properly identified and formally published.

In Alexandria, Greek and Egyptian religions mingled. This sardonyx cameo depicts a Hellenized river god lifting a cornucopia, symbolic of the Nile's bounty.

In 1798 Napoleon launched his bravura invasion of the valley of the Nile. It swiftly aroused in Europe not only an interest in the hoary land but an appetite for collecting its hoary antiquities. During the next half century a stream of objects, enthusiastically carried off by resident diplomats, merchants, and casual visitors, flowed from Egypt to Europe. The big game were the statues, jewelry, stones inscribed with hieroglyphics, and the like, but every now and then specimens of papyrus paper were included in the booty, some with Egyptian writing on them but more with Greek. One lucky collector got himself a copy of the *Iliad*, but most of the pieces were, like the list of dike workers, humdrum documents—bills of sale, accounts, letters, etc.

Then, in 1877, just a century after Cardinal Borgia had received his gift, there suddenly appeared on the antiquities market in Cairo a huge number of papyrus documents written in a variety of ancient languages, Syriac, Hebrew, Arabic, Latin, but especially Greek. Peasants of the Fayum had come upon them while rummaging through ancient piles of refuse, the source of a kind of rich earth they favored as fertilizer.

By now the world of scholarship was becoming aware of the unique historical value of these pieces. They were far too precious to leave their collecting to the random activity of peasants and their distribution to the greed of antiquities dealers. Archaeologists at work in Egypt were alerted to keep their eyes open for them. The first to make a strike was the renowned Sir Flinders Petrie. What is more, he was able to add yet another source besides rubbish heaps where papyrus documents were to be found. The ancients, he discovered, had at least one way of recycling their waste paper: digging at a site in the north of the Fayum during the years 1889 and 1890 he came upon mummies that had been laid to rest in papier-mâché cases, cases made out of discarded papyri glued together to form a kind of cardboard. Unsticking them without destroying the writing presented a problem, but technicians solved it.

Then a pair of English excavators hit an archaeological gusher. Bernard P. Grenfell and Arthur S. Hunt, while excavating Oxyrhynchus south of the Fayum, the site of what had once been a flourishing provincial Roman capital, unearthed a staggering number of pieces. The pair spent thirty years publishing seventeen volumes of transliterations and translations, their successors have pushed the number of volumes past forty, and there is still a way to go. Grenfell and Hunt were successful as well at the ruins of a village in the Fayum called Tebtunis. This had been in ancient times a center for the worship of the sacred crocodiles, and in it was a cemetery full of their mummified remains; a gratifying number, it turned out, had been packed in cases of recycled papyri. Other archaeologists from all over—France, Germany, Italy, America—joined the search for this new kind of archaeological treasure. Philologists interested themselves in the writing and language of the documents, historians in the contents. Centers and institutes sprang up in various universities and museums. A new scholarly discipline had come into being—papyrology, the study of ancient Egypt's waste paper.

Papyrus paper was made from the reeds that grow in profusion along the Nile. Today they have retreated to Upper Egypt, but in ancient times they were everywhere, being especially dense along the manifold streams of the delta area. They are the reeds that we see in Egyptian tomb pictures, with Egyptian nobles gliding through them in their canoes on the hunt for marsh birds; they are the bulrushes of which Moses' cradle was made. The first step in turning them into paper was to take the stems and slice them along their length, cutting off long, razor-thin strips. The strips were laid side by side to the width the sheet was to be, usually between four and ten inches. Then a second layer was put over the first, this time with short strips running at right angles to the other layer. The long and narrow sheet that resulted, now two-ply as it were, was next put in a press and squeezed till the juices of the plant, which has some gum in its make-up, permeated the whole evenly; then it was taken out and put in the sun to dry. The finished sheets were pasted end to end and rolled up, twenty to a roll. Authors of books might buy whole rolls, but anyone who just wanted some stationery had a piece of the desired length snipped off. Papyrus paper is heavier and thicker than the paper of today but, if of good quality, not a bit inferior. It is certainly tough. Its mortal enemy is damp; saved from that, it can lie in the sand or in a tomb for thousands of years and emerge in fine shape, able to be handled with no more than ordinary care.

The writing was done by reed pen with split point dipped in an ink made of lampblack and gum and water. The ink is as tough as the paper; excavators have dug up many a piece with the writing as black as the day it was set down.

Until late in the last century, students of the ancient world had little more to go on than the works of its historians, of Herodotus, Thucydides, Livy, Tacitus, and so on. These men were not interested in anything other than the large-scale, the grandly important: the fate of nations, the doings of kings and statesmen, widespread natural disasters. Occasionally they would mention ordinary people but only in generalized terms: how these had been affected en masse by the overthrow of a government that ruled them, by the arrival of a new leader among them, by the tide of a war that swept over them, by a plague that hit them. In the nineteenth century two new scholarly disciplines arose that considerably expanded our stock of information—archaeology and epigraphy. But they too tended to concentrate on the high and the mighty. Excavators kept laying bare the remains of grandiose temples and palaces, only occasionally of private dwellings, and practically never of slums. Epigraphy, the study of inscriptions on stones, was somewhat more helpful. Although the fullest and most important usually detailed the doings of governments, kings, magistrates, etc., many came from tombstones, including those over graves of the humble as well as the haughty. Such an inscription often gives the deceased's métier, occasionally some details about it, and the stone itself, by its size and material and workmanship, provides some indication of financial status. Scant information, to be sure, but better than none at all.

Then came the discovery of Egypt's papyrological riches. Here were pieces of writing which, since they were found in the nation's waste dumps, were totally haphazard; they ran the gamut from outdated files of lofty government officials to scribbled lovers' notes, from pages with formal columns of figures ripped out of discarded tax registers to scraps with the scrawled incoherent curses irate Egyptians hurled against their enemies, from elegant missives beautifully written by professional secretaries to the ungainly copy sheets of schoolboys. All of this suddenly opened up to us a world that had been totally lost, the world of the ordinary folk of the past. Suddenly we were able to follow,

from birth to death, the vicissitudes of the Toms, Dicks, and Harrys of Egypt, particularly in the days from about 300 B.C. to A.D. 500, when first the Greeks and then the Romans ruled the land.

We grumble today about how the government keeps track of our every move, how we do nothing but fill out forms, how we will all end up buried in paper. If it is any consolation, things were much the same two thousand years ago. The documents found in Egypt show, in discouraging abundance, that the files of the Roman Empire's bureaucracy bulged with papyrus scrolls recording the doings of all, high and low, from cradle to grave.

To begin with, births were registered every bit as carefully then as now. If you were a Roman subject but not a citizen, as most living in Egypt were, you made a formal declaration to the authorities of the local district headquarters. "To Socrates and Didymus . . . clerks of the metropolis, from Ischyras . . . and his wife Thaisarion," a typical example begins. The couple identify themselves by father's name and mother's name and paternal grandfather's name, by age, and by distinguishing features—and here alone does their practice differ from ours: they prefer to use scars and birthmarks

In marshes along the Nile workers harvest papyrus reeds to be made into paper. The writing tool was a fine pen like that shown below in a stand with water pot and double inkwell. Once a monopoly of the scribe (opposite page), writing was later practiced by Egyptians of all classes.

instead of color of eyes and hair. After identification comes the meat of the document: "We hereby register the son, Ischyras, born to us and being one year of age in the present fourteenth year of Emperor Antoninus Caesar [A.D. 150 or 151]." Ischyras Jr. kept this precious piece of papyrus all his life; it was proof, among other things, that he was freeborn, not a slave.

Ischyras's birth declaration was written in Greek, as were the vast majority of the documents from Egypt. Alexander the Great had conquered the land in 332 B.C., and in his wake waves of Greeks flooded in, gradually becoming the country's social upper crust. In 30 B.C., after Mark Antony had fallen on his sword and Cleopatra had put an asp to her bosom, the Romans made Egypt into one of the provinces of their empire, and soon thereafter a new uppermost crust was formed of Roman citizens, not only Romans who settled down there but local Greeks who managed to achieve naturalization.

Even illegitimate children were registered—not, however, by entry in the official archive but just by a carefully witnessed affidavit. "Sempronia Gemella," reads a document written in A.D. 145,

"who is under the guardianship of Gaius Julius Saturninus, has called upon the witnesses signing below [the document ends with signatures of seven such witnesses] to testify that, on the twelfth day before the Kalends of April [March 21], she gave birth, from father unknown, to twin sons and that she has named these Marcus Sempronius Sarapio and Marcus Sempronius Socratio." Having no father's name to give the boys, she willy-nilly gave them her own family name, Sempronius.

Had Sempronia been raped? Or had she had a passionate moment with some passing fancy? Or was that Roman guardian of hers the father? All we know is that the twins were wanted, that the mother took legal steps to establish their identity. They were lucky. Unwanted children were ruthlessly got rid of. There is an oft-quoted letter written sometime in the first century B.C. by a husband off in Alexandria to his wife up the Nile at Oxyrhynchus. He was a loving husband who closes his missive with the words, "You told me not to forget you. How can I ever forget you?" In the very sentence before this he writes: "Do, please, take care of the little one. As soon as we receive our pay, I'll send it up to you. If, as could well happen, you give birth, if it's a male, let it be, if it's a female, cast it out."

It would have been cast out on the town dump, where it could be picked up by those who were seeking slaves and, instead of buying them fully grown, were willing to pay for raising them from birth and to accept the risk of their dying before reaching a usable age. Such slaves crop up often in the documents; "foundlings from the dunghill" they are called. The mistress of a house that took in one of these infant rejects could hardly be expected to suckle it; the usual practice was to turn it over to a wet nurse, as we know from finding examples of the contracts that were drawn up on such occasions. Here, for instance, are the key passages of an agreement drawn up in A.D. 26 between a wet nurse named Taseus and a man named Paapis. Taseus goes on record that

She has received from him a female infant which he picked up from the dunghill for service as a slave, and to which he had given the name Thermutharion, that she will raise and suckle it with her own milk, that she will, furthermore, nurse it for a period of two years commencing with the present seventeenth of Pachon [May 12], on the understanding that Paapis shall give her sixty drachmas yearly for food, clothing, and all other expenses on behalf of the infant, and she hereby acknowledges . . . receipt from Paapis of sixty drachmas, cash, as payment in full for the first year. . . . She binds herself to provide total protection and care for it, as is proper, not to have sexual intercourse in order to avoid spoiling her milk, not to get pregnant, not to take on the suckling of a second infant . . . and to restore the infant to Paapis duly cared for, as is proper. If some human misfortune should happen which is manifestly such [i.e., the infant should die of natural causes], she shall not be held liable. . . .

Despite all legal precautions, the death of these foundlings could cause infinite trouble, as we learn from a document found in the ruins of Oxyrhynchus. It is a stenographic record of a trial held in A.D. 49 before a local magistrate named Tiberius Claudius Pasion: *Pesouris v. Saraeus.*

Aristocles, lawyer for Pesouris: My client Pesouris, in the seventh year of the reign of the Emperor Claudius [A.D. 47], picked up from the dunghill a male infant named Heracles. He entrusted it to the defendant. . . . She received her wages for the first year. When the due date for the second year arrived, she again received her wages. . . . However, since the infant was being starved, Pesouris took it away from her. Then she, finding just the right moment, managed to enter our house and carried the infant off. . . .

Saraeus: I had weaned my own child, and these people's infant was entrusted to me. I received from them my total wage. After that the foundling died, while a balance of the money was still in my hands. Now they want to take my own child from me.

The situation called for a judgment of Solomon: the Roman magistrate was in exactly the same predicament. There had been two children in Saraeus's house when she was serving as wet nurse, her own and Pesouris's foundling. One died. Pesouris carried the survivor off, claiming it was the foundling, but Saraeus managed to get it back, claiming it was her own son. The document concludes with Pasion's verdict:

The magistrate: Inasmuch as the child, from its features, seems to be Saraeus's, if she and her husband will attest in writing that the foundling entrusted to her by Pesouris died, my judgment following the decisions of His Honor,

From the time of the earliest pharaohs to the time of the Ptolemies, there was little change in the lives of laborers. The bas-relief at left from the Old Kingdom shows farmers plowing with oxen; on the opposite page fishermen haul their catch from the Nile in a net.

the Governor [i.e. of Egypt], is that she shall keep the child as her own but return the money she received.

Not a dramatic Solomonic resolution but an attempt at compromise: Saraeus gets the child after putting down in black and white under oath that it was hers, and Pesouris is to be soothed by recovering all his money, even the part for the period, more than a year, when the foundling was still alive and being suckled.

But Pesouris refused to be soothed, as we learn from a second papyrus found in the same place, the copy of a complaint that Saraeus's husband lodged with the governor shortly thereafter. In it, after reviewing the facts, he states:

My son was returned to me in compliance with your orders . . . as recorded in Pasion's stenographic record. But Pesouris does not wish to comply with the judgment, and he is interfering with me in the practice of my trade [the husband was a weaver]. I therefore am appealing to you, my savior, to obtain justice.

Did he eventually get Pesouris off his back? We will never know; these documents, haphazard pickings that they are, yield generally disconnected fragments, rarely a complete story.

Female foundlings were raised mostly to be household slaves. Males could also be apprenticed out to learn a trade or profession. "I have placed with you," goes an agreement drawn up in A.D. 155 with a specialist in shorthand, "my slave Chaerammon to learn the writing signs that your son Dionysius knows . . . for the fee agreed upon between us, 120 drachmas of silver, holidays excluded." Young Chaerammon, though a slave, was infinitely better off than the children of the free poor. The valley of the Nile was largely given over to agriculture, so most of these were condemned from birth to the peasant's grinding routine, and, of course, to illiteracy. We catch glimpses of them in documents that end with the formula, "Since he does not know letters, I have written for him," followed by the signature of the writer, usually a professional scribe.

Any family that could afford it taught the children to read and write, girls as well as boys. A common practice was to have a tutor live in—hardly in the lap of luxury, to judge by a letter from the head of a household who instructs the recipient to "send to my daughter's teacher . . .

whatever I didn't eat, so he'll be keen on working with her."

The system of teaching was, like ours of a century ago, by rote. This we know from multitudinous examples of written exercises that have turned up, papyri on which appear, in childish hands, *ba be bi bo bu* or *bab, gag, dad, thath,* etc. One hard-working pupil learned his conjugations and declensions by being made to copy out the sentence, "The philosopher Pythagoras, having departed, while teaching letters advised his students to keep away from meat," in all possible grammatical permutations: "To the philosopher Pythagoras, having departed, while teaching letters it seemed right to advise"; "O Philosopher Pythagoras, depart and teach letters and advise"; and so on. Even in the plural: "The Pythagorases, having departed, while teaching letters, advised." And, again as in our schools of the last century, there was much copying out of wise or moral sayings: "It is Zeus who sends us our daily nourishment"; "He who does no wrong needs no law"; "Letters are the greatest beginnings in life"; in this last one we can surely detect the hand of the schoolmaster who set

the assignment. Sometimes the sayings were put in question-and-answer form: "What is pleasing to the gods? Justice"; "What in life is evil? Envy"; "What in life is fresh and wonderful? Man"; "What in life is sweet and must be shunned? Woman."

In well-to-do households, where the parents were often away from home, the children had a chance to put into practice what they had learned through letters to them. Often we find references to these in the parents' correspondence. "My little Heraidous, when she writes her father, doesn't send me any greetings, and I don't know why," complains an aggrieved mother. Sometimes we find the letters themselves. There is a famous one, in an ungainly script and with hair-raising grammar and spelling, of the kind that makes parents wish the children had never learned to write. Theon Sr. had promised to take Theon Jr. along on his next trip and then had, as it were, sneaked out by the back door. Junior writes:

You did a fine thing! You didn't take me with you to the city! If you don't want to take me to Alexandria, I won't write you a letter, I won't talk to you, I won't wish for

Under native pharaohs and foreign rulers alike, the fellahin were held strictly to account for taxes. The levies were usually payable in produce, especially grain and hides, and sometimes also in labor. In this bas-relief from Saqqara, three delinquent taxpayers kneel to receive the judgment of the court while a fourth is whipped for his offense.

114

your good health. What's more, if you go to Alexandria, I won't shake your hand or say Hello to you ever again. So, if you don't want to take me with you, that's what will happen. Mother said to Archelaus [probably a slave attendant], "Take him away! He upsets me!" You did a fine thing: you sent me presents. Big presents! Chicken feed! They pulled a trick on the twelfth, when you sailed. Send for me, please! If you don't send, I won't eat, I won't drink! That's what will happen!

Junior then closes with the Greek equivalent of "Your loving son."

Once having learned their letters, boys were sent to a schoolmaster, often out of town, for the next stage in their education. The prime subject was literature, first and foremost Homer. "I took care," writes a mother to a son studying away from home, "to send to your schoolmaster and find out how you were and to learn what you were reading. He said six." In the context, the number needed no qualification; it meant the sixth book of the *Iliad*. After Homer came Euripides and Aesop. Mathematics was also an important discipline: addition, subtraction, multiplication, fractions, weights, measures, and some simple geometry. Students were set such problems as: How many people can fit as spectators in a hall of such-and-such shape and size? How many measures of grain can fit in a receptacle of such-and-such shape and size? Those interested in getting ahead, in preparing themselves, say, for a government job, went on to study Latin. We have examples of the trots they used, copies of Vergil with translation in Greek.

Judging from what they wrote home, boys who went away to school took their studies seriously and worked hard. "Don't worry, father, about my studies," one reports, "I'm keen about my work. I also take time off." "Look here," writes another to his father, "this is my fifth letter to you, and you haven't written to me except just once . . . and haven't come here. After assuring me, 'I'm coming,' you didn't come to find out whether my teacher was paying attention to me or not. And he asks about you practically every day: 'Isn't he coming yet?' And I just say, 'Yes.' Do your best to come to me quickly, so he'll teach me, as he's eager to do. If you had come up here with me, I would

have been taught long ago." One gathers that the father was to bring not only himself but the tuition as well. Publicly financed education lay centuries and centuries in the future.

When children reached adulthood, they, like their parents before them, were caught in the net of paperwork that the government cast over the land. Every fourteen years there was a "house-to-house census," as it was called. The landlord of each dwelling reported all persons living there as well as the house property any of them owned. Here is a sample, from an apartment or boarding house in the town of Arsinoë. To judge from what the tenants did for a living and their almost total lack of property, the building must have stood in a poorer section of town. The landlord states:

I own in the Moeris quarter a share of a house . . . for which I . . . report for the house-to-house census of the past twenty-eighth year of Emperor Aurelius Commodus Antoninus Caesar [A.D. 189] the following occupants . . .

Pasigenes, son of Theon, grandson of Eutychus, subject to poll tax, donkey driver, age sixty-one

Eutychus, his son by Apollonous who is daughter of Herodes, age thirty

Heracleia, wife of Pasigenes, daughter of Cronion and ex-slave of Didymus who is son of Heron, age forty

Thasis, daughter of both [i.e., Pasigenes and his second wife, Heracleia], age five

Sabinus, son of Heracleia and Sabinus, grandson of Cronion, subject to poll tax, wool carder, age eighteen

Sarapias, son of Heracleia, age twenty-two . . .

Tapesouris, wife of Eutychus, his sister on the father's side, daughter of Isadora, age eighteen. . . . Tapesouris owns in the Moeris quarter a sixth share of a house inherited from her mother.

Whoever purchased or inherited property had to file a declaration with the appropriate authorities. Whoever took up a trade, or wanted to apprentice someone to learn a trade, had to file with the appropriate authorities. To enter the Egyptian priesthood a man underwent circumcision; even that act required approval from the authorities. When a certain Eudaimon, son of Psois and Tiathres, decided that hereafter he would sign himself "son of Heron and Didyme," i.e., the Greek translation of his parents' Egyptian names, presumably to enhance his social status, he had to get permission, in this case from a top treasury official. He submitted his request to the local clerk, who passed it on to the local migistrate; since the local magistrate at the moment happened to be the local clerk acting as such, in perfect Pooh-Bah fashion the clerk in his capacity as clerk wrote a letter to himself in his capacity as magistrate.

The key purpose behind all this bureaucratic paperwork was, as today, the payment of taxes. The dwellers in Egypt paid taxes on land both in cash and kind, taxes on house property, taxes on sheep, pigs, camels, beer, tax on working a trade, tax on certain manufactures. Thousands of receipts for these multifarious levies have been found. All, of course, were made out by hand; the clerks, monotonously repeating the same phrases over and over again, rendered them in an almost indecipherable scrawl on scraps of papyrus or just on fragments of broken pots, the cheapest form of writing material available. The higher social classes enjoyed exemption from some of these burdens, and excavators rummaging about the ruins of houses often find the precious papers that proved the right to such exemption; the holders were careful to put them away in a safe place.

The most privileged group in the land were the Roman citizens. The documents show that this age, in contrast to so many others in man's past, boasted an open society; people were not locked into their social and economic level but could work their way up into money and position. Indeed, not a few of the Greek-speaking subjects of Rome managed to enter the charmed circle of Roman citizens. One path was via the navy; it was slow but it had the great advantage of being open to all, even to boys with native Egyptian blood in their veins. A hitch in the navy was twenty-six years, and citizenship came only at the end, along with discharge, but

Members of the Greek and Roman upper class that ruled Egypt are vividly depicted in "Fayum portraits," named after the district where many of them were painted. The subject commissioned his portrait in the prime of life but saved it to adorn his mummy wrapping. The man on the opposite page is one Artemidorus, of the second century A.D.

that did not discourage able-bodied eager lads.

In 1926, when archaeologists were excavating the little village of Caranis, they came upon two letters that had obviously been carefully preserved by the mother to whom they were addressed. They were written by a young naval recruit and date sometime around the beginning of the second century A.D. In the first he reports that he is "now writing to you from Portus (the harbor of Rome), for I have not yet gone up to Rome and been assigned." The second has the final word:

I want you to know Mother, that I arrived safely at Rome on the twenty-fifth day of Pachon [May 20], and that I was assigned to Misenum. I don't know my ship yet, for I haven't gone to Misenum at the time of writing this letter. Please, Mother, take good care of yourself. And don't worry about me—I've come to a good place!

Quite possibly the mother never saw her son again. Most of these recruits, during their twenty-six years in Italy, took up with local girls, started a family, and established so many bonds that on discharge they preferred to stay where they were.

It helped, as always, to come from a family already a few notches up the ladder—as in the case of young Apion, who signed up sometime in the second century A.D.; he was shipped from Egypt to Misenum and on arrival wrote home:

Apion to Epimachus, his father . . . many greetings. First of all, I hope you are well and will always be well, and my sister and her daughter and my brother. I thank our God Sarapis that, when I was in danger at sea, he quickly came to the rescue. When I arrived at Misenum I received from the government three gold pieces for traveling expenses. I am fine. Please write me, Father, first, to tell me that you are well, second that my brother and sister are well, and third so that I can kiss your hand because you gave me a good education and because of it I hope to get quick promotion, if the gods so will. . . . I have sent you by Euctemon a picture of myself. My name is Antonius Maximus, my ship the *Athenonice*.

The letter closes with regards to various friends and relatives. Like any young recruit in any age, Apion hungers for news from home and sends the family a portrait of himself, very likely showing him resplendent in his new uniform. In these precamera days it has to be a miniature, and in

these pre-postal-service days he must find someone heading for the family's neighborhood to deliver it. Now that he is in the Roman navy he drops his Egyptian name for a good Roman one.

Those who came from the higher social strata had it infinitely easier than an enlistee in the navy. The pride of the Roman army, the legions, were by law open to Roman citizens only. Since this source could not always be counted on to furnish the numbers needed, the sons of upper-class Greek families settled in Egypt were permitted to enlist and, to satisfy the admissions requirement, were given citizenship upon signing up. Not only that but, once in, family connections could smooth the path for them. Take the case of a certain young Pausanias, who was a soldier in the legion stationed at Alexandria at the mouth of the Nile. That was not good enough for him, he wanted to be in a cavalry unit. Pausanias Sr. was able to wangle a transfer to one at Coptos in Upper Egypt, much nearer to home, as he explains in a letter to his brother:

I have written to you before about my boy Pausanias taking service in a legion. However, since he no longer wanted to serve in a legion but in a squadron, on hearing about this I had to go and see him, even though I didn't want to. So, after much pleading on the part of his mother and sister . . . I went to Alexandria and used ways and means till he was transferred to the squadron at Coptos.

It sounds so familar, the adored son expressing a wish, and the mother and sister badgering the poor father till he does something about it.

Here is a letter from another mother's darling, also attached to the legion at Alexandria. Roman servicemen had to provide their own uniforms and equipment; this was obviously much on his mind:

On receiving this letter it would be very nice of you if you sent me 200 drachmas. . . . I had only 20 staters left, but now not one, because I bought a mule carriage and spent all my change on it. I'm writing you this to let you know. Send me a heavy cape, a rain-cape with a hood, a pair of leggings, a pair of leather wraps, oil, and the washbasin, as you promised, . . . and a pair of pillows. . . . For the rest, then, Mother, send me my monthly allowance right away. What you said when I came to

you was, "Before you reach your camp, I will send one of your brothers to you." And you sent me nothing . . . you left me this way without a thing. You didn't say, "I don't have an obol, I have nothing," you just left me this way, like a dog. And when my father came to me, he didn't give me an obol, not a rain-cape, not anything. They all make fun of me: "His father is a soldier, and he's given him nothing." He said he'll send me everything when he gets home. But you two have sent me nothing! Why? Valerius's mother sent him a pair of belts, a jar of oil, a basket of meat, a double-weight garment, and 200 drachmas. . . . So, please, Mother, send me, don't neglect me this way. I've gone and borrowed some change from a buddy and from my sergeant. My brother Gemellus sent me a letter and breeches. I'm sorry I haven't gone anywhere near my brother, and he's sorry I haven't gone anywhere near him. He wrote me a letter scolding me because I went to another camp. I'm writing you this to let you know. It would be very nice of you if, on receiving this letter, you sent right away.

Not all the upper-class boys who entered the service found the going that easy. We have a batch of letters that in the early years of the second century A.D. a certain Terentianus wrote to his father, Claudius Tiberianus. Both parent and son bear good Roman names, and the correspondence is in fluent Latin as well as Greek; but the son is only a sailor serving on the ancient equivalent of a destroyer in the flotilla based at Alexandria, and he is trying as hard as he can to get transferred to a cohort in a legion:

Please, Father, if it seems all right to you, send me from where you are some low-cut boots and a pair of felt socks. Fancy boots are worthless. . . . And I beg you, send me a pickax. The adjutant took from me the one you sent me. . . . God willing I hope to live thriftily and to be transferred to a cohort; but here nothing gets done without money. Letters of recommendation are useless, unless a man helps himself [with money].

Either luck finally smiled on Terentianus or he somewhere found the money to grease palms, because in a later letter he signs as "soldier of the legion."

In 1899 the indefatigable Grenfell and Hunt, while excavating a tiny village, came upon a group of papyri that concerned the doings of someone with the good Roman name of Lucius Bellienus Gemellus. Most were from his hand, in a careless colloquial Greek spelled in hit-or-miss fashion; it is written Greek at about the level of Huck Finn's written English. A contract in which he identifies himself as "veteran of the legion" may provide a clue: he perhaps got what education he had while in the service.

Bellienus was born about A.D. 32, enlisted about A.D. 52, and emerged at the end of his hitch with enough money saved up to buy himself farmland. The papers we have date from A.D. 94 to 110, when he had already made his mark, owning no less than nine pieces of property, including grain land, vineyards, olive orchards, and vegetable gardens. Two he ran by himself, and most of the others through a trusted slave bailiff, Epagathus. He also had the help of a grown son, Sabinus. We have quite a few letters he wrote to these two. Despite the appalling syntax and spelling, they are perfectly clear, mostly a volley of staccato commands closed by his favored coda, "Now you do as I say!" Sabinus's responses are in eminently correct Greek; as so often happens in the families of self-made men, the children get a proper education. The light of Bellienus's life was his grandson, "the little one," as he always calls him. Sabinus, for example, is ordered to send into town for twelve drachmas' worth of fish to celebrate some occasion for the little one.

Right up to the very end, Bellienus was on top of everything and held the reins firmly in his hands. Epagathus gets called down because, instead of transporting a herd of pigs, he drove them on foot and "lost two little pigs because the journey was so hard, even though you had in the village ten animals fit for work. . . . I expressly ordered you to stay at Dionysias for two days until you bought twenty bushels of lotus seed. They say lotus seed is twenty drachmas at Dionysias. Whatever you find the price to be, buy the twenty bushels because we need it. Hurry the irrigating of all the olive orchards . . . and water the row of trees. . . . Now you do as I say." To Sabinus he complains bitterly about the hay one of his donkey drivers bought, "a rotten bundle at twelve drachmas, a little bundle and rotten hay, completely spoiled—no better than

dung!" There was more to Bellienus's success than hard work, care, and a sharp eye for saving a drachma. He was adept in that ancient Near Eastern art, the handling of baksheesh. "I want to let you know," he writes his son, "that Ailouras, the royal clerk, has become deputy for the magistrate Erasus, in accordance with a letter from His Honor, the Governor [of Egypt]. Would you please send him a bushel of olives and some fish, for we need him." And in the last letter we have from him, written when he was seventy-seven in a hand so shaky it is barely legible, he instructs Epagathus to "buy some Isis Day gifts for the ones we usually send to, especially the magistrates."

We hear nothing of Bellienus's wife, but this is accidental. The women of Greco-Roman Egypt were by no means mere household appurtenances, as they were in so many other epochs of man's past. They could come and go as they wanted, handle their own property, pass it on by will to whomever they wished, run their own businesses, even, on occasion, serve as magistrates. When they entered into marriage their interests and rights were protected by written agreement. This was particularly true of women middle-class or higher, who generally brought a substantial dowry to their husbands. Here, for example, are the terms under which Philiskos and Apollonia became man and wife in 92 B.C.:

Philiskos . . . acknowledges to Apollonia . . . that he has received from her in copper money two talents and 4,000 drachmas [16,000 in all], the dowry agreed upon by him for her, Apollonia. Apollonia shall remain with Philiskos, obeying him as a wife should obey her husband, owning their property jointly with him. Philiskos, whether he is at home or away from home, shall furnish Apollonia with everything necessary and clothing and whatsoever is proper for a wedded wife, in proportion to their means. It shall not be lawful for Philiskos to bring home another wife in addition to Apollonia nor to have a concubine or boy-lover, nor to beget children by another woman while Apollonia is alive nor to maintain another house of which Apollonia is not mistress, nor to eject or insult or ill-treat her nor to alienate any of their property with injustice to Apollonia. If he is shown to be doing any of these things or does not furnish her with necessities or clothing or the rest as stipulated, Philiskos shall immediately pay back to Apollonia the dowry of two talents and 4,000 drachmas of copper. Similarly, it shall not be lawful for Apollonia to spend night or day away from the house of Philiskos without Philiskos' knowledge, or to have intercourse with another man, or to ruin the common household or to bring shame upon Philiskos in whatever may cause a husband shame. If Apollonia voluntarily wishes to separate from Philiskos, Philiskos shall pay back to her the bare dowry within ten days from the day it is demanded. If he does not pay it back as stipulated, he shall immediately forfeit the dowry he has received plus one half.

The Roman bureaucracy, with its apparatus for registering Egypt's inhabitants, keeping track of their property and ways of earning a living, and collecting myriads of taxes from them, naturally had an apparatus for taking care of disturbances in the established order of things, for handling crime. That crime exists in all ages is a generalization which hardly needs to be demonstrated. But in Greco-Roman Egypt we are brought face to face with it in the jottings on the police blotter, the statements that victims drew up for the authorities, or the reports of the authorities themselves.

"After being away, upon returning to the village," writes a certain Ptolemaeus to the district magistrate, "I found my house pillaged and everything that had been stored in it carried off. Wherefore . . . I apply to you and request this petition be entered on the register so that, if anyone is proved guilty, he be held accountable to me." The last sentence is the standard legal formula for swearing out a complaint; we find it in more or less the same form in document after document. "Certain parties," runs a statement dated A.D. 176, "with intent to rob came to my house in the village during the night before the twenty-second of the present month Hathyr [November 18], taking the opportunity afforded by my absence owing to mourning for my daughter's husband. Removing the nails from the doors, they carried off everything stored in my house, of which I will present an itemized list at the stated time. Wherefore I apply to you and request," etc. Occasionally we learn exactly how the robbery was carried out: "A

door that opened onto the street and had been bricked up, they broke down, probably using a log to batter it, and, entering the house this way, carried off from what was in the house ten bushels of barley and nothing else; I suspect that these were removed piecemeal through the same door because of marks of the dragging of a rope on it. . . . Wherefore, making application," etc. In this case the housebreakers, like those of today who go only for cameras and television sets, took the one item that was assured of quick and easy sale.

At times the culprits were known to the victims and made no effort to hide their identities; they may have been pursuing some vendetta or perhaps were merely drunk and disorderly. A complaint lodged in A.D. 131 reads:

On the first day of the present month of Thoth [August 29], Orsenouphis and Poueris, both sons of Mieus, and Theon and Sarapas, both sons of Chaeras, and [three more names] . . . brazenly attacked the house I own in the village. . . . While I was parleying with them, they beat me on every limb of my body, and they carried off a white tunic and cloak, a cape, . . . a pair of scissors, beer, a quantity of salt, and other items which at present I do not know.

Outside of the villages and towns the danger was even greater. A husband advises in a letter to his wife, who was to sail up the Nile to join him, to "bring your gold jewelry, but don't wear it on the boat." On the open road there was murder to fear, not merely robbery. "Just as we were rejoicing at being about to arrive home," writes a certain Psois in the latter part of the third century A.D., "we fell into an attack by bandits . . . and some of us were killed . . . Thank God, I escaped with just being stripped clean." Wealthy travelers took along a coterie of armed slaves as protection; poorer ones

Of all Rome's provinces none seemed as fascinating and exotic as Egypt. It was a favorite destination of tourists, a choice post for legionaries. This imaginative scene, part of a large mosaic at Praeneste in Italy, shows Roman soldiers drinking in a pavilion at bottom left, while a religious ceremony is conducted in the small temple at center right. In the rocky landscape at top, behind the large temple, hunters bearing spears and shields attack real or mythological beasts.

moved in groups or waited around until they found some government official headed in the desired direction and attached themselves to his cortege.

Hunters, whose profession required the spending of time alone or nearly alone in desolate places, were particularly vulnerable. "My father," reports Aurelia Tisais on the twenty-sixth of Choiak (December 22) to the chief of police of her village, "who is a hunter, left home with my brother Nilus as long ago as the third of the present month to hunt hares; to date they have not returned. I suspect, therefore, that they have suffered a fatal end. I apply to you . . . so that . . . there be held accountable to me those who may prove guilty." And here is the text of a laconic report from a policeman:

On the fifth of the present month while patrolling the fields near the village I found a pool of blood but no body. I learned from the villagers that Teodotus, son of Dositheus, having set out in that direction, has not yet returned. This is my report.

For some reason he cancelled out the words "but no body." His next sentence shows that he felt there was a connection between the blood and the man who had disappeared; did he omit those words because including them would seem to lessen the implication of murder?

We have a letter from a son to his father, who apparently was being forced to remain at large out of reach of his foreman; the latter, the son informs him, "is looking for you and I suspect has something new against you." So fearful is the son of his father's safety that he observes, "Often, in view of the unsettled state of things, I wished to tell you that I wanted to engrave a mark on you"—in other words, brand him, like an animal, so that in the event of death he might be able to identify the body and give it proper burial.

Floodtime in the Nile Delta was a time of rejoicing and festivity. Peasants herded their animals onto high ground and waited for the waters to deposit a new rich load of silt on their fields. Sportsmen poled and paddled their boats in pursuit of waterfowl. In this segment of the Praeneste mosaic Egyptians recline and play music beneath a fruit-laden trellis.

The streets of a town offered yet another danger. In all ages before the introduction of house plumbing, a common fashion of getting rid of waste was to empty the chamber pots out the window. In 219 B.C. Heracleides lodged an irate complaint:

On Phamenoth 21 [March 16], on my going into Psy on private business . . . an Egyptian woman, whose name is said to be Psenobastis, leaned out from an upper story and emptied urine into the street so that it slopped over me. When I got angry and scolded her, . . . with her right hand she pulled my clothes so that my breast was left bare and she spit in my face, with bystanders present who can testify to my being victim of unjust treatment. When some of the bystanders scolded her, she climbed up to the upper story from where she had poured urine on me.

Egypt, since time immemorial, was saturated with religion, fertile in the proliferation of deities. During the thousands of years in which the pharaohs ruled the land, the priests had formed a well-organized, powerful group. When the Greeks and Romans took over, they extended their authority over the religious bodies and the priesthood, just as they had over everything and everybody else, as we can tell from the documents that deal with such matters. On the one hand, the government astutely subsidized religious institutions: "In accordance with the king's instructions," write the priests of the goddess Hathor, worshiped in the form of a sacred cow, to the minister of finance, "to provide one hundred talents of myrrh for the burial of the Hesir [the sacred cow], will you please order this to be done." On the other hand, the government recouped some of its outlay by auctioning off posts in the priesthood; since these, over and above the dignity they conferred, entitled the holder to a cut of the offerings in cash and kind that the faithful made to the temple, there was usually no lack of candidates. Thus, a certain Pakebkis, already a priest in the temple of the crocodile god, in A.D. 146 writes to a top treasury officer that he wishes

to purchase the office of prophet in the aforesaid temple . . . on the understanding that I shall . . . carry the palm branches and perform the other functions of the Office of Prophet and receive one fifth of the total revenues

123

When the Greeks and later the Romans conquered Egypt, native deities acquired curious new trappings. At left is the falcon-headed god Horus, wearing on his head the double crown of Upper and Lower Egypt but on his body a suit of Roman armor. At right is the temple of Horus at Edfu, erected by the Greek overlords between the third and first centuries B.C.

taken in by the temple, . . . at a price . . . of 2,000 drachmas, which I will pay, upon ratification of my appointment, to the local public bank on the customary dates; furthermore, that my descendants and successors shall have ownership and possession of this office forever with all the same privileges and rights upon payment [by each] of 200 drachmas admission fee.

The businesslike, hard-boiled fashion in which Egypt's religious offices were run did not diminish one whit the power of her gods. The chief deity was Sarapis, a combination of Zeus and the Egyptian bull deity Apis; he had been deliberately created by the first Greek ruler of Egypt, Ptolemy I, around 300 B.C., but his worshipers gave no thought whatsoever to his synthetic origin. Letter after letter includes the phrase, "I thank the God Sarapis," for this or that, even as the young naval recruit Apion whom we mentioned earlier thanked him for being saved from a storm at sea. Sarapis had famous sanctuaries at Alexandria and Memphis, as well as lesser ones elsewhere. That at Memphis included not only a temple but also elaborate living quarters to accommodate worshipers who felt themselves possessed by the god; they would move in and remain until a divine sign signified their release. When a man responded to Sarapis's call, it could not help but work hardship on the family. Here, for example, is a wife's reaction, mostly packed into one long, exasperated sentence:

When I received your letter . . . in which you announce that you have become a recluse in the Sarapeum at Memphis, I immediately thanked the gods at hearing you were well, but your not coming home when all the other recluses have come home, I do not like one bit, because, after having piloted myself and your child through such a bad time and gone to every extremity because of the price of food, I thought that now, at least, with you home, I would get some respite, but you haven't even thought of coming home, haven't given any regard to our circumstances, how I was without everything even while you were here, to say nothing of so long a period passing and such bad times and your not having sent us anything. What's more, Horus, who delivered your letter, reports that you've gotten your release, so I really don't like it at all!

In time Christianity put an end to the worship of Sarapis, Isis, and all the other Egyptian gods. But

Decius in A.D. 250 decided to launch a government-sponsored persecution, he issued an order that all his citizens and subjects were to take, as it were, a loyalty test, were to give public proof of their religious devotion. The orders went out to the provincial governors, they passed them on to the district heads, and they in turn to all communities great and small. In each of these a commission administered the test to everyone without exception, even priests and priestesses of the pagan cults. We know this, for we have recovered at least fifty of the certificates of proper performance that the commissioners issued. Here is a sample:

To the officials in charge of the sacrifices, from Aurelius Sakis of the village Theoxenis, together with his children Aion and Heras, temporarily residents in the village Theadelphia. We have always been constant in sacrificing to the gods, and now, in your presence, in accordance with the regulations, we have sacrificed and poured libations and tasted of the sacred offerings, and we request that you certify this for us below. Farewell.
[Second hand] We, Aurelius Serenus and Aurelius Hermas, saw you sacrificing.
[First hand] The first year of the Emperor Caesar Gaius Messius Quintus Trajanus Decius Pius Felix Augustus, Pauni 23 [June 17, A.D. 250].

Some followers of Christ took their loyalty test with mental reservations. Others managed to obtain certificates through influence or bribery. Those who drew the line at such compromises were executed, a certain number by being sold to impresarios of gladiatorial games who used them for the midday event, the tying up of condemned criminals to stakes to be attacked by wild beasts.

"All the world's a stage/And all the men and women merely players," go Shakespeare's great lines. "The infant, mewling and puking in the nurse's arms, . . . the whining schoolboy, with his satchel, and shining morning face, . . . a soldier, full of strange oaths, . . . the justice . . . with eyes severe"—we have met them all on the streets of Greco-Roman Egypt. They walked the boards of their long-past world, exited into oblivion—but then were resurrected when archaeologists came upon the treasures still preserved in Egypt's damp-free refuse.

the new religion had to fight for its victory. For long its adherents were under constant suspicion, which at times flared up into empire-wide pogroms. The phrase "persecution of the Christians" conjures up in our mind's eye a picture of martyrs thrown to the lions. That did happen—but it was only the tail end of a long bureaucratic process. We have found in Egypt documents that reveal the humdrum administrative paperwork that lay behind martyrdom. A pagan was free to worship any god, to partake of burnt offerings or pour libations for deities of all kinds, Egyptian or Greek or Syrian or the state gods of the Roman Empire. Christians could not. Their religion forbade them to worship any pagan gods, including the gods of Rome. And so, when the Emperor

IN SEARCH OF . . .

The Key to Hieroglyphics

The Rosetta stone

The discovery of the great trove of Egyptian papyrus "scrap paper," described in the preceding chapter, gives us a detailed and intimate glimpse of life in Egypt during one period in its history. But that was a comparatively late period, around the time of Julius Caesar and Jesus Christ. Behind that era lay three thousand years of history that were still locked in the secret of Egypt's native writing.

Unlike the scrap paper, which was written in a peculiar Greek script and which could therefore be read as soon as the script was identified, the older writings were in hieroglyphics and in two derivative scripts called hieratic and demotic. The meaning of these writings had been lost for centuries. They were as much a puzzle to living Egyptians as they were to Europeans.

Actually, the key to the decipherment of hieroglyphics was found only one year after the discovery of the "scrap paper." It was a large, flat black stone turned up in 1799 by a soldier or laborer in the service of Napoleon's army near the village of Rashid, or as the Europeans called it, Rosetta, in the Nile Delta. The stone had been inscribed in the year 196 B.C. to commemorate the coronation of King Ptolemy V. It bore three inscriptions: the top one (partially broken off) in hieroglyphics; the middle one in demotic, the cursive script derived from hieroglyphics; and the bottom one in Greek. The scholars attached to the French expeditionary force correctly assumed that the three inscriptions said the same thing and, since they could easily read the Greek version, expected to have no trouble in deciphering the other two.

It was not so simple. Copies of the Rosetta stone were sent all over Europe and many experts tried to decipher them. Several came up with translations—all quite different from one another. After a while most of them gave up. Meanwhile, after the French army of the Nile capitulated to the British, the stone itself was surrendered as war booty and dispatched to the British Museum.

At the time of the stone's discovery the linguistic genius who would eventually decipher it was only eight years old. Jean François Champollion, the son of a French bookseller, taught himself to read at the age of five, then mastered Latin and Greek on his way to the study of Hebrew, Arabic, Syrian, Aramaic, Persian, and, most importantly, Coptic. When at the age of eleven he first saw examples of hieroglyphic writing and was told that no one could read it, he announced, "I am going to do it."

When he began his task, at the age of nineteen, he was a full professor at the University of Grenoble. By that time other scholars, notably David Åkerblad of Sweden and Thomas Young of England, had taken some steps toward the decipherment of the stone. They had noticed that in many monumental Egyptian inscriptions certain groups of signs are enclosed in a sort of box called a cartouche. Comparing the placement of these cartouches with the Greek texts on the Rosetta stone and on the bilingual inscriptions on an obelisk found at Philae, the scholars deduced that each cartouche enclosed a royal name. But they were still unable to abandon completely a long-standing assumption: that since hieroglyphics appeared to be a kind of picture writing, each glyph must represent a word.

Champollion suspected that something was wrong when he counted the words in the parallel inscriptions and noticed that the number of glyphs in the ancient text exceeded the number of words in the Greek text by nearly three to one. This led to his crucial revelation: that the hieroglyphics of the Rosetta stone were not simply a system of picture writing but that over the centuries the symbols had become increasingly phonetic. For instance, the glyph in the form of a horned snake might stand for fy, the Egyptian word for

Jean François Champollion

viper, but it could also stand simply for the sound "f."

Once he had made this intellectual jump, Champollion was able, by comparing the Rosetta stone with other inscriptions, to begin the process of decipherment. His method may be illustrated by the following example. The cartouche of Ptolemy on the Rosetta stone looks like this:

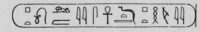

The cartouche of Cleopatra on the obelisk at Philae looks like this:

The second sign, a reclining lion, which would give the *l* in Cleopatra, is exactly the same as the fourth sign in the name of Ptolemy, also an *l*. The fifth symbol in Cleopatra, which must represent the p, is the first sign in the hieroglyphic name Ptolemy.

There were complications. For one thing, there were more signs in the cartouche of Ptolemy than there are sounds in the name. Only later was it realized that the cartouche contained not only Ptolemy's name but signs for his title (Ever-living, Beloved of Ptah, etc.), and that these were intermingled with the letters of the name. The full decipherment of hieroglyphics was a work of many years. Other scholars contributed to the process, but Champollion had one important advantage in his knowledge of Coptic, a language in which he wrote his diary and sometimes talked to himself. Though fallen into obscurity, Coptic was directly descended from the ancient Egyptian and provided many clues to the meaning of signs.

The message on the Rosetta stone had been inscribed by order of the college of priests. The opening lines list the titles of Ptolemy V and epithets proclaiming his devotion to the gods and to the people of Egypt. The second section lists his deeds, which ran from temple gifts and remission of taxes to the sending of military forces overseas and amnesty for rebels. The final section states the resolve of the priests to set up statues in his honor in every Egyptian temple, to establish his shrines, and to declare holidays in his honor.

The message inscribed on the Rosetta stone itself contained nothing of great interest to scholars. But its translation opened the way to reading all the writings of ancient Egypt. The pharaohs and other great figures of Egypt acquired names, the records of the scribes were opened up, and three thousand years of recorded history came to life.

'An Anthology of the
Accounts of Archaeologists
OUT of the EARTH

On the Mesopotamian plain in 1899 Arab workmen bring to light the ziggurat of the ancient city of Nippur.

LAYARD AND THE STONE BEASTS OF NINEVEH

The nineteenth century was the high romantic era of archaeology, and no figure more embodies that romanticism than Austen Henry Layard. After six dull years in a London solicitor's office, he set off for Ceylon by the overland route and decided to stay in the Near East. With a loan of sixty pounds from the British ambassador in Constantinople, Layard started an excavation at the Assyrian capital of Nineveh. In the passage below, Layard describes the discovery and removal of a pair of enormous stone sculptures.

In the morning I had ridden to the encampment of Sheikh Abd-ur-Rahman, and was returning to the mound, when I saw two Arabs of his tribe coming towards me and urging their mares to the top of their speed. On reaching me they stopped. "Hasten, O Bey," exclaimed one of them—"hasten to the diggers, for they have found Nimrod himself. Wallah! it is wonderful but it is true! we have seen him with our eyes. There is no God but God"; and both joining in this pious exclamation, they galloped off. . . .

On reaching the ruins I descended into the newly opened trench, and found the workmen, who had already seen me, as I approached, standing near a heap of baskets and cloaks. Whilst Awad advanced and asked for a present to celebrate the occasion, the Arabs withdrew the screen they had hastily constructed, and disclosed an enormous human head sculptured in full out of the alabaster of the country. They had uncovered the upper part of a figure, the remainder of which was still buried in the earth. I saw at once that the head must belong to a winged lion or bull, similar to those of Khorsabad and Persepolis. It was in admirable preservation. The expression was calm, yet majestic, and the outline of the features showed a freedom and knowledge of art, scarcely to be looked for in works of so remote a period. The cap had three horns, and, unlike that of the human-headed bulls hitherto found in Assyria, was rounded and without ornament at the top.

I was not surprised that the Arabs had been amazed and terrified at this apparition. It required no stretch of imagination to conjure up the most strange fancies. This gigantic head, blanched with age, thus rising from the bowels of the earth, might well have belonged to one of those fearful beings which are described in the traditions of the country as appearing to mortals, slowly ascending from the regions below. One of the workmen, on catching the first glimpse of the monster, had thrown down his basket and had run off towards Mosul as fast as his legs could carry him. I learnt this with regret, as I anticipated the consequences.

Whilst I was superintending the removal of the earth, which still clung to the sculpture, and giving directions for the continuation of the work, the noise of horsemen was heard, and presently Adb-ur-Rahman, followed by half his tribe, appeared on the edge of the trench. As soon as the two Arabs I had met had reached their tents, and published the wonders they had seen, every one mounted his mare and rode to the mound to satisfy himself of the truth of these inconceivable reports. When they beheld the head they all cried together, "There is no God but God, and Mohammed is his Prophet!" It was some time before the Sheikh could be prevailed upon to descend into the pit, and convince himself that the image he saw was of stone. "This is not the work of men's hands," exclaimed he, "but of those infidel giants of whom the Prophet, peace be with him! has said, that they were higher than the tallest date tree; this is one of the idols which Noah, peace be with him! cursed before the flood." In this opinion, the result of a careful examination, all the bystanders concurred.

I now ordered a trench to be dug due south from the head, in the expectation of finding a corresponding figure, and before night-fall reached the object of my search about twelve feet distant. Engaging two or three men to sleep near the sculptures, I returned to the village, and celebrated the day's discovery by a slaughter of sheep, of which all the Arabs near partook. As some wandering musicians chanced to be at Selamiyah, I sent for them, and dances were kept up during the greater part of the night. On the following morning Arabs from the other side of the Tigris, and the inhabitants of the surrounding villages, congregated on the mound. . . .

I formed various plans for lowering the smaller lion and bull, dragging them to the river, and placing them upon rafts. Each step had its difficulties, and a variety of original suggestions were made by my workmen, and by the good people of Mosul. At last I resolved upon constructing a cart sufficiently strong to bear the sculptures. As no wood but poplar could be procured in the town, a carpenter was sent to the mountains with directions to fell the largest mulberry tree, or any tree of equally compact grain, he could find; and to bring back with him beams of it, and thick slices from the trunk.

By the month of March this wood was ready. I purchased from the dragoman of the French Consulate a pair of strong iron axles, which had been used by M. Botta in moving sculptures from Khorsabad. Each wheel was formed of three solid pieces of wood, nearly a foot thick, bound together by iron hoops. Across the axles were laid three beams, and above them several cross-beams. A pole was fixed to one axle, to which were also attached iron rings for ropes, to enable men, as well as buffaloes, to draw the cart.

Simple and rude as this cart was, it became an object of wonder in the town, as carts are unknown in this part of Turkey. Crowds came to look at it, as it stood in the yard of the Vice-consul's khan; and the Pasha's topjis, or artillerymen, who, from their acquaintance with the mysteries of gun carriages, were looked up to as authorities on such matters, daily declaimed on the properties and use of this vehicle, and of carts in general, to a large circle of curious and attentive listeners. As long as the cart was in Mosul, it was examined by every stranger who visited the town. But when the news spread that it was about to leave the gates, and to be drawn over the bridge, the business of the place was completely suspended. The secretaries and scribes of the Pasha left their divans; the guards their posts; the bazaars were deserted; and half the population assembled on the banks of the river to witness the manoeuvres of the cart, which was forced over the rotten bridge of boats by a pair of buffaloes, and a crowd of Chaldaeans and shouting Arabs.

To enable me to move the bull from the ruins, and to place it on the cart in the plain below, a trench or road nearly two hundred feet long, about fifteen feet wide, and, in some places, twenty feet deep, was cut from the entrance, in which stood the sculpture, to the edge of the mound. As I had not sufficient mechanical power at command to raise the bull out of the trenches . . . this road was necessary. It was a tedious undertaking, as a very large accumulation of earth had to be removed. About fifty Arabs and Nestorians were employed in the work.

As the bull was to be lowered, so that the unsculptured side of the slab should be placed on rollers, I removed the walls behind it to form a clear space large enough to receive it when prostrate, and to leave room for the workmen to pass on all sides of it. The principal difficulty was of course to lower it; when once on the ground, or on rollers, it could be dragged forwards by the united force of a number of men; but, during its descent, it could only be sustained by ropes. If these ropes, not strong enough to bear the weight, chanced to give way, the sculpture would be precipitated to the ground, and would, probably, be broken in the fall. The few ropes I possessed had been sent to me, across the desert, from Aleppo; but they were small and weak. From Baghdad I had obtained a thick hawser, made of the fibers of the palm. In addition I had been furnished with two pairs of blocks, and a pair of jackscrews belonging to the steamers of the Euphrates expedition. These were all the means at my command for moving the bull and lion. The sculptures were wrapped in mats and felts, to preserve them, as far as possible, from injury in case of a fall, and to prevent the ropes chipping or rubbing them.

The bull was ready to be moved by the 18th of March. It had been completely isolated, and was now only supported by beams resting against the opposite wall of earth. Amongst the wood obtained from the mountains were several thick rollers. These were placed upon sleepers, formed of the trunks of poplar trees, well greased and laid on the ground parallel to the sculpture. The bull was to be lowered upon these rollers. A deep trench had been cut behind the second bull, completely across the wall, and, consequently, extending from chamber to chamber. Ropes coiled round this mass of earth served to hold two blocks, two others

being attached to ropes wound round the bull to be moved. The ropes, by which the sculpture was to be lowered, were passed through these blocks; the ends, or falls of the tackle, as they are technically called, being held by the Arabs. The cable which was first passed through the trench, and then round the sculpture, was to be gradually slackened by two bodies of men, one at each end. Several of the strongest Chaldaeans placed thick beams against the back of the bull, and were directed to use them in checking it in its descent.

My own people were reinforced by a large number of the Abou-Salman. I had invited Sheikh Abd-ur-Rahman to be present, and he came attended by a body of horsemen. The inhabitants of Naifa and Nimrûd, having volunteered to assist on the occasion, were placed amongst my Arabs. The workmen, except the Chaldaeans who supported the beams, were divided into four parties, two in front of the bull, to hold the ropes, and two at the ends of the cable. They were directed to slack off gradually as the sculpture descended.

The men being ready, and all my preparations complete, I stationed myself on the top of the high bank of earth over the second bull, and ordered the wedges to be struck out from under the sculpture to be moved. Still, however, it remained firmly in its place. A rope having been passed round it, six or seven men easily tilted it over. The thick, ill-made cable stretched with the strain, and almost buried itself in the earth round which it was coiled. The ropes held well. The bull descended gradually, the Chaldaeans propping it up with the beams. It was a moment of great anxiety. The drums and shrill pipes of the Kurdish musicians increased the din and confusion caused by the war-cry of the Arabs, who were half frantic with excitement. They had thrown off nearly all their garments; their long hair floated in the wind; and they indulged in the wildest postures and gesticulations as they clung to the ropes. The women had congregated on the sides of the trenches, and by their incessant screams, and by the ear-piercing *tahlehl*, added to the enthusiasm of the men. The bull once in motion, it was no longer possible to obtain a hearing. The loudest cries I could produce were lost in the crash of discordant sounds. Neither the hippopotamus hide whips of the Cawasses, nor the bricks and clods of earth with which I endeavoured to draw attention from some of the most noisy of the group, were of any avail. Away went the bull, steady enough as long as supported by the props behind; but as it came nearer to the rollers, the beams could no longer be used. The cable and ropes stretched more and more. Dry from the climate, as they felt the strain, they creaked and threw out dust. Water was thrown over them, but in vain, for they all broke together when the sculpture was within four or five feet of the rollers. The bull fell to the ground. Those who held the ropes, thus suddenly released, followed its example, and were rolling one over the other, in the dust. A sudden silence succeeded to the clamour. I rushed into the trenches, prepared to find the bull in many pieces. It would be difficult to describe my satisfaction, when I saw it lying precisely where I had wished to place it, and unbroken! The Arabs no sooner got on their legs again, than, seeing that the sculpture was uninjured and safely placed on the rollers, they darted out of the trenches, and, seizing by the hands the women who were looking on, formed a large circle, and, yelling their war-cry with redoubled energy, commenced a most mad dance. The musicians exerted themselves to the utmost; but their music was drowned by the cries of the dancers. Even

Abd-ur-Rahman shared in the excitement, and, throwing his cloak to one of his attendants, insisted upon leading off the *debké*. It would have been useless to endeavour to put any check upon these proceedings. I preferred allowing the men to wear themselves out—a result which, in consequence of the amount of exertion and energy displayed by limbs and throat, was not long in taking place.

I now prepared, with the aid of Behnan, the Bairakdar, and the Nestorians, to move the bull into the

long trench which led to the edge of the mound. The rollers were in good order; and as soon as the excitement of the Arabs had sufficiently abated to enable them to resume work, the sculpture was dragged out of its place by ropes.

Sleepers were laid to the end of the trench, and fresh rollers were placed under the bull as it was pulled forwards by cables, to which were fixed the tackles held by logs buried in the earth, on the edge of the mound. The sun was going down as these preparations were completed. I deferred any further labour to the morrow. The Arabs dressed themselves; and, placing the musicians at their head, marched towards the village, singing their war-songs, occasionally raising a wild yell, throwing their lances into the air,

and flourishing their swords and shields over their heads.

I rode back with Abd-ur-Rahman. Schloss and his horsemen galloped round us, playing the jerrid, and bringing the ends of their lances into a proximity with my head and body which was far from comfortable; for it was evident enough that had the mares refused to fall almost instantaneously back on their haunches, or had they stumbled, I should have been transfixed on the spot. As the exhibition, however, was meant as a compliment, and enabled the young warriors to exhibit their prowess, and the admirable training of their horses, I declared myself highly delighted, and bestowed equal commendations on all parties.

The Arab sheikh, his excitement once cooled down, gave way to moral reflections. "Wonderful! wonderful! There is surely no God but God, and Mohammed is his Prophet," exclaimed he, after a long pause. "In the name of the Most High, tell me, O Bey, what you are going to do with those stones. So many thousands of purses spent upon such things! Can it be, as you say, that your people learn wisdom from them; or is it, as his reverence the Cadi declares, that they are to go to the palace of your Queen, who, with the rest of the unbelievers, worships these idols? As for wisdom, these figures will not teach you to make any better knives, or scissors, or chintzes; and it is in the making of those things that the English show their wisdom. But God is great! God is great! Here are stones which have been buried ever since the time of the holy Noah—peace be with him! Perhaps they were under ground before the Deluge. I have lived on these lands for years. My father, and the father of my father, pitched their tents here before me; but they never heard of these figures. For twelve hundred years have the true believers (and, praise be to God! all true wisdom is with them alone) been settled in this country, and none of them ever heard of a palace under ground. Neither did they who went before them. But lo! here comes a Frank from many days' journey off, and he walks up to the very place, and he takes a stick (illustrating the description at the same time with the point of his spear), and makes a line here, and makes a line there. Here, says he, is the palace; there, says he, is the gate; and he shows us what has been all our lives beneath our feet, without our having known anything about it. Wonderful! wonderful! Is it by books, is it by magic, is it by your prophets, that you have learnt these things? Speak, O Bey; tell me the secret of wisdom."

RAWLINSON ON THE CLIFF OF BEHISTUN

Henry Creswicke Rawlinson (1810–1895), soldier, diplomat, and member of Parliament, brought both intellectual and physical boldness to solving the puzzle of the cuneiform inscription at Behistun, Iraq. The inscription, which turned out to contain more information about the ancient Persian monarchs than all the classical sources combined, was in three languages—Old Persian, Babylonian, and Elamite (which Rawlinson here calls Scythic). Rawlinson's translation of the Old Persian and Babylonian texts was the great breakthrough that led to the complete decipherment of cuneiform. His description of how he and a young Kurdish boy copied the Behistun inscription in 1847 is quite literally a cliffhanger.

This rock of Behistun is a very remarkable natural object on the high road between Ecbatana and Babylon. It was probably in the very earliest times invested with a holy character; for the Greek physician, Ctesias, who must have visited this spot in the fourth century before Christ, ascribes the most remarkable of the antiquities to be found there to the Assyrian queen Semiramis.

. . . The rock of Behistun doubtless preseved its holy character in the age of Darius, and it was on this account chosen by the monarch as a fit place for the commemoration of his warlike achievements. . . . When I was living at Kermanshah fifteen years ago, and was somewhat more active than I am at present, I used frequently to scale the rock three or four times a day without the aid of a rope or a ladder: without any assistance, in fact, whatever. During my late visits I have found it more convenient to ascend and descend by the help of ropes where the track lies up a precipitate cleft, and to throw a plank over these chasms where a false step in leaping across would probably be fatal. On reaching the recess which contains the Persian text of the record, ladders are indispensable in order to examine the upper portion of the tablet; and even with ladders there is considerable risk, for the foot-ledge is so narrow, about eighteen inches or at most two feet in breadth, that with a ladder long enough to reach the sculptures sufficient slope cannot be given to enable a person to ascend, and, if the ladder be shortened in order to increase the slope, the upper inscriptions can only be copied by standing on the topmost step of the ladder, with no other support than steadying the body against the rock with the left arm, while the left hand holds the notebook, and the right hand is employed with the pencil. In this position I copied all the upper inscriptions, and the interest of the occupation entirely did away with any sense of danger.

To reach the recess which contains the Scythic translation of the record of Darius is a matter of greater difficulty. On the left-hand side of the recess alone is there any foot-ledge whatever; on the right hand, where the recess, which is thrown a few feet further back, joins the Persian tablet, the face of the rock presents a sheer precipice, and it is necessary therefore to bridge this intervening space between the left-hand Persian tablet and the foot-ledge on the left-hand of the recess. With ladders of sufficient length, a bridge of this sort can be constructed without difficulty; but my first attempt to cross the chasm was unfortunate, and might have been fatal, for, having previously shortened my only ladder in order to obtain a slope for copying the Persian upper legends, I found, when I came to lay it across to the recess in order to get at the Scythic translation, that it was not sufficiently long to lie flat on the foot-ledge beyond. One side of the ladder would alone reach the nearest point of the ledge, and, as it would of course have tilted over if a person had attempted to cross it in that position, I changed it from a horizontal to a vertical direction, the upper side resting firmly on the rock at its two ends, and the lower hanging over the precipice, and I prepared to cross, walking on the lower side, and holding to the upper side with my hands. If the ladder had been a compact article, this mode of crossing, although far from comfortable, would have been at any rate practicable; but the Persians merely fit in the bars of their ladders without pretending to clench them outside, and I had hardly accordingly begun to cross over when the vertical pressure forced the bars out of their sockets, and the lower and unsupported side of the ladder thus parted company from the upper, and went crashing down over the precipice. Hanging on to the upper side, which still remained firm in its place, and assisted by my friends, who were anxiously watching the trial, I regained the Persian recess, and did not again attempt to cross until I had made a bridge of comparative stability. Ultimately I took the cast of the Scythic writing by laying one long ladder, in the first instance, horizontally across the chasm, and by then placing another ladder, which rested on the bridge, perpendicularly against the rock.

The Babylonian transcript at Behistun is still more difficult to reach than either the Scythic or the Persian tablets. The writing can be copied by the aid of a good telescope from below, but I long despaired of obtaining a cast of the inscription; for I found it quite beyond my powers of climbing to reach the spot where it was engraved, and the cragsmen of the place, who were accustomed to track the mountain goats over the entire face of the mountain, declared the particular block inscribed with the Babylonian legend to be unapproachable. At length, however, a wild Kurdish boy, who had come from a distance, volunteered to make the attempt, and I promised him a considerable award if he succeeded. The mass of the rock in question is scarped, and it projects some feet over the Scythic recess, so that it cannot be approached by any of the ordinary means of climbing. The boy's first move was to squeeze himself up a cleft in the rock a short distance to the left of the projecting mass. When he had ascended some distance above it, he drove a wooden peg firmly into the cleft, fastened a rope to this, and then endeavoured to swing himself across to another cleft at some distance on the other side; but in this he failed, owing to the projection of the rock. It then only remained for him to cross over to the cleft by hanging on with his toes and fingers to the slight inequalities on the bare face of the precipice, and in this he succeeded, pass-

ing over a distance of twenty feet of almost smooth perpendicular rock in a manner which to a looker-on appeared quite miraculous. When he had reached the second cleft the real difficulties were over. He had brought a rope with him attached to the first peg, and now, driving in a second, he was enabled to swing himself right over the projecting mass of rock. Here with a short ladder he formed a swinging seat, like a painter's cradle, and, fixed upon this seat, he took under my direction the paper cast of the Babylonian translation of the records of Darius which is now at the Royal Asiatic Society's rooms, and which is almost of equal value for the interpretation of the Assyrian inscriptions as was the Greek translation of the Rosetta Stone for the intelligence of the hieroglyphic texts of Egypt.

JEFFERSON DIGS AN INDIAN MOUND

Perhaps the least-known of Thomas Jefferson's astonishing number of achievements is his work as an archaeologist. In 1784 he excavated an Indian burial site and took careful note of its stratifications—a method of scientific observation that European archaeologists did not adopt until another century had passed.

I know of no such thing existing as an Indian monument: for I would not honor with that name arrow points, stone hatchets, stone pipes, and half-shapen images. Of labor on the large scale, I think there is no remain as respectable as would be a common ditch for the draining of lands: unless indeed it be the Barrows, of which many are to be found all over this country. These are of different sizes, some of them constructed of earth, and some of loose stones. That they were reposi-

tories of the dead, has been obvious to all: but on what particular occasion constructed, was matter of doubt. Some have thought they covered the bones of those who have fallen in battles fought on the spot of internment. Some ascribed them to the custom, said to prevail among the Indians, of collecting, at certain periods, the bones of all their dead, wheresoever deposited at the time of death. Others again supposed them the general sepulchres for towns, conjectured to have been on or near these grounds; and this opinion was supported by the quality of the lands in which they are found (those constructed of earth being generally in the softest and most fertile meadow grounds on river sides), and by a tradition, said to be handed down from the Aboriginal Indians, that, when they settled in a town, the first person who died was placed erect, and earth put about him, so as to cover and support him; that, when another died, a narrow passage was dug to the first, the second reclined against him, and the cover of earth replaced, and so on.

There being one of these in my neighborhood, I wished to satisfy myself whether any, and which of these opinions were just. For this purpose I determined to open and examine it thoroughly. It was situated on the low grounds of the Rivanna, about two miles above its principal fork, and opposite to some hills, on which had been an Indian town. It was of spheroidical form, of about forty feet diameter at the base, and had been of about twelve feet altitude, though now reduced by the plough to seven and a half, having been under cultivation about a dozen years. Before this it was covered with trees of twelve inches diameter, and round the base was an excavation of five feet depth and width, from whence the earth had been taken of which the hillock was formed.

Notes on the State of Virginia by Thomas Jefferson, edited by William Peden. Copyright © 1955 by The University of North Carolina Press. Published for the Institute of Early American History and Culture, Williamsburg.

I first dug superficially in several parts of it, and came to collections of human bones, at different depths, from six inches to three feet below the surface. These were lying in the utmost confusion, some vertical, some oblique, some horizontal, and directed to every point of the compass, entangled, and held together in clusters by the earth. Bones of the most distant parts were found together, as, for instance, the small bones of the foot in the hollow of a scull, many sculls would sometimes be in contact, lying on the face, on the side, on the back, top, or bottom, so as, on the whole, to give the idea of bones emptied promiscuously from a bag or basket, and covered over with earth.

The bones of which the greatest numbers remained, were sculls, jawbones, teeth, the bones of the arms, thighs, legs, feet, and hands. A few ribs remained, some vertebrae of the neck and spine, without their processes, and one instance only of the bone which serves as a base to the vertebral column. The sculls were so tender, that they generally fell to pieces on being touched. The other bones were stronger. There were some teeth which were judged to be smaller than those of an adult; a scull, which, on a slight view, appeared to be that of an infant, but it fell to pieces on being taken out, so as to prevent satisfactory examination; a rib, and a fragment of the under-jaw of a person about half grown; another rib of an infant; and part of the jaw of a child, which had not yet cut its teeth.

This last furnishing the most decisive proof of the burial of children here, I was particular in my attention to it. It was part of the right-half of the under-jaw. The processes, by which it was articulated to the temporal bones, were entire; and the bone itself firm to where it had been broken off, which, as nearly as I could judge, was about the place of

the eyetooth. Its upper edge, wherein would have been the sockets of the teeth, was perfectly smooth. Measuring it with that of an adult, by placing their hinder processes together, its broken end extended to the penultimate grinder of the adult. This bone was white, all the others of a sand color. The bones of infants being soft, they probably decay sooner, which might be the cause so few were found here.

I proceeded then to make a perpendicular cut through the body of the barrow, that I might examine its internal structure. This passed about three feet from its center, was opened to the former surface of the earth, and was wide enough for a man to walk through and examine its sides. At the bottom, that is, on the level of the circumjacent plain, I found bones; above these a few stones, brought from a cliff a quarter of a mile off, and from the river one-eighth of a mile off; then a large interval of earth, then a stream of bones, and so on. At one end of the section were four strata of bones plainly distinguishable; at the other, three; the strata in one part not ranging with those in another. The bones nearest the surface were least decayed. No holes were discovered in any of them as if made with bullets, arrows, or other weapons. I conjectured that in this barrow might have been a thousand skeletons.

Every one will readily seize the circumstances above related, which militate against the opinion, that it covered the bones only of persons fallen in battle; and against the tradition also, which would make it the common sepulchre of a town, in which the bodies were placed upright, and touching each other. Appearances certainly indicate that it has derived both origin and growth from the accustomary collection of bones, and deposition of them together; that the first collection had been deposited on the common

surface of the earth, a few stones put over it, and then a covering of earth, that the second had been laid on this, had covered more or less of it in proportion to the number of bones, and then also covered with earth; and so on. The following are the particular circumstances which give it this aspect. 1) The number of bones. 2) Their confused position. 3) Their being in different strata. 4) The strata in one part have no correspondence with those in another. 5) The difference in the time of inhumation. 6) The existence of infant bones among them.

WOOLLEY AT THE DEATH PIT OF UR

Leonard Woolley's eighty-year lifetime (1880–1960) encompassed not only a distinguished career as an archaeologist but also service in British intelligence during World War I that landed him in a Turkish prison for two years. Starting in 1922 he devoted thirteen years to excavations at Ur, where he discovered evidence of the Flood and the rich, but ghastly, grave of the Sumerian Queen Shub-Ad.

Ur lies about half-way between Baghdad and the head of the Persian Gulf, some ten miles west of the present course of the Euphrates. A mile and a half to the east of the ruins runs the single line of railway which joins Basra to the capital of Iraq, and between the rail and the river there is sparse cultivation and little villages of mud huts or reed-mat shelters are dotted here and there; but westwards of the line is desert blank and unredeemed. Out of this waste rise the mounds which were Ur, called by the Arabs after the highest of them all, the Ziggurat hill, "Tel al Muqayyar," the Mound of Pitch. . . . It seems incredible that such a wilderness should ever have been habitable for man, and yet the weathered hillocks at one's feet cover the temples and houses of a very great city. . . .

The greater part of three seasons' work has been devoted to the clearing of the great cemetery which lay outside the walls of the old town and occupied the rubbish heaps piled up between them and the water-channel, and the treasures which have been unearthed from the graves during that time have revolutionised our ideas of the early civilization of the world. . . .

In 1927–8 we found five bodies lying side by side in a shallow sloping trench; except for the copper daggers at their waists and one or two small clay cups, they had none of the normal furniture of a grave, and the mere fact of there being a number thus together was unusual. Then, below them, a layer of matting was found, and tracing this along we came to another group of bodies, those of ten women carefully arranged in two rows; they wore head-dresses of gold, lapis lazuli, and carnelian, and elaborate bead necklaces, but they too possessed no regular tomb furnishings. At the end of the row lay the remains of a wonderful harp, the wood of it decayed but its decoration intact, making its reconstruction only a matter of care; the upright wooden beam was capped with gold, and in it were fastened the gold-headed nails which secured the strings; the sounding-box was edged with a mosaic in red stone, lapis lazuli and white shell, and from the front of it projected a splendid head of a bull wrought in gold with eyes and beard of lapis lazuli; across the ruins of the harp lay the bones of the gold-crowned harpist.

By this time we had found the earth sides of the pit in which the women's bodies lay and could see that the bodies of the five men were

on the ramp which led down to it. Following the pit along, we came upon more bones which at first puzzled us by being other than human, but the meaning of them soon became clear. A little way inside the entrance to the pit stood a wooden sledge chariot decorated with red, white, and blue mosaic along the edges of the framework and with golden heads of lions having manes of lapis lazuli and shell on its side panels; along the top rail were smaller gold heads of lions and bulls, silver lionesses' heads adorned the front, and the position of the vanished swingle-tree was shown by a band of blue and white inlay and two smaller heads of lionesses in silver. In front of the chariot lay the crushed skeletons of two asses with the bodies of the grooms by their heads, and on the top of the bones was the double ring, once attached to the pole, through which the reins had passed; it was of silver, and standing on it was a gold "mascot" in the form of a donkey most beautifully and realistically modelled.

Close to the chariot were an inlaid gaming-board and a collection of tools and weapons, including a set of chisels and a saw made of gold, big

bowls of gray soapstone, copper vessels, a long tube of gold and lapis which was a drinking tube for sucking up liquor from the bowls, more human bodies, and then the wreckage of a large wooden chest adorned with a figured mosaic in lapis lazuli

and shell which was found empty but had perhaps contained such perishable things as clothes. Behind this box were more offerings, masses of vessels in copper, silver, stone (including exquisite examples of volcanic glass, lapis lazuli, alabaster, and marble), and gold; one set of silver vessels seemed to be in the nature of a communion-service, for there was a shallow tray or platter, a jug with tall neck and long spout such as we know from carved stone reliefs to have been used in religious rites, and tall slender silver tumblers nested one inside another; a similar tumbler in gold, fluted and chased, with a fluted feeding-bowl, a chalice, and a plain oval bowl of gold lay piled together, and two magnificent lions' heads in silver, perhaps the ornaments of a throne, were amongst the treasures in the crowded pit. The perplexing thing was with all this wealth of objects we had found no body so far distinguished from the rest as to be that of the person to whom all were dedicated; logically our discovery, however great, was incomplete.

The objects were removed and we started to clear away the remains of the wooden box, a chest some six feet long and three feet across, when under it we found burnt bricks. They were fallen, but at one end some were still in place and formed the ring-vault of a stone chamber. The first and natural supposition was that here we had the tomb to which all the offerings belonged, but further search proved that the chamber was plundered, the roof had not fallen from decay but had been broken through, and the wooden box had been placed over the hole as if deliberately to hide it. Then, digging round the outside of the chamber, we found just such another pit as that six feet above. At the foot of the ramp lay six soldiers, orderly in two ranks, with copper spears by their sides and copper helmets crushed flat on the broken skulls; just inside, having evidently been backed down the slope, were two wooden four-wheeled waggons each drawn by three oxen—one of the latter so well preserved that we were able to lift the skeleton entire; the waggons were plain, but the reins were decorated with long beads of lapis and silver and passed through silver rings surmounted with mascots in the form of bulls; the grooms lay at the oxen's heads and the drivers in the bodies of the cars; of the cars themselves only the impression of the decayed wood remained in the soil, but so clear was this that a photograph showed the grain of the solid wooden wheel and the grey-white circle which had been the leather tyre.

Against the end wall of the stone chamber lay the bodies of nine women wearing the gala head-dress of lapis and carnelian beads from which hung golden pendants in the forms of beech leaves, great lunate earrings of gold, silver "combs" like the palm of a hand with three fingers tipped with flowers whose petals are inlaid with lapis, gold, and shell, and necklaces of lapis and gold; their heads were leaned against the masonry, their bodies extended on to the floor of the pit, and the whole space between them and the waggons was crowded with other dead, women and men, while the passage which led along the side of the chamber to its arched door was lined with soldiers carrying daggers, and with women. Of the soldiers in the central space one had a bundle of four spears, and by another there was a remarkable relief in copper with a design of two lions trampling on the bodies of two fallen men which may have been the decoration of a shield. . . .

Inside the tomb the robbers had left enough to show that it had contained bodies of several minor people as well as that of the chief person, whose name, if we can trust the inscription on a cylinder seal, was A-bar-gi; overlooked against the wall we found two model boats, one of copper now hopelessly decayed, the other of silver wonderfully well preserved; some two feet long, it has high stern and prow, five seats, and amidships an arched support for the awning which would protect the passenger, and the leaf-bladed oars are still set in the thwarts; it is a testimony to the conservatism of the

East that a boat of identical type is in use to-day on the marshes of the Lower Euphrates, some fifty miles from Ur.

The king's tomb-chamber lay at the far end of this open pit; continuing our search behind it we found a second stone chamber built up against it either at the same time or, more probably, at a later period. This chamber, roofed like the king's with a vault of ring arches in burnt brick, was the tomb of the queen to whom belonged the upper pit with its ass chariot and other offerings: her name, Shub-ad, was given us by a fine cylinder seal of lapis lazuli which was found in the filling of the shaft a little above the roof of the chamber and had probably been thrown into the pit at the moment when the earth was being put back into it. The vault of the chamber had fallen in, but luckily this was due to the weight of the earth above, not to the violence of tomb-robbers; the tomb itself was intact.

At one end, on the remains of a wooden bier, lay the body of the queen, a gold cup near her hand; the upper part of the body was entirely hidden by a mass of beads of gold, silver, lapis lazuli, carnelian, agate, and chalcedony, long strings of which, hanging from a collar, had formed a cloak reaching to the waist and bordered below with a broad band of tubular beads of lapis, carnelian, and gold: against the right arm were three long gold pins of lapis heads and three amulets in the form of fish, two of gold and one of lapis, and a fourth in the form of two seated gazelles, also of gold.

The head-dress whose remains covered the crushed skull was a more elaborate edition of that worn by the court ladies; its basis was a broad gold ribbon festooned in loops round the hair—and the measurement of the curves showed that this was not the natural hair but a wig padded out to an almost grotesque size; over this came three wreaths, the lowest hanging down over the forehead, of plain gold ring pendants, the second of beech leaves, the third of long willow leaves in sets of three with gold flowers whose petals were of blue and white inlay; all these were strung on triple chains of lapis and carnelian beads. Fixed into the back of the hair was a golden "Spanish comb" with five points ending in lapis-centered gold flowers. Heavy spiral rings of gold wire were twisted into the side curls of the wig, huge lunate earrings of gold hung down to the shoulders, and apparently from the hair also hung on each side a string of large square stone beads with, at the end of each, a lapis amulet, one shaped as a seated bull and the other as a calf. Complicated as the head-dress was, its different parts lay in such good order that it was possible to reconstruct the whole. . . .

The discovery was now complete and our earlier difficulty was explained: King A-bar-gi's grave and Queen Shub-ad's were exactly alike, but whereas the former was all on one plane, the queen's tomb-chamber had been sunk below the general level of her grave-pit. Probably they were husband and wife: the king had died first and been buried, and it had been the queen's wish to lie as close to him as might be; for this end the grave-diggers had reopened the king's shaft, going down in it until the top of the chamber vault appeared; then they had stopped work in the main shaft but had dug down at the back of the chamber's pit in which the queen's stone tomb could be built. But the treasures known to lie in the king's grave were too great a temptation for the workmen; the outer pit where the bodies of the court ladies lay was protected by six feet of earth which they could not disturb without being detected, but the richer plunder in the royal chamber itself was separated from them only by the bricks of the vault; they broke through the arch, carried off their spoil, and placed the great clothes-chest of the queen over the hole to hide their sacrilege.

Nothing else would account for the plundered vault lying immediately below the untouched grave of the queen, and the connecting of Shub-ad's stone chamber with the upper "death-pit," as we came to call these open shafts in which the subsidiary bodies lay, made an exact parallel to the king's grave and, in a lesser degree, to the other royal tombs. Clearly, when a royal person died, he or she was accompanied to the grave by all the members of the court: the king had at least three people with him in his chamber and sixty-two in the death-pit; where there was a larger stone building with two or four rooms, then one of these was for the royal body and the rest for the followers sacrificed in precisely the same way; the ritual was identical, only the accommodation for the victims differed. . . .

On the subject of human sacrifice more light was thrown by the discovery of a great death-pit excavated last winter. At about twenty-six feet below the surface we came upon a mass of mud brick not truly laid but rammed together and forming, as we guessed, not a floor but a stopping, as it were, of a shaft. Immediately below this we were able to distinguish clean-cut earth sides of a pit, sloping inwards and smoothly plastered with mud; following these down, we found the largest death-pit that the cemetery has yet produced. The pit was roughly rectangular and measured thirty-seven feet by twenty-four at the bottom, and was approached as usual by a sloped ramp. In it lay the bodies of six men-servants and sixty-eight women; the men lay along the side of the door, the bodies of the women were disposed in regular rows across the floor, every one lying on her side with legs slightly bent and hands brought up near the face, so close together that the heads of those in one row rested on the legs of those in the row above. Here was to be observed even more clearly what had been fairly obvious in the graves of Shub-ad and her husband, the neatness with which the bodies were laid out, the entire absence of any signs of violence or terror.

We have often been asked how the victims in the royal graves met their death, and it is impossible to give a decisive answer. The bones are too crushed and too decayed to show any cause of death, supposing that violence had been used, but the general condition of the bodies does supply a strong argument. Very many of these women wear headdresses which are delicate in themselves and would easily be disarranged, yet such are always found in good order, undisturbed except by the pressure of the earth; this would be impossible if the wearers had been knocked on the head, improbable if they had fallen to the ground after being stabbed, and it is equally unlikely that they could have been killed outside the grave and carried down the ramp and laid in their places with all their ornaments intact; certainly the animals must have been alive when they dragged the chariots down the ramp, and if so, the grooms who led them and the drivers in the cars must have been alive also; it is safe to assume that those who were to be sacrificed went down alive into the pit.

That they were dead, or at least unconscious, when the earth was flung in and trampled down on the top of them is an equally safe assumption, for in any other case there must have been some struggle which would have left its traces in the attitude of the bodies, but these are always decently composed; indeed, they are in such good order and alignment that we are driven to suppose that after they were lying unconscious someone entered the pit and gave the final touches to their arrangement—and the circumstances that in A-bar-gi's grave, the harps were placed on the top of the bodies proves that someone did enter the grave at the end. It is most probable that the victims walked to their places, took some kind of drug—opium or hashish would serve—and lay down in order; after the drug had worked, whether it produced sleep or death, the last touches were given to their bodies and the pit was filled in. There does not seem to have been anything brutal in the manner of their deaths. . . .

It must have been a very gaily dressed crowd that assembled in the open mat-lined pit for the royal obsequies, a blaze of colour with the crimson coats, the silver, and the gold; clearly these people were not wretched slaves killed as oxen might be killed, but persons held in honour, wearing their robes of office, and coming, one hopes, voluntarily to a rite which would in their belief be but a passing from one world to another, from the service of a god on earth to that of the same god in another sphere.

This much I think we can safely assume. Human sacrifice was confined exclusively to the funerals of royal persons, and in the graves of commoners, however rich, there is no sign of anything of the sort, not even such substitutes, clay figurines, etc., as are so common in Egyptian tombs and appears there to be reminiscent of an ancient and more bloody rite. In much later times Sumerian kings were deified in their lifetime and honoured as gods after their death: the prehistoric kings of Ur were in their obsequies so distinguished from their subjects because they too were looked upon as superhuman, earthly deities; and when the chroniclers wrote in the annals of Sumer that "after the Flood kingship again descended from the gods," they meant no less than this. If the king, then, was a god, he did not die as men die, but was translated; and it might therefore be not a hardship but a privilege for those of his court to accompany their master and continue in his service.

A SCHOOLBOY FINDS THE PAINTED CAVE OF LASCAUX

In September 1940 four fifteen-year-old French schoolboys were wandering in the woods of the Dordogne Valley in southwest France with a dog named Robot. When the dog disappeared in a hole the boys went to his rescue and in so doing discovered the now famous painted cave of Lascaux. Modern man's first glimpse of these Paleolithic works of art is described here in a letter written by one of the boys, Marcel Ravidat, to their schoolmaster, Léon Laval.

I threw some large stones into the hole and was amazed at how long they took to hit bottom and was also surprised at the loud echo they made as they fell. Armed with a large cake knife, the blade well honed by me, I started to dig around the hole to make it big enough for me to get through. After an hour of very hard work, I tried to get into the hole. I thought that all that hard work was lost, my shoulders were too large! But by trying another tactic I managed to push my way in as far as five to six feet, but vertically, head first. It's hardly worth telling you all the trouble I had to even go that distance.

Then I turned on my flashlight and looked around me. I had hardly taken a step forward when I tripped on some loose clay that had been dislodged from the walls and I fell straight to the bottom. I got up, stiff from the fall, and relit my flashlight which I had the sense to hold on to.

After checking first to see if it was safe to climb down, I called to my three pals to join me but warned them to be careful.

Once reunited we started to explore the cave. Looking to the right and to the left we slowly walked across the cave. Our progress was slow because as we walked, the beam from the flashlight was weaving drunkenly around. There were no obstructions as we made our way across a large chamber, finally finding ourselves in a narrow passage with quite a high ceiling. We flashed the light high up onto the walls and it is then that we noticed, by its flickering light, several different colored drawings.

Fascinated by these outlines, we started to examine them very closely and we discovered several figures that looked like large animals. It was then that we realized that we had discovered a cave with prehistoric paintings. Encouraged by our success we proceeded through the rest of the cave making more and more discoveries.

Our joy was indescribable. We were like a band of savages doing a war dance. We decided to say nothing about our discovery to anyone and to return with a stronger light.

The following day armed with all we needed, one by one we left, each at ten minute intervals, each taking different routes, like a band of Indians hiding their tracks.

Arriving at our "treasure" (that's the name we gave our discovery) we

set off again into the unknown. Going from one wonder to another, we came to a passage that went down vertically so deep we couldn't see the bottom. There we stopped. "Who will be the first to go down?" My friends were afraid that they couldn't get back up again. One could only get up by holding on to a slippery rope. But it wasn't that that made me hesitate, for I knew my arms were strong. It was the strength of my friends who had to hold my seventy kilos with only their arms and with nothing to lean against. In spite of my doubts, the three managed to lower me down, and with my heart beating fast, I reached the bottom.

I looked up and saw that I'd come down a long way, at least a dozen meters. Off I went again on this new adventure. I hadn't gone more than twenty to thirty meters when I hit a landslide. I circled around again inspecting the walls. There to my great surprise, I saw a human figure with the head of a bird and with only four fingers on each hand, being knocked down by a bison. All of it forming a picture of about two meters in size.

After exploring every crevice, I

climbed back up, not without enormous trouble, reaching the place where my friends were waiting. As soon as I told them of my discovery they all wanted to go down and see it. I didn't want to stop them, although I warned them of the difficulties of getting back up again.

They had such confidence in my strength that, one by one, they descended into the well. But climbing back up was another story. I had to hoist each one up with my hands alone, never really being sure of my balance. Finally I managed to get them all back up and it was with very pale faces that they told me the effect the unexpected paintings had on them.

MASPERO FINDS A HOARD OF ROYAL MUMMIES

During his tenure in the 1880's as director general of excavations and antiquities of Egypt, Gaston Maspero (1846–1916) waged an energetic war on tomb robbers. In this excerpt from an 1881 article in the Institut Egyptien Bulletin *Maspero describes how his assistant, Emile Brugsch, broke up a ring of tomb robbers and found the source of the grave goods they had been selling. The robbers, it turned out, had uncovered not just the tomb of a single pharaoh but a chamber piled with the mummies of great kings and queens.*

The history of this unique hoard went back to about 1000 B.C. Alarmed by the depredations of the grave robbers of that time, the high priests of the twenty-first dynasty had removed the mummies of many important rulers and secreted them in a deep, unmarked shaft originally dug for one obscure queen. This was the hiding place that the latter-day robbers had discovered.

For some several years past it had been realised that the Arabs of Gurna had found one or two royal tombs whose whereabouts they refused to divulge. In the spring of 1876 an English general named Campbell had shown me the hieratic ritual papyrus of the high-priest Pinotem, bought in Thebes for £400. In 1877 M. de Saulcy sent me on behalf of one of his friends in Syria, photographs of a long papyrus belonging to Queen Notmit, mother of Herihor, the end of which is now in the Louvre and the beginning in England. M. Mariette had also nego-, tiated at Suez the purchase of two other papyri written in the name of a Queen Tiuhathor Henttaui. About the same time funerary statuettes of King Pinotem appeared on the market, some of fine workmanship and the others coarse. Briefly the fact that a discovery had been made became so certain that [in] 1878 I could definitely state concerning a tablet belonging to Rogers Bey that "it came from a tomb close to the, as yet, unlocated tombs of the Herihor family". . . .

To find the site of these royal tombs was therefore, if not the main, at least one of the principal objects of a trip which I made to Upper Egypt during March and April 1881. My intention was not to carry out any sondages or to settle down to excavations in the Theban necropolis; the problem was far more difficult. It was necessary to extract from the fellahin the secret which they had so zealously guarded until now. I had learnt only one thing: the principal dealers in antiquities were a certain Abd-er-Rassoul Ahmed, of Sheik Abd-el-Gurna, and a certain Mustapha Aga Ayad, vice-consul of England and Belgium at Luxor. I returned to Europe but left M. Emile Brugsch, my assistant curator, the necessary powers to act for me in my stead. He left for Thebes on Saturday, 1st July, accompanied by a trustworthy friend and Ahmed Effendi

Kamal, the Museum secretary-interpreter. A surprise awaited him at Qena: Daud Pasha [the governor] had seized several precious objects at the house of the Abd-er-Rassoul brothers including three papyri of Queen Makere, Queen Isiemkheb and the princess Nesikhonsu. It was a promising beginning. To ensure the happy outcome of this delicate operation that was just beginning, His Excellency had placed his *wekil* at the service of our agents and also several employees of the Mudir. . . .

On Wednesday, the 6th, Messrs. Emile Brugsch and Ahmed Effendi Kamal were led by Mohammed Ahmed Abd-er-Rassoul directly to the place where the funeral vault was located. The Egyptian engineer who had excavated it so long ago had laid his plans in a most skilful manner; never was a hiding place more cleverly concealed. The line of hills which separates the Biban-el-Moluk [Valley of the Kings] from the Theban plain here forms a series of natural circular clefts between the Assassif and the Valley of the Queens, of which the best known is that where the temple of Deir el-Bahari was built. In the rock face which separates Deir el-Bahari from the next cleft just behind the hill of Sheikh Abd-el-Gurna, about sixty metres above the level of the cultivated ground, a shaft eleven and a half metres deep and about two metres in diameter had been dug. At the bottom of the shaft, on the west side was the entrance to a passage 1.4 metres wide and 80 cm high. After running for 7.4 metres it turned suddenly northwards and continued for another 60 metres, the measurements never remaining constant: in places the passage was two metres wide and in others not more than 1.3 metres; near the middle five or six roughly cut steps showed a marked change of level, and on the right hand side an unfinished niche indicated that another change in direc-

"A Hoard of Royal Mummies," by Gaston Maspero, *Institut Egyptien Bulletin, 1881.* Translated by P. A. Clayton in *The World of Archaeology,* edited by C. W. Ceram. Copyright © 1966. Reprinted by permission of Thames & Hudson Ltd.

tion of the passage had at one time been considered. Finally it opened out into an irregular, oblong chamber about eight metres long.

The first object which had presented itself to M. Emile Brugsch's gaze when he reached the bottom of the shaft was a white and yellow coffin inscribed with the name Nesikhonsu. It was in the passage about sixty centimetres from the entrance; a little farther on was a coffin of XVII dynasty style, then the

Queen Tiuhathor Henttaui, then Seti I. Beside the coffins and scattered on the ground were wooden funerary statuettes, canopic jars, bronze libation vases, and, at the back in the corner angle made by the passage as it turned northward was the funeral tent of Queen Isiemkheb bent and crumpled like a valueless object, which a priest in a hurry to get out had thrown carelessly into a corner. The entire length of the main passage was similarly obstructed and disordered: it was necessary to advance on all fours not knowing where one was putting hands and feet. The coffins and the mummies rapidly glimpsed by the light of the candle bore historic names, Amenhetep I, Tuthmoses II, in the niche near the steps, Ahmose I and his son Siamun, Sequenre, Queen Ahotpe, Ahmose, Nefertari and others. The chamber at the end was the height of confusion but it was possible to see at first glance that the style of the XXth dynasty predominated. Mohammed Ahmed Abd-er-Rassoul's report which had at first seemed exaggerated hardly expressed the truth: where I had expected to find one or two minor kings, the Arabs had dug up a vault full of Pharaohs. And what Pharaohs! Probably the most famous in the history of Egypt, Tuthmoses III and Seti I, Ahmose the Liberator and Ramesses II the Conqueror. M. Emile Brugsch thought that he must be dreaming coming upon such an assemblage so suddenly. Like him I still ask myself if it is true and if I am dreaming when I see and touch the bodies of all these people when we never thought to know more than their names.

Two hours were sufficient for the preliminary examination, then the work of getting the coffins out began. Three hundred Arabs were quickly assembled by the Mudir's officials and put to work. The Museum's boat, hastily summoned, had not yet arrived; but one of its pilots, Reis Mohammed, who was perfectly trustworthy, was present. He descended to the bottom of the shaft and supervised the removal of its contents. Messrs. Emile Brugsch and Ahmed Effendi Kamal received the objects and sorted them out as best they could on the ground without relaxing their vigilance for a moment, then the objects were carried to the bottom of the hill and laid side by side. Forty-eight hours of hard work got everything out of the cache; but the task was by no means finished. It was still necessary for the convoy to cross the Theban plain to the river's edge near Luxor. Several of the coffins, lifted only with the greatest difficulty by a dozen or sixteen men, took seven to eight hours to make the journey to the river, and it can easily be imagined what such a journey was like in the dust and heat of July.

At last, on the evening of the eleventh, all the mummies and coffins were at Luxor, carefully wrapped in matting and canvas. Three days later the Museum's steamer arrived and no sooner was it loaded than it set sail back to Bulaq with its cargo of kings. A strange thing happened! From Luxor to Quft on both banks of the Nile the wailing fellahin women with dishevelled hair followed the boat and the men fired off their guns, just as they do at funerals. Mohammed Abd-er-Rassoul was rewarded with five hundred pounds sterling, and I thought it best to appoint him reis of excavations at Thebes: if he serves the Museum with the same skill which he had used for so many years against it, we may hope for some magnificent discoveries.

CARTER OPENS THE TOMB OF TUTANKHAMEN

Without any doubt the most sensational archaeological find of this century was Howard Carter's discovery of the tomb of the pharaoh Tutankhamen in Egypt's Valley of the Kings in 1922. His account of the discovery and opening of the tomb reveals that he was a remarkably patient man—he held up the digging for two weeks until the arrival of his sponsor, Lord Carnarvon—as well as a meticulous excavator and a master of the suspense story.

This was to be our final season in The Valley. Six full seasons we had excavated there, and season after season had drawn a blank; we had worked for months at a stretch and found nothing, and only an excavator knows how desperately depressing that can be; we had almost made up our minds that we were beaten, and were preparing to leave The Valley and try our luck elsewhere; and then—hardly had we set hoe to ground in our last despairing effort than we made a discovery that exceeded our wildest dreams.

I [had] arrived in Luxor on October 28th, and by November 1st I had enrolled my workmen and was ready to begin. Our former excavations had stopped short at the northeast corner of the tomb of Ramses VI, and from this point I started trenching southwards. It will be remembered that in this area there were a number of roughly constructed workmen's huts, used probably by the labourers in the tomb of Ramses. These huts, built about three feet above bed-rock, covered the whole area in front of the Ramesside tomb, and continued in a southerly direction to join up with a similar group of huts on the opposite side of The Valley, discovered by [Theodore] Davis in connexion with his work on the Akhenaten cache. By the evening of November 3rd we had laid bare a sufficient number of these huts for experimental purposes, so, after we had planned and noted them, they were removed, and we were ready to clear away the three feet of soil beneath them.

Hardly had I arrived on the work next morning (November 4th) than the unusual silence, due to the stoppage of the work, made me realize that something out of the ordinary had happened, and I was greeted by the announcement that a step cut in the rock had been discovered underneath the very first hut to be attacked. This seemed too good to be true, but a short amount of extra clearing revealed the fact that we were actually in the entrance of a steep cut in the rock, some thirteen feet below the entrance to the tomb of Ramses VI, and a similar depth

from the present bed level of The Valley. The manner of cutting was that of the sunken stairway entrance so common in The Valley, and I almost dared to hope that we had found our tomb at last. Work continued feverishly throughout the whole of that day and the morning of the next, but it was not until the afternoon of November 5th that we succeeded in clearing away the masses of rubbish that overlay the cut, and were able to demarcate the upper edges of the stairway. . . .

The cutting was excavated in the side of a small hillock, and, as the work progressed, its western edge receded under the slope of the rock until it was, first partially, and then completely, roofed in, and became a passage, 10 feet high by 6 feet wide. Work progressed more rapidly now; step succeeded step, and at the level of the twelfth, towards sunset, there was disclosed the upper part of a doorway, blocked, plastered, and sealed.

A sealed doorway—it was actually true, then! Our years of patient labour were to be rewarded after all, and I think my first feeling was one of congratulation that my faith in The Valley had not been unjustified. With excitement growing to fever heat I searched the seal impressions on the door for evidence of the identity of the owner, but could find no name: the only decipherable ones were those of the well-known royal necropolis seal, the jackal and nine captives. Two facts, however, were clear: first, the employment of this royal seal was certain evidence that the tomb had been constructed for a person of very high standing; and second, that the sealed door was entirely screened from above by workmen's huts of the Twentieth Dynasty was sufficiently clear proof that at least from that date it had never been entered. With that for the moment I had to be content. . . .

Naturally my wish was to go

straight ahead with our clearing to find out the full extent of the discovery, but Lord Carnarvon was in England, and in fairness to him I had to delay matters until he could come. Accordingly, on the morning of November 6th I sent him the following cable:—"At last have made wonderful discovery in Valley; a magnificent tomb with seals intact; re-covered same for your arrival; congratulations."

. . . On the 23rd Lord Carnarvon arrived in Luxor with his daughter, Lady Evelyn Herbert, his devoted companion in all his Egyptian work, and everything was in hand for the beginning of the second chapter of the discovery of the tomb. [A. R.] Callender had been busy all day clearing away the upper layer of rubbish, so that by morning we should be able to get into the staircase without any delay.

By the afternoon of the 24th the whole staircase was clear, sixteen steps in all, and we were able to make a proper examination of the sealed doorway. On the lower part the seal impressions were much clearer, and we were able without any difficulty to make out on several of them the name of Tutankhamen. Now . . . it was possible to discern a fact that had hitherto escaped notice—that there had been two successive openings and re-closings of a part of its surface. . . . The tomb then was not absolutely intact. . . .

On [November 25th] the sealed doorway was to be removed, so Callender set carpenters to work making a heavy wooden grille to be set up in its place. Mr. Engelbach, Chief Inspector of the Antiquities Department, paid us a visit during the afternoon, and witnessed part of the final clearing of rubbish from the doorway.

On the morning of the 25th the seal impressions on the doorway were carefully noted and photographed, and then we removed the actual blocking of the door, consisting of rough stones carefully built from floor to lintel, and heavily plastered on their outer faces to take the seal impressions.

This disclosed the beginning of a descending passage (not a staircase), the same width as the entrance stairway, and nearly seven feet high. . . . It was filled completely with stone and rubble, probably the chip from its own excavation. This filling showed distinct signs of more than one opening and reclosing of the tomb, the untouched part consisting of clean white chip, mingled with dust, whereas the disturbed part was composed mainly of dark flint. It was clear that an irregular tunnel had been cut through the original filling at the upper left corner. . . .

As we cleared the passage we found, mixed with the rubble of the lower levels, broken potsherds, jar sealings, alabaster jars, whole and broken, vases of painted pottery, numerous fragments of smaller articles, and water skins, these last having obviously been used to bring up the water needed for the plastering of the doorways. These were clear evidence of plundering, and we eyed them askance. By night we had cleared a considerable distance down the passage, but as yet saw no sign of second doorway or chamber.

The day following (November 26th) was the day of days, the most wonderful that I have ever lived through, and certainly one whose like I can never hope to see again. Throughout the morning the work of clearing continued, slowly perforce, on account of the delicate objects that were mixed with the filling. Then, in the middle of the afternoon, thirty feet down from the outer door, we came upon a second sealed doorway, almost an exact replica of the first. The seal impressions in this case were less distinct, but still recognizable as those of Tutankhamen and of the royal necropolis.

Here again the signs of opening and re-closing were clearly marked upon the plaster. We were firmly convinced by this time that it was a cache that we were about to open, and not a tomb. The arrangement of stairway, entrance passage and doors reminded us very forcibly of the cache of Akhenaten and Tiy material found in the very near vicinity of the present excavation by Davis, and the fact that Tutankhamen's seals occured there likewise seemed almost certain proof that we were right in our conjecture. We were soon to know. There lay the sealed doorway, and behind it was the answer. . . .

Slowly, desperately slowly it seemed to us as we watched, the remains of passage debris that encumbered the lower part of the doorway were removed, until at last we had the whole door clear before us. The decisive moment had arrived. With trembling hands I made a tiny breach in the upper left hand corner. Darkness and blank space, as far as an iron testing-rod could reach, showed that whatever lay beyond was empty, and not filled like the passage we had just cleared. Candle tests were applied as a precaution against possible foul gases, and then, widening the hole a little, I inserted the candle and peered in, Lord Carnarvon, Lady Evelyn and Callender standing anxiously beside me to hear the verdict. At first I could see nothing, the hot air escaping from the chamber causing the candle flame to flicker, but presently, as my eyes grew accustomed to the light, details of the room within emerged slowly from the mist, strange animals, statues, and gold—everywhere the glint of gold. For the moment—an eternity it must have seemed to the others standing by—I was struck dumb with amazement, and when Lord Carnarvon, unable to stand the suspense any longer, inquired anxiously, "Can you see

anything?" it was all I could do to get out the words, "Yes, wonderful things." Then widening the hole a little further, so that we both could see, we inserted an electric torch.

I suppose most excavators would confess to a feeling of awe—embarrassment almost—when they break into a chamber closed and sealed by pious hands so many centuries ago. For the moment, time as a factor in human life has lost its meaning. Three thousand, four thousand years maybe, have passed and gone since human feet last trod the floor on which you stand, and yet, as you note the signs of recent life around you—the half-filled bowl of mortar for the door, the blackened lamp, the finger-mark upon the freshly painted surface, the farewell garland dropped upon the threshold—you feel it might have been but yesterday. The very air you breathe, unchanged throughout the centuries, you share with those who laid the mummy to its rest. Time is annihilated by little intimate details such as these, and you feel an intruder.

That is perhaps the first and dominant sensation, but others follow thick and fast—the exhilaration of discovery, the fever of suspense, the almost overmastering impluse, born of curiosity, to break down seals and lift the lids of boxes, the thought—pure joy to the investigator—that you are about to add a page to history, or solve some problem of research, the strained expectancy—why not confess it?—of the treasure-seeker. Did these thoughts actually pass through our minds at the time, or have I imagined them since? I cannot tell. It was the discovery that my memory was blank, and not the mere desire for dramatic chapter-ending, that occasioned this digression.

Surely never before in the whole history of excavation had such an amazing sight been seen as the light of our torch revealed to us. . . . imagine how [it] appeared to us as we looked down from our spy-hole in the blocked doorway, casting the beam of light from our torch—the first light that had pierced the darkness of the chamber for three thousand years—from one group of objects to another, in a vain attempt to interpret the treasure that lay before us. The effect was bewildering, overwhelming. I suppose we had never formulated exactly in our minds just what we had expected or hoped to see, but certainly we had never dreamed of anything like this, a roomful—a whole museumful it seemed—of objects, some familiar, but some the like of which we had never seen, piled one upon another in seemingly endless profusion.

Gradually the scene grew clearer, and we could pick out individual objects. First, right opposite to us—we had been conscious of them all the while, but refused to believe in them—were three great gilt couches, their sides carved in the form of monstrous animals, curiously attenuated in body, as they had to be to serve their purpose, but with heads of startling realism. Uncanny beasts enough to look upon at any time: seen as we saw them, their brilliant gilded surfaces picked out of the darkness by our electric torch, as though by limelight, their heads throwing grotesque distorted shadows on the wall behind them, they were almost terrifying. Next, on the right, two statues caught and held our attention; two life-sized figures of a king in black, facing each other like sentinels, gold kilted, gold sandalled, armed with mace and staff, the protective sacred cobra upon their foreheads. . . .

By the middle of February our work in the antechamber was finished. With the exception of the two sentinel statues, left for a special reason, all its contents had been removed to the laboratory, every inch of its floor had been swept and sifted for the last bead or fallen piece

of inlay, and it now stood bare and empty. We were ready at last to penetrate the mystery of the sealed door.

Friday, the 17th, was the day appointed, and at two o'clock those who were to be privileged to witness the ceremony met by appointment above the tomb. . . . By a quarter past two the whole company had assembled, so we removed our coats and filed down the sloping passage into the tomb.

. . . There before us lay the sealed door, and with its opening we were to blot out the centuries and stand in the presence of a king who reigned three thousand years ago. My own feelings as I mounted the platform were a strange mixture, and it was with a trembling hand that I struck the first blow.

My first care was to locate the wooden lintel above the door: then very carefully I chipped away the plaster and picked out the small stones which formed the uppermost layer of the filling. The temptation to stop and peer inside at every moment was irresistible, and when, after about ten minutes' work, I had made a hole large enough to enable me to do so, I inserted an electric torch. An astonishing sight its light revealed, for there, within a yard of the doorway, stretching as far as one could see and blocking the entrance to the chamber, stood what to all appearance was a solid wall of gold. For the moment there was no clue as to its meaning, so as quickly as I dared I set to work to widen the hole. This had now become an operation of considerable difficulty, for the stones of the masonry were not accurately squared blocks built regularly upon one another, but rough slabs of varying size, some so heavy that it took all one's strength to lift them: many of them, too, as the weight above was removed, were left so precariously balanced that the least false movement would have sent

them sliding inwards to crash upon the contents of the chamber below. We were also endeavouring to preserve the seal-impressions upon the thick mortar of the outer face, and this added considerably to the difficulty of handling the stones. [Arthur C.] Mace and Callender were helping me by this time and each stone was cleared on a regular system. With a crowbar I gently eased it up, Mace holding it to prevent it falling forwards; then he and I lifted it out and passed it back to Callender, who transferred it on to one of the foremen, and so, by a chain of workmen, up the passage and out of the tomb.

With the removal of a very few stones the mystery of the golden wall was solved. We were at the entrance of the actual burial-chamber of the king, and that which barred our way was the side of an immense gilt shrine built to cover and protect the sarcophagus. It was visible now from the Antechamber by the light of the standard lamps, and as stone after stone was removed, and its gilded surface came gradually into view, we could, as though by electric current, feel the tingle of excitement which thrilled the spectators behind the barrier. . . .

In clearing away the blocking of the doorway we had discovered that the level of the inner chamber was about four feet lower than that of the Antechamber, and this, combined with the fact that there was but a narrow space between the door and shrine, made an entrance by no means easy to effect. Fortunately, there were no smaller antiquities at this end of the chamber, so I lowered myself down, and then, taking one of the portable lights, I edged cautiously to the corner of the shrine and looked beyond it. At the corner two beautiful alabaster vases blocked the way, but I could see that if these were removed we should have a clear path to the other end of the chamber; so, carefully marking the spot on which they stood, I picked them up—with the exception of the king's wishing-cup they were of finer quality and more graceful shape than any we had yet found—and passed them back to the Antechamber. Lord Carnarvon and M. Lacau now joined me, and, picking our way along the narrow passage between shrine and wall, we investigated further.

It was, beyond question, the sepulchral chamber in which we stood, for there, towering above us, was one of the great gilt shrines beneath which kings were laid. So enormous was this structure (17 feet by 11 feet, and 9 feet high, we found afterwards) that it filled within a little the entire area of the chamber, a space of some two feet only separating it from the walls on all four sides, while its roof, with cornice top and torus moulding, reached almost to the ceiling. From top to bottom it was overlaid with gold, and upon its sides there were inlaid panels of brilliant blue faience, in which were represented, repeated over and over, the magic symbols which would ensure its strength and safety. Around the shrine, resting upon the ground, there were a number of funerary emblems, and, at the north end, the seven magic oars the king would need to ferry himself across the waters of the underworld. The walls of the chamber, unlike those of the Antechamber, were decorated with brightly painted scenes and inscriptions, brilliant in their colors, but somewhat hastily executed.

These last details we must have noticed subsequently, for at the time our one thought was of the shrine and of its safety. Had the thieves penetrated within it and disturbed the royal burial? Here, on the eastern end, were the great folding doors, closed and bolted, but not sealed, that would answer the question for us. Eagerly we drew the bolts, swung back the doors, and

there within was a second shrine with similar bolted doors, and upon the bolts a seal, intact. This seal we determined not to break, for our doubts were resolved, and we could not penetrate further without risk of serious damage to the monument. I think at the moment we did not even want to break the seal, for a feeling of intrusion had descended heavily upon us with the opening of the doors, heightened, probably, by the almost painful impressiveness of a linen pall, decorated with golden rosettes, which drooped above the inner shrine. We felt that we were in the presence of the dead King and must do him reverence, and in imagination could see the doors of the successive shrines open one after the other till the innermost disclosed the King himself. Carefully, and as silently as possible, we re-closed the great swing doors, and passed on to the farther end of the chamber.

Here a surprise awaited us, for a low door, eastwards from the sepulchral chamber, gave entrance to yet another chamber, smaller than the outer ones and not so lofty. This doorway, unlike the others, had not been closed and sealed. We were able, from where we stood, to get a clear view of the whole of the contents, and a single glance sufficed to tell us that here, within this little chamber, lay the greatest treasures of the tomb. Facing the doorway, on the farther side, stood the most beautiful monument that I have ever seen—so lovely that it made one gasp with wonder and admiration. The central portion of it consisted of a large shrine-shaped chest, completely overlaid with gold, and surmounted by a cornice of sacred cobras. Surrounding this, free-standing, were statues of the four tutelary goddesses of the dead—gracious figures with outstretched protective arms, so natural and lifelike in their pose, so pitiful and compassionate the expression upon their faces, that

one felt it almost sacrilege to look at them. One guarded the shrine on each of its four sides, but whereas the figures at front and back kept their gaze firmly fixed upon their charge, an additional note of touching realism was imparted by the other two, for their heads were turned sideways, looking over their shoulders towards the entrance, as though to watch against surprise. There is a simple grandeur about this monument that made an irresistible appeal to the imagination, and I am not ashamed to confess that it brought a lump to my throat. It is undoubtedly the canopic chest and contains the jars which play such an important part in the ritual of mummification. . . .

How much time we occupied in this first survey of the wonders of the tomb I cannot say, but it must have seemed endless to those anxiously waiting in the Antechamber. Not more than three at a time could be admitted with safety, so, when Lord Carnarvon and M. Lacau came out, the others came in pairs: first Lady Evelyn Herbert, the only woman present, with Sir William Garstin, and then the rest in turn. It was curious, as we stood in the Antechamber, to watch their faces as, one by one, they emerged from the door. Each had a dazed, bewildered look in his eyes, and each in turn, as he came out, threw up his hands before him, an unconscious gesture of impotence to describe in words the wonders that he had seen. They were indeed indescribable, and the emotions they had aroused in our minds were of too intimate a nature to communicate, even though we had the words at our command. It was an experience which, I am sure, none of us who were present is ever likely to forget, for in imagination—and not wholly in imagination either—we had been present at the funeral ceremonies of a king long dead and almost forgotten.

In the tomb of Tutankhamen in 1925 Howard Carter opens one of four shrines guarding the king's sarcophagus.

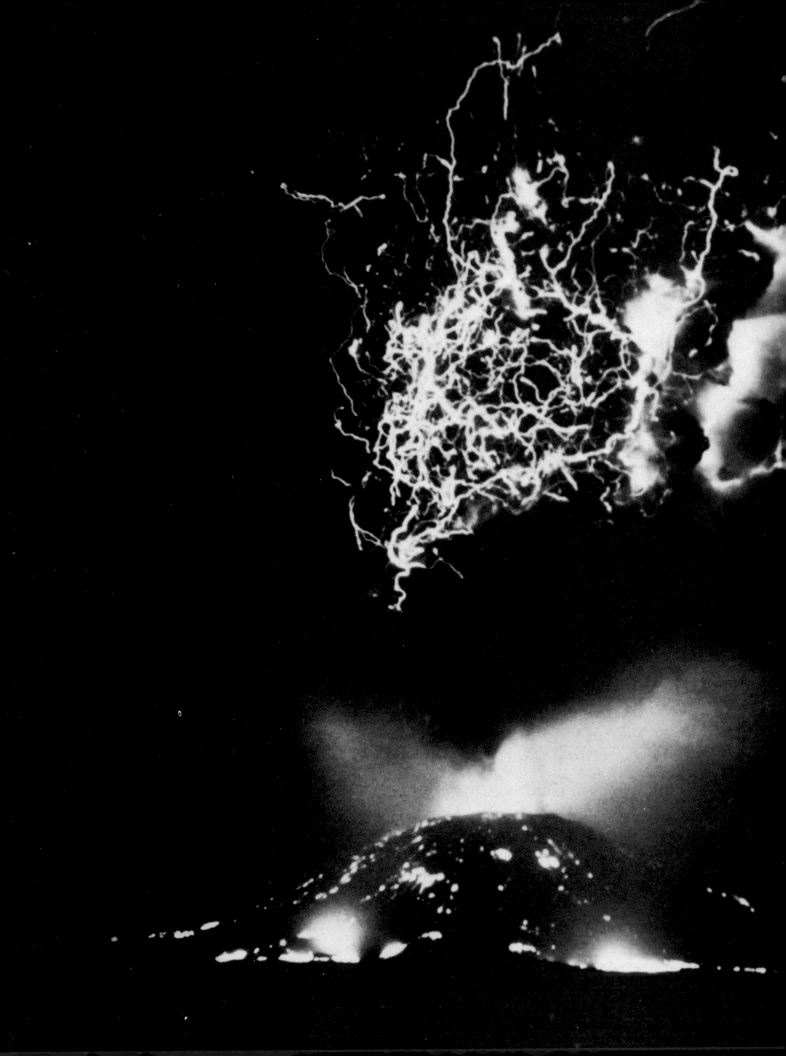

6: Time Stopped at Pompeii

by MICHAEL GRANT

The night sky in the background picture was lit by electrical storms and flaming lava during the last great eruption of Vesuvius, in 1944. The mosaic above, from a Pompeii villa, depicts an actor's mask of tragedy.

Just nineteen hundred years ago a group of small cities beside the Bay of Naples, in the smiling, fertile Italian territory of Campania, were obliterated and buried in the depths of the earth by the savage action of Mount Vesuvius. It was an event which has had the strange result of preserving, for our eventual study, a unique amount of information about the ancient world. It has also exercised an almost incalculably large effect on the art, literature, and taste of people of many nations, from the eighteenth century up to our own time—and has stirred their heartfelt philosophical thoughts and emotions as well, because nothing in the world seems better able to illustrate the precariousness of human fortunes. The cities destroyed were Pompeii and Herculaneum, together with many great country houses (villas) round about, notably at Stabiae and Oplontis, which have been the scenes of remarkable recent discoveries.

The volcano had perhaps been extinct since before the beginnings of history, although several ancient writers of the first century B.C. were aware that it had once been active. Moreover, seventeen years before the fatal outburst a dire warning had been offered by nature. For on a sunny day in February A.D. 62 the area was convulsed by a fierce earthquake, which caused loss of life and gravely damaged many buildings. But neither this sinister occurrence nor anything else caused the people of the area to foresee or expect the terrifying disaster of August 24, 79.

By chance, we have a vivid description of what happened, written by the Latin writer Pliny the Younger. A youth of about eighteen at the time, he was staying at Misenum, at the northern end of the Bay of Naples, as a guest of his uncle, the elder

Pliny, who was an erudite historian and scientist and happened also to be the admiral in command of the great Roman naval base beside the port. Another and even more eminent historian, Tacitus, later asked the younger Pliny to send him a report on the eruption, and he responded by providing an unforgettable description. He tells how his uncle, after seeing a huge cloud "like an umbrella pine" rise to the sky at the other end of the bay, had received a panic-stricken appeal for help from a woman friend, or friend's wife, whose house was at the foot of the mountain; whereupon the commander gave orders to launch the warships, and took them straight to the danger zone.

Ashes were already falling, hotter and thicker as the ships drew near, followed by bits of pumice and blackened stones, charred and cracked by the flames; then suddenly they were in shallow water, and the shore was blocked by the debris from the mountain.

However, the elder Pliny managed to beach his ship beside Stabiae, and spent the night composedly at the house of a friend. "Meanwhile, on Mount Vesuvius broad sheets of fire and leaping flames blazed at several points, their bright glare emphasized by the darkness of the night." After endeavoring to calm the fears these phenomena aroused in his host's household, he went to bed and slept, snoring loudly, since he was a stout man with respiratory troubles. This sound, indicating that he saw no need to keep awake, had a reassuring effect on the others. In the morning he was called and joined the rest of his party, who had been up all night. By this time the buildings were rocking and swaying to and fro,

This bronze statue of an athlete, found at Herculaneum, is probably a copy of a Greek original.

and porous volcanic stones (pumice) were raining from the sky, which was now as black as night. The elder Pliny decided to go down to the shore to see if the party could embark, but found the waves still mountainously high. The air all around was crackling with flames and stinking of sulphur. Soon Pliny, who was leaning on the shoulders of two slaves, was overcome by the fumes; he collapsed and died. Everyone else got away, and two days later, when a yellowish daylight was at last beginning to shine on the scene once again, his body was found still lying on the beach. Nowadays, perhaps, if he had survived, he might have been in trouble for taking out the imperial fleet to rescue a lady in distress, and his loyal nephew is at pains to point out that he only did so in order to save others as well.

Pliny the Younger does not refer to the very first of the unpleasant phenomena accompanying the eruption, which is recorded by a Latin poet and a Greek historian. This was an enormous crashing reverberation, as the pressure of internal gases caused the crater (which had hitherto been closed for as far back as anyone knew) to break open and the whole mountain to burst and split apart. The explosion hurled incandescent rocks and stones thousands of feet in the air. Next, seething clouds of debris and dust followed in their wake, and then came down again, snowing torridly over the entire Vesuvian region, so that day was turned into night. The younger Pliny refers to terrifying electrical storms that erratically lit up the darkness.

By the time that his uncle, setting out with his flotilla, reached the other side of the bay, Pompeii had already been buried, first by a rain of volcanic pebbles that covered the ground to a height of half a dozen feet or more, and then by a second fall of the same volume, consisting of a layer of ash (all this was covered over, during the centuries that have elapsed since that time, by an equivalent quantity of solid earth). The sinister shower provided a strangely tender form of obliteration, considerate to posterity. For so delicate was the steady downpour that even loaves of bread in a bakery's oven, though carbonized, remained essentially intact, as did fruit in glass containers, and fish and eggs on dining-room tables.

Delicate, too, was the overwhelming of Herculaneum, though it came about in a strangely different fashion. For what blotted out Herculaneum, after the same initial crash of rocks falling from the sky, was not pumice and ash at all, but mud. The mountain, in its convulsion, had vomited upward a huge funnel of boiling steam, which, mingling with the torrential spray uplifted from the mountainous sea, then beat down upon the countryside in atrocious scorching rainstorms. These downpours churned up the lava surface of Vesuvius into hot, glutinous rivers of mud, and it was these rivers, making their way down the mountain slopes, that buried Herculaneum to a depth of fifty feet. Yet the streams of mud lava equaled the pumice and ashes that fell upon Pompeii, in the weird circumspection with which they performed their task. For the inexorable ooze moved so gradually upon Herculaneum that it allowed beams and planks of wood to survive. Even fabrics and ropes and fishermen's nets and wax tablets, though scorched and carbonized, were not destroyed. At one house in Herculaneum the occupants were evidently eating a lunch of bread, salad, and fruit when the mud wave moved in on them. When the archaeologists of a later age came upon the scene, the whole lunch was still recognizably there.

The people who had been eating the meal, on the other hand, very probably got away in time, because the mud invasion, though relentless, was slow. At least they got out of town; what happened afterward is anyone's guess, since many dead have been found in the countryside and harbor. But within Herculaneum itself not more than about thirty skeletons have been found. The casualties at Pompeii were far larger, amounting to at least two thousand, which was perhaps nearly ten per cent of the total population. Within the boundaries of the town, excavators found abundant evidence of human fatalities.

In 1864 one of these archaeologists, Giuseppe Fiorelli, discovered a unique way of focusing our attention upon such tragedies for all time to come. He noted that when someone at Pompeii had fallen down and died during the eruption, the ash had subsequently solidified round the corpse, so that after decomposition, the exact *outline* of its flesh still remained perfectly preserved. So Fiorelli removed the bones and then pumped into the vacuum a solution of liquid plaster, which subsequently hardened and reproduced exactly, in every detail, the shape of the body—hair, tormented facial expression, clothes, sandals and all. The examples of his technique, to be seen at Naples and Pompeii today—and there are agonized dead dogs, too, as well as men, women, boys, and girls—are relics that strike those who come upon them with an impact of appalling, heart-wrenching immediacy.

The Roman emperor Titus, who had just begun his reign at the time of the eruption, took steps to house the numerous destitute refugees but did not attempt to rebuild on the obliterated sites. But rescue parties or looters burrowed down into the shambles to extract whatever statues and other valuables they could find; and they left grim graffiti behind them, one of which, "Sodom and Gomorrah," suggests that its writer was Jewish.

For more than sixteen centuries thereafter, the sites and even the names of Pompeii and Herculaneum were more or less forgotten, except by cartographers and a few people offering casual conjectures. Attention to Herculaneum was finally revived by Emmanuel Maurice of Lorraine, prince of Elbeuf and duke of Guise, an Austrian cavalry commander in the service of the court of Naples. While a farm worker was digging a well in 1710 or 1711, near a country house the prince was building for himself, he came upon a mass of expensive-looking marble sculptures. Advised by a Frenchman that the material was important, Elbeuf purchased the well and continued explorations on his own account. Without knowing it, he had hit on the amphitheater of Herculaneum. And then for seven years he persistently plundered the precious contents of the buildings, sending much

of his loot to his commander-in-chief, Prince Eugene of Savoy, in whose palace at Vienna statues of women from the site attracted much admiration, as they continued to do when transferred to the Antikensaal at Dresden later on.

Then in 1834 a young Spanish Bourbon, Prince Charles, became king of Naples. His bride was the art-loving Maria Amalia of Saxony, who knew Eugene's statues and, on arrival at Naples, helped to arrange that the work of rediscovery should be resumed.

As news of what was happening began to spread through Europe, foreign visitors came to inspect the excavations. Horace Walpole, although distressed by the ignorance, crossness, and jealousy he thought he detected in those in charge of the work, concluded nevertheless that Herculaneum was "perhaps one of the noblest curiosities that has ever been discovered. There is nothing of the kind known in the world."

Then in 1748 excavations began at Pompeii, (wrongly believed at that time to be Stabiae). Twelve Moslem slaves, chained together in pairs, were assigned to the task. The ground was easier here than at Herculaneum, and a good deal of progress was made, including the correct identification of the place by means of an inscription that recorded its name.

The next major discovery was a sensational one. This was the Villa of the Papyri outside Herculaneum, where prolonged digging disclosed fabulous and unparalleled collections of papyri and bronze statues. But in 1765 work at the villa was discontinued and the site covered over, partly because the emergence of poisonous gases and vapors (*mofeta*) that had been trapped for centuries in the depths of the ground discouraged further attempts at excavation. And that, more or less, is how the Villa of the Papyri remains today. So it is particularly fortunate that the excavators left an excellent detail plan of the site—on which the design of the J. Paul Getty Museum at Malibu, California, has been based in our own time.

The excavation of the cities and villas buried by Vesuvius, continuing to the present, has revealed in ever greater detail the life of the ancient Romans. Thanks to Fiorelli's ingenious technique, we can see the people themselves, preserved in three-dimensional silhouettes at one catastrophic moment. They are tragic representatives of the human condition; and their humanity is pathetically emphasized by the many small objects that have survived in their midst, not only their food but their bottles and jugs and lamps, the knucklebones and dice they used for their games, the instruments employed every day by doctors and jewelers and carpenters.

Quite recently, in convenient response to modern sociological trends and tastes, excavations have brought to light far more extensive evidence than hitherto of the houses and apartments of the poor—including the slaves who formed the lowest levels of ancient society. And it has for some time been clear how some of the larger houses, especially in the later days of Herculaneum, were divided up into much smaller units to accommodate the less privileged sections of the population.

But it is the dwellings of the rich and fairly rich that have survived better and provide us with a far greater mass of varied information. The architects and designers of these larger houses had to protect their occupants from the heat of the south Italian summer. So the houses did not look outward onto the dusty, noisy streets but faced inward, drawing their light from a cool interior courtyard, known as the *atrium*. The atrium was covered in, but generally there was an opening in the middle of its roof, with a stone basin just below for the retention of rain water. The principal rooms of the house were grouped around the atrium.

These houses sometimes occupied quite a lot of ground, occasionally as much as six thousand square feet. To modern eyes they seem to display an extraordinary mixture of discomfort and elegance. The dining rooms, of which there were sometimes several in a single house—to suit the changing seasons—seem deplorably cramped, es-

The forms of Pompeii victims were preserved at the moment of death by the ash that engulfed them.

151

pecially when one bears in mind that guests were accustomed to bring their own slaves to help. (No wonder that the walls of one such room bear written injunctions to the diners in these crowded quarters to mind their behavior and manners!) Furthermore, there was very often nothing better than a corner of the house to serve as a kitchen. The cooks, when they got to work on their elaborate confections—relying on strong sauces to kill the taste of rotting meat and fish—had to make do with makeshift, portable facilities. As for the sanitary arrangements, if they deserve this term, they were such, even in the grandest houses, as to make the toughest modern holidaymaker blench.

Besides, although the houses were cleverly designed for protection against the hot summers, strangely little endeavor was made to cope with the winters, which as many visitors to Neapolitan hotels can testify, are often perishingly chilly. The heating of the private houses was entirely inadequate, being provided by smelly and dangerous braziers. Moreover, windows were never or very rarely glazed in private dwellings; the only way to close the openings was by sealing them up suffo-catingly with wooden shutters like the *scuri* that are attached to Italian window frames today. The artificial lighting, too, would have seemed to us dreadful. The lamps or torches or tapers or tallow candles that provided such light as existed were smoky and malodorous. Even with good lights, reading was a considerable problem in ancient times. In the absence of spectacles, most older people needed a young slave to read aloud to them. But even the keenest slave would have found it hard to read much after dark at Pompeii or Herculaneum.

On the other hand, the internal decoration of these disconcerting habitations was attractive, bearing witness to a general level of taste among the prosperous and fairly prosperous that compares more than favorably with our own time. But the assumptions according to which the decoration of these houses was undertaken were entirely alien to modern ideas or practices. Panel pictures, such as we have today, were not favored, since they would have been regarded as interfering with the architectural conception as a whole. Instead, the rooms were adorned with frescoes painted

The opulent cityscape above adorned a wall at Boscotrecase. On the opposite page is a room from a villa at Boscoreale, now reconstructed at New York's Metropolitan Museum.

directly on the walls and ceilings, thus forming an integral part of the design of the house. The painters had a difficult technique to master, involving a careful mixing of colors followed by the addition of glue to impart a brilliant gloss. The artists—many of them Greeks, it may be, but including some Romans as well—provided the many and varied paintings, some copied from Greek models but others distinctly original, that are among the principal glories of the cities of Vesuvius. A graceful alternative to wall paintings was low stucco relief, which has left us some alluring works of art.

Just as a detachable panel painting would have upset the design of the walls, it was felt that furniture must remain sparse, so as not to distract the eye from the overall pattern of decoration. A vital element in that pattern was the floor, and that, too, must for the same reasons be kept as free as possible of rugs or carpets. Just as the surfaces of the walls and ceilings were directly covered with paintings, the expanses of the floors were inlaid with mosaics. These were constructed of innumerable small cubes of colored stone and marble attached to beds of cement. The Greeks, experimenting with this technique, had also covered their floors with mosaics but had generally restricted the decorative, figurative portions to panels of limited size—solid versions, as it were, of the rugs and mats that were not there. But the designers of the houses at Pompeii and Herculaneum tended, more ambitiously, to see the entire floor as a single, homogeneous unit to be "carpeted" all over by a mosaic pattern. Some of the results are so astonishing and satisfying that mosaics have been hailed as one of the most notable of all Roman arts.

Another peculiarly successful feature of the houses of the Vesuvian cities was the garden. For at the back of these residences, whenever sufficient room existed, there was a second enclosed space, supplementing the atrium on a more substantial scale: that is to say, a colonnaded garden court, further supplemented in the case of the largest houses by an orchard or open garden

Vine-covered trellises gave shade to the waterways, pools, and fountains in this Pompeii garden.

behind. The contents of these gardens have been arrestingly reconstructed by Fiorelli's technique—pouring plaster into the empty spaces left by the long-since disintegrated roots of trees, plants, and flowers. It was possible to expand such gardens into wide and gracious parklands, with splendid views, at the much larger residences outside the urban areas. These villas, numbered in the dozens, belonged to the richest citizens of the region and to important men of Rome. Such mansions, and the farmhouses attached to them, suffered total obliteration in the eruption of A.D. 79, but many of the most luxurious of them have been disinterred in modern times.

The public buildings of Pompeii and Herculaneum are, in their way, just as remarkable as their private counterparts. And what is so particularly noteworthy is that two towns of such modest dimensions, with about 25,000 and 10,000 inhabitants respectively, should have possessed such a

This bucolic idyl, with a goddess and a goatherd, was painted on the wall of a villa.

lavish array of these public, municipal amenities—an array that would put to shame almost any place of the same size today. At Pompeii there was an amphitheater, devoted to the gladiatorial games, and two stone theaters for plays. Ten temples, too, are known. But the grandest of the public buildings in a Roman city of the time was the basilica, a legal, commercial, and social meeting place that combined the functions of modern law courts, stock exchanges, and marketplaces (like the *galerei* of Italy). The Pompeii basilica, a very early example of its kind, stands on the wide, colonnaded forum, one of the ancestors of the spacious Italian squares that can be seen today.

No fewer than four sets of elaborate public baths have come to light in Pompeii, and two at Herculaneum. These establishments played an enormous part in the lives of the two towns, providing not only cold, tepid, hot, and steam rooms for bathers but also social activities of many kinds. The built-in heating arrangements were sophisticated, and the baths were furnished with a wide range of comfortable club facilities. The baths add considerably to our knowledge of how the people lived—and not only the upper class, because admission to the baths seems to have been fairly liberal.

Even more can be learned from the inscriptions on the walls of the buildings. For one thing, at Pompeii an astonishing array of election posters has survived. Such towns were self-governing and elected their own municipal officials. Similar elections at Rome itself were somewhat muted owing to the overwhelming proximity of the emperor. But at Pompeii the elections were very freely and sharply contested. At the time of the fatal eruption, a political campaign was just getting into its stride, as can be seen from the written appeals of innumerable canvassers; and very vigorous reading they make. Some of these propagandists are fifth-column saboteurs within the ranks—electioneers who pretend to be recommending a candidate, whereas in reality they are doing the opposite. One such poster-writer, for example, asserts that she is the "little girlfriend" of the man she is claiming to help, a boast that may have been intended to publish an uncomfortable secret fact about his life. Another inscription declares, disingenuously, that a personage who is seeking office is supported by all the "late drinkers" and "heavy sleepers," who may not have been, by any means, the backers he was hoping for or wanted to proclaim to the world.

Another, uniquely important source of information about Pompeii is the graffiti that were scratched by the population on its walls. The visitor to the place will not see much of these scrawls, because they are nowadays hard to discern and decipher—and, indeed, the walls themselves, which formerly preserved them, have sometimes crumbled away. Yet some specimens are still there on the spot, others can be seen at the National Archaeological Museum in Naples, and almost every one of the graffiti has been carefully recorded in the Corpus of Latin Inscriptions. From these informal documents we really seem to be obtaining deep insight into the minds and emotions and longings of the men and women, boys and girls, of Pompeii. Politics is there, and literature, but above all, as today, an enormous abundance of lavatory humor and sex.

The sexual habits of Pompeii and Herculaneum deserve a little further comment. Sex, sometimes of the most explicit kind, figures abundantly not only in the graffiti of the two cities but in their sculpture and painting as well: representations of the male organ, intended to have encouraging magical effects, are particularly frequent. Moreover, at least seven brothels, lavishly decorated with pornographic designs, have been discovered at Pompeii. This seems rather a lot for a relatively small town—and there may be other similar institutions that have not yet been found. Sex was evidently a subject on which people concentrated

This fresco depicts the climax of the initiation rites of a Dionysiac cult. As two hands reach out to unveil an image of the sacred phallus, which is covered by a cloth, a figure wearing huge wings raises her whip to flagellate a postulant (seen on the following page).

with great gusto, and, to judge from the designs and graffiti, they devoted to its enjoyment a professional versatility in thought and deed alike. Whether this was a phenomenon to be found all over the Roman Empire it is hard to say. Perhaps the theme received special emphasis in this hedonistic, Hellenized region of beautiful Campania and was expressed here with particular artistic virtuosity.

The excavation of the buried cities is important not only for what it has revealed of ancient Roman life but for the strong and lasting impact of that revelation on the cultural life of western Europe. The two sites were first given their due by Johann Winckelmann, whose *History of the Art of Antiquity* (1764) and other works made him the first to apply historical method to the study of classical art. In Italy, where he arrived in 1755, he felt he had found a new key to unlock the inner meaning of the art of the ancients: and he became sure of this three years later, when he visited Pompeii and Herculaneum. Winckelmann was eventually murdered in a Trieste hotel. Yet, before that, it was he more than anyone else who turned the taste of European art and decoration from the prevailing baroque forms of the time to the classical style of the ancient Greco-Roman world.

In the wave of enthusiasm for classical forms that swept the European cultural world in the last years of the eighteenth century, fine distinctions were lost. The new style was labeled indiscriminately Greek, Roman, and Etruscan. The confusion was natural, since most of the painting found at Pompeii derived from the Greek in both style and theme, while the Roman style of architecture owed much to the Etruscan. The excavations at Pompeii and Herculaneum brought all this classical treasure to the eyes of western Europe.

One of the most influential admirers of the

In this fresco the postulant kneels to receive on her back the lash of the whip wielded by the winged personage on the preceding page. Meanwhile a bacchante dances to the clash of cymbals. The frescoes come from the Villa of Mysteries at Pompeii.

ancient style was Robert Adam, the favorite architect and interior decorator of the English aristocracy. His Etruscan Room, opened in 1775 at the Courtauld Institute in London, was a showcase of Pompeian motifs in wall paintings and furniture design, as well as "Etruscan" (really Greek) vases. With his brother James he designed the interiors of the greatest country houses then being built: Syon House, Kedleston Hall, Osterley Park, Lansdowne House, Harewood House, Luton Hoo, and others. "The whole town," complained a rival, "is run mad after Adam."

Another formidable tastemaker was Josiah Wedgwood, the maker of fine pottery. In his early manufactures Wedgwood had followed the patterns of the great European designers at Meissen and Sèvres. But after he had seen the treasures of Pompeii and Herculaneum, those became the inspiration for his most successful designs. Out went the fanciful swirls and bright colors of the Continental rococo porcelain. In came the more restrained designs of his Etruscan ware—classical robed figures, with borders and garlands, against rich blue or green backgrounds.

For thirty-six years, from 1764 to 1800, the craze for Pompeian antiquities was promoted by Sir William Hamilton, the British ambassador to the court of Naples. A student and collector of antiquities himself, he played host to a steady stream of British visitors, ranging from young noblemen on the Grand Tour to the distinguished men of arts and letters who called themselves the Society of the Dilettanti. Workmen in the excavations had learned the congenial trick of leaving bronze or marble "finds" lightly buried until Sir William came by with his English milords, and then unearthing them to the accompaniment of joyous cries and generous tips. Sir William's guests might be entertained by his lovely young wife, Emma (later Nelson's mistress), in an after-dinner program of her own invention. Clothed in filmy drapes and standing within a gold frame against a black background, she assumed the poses of figures from newly found wall paintings. These "Grecian attitudes," widely imitated in the grand houses of Europe, helped to spread not only her own reputation but the influence of the buried cities.

Men of letters have seldom failed to respond, often at great length, to the revelations of the Vesuvian cities. Pre-eminent among the early travelers was Johann Wolfgang von Goethe. His twenty-month-long first visit to Italy, begun in 1786 when he was thirty-seven and recalled with deep feeling in his *Italian Journey* nearly thirty years later, seemed to him to provide the perfect fusion between the natural philosophy that he had been studying and the classical world that was the greatest of his loves. Above all else, he never forgot his visits to Pompeii, which became his symbol of this beloved world—and prompted him also to remark that no calamity had ever brought so much pleasure and entertainment to subsequent generations. Nevertheless, his enthusiasm was tempered by reservations. Thus Pompeii, while fascinating him, also brought feelings of disquiet; it

was a "mummified city," he said, made up of dolls' houses that left rather a disagreeable impression. As for Herculaneum, he remarked, a little chauvinistically, that he would have much preferred to see Germans doing the excavations, instead of those currently occupied in the task, whom he regarded as inefficient and rapacious.

In 1821 the poet Percy Bysshe Shelley conferred on Pompeii the supreme accolade of Romanticism, then come to its zenith. The Pompeian paintings appeared to him to reflect an "ideal life" and "atmosphere of mental beauty" in which "every human being caught a splendour not its own." But, most of all, it was the Street of the Tombs, the road outside Pompeii lined by the graves of the dead, that moved him, as along the broad pavestones "you hear the late leaves of autumn shiver and hustle in the stream of the inconstant wind, as it were, like the step of ghosts." It was this visit that inspired the imagery of his "Ode to Naples":

The first extensive excavation of Herculaneum was carried on in the eighteenth century by order of the king of Naples. Some of the Moslem galley slaves who worked on the job may be seen in the engraving above. The photograph below shows the north end of the forum, with the temple of Jupiter in the foreground and Vesuvius in the distance. The peak at left is the present cone of the volcano, formed in the eruption of A.D. 79; at right is the old cone, now inactive.

I stood within the City disinterred;
       And heard the autumn leaves like light footfalls
Of spirits passing through the streets; and heard
       The mountain's slumberous voice at intervals
Thrill through those roofless halls;
       The oracular thunder penetrating shook
The listening soul in my suspended blood;
       I felt that Earth out of her deep heart spoke—
I felt, but heard not: through white columns glowed
       The isle-sustaining ocean-flood,
A plane of light between two heavens of azure.

Thirteen years later, in 1833, the aging Sir Walter Scott proved a much less responsive visitor, merely mumbling the words "City of the Dead" over and over again. But in the following year the visit of another highly romantic English novelist, Edward Bulwer-Lytton, bore much more abundant fruit. For he went home to write his phenomenally popular *The Last Days of Pompeii*. The House of Glaucus in the book was closely modeled on a mansion excavated at Pompeii (known as the House of the Tragic Poet). Lytton's novel is full of stilted, bogus archaisms of the "prithee" or "forsooth" type ("Daughter of Etruria, whither wendest thou?"); and it abounds in glutinously soulful philosophizings (" 'How beautiful,' said Glaucus in a half-whispered tone, 'is that expression by which we call Earth our mother.' ") But the final scene of the eruption still retains its compelling power— when the ashes rain down from heaven and the blind flower girl, the only person in Pompeii who can find her way through the lethal all-encompassing darkness, guides the man she loves, and the woman to whom he is betrothed, to safety and a future in which she herself can have no part.

In 1836 the Italian poet Giacomo Leopardi wrote *La Ginestra* ("The Broom"), which is one of the most impressive, if not the most cheering, products of the world's meditations on Pompeii's doom; perhaps Leopardi was affected by the catastrophe all the more deeply because he had been obliged to flee from a cholera epidemic at Naples to the house of a friend outside the city. In contrast to the volcano's destructive might, he sees human life as an insignificant phenomenon—especially when it is falsely puffed up by the illusion of "inevitable, permanent progress." He likens human life to an ant heap, which can be wiped out at any moment by an apple falling from a tree. And he concludes that the most suitable and dignified manner in which we can confront our common predicament is suggested by that unpretentious shrub called broom, making its gradual way up through the lava, where a new catastrophe will one day reduce it to extinction. Unlike humankind, Leopardi is saying, the plant makes no claim to be permanent or immortal; it just lives quietly and sensibly for the hour.

Charles Dickens, too, in *Pictures from Italy* (1845), was deeply affected by the "strange and melancholy sensation of seeing the Destroyed and the Destroyer making this quiet picture in the sun. Then, ramble on, and see, at every turn, the little familiar tokens of human habitation and everyday pursuits . . . all rendering the solitude and deadly lonesomeness of the place ten thousand times more solemn than if the volcano, in its fury, had swept the city from the earth and sunk it in the bottom of the sea."

Queen Marie Antoinette of France had her boudoir (opposite page) decorated with motifs from Pompeii. The porcelain inlays in her commode were copied from the paintings of bacchantes (left) found in the so-called Villa of Cicero.

Lady Hamilton, the beautiful wife of the English ambassador to Naples (and later mistress of Lord Nelson) was painted by Romney (opposite page) in a pose inspired by Pompeian bacchante figures (right). At dinner parties she entertained her guests by appearing in such "Grecian attitudes" copied from frescoes at Pompeii.

All this emphasis on the downfall of Pompeii and Herculaneum, combined with the abundance of sexuality in their art, led to a widespread conviction, in moralistic nineteenth-century Europe, that the cities had been exceptionally wicked, which was why they had been struck down. Thus the famous, earnest, reforming English headmaster Dr. Thomas Arnold saw the Bay of Naples, in 1840, as the scene of a "fearful drama of Pleasure, Sin and Death"; and his son Matthew Arnold put forward the argument that the continuous series of sensual indulgences that the inhabitants of Pompeii and Herculaneum had obviously permitted themselves must surely in the end have "fatigued and revolted them." Herman Melville, too, on a visit in 1857, compared Pompeii with sinful Paris—the city struck down in life, and the city ripe unto death.

While Pompeii and Herculaneum continued to prompt so many reflections among writers and thinkers, the stream of tourists inspecting the sites continued unabated. King Ludwig I of Bavaria (1825–48) was a particularly frequent and assiduous visitor; at Aschaffenburg, in his own country, he built a residence, the Pompeianum, imitating one of the ancient houses. It was then that the fashion for "Pompeian" design stood at its height among Germans; striking examples continued to appear in the work of Karl Friedrich Schinkel, and in Leo von Klenze's plans for the Maxpalais and the Hofgarten arcades at Munich (1840).

But some visitors to the Vesuvian cities were by no means uncritical. In 1851 Maximilian, the ill-starred future emperor of Mexico, felt deeply the shocking confrontation of life and death which thoughtful people often see as the essence of the scene. The seascape was enchanting, Maximilian saw, and Pompeii extraordinary. "But it is terrible as well. The diminutive rooms still glitter in their garish colours like painted corpses." Mark Twain, on the other hand, who paid the region a visit in 1867, felt sad because the hard labors of all those generations, one after another, had left so pathetically little trace. He was also indignant because the state of the ancient Pompeian streets showed that men in charge of looking after them had swindled the local taxpayers. Worse still, Augustus Hare, in his *Cities of Southern Italy and Sicily* (1883), crudely declared that the little windowless houses of the place looked to him like nothing better than ruined cow sheds or pig sties.

On the other hand, as Raleigh Trevelyan records in his book *The Shadow of Vesuvius*, the French painter Auguste Renoir, on a visit in 1881, found the ancient frescoes significantly fruitful for his own artistic tastes and methods. Pictures of "priestesses in grey-green tunics" somewhat unexpectedly reminded him of Corot's nymphs. When he visited the area he liked to paint out of doors, so as to catch the winter sun and "the grand harmonies," instead of bothering about small details which "obscure the sun rather than brighten it."

Since the invention of the movie camera there have been notable films about Pompeii. The production that particularly comes to mind is Federico Fellini's *Satyricon*. It does not set out to depict the city itself but to adapt Petronius's great novel of the same name. Petronius had been describing some other place, not far away; but it was not unlike Pompeii, and Fellini provides a peculiarly pungent interpretation of what he saw as the gamy Pompeian way of life.

Through all these years the fortunes of the excavations underwent their ups and downs. In 1790, in response to fears that another eruption might rebury Pompeii, the Naples museum was remodeled to provide a permanent home for the greatest treasures. In 1860 the directorship of the excavations, and of the museum, was conferred upon Alexandre Dumas, senior, the prolific French author, as a reward for his enthusiastic reports in Garibaldi's war of national liberation. The Neapolitans showed that they were not happy about the arrival of this eccentric personage, who although he worked quite hard (at cataloguing the pornographic collection, for example) was too free with their money. He also tried to open a restaurant; and he was attended on his yacht by a young girl described as "a very charming midshipman who appears for duty in jacket and trousers."

A new archaeological era began when King Victor Emmanuel II conferred the directorship upon Giuseppe Fiorelli in 1864. In 1848, the year of revolutions, Fiorelli had been obliged to retrain his twenty archaeological diggers as artillerymen. But now, after his new appointment, he came into his own. It was he who not only made the extraordinary reconstructions of the Pompeian dead by plaster casts but introduced scientific discipline to the excavation. During the last five years of the nineteenth century, large and luxurious ancient country villas at Boscoreale and Boscotrecase came to light; in 1903 one whole beautiful painted

The hedonistic spirit of Pompeii found expression in these two sculptures. The bronze fountain figure at left is a satyr carrying a wineskin. The white marble Venus removing her sandal, on the opposite page, still bears more than traces of the gold that was applied to her hair and bits of bodily adornment. Beneath her missing left hand is the god Priapus and at her feet, a baby Eros.

room found its way to the Metropolitan Museum of Art in New York.

A highlight of later excavations was the emergence of huge Roman country mansions at Stabiae. A series of interesting houses and apartments belonging to less prosperous people were also unearthed. At Herculaneum the main street began to be uncovered in 1966; two years later systematic work began at the Wrestling School (Palaestra); and an exceptional example of the Italian taste for bathing establishments, the Suburban Baths, has been restored. Altogether something approaching half of Herculaneum has been revealed, compared with approximately three fifths of Pompeii.

But the most striking discovery of all, in the 1960's and 1970's, was the whole lost site of Oplontis, three miles east of Pompeii. Oplontis was named in old documents as one of the major centers that suffered destruction in A.D. 79. Oplontis and Stabiae were probably conglomerations of rich country villas with farms, rather than towns. At Oplontis, a spacious mansion has now come to light, fronted to the south by a continuous colonnade facing the sea; more than fifty of its rooms have been uncovered. The palatial residence includes room after room containing wall paintings that display sophisticated, illusionistic architectural vistas. It is thought that at one time its owner may have been the emperor Nero's wife Poppaea, whose family was prominent in the area. Extensive damage was caused by the earthquake of A.D. 62 (three years before her death), and then the eruption of 79 buried the entire structure beneath six feet of ash and pumice, topped by fifteen feet more of volcanic mud.

During the Second World War, the buildings and valuables of the cities of Vesuvius ran into graver hazards than at any time since A.D. 79. First, in September 1943, Allied air pilots, for reasons that have been hotly disputed, dropped 162 bombs on Pompeii, inflicting severe damage (but uncovering, in the process, some further ancient buildings). Then, in the same period, after the landings of the Allies at Salerno, 187 cases of objects from the Naples museum, including the bulk of the

material from Pompeii and Herculaneum, were dispatched for safety to Monte Cassino. But from there, when the place was attacked in the following year, they had to be hastily evacuated and subsequently underwent perils of all kinds as they were ferried from place to place across Europe; eighteen of the cases, which had gone astray in the meantime, were eventually discovered by American troops in May 1945, hidden in a salt mine at Alt Aussee in Germany.

Since then a new chapter has been written in the long odyssey of the treasure collected in the eighteenth century by Sir William Hamilton. In 1772 he sent his first magnificent collection to the British Museum. By 1796 he had amassed a second collection of one thousand vases and other antiquities. Two years later, however, he and Emma had to flee from Naples, which was faced by the imminent threat of Napoleonic invasion; and so his antiques were packed and moved onto a British ship, H.M.S. *Colossus*. While returning to England, however, the vessel had the misfortune to run into a fierce December storm off the Scilly Islands and sank to the bottom of the sea. But during the years 1975-7 divers went down and recovered 32,000 fragments of vases. They date from the seventh to the fourth centuries B.C. and thus show how extensively the rich Pompeians and others collected older works. With the help of outline drawings by J. H. W. Tischbein, commissioned and published by Hamilton, the British Museum, which has been lent all these objects, has gone ahead with the extremely difficult, fascinating process of reconstruction.

In this case an alien sea was the destroyer. But in the Bay of Naples itself it has always been the mountain. Since the great disaster of A.D. 79 Vesuvius has erupted, less savagely but frighteningly all the same, on no fewer than seventy occasions, at irregular intervals. The most serious of these outbreaks was in 1631, when lava poured from the crater in seven streams and nearly all the towns at the foot of Vesuvius were overwhelmed; the death roll has been variously estimated at 3,000 and 18,000. The whole mountain changed its shape. It

had done the same in 79, and since 1631 it has assumed new forms on several occasions.

Sir William Hamilton (who climbed to the top of Vesuvius no less than sixty-eight times) witnessed from close-by the eruptions of 1766, 1767, and 1794. He wrote, on the first of these occasions, that "the lava had the appearance of a river of red-hot and liquid metal on which were large floating cinders, half-lighted, and rolling one over another with great precipitation down the mountain, forming a most beautiful and uncommon cascade."

The most recent eruptions of Vesuvius occurred during the Second World War, and nature's fireworks achieved less notice than usual because of the rival human holocausts round about. But the English poet Gavin Ewart happened to be at Naples at the time as a soldier, and later wrote on the theme:

It looked very splendid at night,
crushing the villas and trees, and the ash came down, a
red-purple,
To the depth of an old-fashioned foot. We moved
the trucks and guns
to safety. But our letters home were security-minded. No
mention
You needed a four-wheel drive to churn through
that stuff on the road.

This was in March '44 (as the clubland talks would
remind you)
Of Europe's one active volcano the last recorded
display.

The last for how long? During the past nineteen centuries, depending on methods of calculation and the chronological limits that are selected, Vesuvius has erupted, on an average, either every twenty-five years or every seventeen. The crater is now closed; the famous plume of smoke, beloved by painters, no longer crowns the mountain. That means, as was all too apparent in A.D. 79 and in 1944, when the vast underground pressures had to force themselves through a blocked crater, that the next eruption will probably be a severe one. The present inhabitants of the villages around the base can only hope that they will have more warning than the ancients had.

In a recent excavation, a Pompeian beauty emerges from the volcanic rubble.

IN SEARCH OF . . .
The Truth About Etruscan Women

To the ancient Greeks and Romans there was something scandalous about the Etruscans and especially about Etruscan women. Theopompus, the gossipy Greek historian of the fourth century B.C., reported that the women enjoyed all the freedoms men had. In the streets they walked boldly beside the men, and at dinner they reclined beside them. They took great care of their faces and bodies, removed hair from their skin with melted wax, and took their exercise in the nude. For the Etruscans "there is no shame," said Theopompus, "to be seen committing a sexual act in public. . . . when they are at a gathering of friends, this is what they do: first of all, when they have finished drinking and are ready for bed and while the torches are still lighted, the servants bring in sometimes courtesans, sometimes handsome boys, sometimes their own wives. They all engage in making love, some watching one another, some isolating themselves with rattan screens set up round the couches, each couple wrapped in one cover."

In view of all this permissiveness,

Theopompus was not surprised to learn that Etruscan women "brought up together all those children that are born to them, regardless of who their fathers might be." Roman historians, especially Livy, censured this disregard for the rights and status of the paterfamilias. In contrast to Roman fathers, who held the power of life and death over all family members, Etruscan fathers indulged their sons and accepted their wives as equals. Livy contrasts the virtuous Roman mother, working all evening at her loom, with the Etruscan ladies reclining on their banquet couches.

In the absence of any accounts to the contrary, the Greek and Roman views prevailed. It may well be that a more balanced report was contained in a twenty-volume history of the Etruscan people, written by the enlightened Emperor Claudius in the first century A.D., but this did not survive the fall of Rome.

It was archaeology, beginning in the nineteenth century, that finally came to the rescue of the Etruscan reputation. By that time little remained above ground of the splen-

did cities that had crowned the Italian hills north of Rome during the Etruscan heyday from the seventh to the fourth centuries B.C. They had been ravaged by invading barbarians, plundered for building materials by medieval tyrants, and plowed under by local farmers. But beneath the Tuscan earth were cities of the dead almost as vast and sumptuous as the living cities must have been. Many of these tombs had been robbed of their furnishings, but not all. In 1836 two amateur archaeologists, Father Alessandro Regolini and General Vincenzo Galassi, uncovered near the ruins of Caere the tomb of an Etruscan noblewoman. The contents of the tomb, including a vast array of gold ornaments and jewelry, bronze figurines, caldrons, shields and javelins, as well as a bronze couch and funeral wagon, form the core collection of the Gregorian Etruscan Museum at the Vatican.

But the most revealing discoveries—in plundered as well as unplundered tombs—are the wall paintings. It is evident that in these paintings

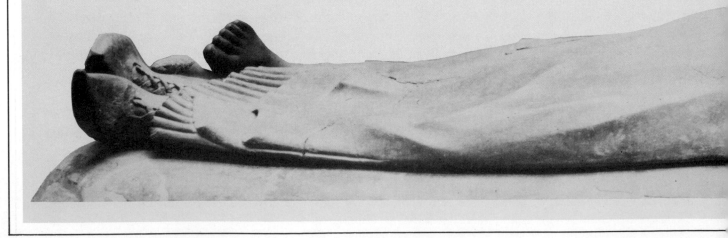

An Etruscan wife and husband, reclining in effigy on their sarcophagus aristocratic Etruscans sought to re-create for departing family members the life they had lived above ground. Diners recline on couches, eating and drinking, listening to music, playing at darts, throwing scraps to pet dogs. There are scenes of dancing, playing pipes, running and wrestling, hunting waterfowl, and diving into the sea. They depict a life of grace, pleasure, and luxury, a far cry from the orgies that might be imagined from ancient accounts. While they do not directly contradict what the Greeks and Romans wrote, they put Etruscan life in a far more wholesome and appealing light.

The opening up of Etruscan tombs brought streams of visitors to Tuscany. None was more lyrical than D. H. Lawrence, who described the Tomb of the Leopards thus:

"The walls of this little tomb are a dance of real delight. The room seems inhabited still by Etruscans of the sixth century before Christ, a vivid, life-accepting people, who must have lived with real fullness. . . .

"The dancers on the right wall move with a strange, powerful alertness onwards. They are men dressed only in a loose coloured scarf, or in the gay handsome chlamys draped as a mantle. The *subulo* plays the double flute the Etruscans loved so much, touching the stops with big, exaggerated hands, the man behind him touches the seven-stringed lyre, the man in front turns round and signals with his left hand, holding a big wine-bowl in his right. And so they move on, on their long, sandalled feet, past the little berried olive-trees, swiftly going with their limbs full of life, full of life to the tips.

"This sense of vigorous, strong-bodied liveliness is characteristic of the Etruscans, and is somehow beyond art. You cannot think of art, but only of life itself, as if this were the very life of the Etruscans, dancing in their coloured wraps with massive yet exuberant naked limbs, ruddy from the air and the sea-light, dancing and fluting along through the little olive-trees . . . ."

The censorious view taken by the Greeks and Romans may be attributed in some part to military rivalry and economic jealousy. The Etruscans traded with the Greeks and collected their art (Etruscan tombs have yielded more sixth-century Greek vases than have ever been found in Greece), but they also joined with the Carthaginians to fight and defeat them at sea. The Etruscans taught the Romans much of what they knew about art and culture and graceful living, but they also sent kings to rule them when Rome was still a struggling city-state. Even so, the Greek and Roman accounts seem to contain more than the usual bias of histories written by enemies.

Nor is it easy to accept at face value the contrast drawn by Greek and Roman writers between their own stern morals and the licentious behavior of the Etruscans. The Greeks were notoriously tolerant of

On the walls of tombs at Tarquinia: dancers (above) and an elegant lady (opposite page)

homosexual love, whereas the Etruscans, on the evidence of the tomb paintings, were exuberantly heterosexual. And Livy, though he wrote of the puritanical early republic, lived in the Augustan age, when Roman luxury surpassed anything known in Etruscan times.

What, then, had so offended the Greeks and Romans? In recent years some modern scholars, under the influence of the women's liberation movement, have taken another look at the evidence and come up with a more sharply focused answer. The cause of the enmity, they say, was not sexual license but the position accorded to women in Etruscan life. Professor Larissa Bonfante of New York University writes: "To Theopompus, seeing husbands and wives so unexpectedly together must have seemed a serious breach of culture and good taste." In Greece women never dined with men. A recently discovered painting at Paestum, an ancient Greek city in southern Italy, displays the difference. As Professor Bonfante writes: "The South Italian scene shows men courting a handsome young boy with bright red lips and cheeks. No women appear, not even as dancers or attendants. In striking contrast, Etruscan art seems to show a world of married couples."

Etruscan women did not take their husband's name as Roman women did, but retained their own through life. And if, as Theopompus implies, they raised all their children, without regard to legitimacy or their husband's consent, they must have enjoyed a legal position far superior to that of Roman women. The threat to male status and authority, Professor Bonfante concludes, was the root cause of the ancient enmity toward the Etruscans. It was, she says, "Rome's first 'cultural shock.'"

7: The Mysterious Celts

by GEOFFREY BIBBY

In the background picture the remains of a Celtic fort stand in concentric crescents on the coast of Inishmore, largest of the Aran Islands. Above is a Roman figurine of a Celtic warrior, his arm raised to throw a spear. To the Romans' astonishment, the Celts sometimes went into battle naked.

The delicacy of Celtic art is displayed in the tendril engraving on a bronze mirror found in England.

In the story of every country and every region of the world there exists a "twilight zone," a period of half-light that precedes the full dawn of history. For history, with its names of peoples and of kings, its known sites of battles, its dates and descriptions, starts when written records are first made, or when contemporary events are first chronicled. For the period before contemporary records we have only such lays and legends, folk traditions and genealogies, myths and customs, as were current at the time of the first historians, and of them only as much as those historians thought worth recording. We know that these myths and legends contain some truth and some poetic invention—but we seldom know which is which. Sometimes we can seek assistance through studies of language, or of place names, or through chance references by earlier historians of adjacent areas; but such oblique light rarely succeeds in resolving doubts, and often casts as many shadows as it dispels.

Nowhere is this twilight zone more tantalizing than in the hinterland of Europe. Here, north of the Alps and the Balkans, history dawns with the expansion of the Roman Empire in the first century B.C. And if we look back beyond this dawn, we see in the half-light of pre-Roman Europe the vague outline of the Celts. During several centuries before the birth of Christ, while Greece and then Rome were extending their sway over the Mediterranean world, Celtic tribesmen swept across the breadth of northern Europe from the Black Sea to the Atlantic, asserting a hegemony over the native inhabitants of that large territory wherever they could. Classified as barbarians by the classical world, these warlike peoples nevertheless were carriers of a distinctive culture that has gradually been rediscovered during past generations—a culture whose enduring impress may, in some areas at least, be discerned in our own day.

That the Celts have stayed in the half-light is entirely their own fault, since they are singularly silent about themselves. For at least five hundred years they existed on the borders of— and in close contact with—a variety of nations possessing developed literary and historical traditions, and easily assimilated written languages. Yet the Celts never developed a written language of their own and never wrote anything down while they existed as a people. Our only historical evidence of the Celts is in what other nations wrote about them.

About 500 B.C. the Greek historian Hecataeus mentions that the Greek colony of Marseilles lies in the country of the Ligurians close to the country of the Celts. Some fifty years later Herodotus, who gives us such detailed accounts of other countries and peoples of the ancient world, reports briefly that the source of the Danube is said to lie in Celtic country, near "Pyrene," which is believed to be the Pyrenees! He adds that the Celts are the most westerly of the peoples of Europe except for the Cynetes, who apparently occupied the southern part of Portugal, and that you will meet Celts if you sail beyond the Strait of Gibraltar.

Not very much later the Celts erupt into history. In 425 B.C. four tribes from beyond the Alps invade northern Italy, and thirty-five years later sack Rome. Admittedly the Romans call these invaders Gauls (*Galli*), not Celts. But although it is a full third of a millennium later before Julius Caesar tells us that the tribes that the Romans call Galli call themselves Celtae, it is reasonable to assume the indentification at the earlier date, too. For it seems that by then the Celts were already a power north of the Alps, and moreover that they were in a state of ferment. In the fourth century B.C. Ephorus, another Greek historian, lists them, indeed, as one of the four great barbarian peoples of the world, along with the Scythians, the Indians, and the Ethiopians; and about the same time we meet bands of Celtic warriors serving as mercenaries in Greece. In the meantime, the Gallic raids in Italy continued, and Celts from Gaul were fully settled in the valley of the Po and apparently around the head of the Adriatic, whence Celtic envoys went to meet Alexander the Great when he was campaigning in Bulgaria in 335 B.C.

Almost sixty years later all Celts erupted again. Three Celtic tribes, each with its own name but all calling themselves Galatians (like Galli, an equivalent name for Celtae), descended into Macedonia with their families and wagons in the middle of the winter of 280 B.C., looting and seeking to settle. In the following year they sacked Delphi but were defeated and crossed to Asia Minor, where after a period of widespread raiding they settled down in the region of present-day Ankara, a region that received the name of Galatia.

This raid of 279 B.C. appears to have been a venture of desperation by a tribal confederacy forced to find a new place to settle. It was the last act of Celtic aggression. For the next two hundred years the Celts were on the defensive, gradually losing ground. In 225 B.C. at Telamon the Romans decisively defeated the Celts—or the Gauls, as they continued to call them—of northern Italy and their confederates north of the Alps, and in 192 B.C., with the capture of Bologna, Rome extended her rule over all the Gauls of the Po Valley. Nearly seventy years later, in 124 B.C., the Romans conquered Provence, the area closest to Italy inhabited by "the Gauls beyond the Alps." And nearly seventy years after that, in 58 B.C., Julius Caesar began the seven-year campaign that reduced the whole of Gaul to a Roman province.

Meanwhile, however, the Celts in Gaul had been under attack from another side, the north. In 115 B.C. three migratory peoples—the Cimbri, the Teutones, and the Ambrones—descended upon the Boii, a Celtic tribe in Bohemia, were repulsed with difficulty, and then moved slowly westward, plundering and crushing any organized opposition. We can see the impact of the Cimbri and the Teutones, for they pressed deep enough into Celtic territory to meet the Romans and to be recorded in Roman history. They defeated three Roman armies before they were turned back.

Pressure upon the Celts from both north and east seems to have continued. In Caesar's famous description of Gaul at the time of his campaigns in the fifties of the first century B.C., he divides Gaul into three parts: the southwest, inhabited by the Aquitani; the center, inhabited by the Celts; and the northeast, inhabited by the Belgae. And the Belgae, he says, were Germanic, and had come from across the Rhine.

So much do we know of the Celts from classical sources. Clearly they were the major power in Europe throughout the classical period. When the Greeks defeated the might of the Persian Empire at Marathon, while Pericles was building the Parthenon, when Alexander the Great campaigned to India, while the Romans were warring against Carthage and establishing their empire around the Mediterranean—all this time north of the Alps the Celts were dominant, and were undoubtedly waging wars just as great and just as significant as those to the south. They had no historians, and their wars are forgotten. But for at least five hundred years they held sway from the Carpathians to the Pyrenees, and raided and even settled, when the opposition was not too strong, in Spain, Italy, Greece, and Asia Minor.

But who were they, and how did they arise? For that matter, when did they arise? For we only know that when the first Greek historians began to write their first histories about 500 B.C., the Celts were already fully established. They may well have existed as a power long before that.

Clearly they were not a nation in the modern sense. As indicated earlier, there were many tribes in the European hinterland, each with its own tribal name, that were recognized by the Greeks and Romans as Celts. There were also many tribes that were recognized as non-Celts, some classified by the Romans as belonging to a people they called Germani. Those classed as Celts did not constitute a political entity. They had no common ruler or federal organization, and they did not act in concert. Some would be at peace with Rome, while others were at war—sometimes at war with one another.

They apparently had a common language, but it seems that this was also spoken by other peoples. The chieftains of the Cimbri and the Teutones, sworn enemies of both Celts and Romans, bear Celtic names; so do the Belgae of northeast Gaul who, according to Caesar, prided themselves on their Germanic, non-Celtic origin. It is even uncertain that all who were known as Celts spoke "Celtic." In fact, it appears that the term *Celt* had no necessary linguistic, ethnic, or "national" connotation.

By what criteria did the Greeks and Romans distinguish the Celts from other barbaric tribesmen, and how can we recognize them as a separate group? Two possibilities remain. The Celts may have shared a common religion, and they may have had in common what the archaeologist calls a culture: they may have worn the same clothes, used the same type of equipment, built the same sort of houses, had the same burial customs, produced the same kind of art and ornament.

Oddly enough, we know a lot about the religion of the Celts—a lot, that is, compared to what we know of other aspects of their culture. The classical writers show considerable interest in the Celtic gods, and in their priests, the Druids, and such representational art as the Celts had is almost

At its peak around the third century B.C., Celtic culture (tinted brown in the map below) stretched across Europe from modern Turkey to Ireland. The small map locates the remnants of Celtic culture and language today.

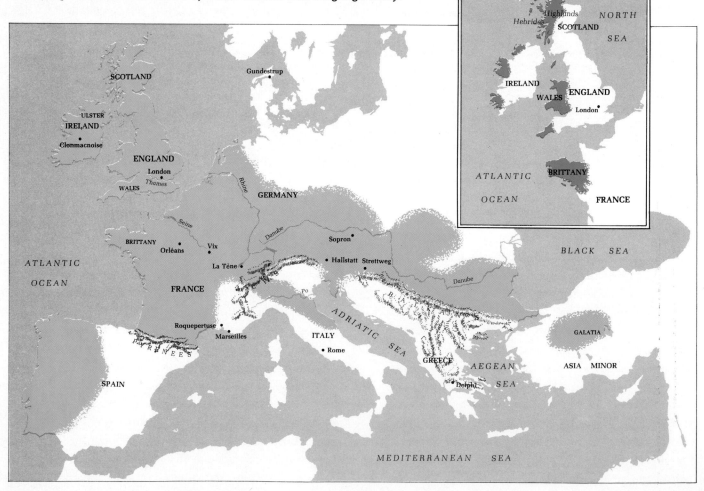

entirely devoted to objects of religious significance. Moreover, when the main areas of Celtic habitation were absorbed into the Roman Empire, the Celts did finally learn to write—in Latin—and since they preserved their religion, a large number of altars and dedicatory tablets have been found bearing images and names of Celtic deities.

But if we look for a religion common to all the Celts and distinguishing them from non-Celts, we will look in vain. The most characteristic feature of Celtic religion is its local nature. Every region and every tribe appears to have had its own particular gods and goddesses. Yet behind the diversity of names, certain characteristics and attributes recur. Goddesses often appear to be connected with water, to be the divinities of rivers and springs. A god with deer antlers occurs frequently; in Gaul he was named Cernunnos, the horned one. We find gods associated with the bull, and the pig, and the wheel, and the caldron. Again and again a three-faced god is found portrayed—in Ireland, in France, in Yugoslavia, and even in Denmark—well outside the area normally considered Celtic.

In fact the most fascinating portrayal of the deities of the Celts comes from Denmark, though it is generally recognized as having originated in the traditionally Celtic area of the Danube Valley and to have reached Denmark, perhaps as booty, at about the time of the campaigns of the Cimbri, around 100 B.C. This is the great silver caldron of Gundestrup, ornamented inside and out with plates of embossed silver. These plates show animals, both real and mythical, ranks of horsemen and foot soldiers with Celtic armament, and a whole series of figures of gods and goddesses. Many of the latter are well known from other Celtic sources, and include the horned god, the god of the wheel, and the god with the caldron, in this case shown dropping a soldier headfirst into his kettle!

The temples from which the Cimbri may have plundered such treasures were not made with hands. No certain temple building of earlier than Roman date is known anywhere in the Celtic area, and the classical authors unanimously describe the

This twenty-seven-inch-wide silver bowl, called the Gundestrup caldron, was found in a Danish bog, but scholars believe it was made somewhere in central Europe and carried north, perhaps as war booty.

main religious practices of the Celts as taking place in woods and sacred groves. The late professor T. G. E. Powell pointed out in this connection the significance of the work *nemeton*, which in Celtic appears to mean "a sacred wood," and which is found incorporated in important place names from Spain to Galatia. In Galatia, for example, Drunemeton was the main sanctuary of the Celts of Asia Minor, and must mean "the sacred oak grove," using the same word for oak, *dru*, that also occurs in the name of the Celtic priests, the Druids. This would agree with Pliny's account of the association of the Druids with the oak—the Druids cutting mistletoe from the oak with a golden sickle, accompanied by sacrifices of bulls.

Much nonsense has been talked about Druids. From the time when Caesar described the Druids of Gaul as members of colleges of priests who had long periods of training at "seminaries" as far away as Anglesey in Wales, and who could arbitrate between contending kings, there has been a tendency to regard them as repositories of an ancient wisdom and power, transcending the petty divisions of Celtic society and the narrow preoccupations with violence of a warrior age. William Stukeley, eighteenth-century surgeon and antiquary, and a close friend of Sir Isaac Newton, even considered the religion of the Druids to be that "aboriginal patriarchal religion" out of which all religions derive, and counted it his mission in life to reconcile this religion with Christianity.

Actually the Druids seem to have been shamans and necromancers. Their supratribal influence was apparently of the same type as that of the oracles of Greece, which was based on a claim to be able to foresee the future, and their long period of training consisted of memorizing the genealogies and epics which are the literature of a people without writing. (They had, of course, no connection whatever with Stonehenge, the stone-built temple of a sun cult nearly twice as old as the first mention of the Druids.)

The Druids and the sacred groves do perhaps bring some sort of unity into the plurality of Celtic religion. They are by no means a pan-Celtic phenomenon, for the influence of the Druids extended only over confederacies of tribes in a restricted area. But the attested connection between the Druids of the Celts of Gaul and the Druids of Wales does suggest that a consciousness of underlying unity, based on common language and common creeds, existed over large areas despite local wars and rivalries—much as the city-states of Greece were always conscious, despite their wars with one another, that they were one people, possessing one religion and fundamentally one culture.

If we turn now to examine the culture of the Celts, we must seek evidence in archaeology, in the material relics dug up from the earth, and we must call in the testimony of the spade to bear witness to who was Celt and who was not. Ask an archaeologist who the Celts were and he will answer that they were the bearers of the La Tène culture.

La Tène is a tiny village in Switzerland, lying where the River Thiele drains the Lake of Biel into the Lake of Neuchâtel. Willow thickets still cover the low-lying land between the two lakes, just as they must have done more than a hundred years ago, when Colonel Friedrich Schwab, a distinguished citizen of Biel and a prominent antiquarian, discovered in 1857 a hoard of weapons lying in the mud of the lake bottom, close to the mouth of the Thiele.

Among the hundreds of iron weapons and other objects—blacksmiths' and carpenters' tools, harness, bronze caldrons, and parts of wagons—there were as many as fifty iron swords, some still in their scabbards. The scabbards in many cases were decorated with designs of intertwined tendrils and stylized but oddly curvilinear animals. The style of the objects found, and in particular the tendril ornamentation, classified La Tène with other, lesser sites from which the same sorts of things had recently been turning up. A magnificent bronze shield, dredged up from the Thames near Battersea and now displayed in the British Museum, showed similar ornamentation; and a number of swords identical with those from La Tène had been found ten years before not far away at Tiefenau near Bern, together with coins of republican Rome. In 1861, the year after Colonel Schwab finished dredging at La Tène, excavations begun in Burgundy by order of Napoleon III resulted in the discovery, in the ditch of the Roman camp of Mont Réa, of swords of the La Tène type and Roman coins, the latest of which was dated 54 B.C. The discovery at Mont Réa was decisive. The men who had died in an attack on a Roman fort in Burgundy not long after 54 B.C. could only have been Celtic tribesmen resisting Julius Caesar's conquest of Gaul in that very year. And those Celts used swords of the La Tène type.

The weapons from La Tène could logically be classed as Helvetian, the armament of the Celtic tribe of the Helvetii, who were known to have occupied Switzerland during the first half of the last century before Christ. In general it began to appear that wherever they were found, objects of a type similar to the La Tène weapons could be ascribed most fittingly to the immediately pre-Roman period. And objects of the La Tène type, or decorated with the La Tène ornamentation, were appearing over an area that extended from northern France and southern England to the Po Valley in Northern Italy, and far into Germany, Austria-Hungary, and the Balkans. They were even appearing, as we have seen, in Denmark.

In 1874 an international congress of anthropologists officially recognized La Tène as the type site for the pre-Roman culture of central and western Europe, which has since gone under that name. By then it was already clear that there was a very close correspondence, both geographically and chronologically, between the La Tène culture and the Celts. Wherever the Celts were known to have been, objects of the La Tène type were found; and wherever the La Tène culture dominated, Celts were known to have been at some time dominant.

Moreover, it was becoming clear that the famous Dark Age art of Ireland—the illuminated manuscripts and carved stone crosses—was in fact a development of La Tène art, appearing in the only area in Europe where the La Tène culture had not been broken off short by Roman conquest. Thus on every count it seemed beyond reasonable doubt that the bearers of the La Tène culture were the Celts. And this was important. For if we could find archaeological evidence for the origins and antecedents of the La Tène culture we could push back our knowledge of the history and origins of the Celts beyond the time when they first appear, fully fledged, in the Greek histories of 500 B.C..

During the hundred and more years since the discovery at the site of La Tène, innumerable excavations across the length and breadth of Europe have added pieces to the jigsaw puzzle of La Tène origins, and evidence has gradually accumulated for a theory that would make the dawn of the Celts at least as mystical and romantic as the "Celtic twilight" ever was. We must go back to 1000 B.C.

At this time east and central Europe, from the Black Sea to the Pyrenees, was inhabited by peoples with a fairly uniform culture, which archaeologists have called the Urnfield culture. It is an uninspiring name for what, by and large, seems to have been an uninspiring culture. The Urnfield peoples lived in small villages of round or square wooden houses, all of much the same size; the men wore a wrap-around kilt or sarong, with a cloak above, the women a long or short skirt

THE DIGGING DUCHESS

The elegant archaeologist above, in her Edwardian digging coat and her wide-brimmed hat, is the Duchess of Mecklenburg, born Princess Marie of Windischgrätz. She is kneeling in the dirt beside the tomb of an Iron Age warrior dating from the first millennium B.C.

During the decade before World War I the duchess excavated about one thousand such tombs, many of them in and around her estate in what is now Yugoslavia but was then part of the Austro-Hungarian Empire. With her crew of twenty or thirty workmen she also dug at Hallstatt in Austria. The Hallstatt site, which gave its name to the earliest Celtic culture, has turned up such prizes as the bronze bowl below, its handle fashioned in the form of a cow and calf.

In February, 1914, the duchess received a fan letter which read in part: "The descriptions you make of your work . . . read like a romance." The writer was her cousin, Kaiser Wilhelm II, who six months later brought an abrupt end to the duchess's work as well as to the peace of Europe.

and a blouse, all of plain woolen weave; they farmed a small area of uniformly sized fields, plowing with an ox-drawn plow that had no moldboard and did not turn the sod; and when they died they were cremated and the ashes were buried in a pottery vessel in large communal cemeteries, the urn fields which have given the culture its name. They were not poor, these Urnfield peoples, and not necessarily peaceful. Bronze working was widespread, with exploitation of the copper of Ireland and the Carpathians, and the tin of Cornwall; long-swords of bronze, an innovation in Europe, are commonly found. But they appear to have been an egalitarian population, with no great extremes of wealth and poverty, and with no signs of large-scale wars or empire building.

Farther south and east the situation was very different. Less than two hundred years earlier many of the great powers of the Near East—Mycenae and Troy and the Hittite Empire—had fallen, apparently before invaders from the north and northwest. Egypt itself had suffered inroads from the warriors of what they called the Sea Peoples, fleets of apparently homeless peoples from the northern shores of the Mediterranean. Farther east the Assyrian Empire was beginning its expansion, with wars against the Urartaeans of Armenia, between the Black Sea and the Caspian. And north of Armenia the Cimmerian horsemen of the south Russian steppes were beginning to feel the pressure of the great Scythian nation to the east. These warrings and movements of nations would sooner or later impinge upon the settled culture of central Europe.

It is about 800 B.C. that the first signs of outside interference appear among the Urnfield peoples. Scattered among the thousands of burial urns of this period are found a few, perhaps sixty in all, containing bronze horse trappings, especially bits, of a remarkable type. They are remarkable because they are well known—somewhere else. They are the horse-bits, with ornamental cheekpieces, depicted on Assyrian reliefs from the eighth century B.C. in northern Mesopotamia. Now, these horse trappings were new in Assyria also, and there seems little doubt that they were introduced from the north, from the Cimmerian and Scythian horsemen who at this time were contending for grazing grounds north of Armenia and north of the Black Sea. It would seem that a very small number of these warrior horsemen, Cimmerians and possibly even Scyths, penetrated into Europe in this century. They were probably originally mercenaries, perhaps even veterans from the Assyrian armies. But they rapidly attained positions of some prominence among the peoples whom they served. From about 700 B.C. we find their burials.

A greater contrast to the urn fields would be difficult to imagine. In an excavation below a barrow a wooden mortuary house was built, and therein was interred the uncremated body of the dead warrior. He lies beside, or upon, a four-wheeled wagon, and while horses were still too valuable to be sacrificed in their master's grave, the harness lies there, not only of the two horses that drew the wagon, but also of a third horse, the warrior's charger. The bodies were buried with long broadswords and with spears of iron, for it was at this time that iron was introduced into Europe from the Middle East. The bits of the

Celtic arms and armor served aesthetic and religious as well as military purposes. The helmet with conical horns and the shield were both dredged up from the river Thames. Made of thin bronze, with glass and enamel inlays, they seem too light for use in warfare. Experts think they may have been used in ceremonies or thrown into the river as votive offerings. The sword hilt at left is believed to be made in the image of some deity. The Celtic warriors on the opposite page are redrawn from the scabbard of a sword found at Hallstatt, Austria.

The Celts made a practice of cutting off their enemies' heads in battle. They not only hung them from their saddles or carried them on spears as trophies of war but preserved them as objects of a mystical cult. It was their belief that the human head retained, even after death, some magical power to ward off evil spirits. The skull below peers from a niche, made especially to hold it, in a stone pillar at the sanctuary of Roquepertuse in France.

horses were of the Cimmerian type, and indeed the whole burial was of a type that had been known for a thousand years on the steppes of southern Russia.

The practice of burying chieftains in rich graves each containing a four-wheeled wagon, continued for about two hundred years. Significantly, the sites of such graves move ever westward. In the seventh century B.C. they were located in the area of the eastern Alps. In the sixth, we find them around the western Alps, in Switzerland, the Black Forest, and the Upper Rhine Valley. The latest, the most westerly, and the richest of these wagon graves, dating from the end of the sixth century B.C., was that of a Celtic princess at Vix on the upper Seine. Here the body of a woman in her early thirties lay upon a light wooden carriage ornamented with bronze. The carriage was similar to other richly ornamented wagons found in Denmark, and of too flimsy a construction to have been useful for everyday purposes. It has been suggested that it was a ritual carriage used only in religious processions, and that the princess was perhaps a priestess. Whatever her rank may have been, she bore fine adornment: armlets, anklets, brooches, and necklaces of bronze inlaid with amber and coral, and a diadem of gold. And in her grave were her greatest treasures, vessels of bronze and pottery imported from the civilized world that lay to the south. There were three bronze drinking cups and a bronze jug of Etruscan origin. There were two painted vases from Athens, one with a Greek combat scene that dated it close to 525 B.C. And above all there was an immense Greek krater of bronze, over five feet high and three feet in diameter, ornamented around the neck with chariot scenes. It is probably the most magnificent example of Greek bronzework surviving anywhere.

The record of archaeology is of necessity impersonal, a catalogue of artifacts, house foundations, and the contents of the graves of nameless persons. But seldom do we feel the absence of names so deeply as in this record of the rise of the Celts as a power. Behind the list of horse bits of eastern type, of wagon burials and chariot burials, we can glimpse the shadowy outlines of heroes and kings and dynasties whose exploits must have been sung for centuries in lost epics, lost because they were never written down. How often did a warrior prince, riding out of the east, save a kingdom from peril and win the hand of the king's daughter? What dynastic quarrels and revolts of vassals or younger sons accompanied the move of the chieftains from southeast Germany to eastern France? Even the little that the classical writers cared to tell us about the Celts during the last four hundred years before Christ gives a picture that is clear compared to what we have been able to learn about Celtic origins during the four hundred years before that.

For this is where we came in. The princess of Vix was buried, with all her Greek and Etruscan treasures, at almost the same time that Hecatáeus named the Celts for the first time, as the people living inland from the Greek trading city of Marseilles in the south of France. We are still over four hundred years before La Tène, and only at the beginning of the period when the Celts were to menace the civilized peoples of the Mediterranean world. But clearly over the last four hundred years the Urnfield people have become the Celts.

They probably always were the Celts, in the sense that the Urnfield peoples probably spoke a Celtic language (or several Celtic languages), but during those four centuries they changed out of all recognition. The former egalitarian husbandmen were now ruled by a warrior aristocracy, mounted on chargers or fighting from two-horse chariots. From Roman and Greek statues, and from their own representations in effigies of stone or figures upon metal caldrons, we know what they looked like. They no longer wore kilts but had adopted the trousers of the riders of the steppes. They were clean-shaven apart from an elaborately curled mustache, and their long hair was pomaded into a stiff, backward-streaming mane. They frequently went naked into battle, but they were never depicted without a torque (a hoop of gold or bronze, or very occasionally silver, worn about the neck). In its simplest form the torque was open-ended, with the two ends almost meeting and thickened into knobs, but the form of both the hoop and the knobs was capable of much variation. Occasionally it was a complete hoop with a hinged portion, but even that must almost have required a blacksmith to put it on. The torque appears to have had a religious, or at least a social, significance—it was worn only by men (among all the jewelry of the princess of Vix there was no torque), and apparently by all freemen, but both gods and goddesses were depicted wearing it.

It was not only their appearance that had changed. They were more free-ranging than before. We often catch glimpses, through the eyes of the classical writers, of whole nations of Celts on the move, with covered wagons, wives and children, flocks and herds. The farmers of prehistoric Europe were admittedly more mobile than those of today, with a less rigid system of ownership of land and fewer possibilities for keeping the same plot of land in production indefinitely. But the constant fermentation among the Celts looks like more than this. There was probably the pressure of population growth, combined with the exhaustion of marginal lands—for the European climate became quite suddenly wetter in the last 500 years B.C., and the ecological balance of farmland and pasture was disturbed. There was also the emphasis on herding rather than tillage that had come in with the Cimmerians. And there was quite simply the nomad tradition of the steppes. All these combined to make Europe literally an unsettled area in the middle years of the first millennium B.C.

Now, movements of peoples mean wars, and a warrior aristocracy implies wars. And so we come to that aspect of the Celts which cannot be ignored but which is the most difficult for a historian to pin down, to quantify, and to explain—the Celtic character, the heroic, tragicomic spirit which throughout history has been associated with the Celts. "For the great Gaels of Ireland," wrote G. K. Chesterton, "Are the men that God made mad,/ For all their wars are merry,/ And all their songs are sad." And for twenty-five centuries those who have met or heard of the Celts have been saying much the same. "The whole nation . . . is war-mad," wrote Strabo in the first century B.C., "and both high-spirited and quick for battle, although otherwise simple and not uncouth." Posidonius at much the same time called them "boasters and threateners and given to bombastic self-dramatization." Since the Celts themselves wrote nothing down, we know nothing of how they viewed themselves in these early centuries. That they had a rich oral tradition of heroic lays and epics can hardly be doubted, and it is one of the tragedies of the Celts that this is lost to us and to them.

The probable richness of this lost heritage is attested in Ireland, where cycles of lays have survived, though belonging to a later date. The Fenian Cycle and the Ulster Cycle—which deals with the exploits of the champions of the Red Branch, whose leader is Cúchulainn, the Hound of Ulster—were first written down in the twelfth century A.D., but their language is that of the sixth to eighth centuries, and the events they record appear to have taken place at the beginning of the Christian era. The society depicted agrees closely with the Greek and Roman estimation of the Celts. It could be said with some truth that Cúchulainn never did a day's work in his life. On the other hand, his training in warfare, especially in single combat and more particularly in chariot combat, was comprehensive, strenuous, and dangerous. His life was spent in fighting the enemies of Ulster, in feasting and wenching and cattle-raiding, all apparently to the accompaniment of laudatory lays composed for the occasion by a body of court poets who ranked scarcely, if at all, below the warriors of the court. Indeed, some of the poets were themselves famous warriors, and any warrior of repute was expected to be able to produce, when occasion demanded (for example, in his death throes), an appropriate couplet or at least a memorable aphorism.

It can legitimately be questioned to what degree this Celtic temperament—which is recognizable to this day among the Celtic-speaking peoples of the British Isles and their descendants abroad, and which is even assiduously cultivated, perhaps especially among the Irish—extended beyond the warrior aristocracy surrounding the tribal chieftains. The descriptions of Strabo and Posidonius, admittedly, refer to the whole of the population, and there was probably, then as now, a cultivation by all classes of society of the traditional attributes of the national character. But there must have been a large substratum of the population that was concerned with ordinary husbandry. Indeed, some of the more fascinating excavations of recent years have uncovered whole villages and farmsteads of the Celts, and there are even experiments in progress at the present time to reproduce and operate Celtic settlements in order to work out on a statistical basis the ecological and economic background of Celtic life.

The picture that archaeology gives of the daily life of the Celts is almost comically in contrast with the picture of them presented in lay and legend, and in the accounts of the classical historians—though perhaps no more so than the contrast, for example, between the daily life of an eighteenth-century Scottish crofter and the legends of the Forty-five. Through the length of Europe, from the green water meadows of Ireland to the sheep-cropped foothills of the Alps, while their chieftains were plotting their raids and the gentlemen-at-arms of the courts were carousing, the peasantry were going about their immemorial business. Their business was not quite the same, of course, from one end of Europe to the other. In the heart of Europe the farmers still lived in villages of square-built timber or wattle houses. In Britain and Ireland, on the other hand, houses were, by a tradition at least a thousand years old, round and often stone-built. They were often not grouped in villages but formed isolated farmsteads of three or four houses, surrounded by the pattern of small squarish fields, a form dictated by the necessity of cross-plowing.

The family shared its house with the cattle and

Tales of the Druids, who were priests or shamans of the Celtic religion, have fascinated Europeans ever since Roman times. The macabre scene at top comes from a work by the seventeenth-century historian Elias Schedius. A Druid priest, holding a goblet in one hand and a knife in the other, stands amid a welter of corpses and severed heads in a forest glade, while his female companion beats a drum with human thigh bones.

The Celts' own view of their priests may be represented by the robed figure at right, unearthed near Orléans in France. Still another conception may be found in the cartoon figure of Panoramix, at left. He appears in the popular French comic strip Astérix le Gaulois, whose creators pride themselves on historical accuracy.

other livestock, and indeed the animals were an integral part of the heating system of the houses. Small wide-horned cattle were kept, and an abundance of sheep and goats, for milk and cheese were staple foods. Pigs were common, and the boar—though perhaps the wild boar—seems to have been of more than culinary significance, being often represented as a helmet crest. Chickens were rare, having only recently been introduced into Europe from the east, but geese were plentiful. Horses were probably still the prerogative of the nobility, but dogs, of a mastiff or Irish wolfhound type, were common, and cats were known. Bees were probably kept, to provide wax for bronze casting and honey for sweetening and for the production of mead, like beer and milk a common drink of the masses. Wine was imported, but only for the nobility. The main crops were barley—for beer as well as for bread—and emmer and spelt, two early forms of wheat, though oats were also known. Vegetables were few, but beans were extensively cultivated, as was vetch, probably mainly as cattle feed. Flax was grown for the weaving of linen, but most woven cloth was of wool.

Such, then, were the Celts. A settled peasant populace whose nomadic tradition tended to make migration the natural answer to climatic or population crises. A tribal organization with a harddrinking, hard-riding aristocracy at constant feud with their neighbors. An artistic race including many craftsmen in wood and metal, with an artistic tradition going back to the animalistic decoration of the Russian steppe. A people with no writing but with a wealth of lays and legends transmitted by word of mouth and constantly renewed. And this rich and colorful culture disappeared completely—except for a remnant in the westernmost fringe of the British Isles—before the advance of the Roman Empire.

The deathblow was given by the conquest of Gaul by Julius Caesar in 58–52 B.C., but for a hundred years before that, as we have seen, the Celts had been on the defensive before the rising power of Rome to the south and the inroads of Germanic-speaking peoples from the east. In fact Julius Caesar was invited into Gaul by the Celtic tribe of the Aedui in order to help them repel an invasion of Germans from across the Rhine. This he did, but the Celts only exchanged a German conqueror for a Roman. In the course of the next two years Caesar subdued the whole of present-day France and established the Rhine as the dividing line between the Roman and the German spheres of influence. This left the Celts with nowhere to be, and they united under their last great leader, Vercingetorix, in a desperate attempt to stave off the inevitable. But Caesar called in German cavalry to oppose the chariotry of the Celts, and in the storming of the hill-fortress of Alesia the hope of the Celts went down.

Some would say that at Alesia, too, poetry fell to prose, art to science, and glory to technocracy. For that the military and political power of the Celts broke before the organized legions and bureaucratic administration of Rome is not so surprising. Other powerful nations had suffered the same fate. What is surprising is that the whole culture, the language, and the art of the Celts succumbed just as thoroughly and just as suddenly. Within a

This miniature bronze wagon, bearing a nature goddess and her attendants, was buried with an Alpine chieftain at Strettweg, Austria, in the seventh century B.C. On the opposite page is an enlarged view of the ten-inch goddess, who holds a shallow basin on her head, standing among spearmen and axmen.

188

LIVING LIKE CELTS

The compound included the round house and thatched huts for livestock.

How did the prehistoric people of Britain live in the Iron Age? To answer that question a television producer for the British Broadcasting Corporation set out two years ago to recreate a Celtic community of the third century B.C.

The experiment began on a cold March day when a band of fifteen young Britons, including three children, were set down on a thirty-five-acre tract of woods and meadows in southern England. To get them going, the BBC provided temporary tents, clothing, rations, some simple iron tools, and medical supplies. For starting animals they had three cows, four pigs, nine goats, twenty-five sheep, forty chickens, and a swarm of bees.

Following Celtic tradition, the settlers built a large round house with a conical thatch roof reaching almost to the ground. In the center of the house they built a hearth for warmth and cooking. At night they slept under the skins of animals.

By the end of the summer they were eating quite well on a diet of grains and vegetables grown in their garden, as well as meat from animals they raised or caught in the woods. They brewed beer and made mead with honey, water, and wine.

hundred years Roman roads and Roman towns and the large-scale Roman farms, slave-run to feed the towns, had spread over the new provinces of Gallia and were beginning to spread over the newly conquered province of Britannia. The Celtic languages disappeared from the mainland of Europe, and today languages derived from Latin are spoken in the former Celtic lands. (Breton, the Celtic language of Brittany, was later reintroduced from southwest England.) And after La Tène, there was no more Celtic art.

The archaeologist Stuart Piggott has in his *Ancient Europe* given the reason. The eclipse of Celtic art was "not so much the shrinking of the sensitive Celtic artist from the 'uniform and sordid ugliness of drab Romano-British daylight' as the removal by Roman civilisation of the aristocratic patronage of a barbaric and flamboyant martial tradition. The panoply and equipment of the battle-drunk, screaming tribal chieftain in his chariot hung with the decapitated heads of his foes, the air raucous with the sound of the *baritus* and the *carnyx*, was hardly appropriate for the new Romano-British world with the chieftain now a Celtic country gentleman in reduced circumstances taking a quiet stroll round the forum of his market town."

The Celts had been civilized, de-Celticized, and, many would say, denaturized. The only regions of the original Celtic realm that were not under

Cattle pull a cart made with crude iron tools. The settlers spun raw wool for clothing (above, right) and ground corn with mortar and pestle (below).

The clothes they made from the wool of their sheep kept them warm through the winter. But shoes were a problem. They tried making them out of skins but these leaked and quickly wore out. Often they went barefoot, ankle-deep in cold mud. "The Celts must have had better shoes," they decided.

There were other hardships. The soap they made from animal fats did not clean well. The iron tools they forged were too soft to cut wood. Their home-fired pottery crumbled. "Give us another ten years," they concluded, "and we would have all the skills the Celts must have had."

Most of the settlers stuck it out for a full year. At the end many said they had liked the peace and quiet, the absence of cars and television, the convivial evenings of talk and song. Some of them were sorry to return to the modern world.

Roman or German dominion by the second century A.D. were Ireland and Scotland. They deserve a final word, for they show something of the potentialities that lay in the Celtic culture if left to itself. Not that they were left to themselves. The Romans made one full-scale attempt to conquer Scotland and many minor campaigns north of Hadrian's Wall. And in the last expansion of the Germanic-speaking peoples, the Viking movement of the ninth and tenth centuries A.D., both Scotland and Ireland were invaded and partially colonized. And—since they were after all Celtic lands—Scottish and Irish principalities were often at war with one another, both internally and between the two countries.

But in the first four hundred years of the Christian era, while western Europe was being Romanized, Ireland remained free to develop in as much peace as Celtic peoples ever allow themselves. It is to these centuries that the lays of the House of Ulster would seem to refer, though as we have seen they appear to have been composed some centuries later and first written down in the early years of the present millennium. This fiercely warring, cattle-herding (and rustling) society was still in full vigor when the collapse of Roman rule in Britain and western Europe gave the opportunity for a last Celtic revival. As the Anglo-Saxons—again, a Germanic people—poured into eastern England and southern Scotland, and the Roman-

ized Celts of Wales were reinforced by Romanized Celtic refugees from England, the Irish too moved into the vacated lands. There was considerable Irish settlement in southern Wales, while the kings of northeast Ireland established the kingdom of Dalriada in western Scotland. At this time, too, the Scotti from Ireland invaded Scotland and gave the land their name. It is from these invasions, rather than from the surviving Celtic "natives," that the Gaelic languages of Wales and Scotland received the impetus that enabled them to survive into modern times.

It was at this time when the Roman legions were withdrawing from Britain that Christianity reached Ireland. Saint Patrick was by tradition the son of a Romanized Welsh family, who converted a king of Ireland at a pagan spring festival at Tara about 432. It is perhaps because Patrick was himself a Celt, though trained as a missionary in the south of France, that there was a unique feature to the conversion—the schools of Druids and minstrels, which guarded the wealth of Ireland's culture, were allowed to continue. The special position of the "lay universities" of Ireland was confirmed by Saint Columba a century and a half later, and thus for a further thousand years the oral traditions and the poetry of the Celts were honored and maintained. At the same time, the monasteries established by Saint Patrick and his successors in Ireland, and spread throughout Wales, Scotland, and northern England by Saint Columba and his successors, inherited the art of La Tène, which the Celts had once spread through Europe; and the school of ornamentation which had its origins among Scythian horsemen two thousand years before reached its final flower in the illuminated manuscripts of the Irish monks, in such masterpieces as the Book of Kells.

The ruined monastery of Clonmacnoise in central Ireland bears witness to the influence of Celtic tradition within the Christian church. The ancient Celtic symbol of the circle is here united with the symbol of Christ in the characteristic Gaelic cross.

The Real King Arthur

When the Romans withdrew their legions from Britain in the fifth century A.D. they left behind a political and military vacuum. After four centuries of Roman rule and Roman protection, the predominantly Celtic people of Britain had to see to their own government and their own defenses. From the neighboring coasts of northern Europe they were being attacked by the aggressive tribes of Angles, Saxons, and Jutes, themselves driven westward by German pressures from the east. Most of Britain was soon conquered, but in the mountains of Wales and in southwest England the invaders found fierce resistance.

The struggles that followed are cloaked in the gloom of England's dark age. But out of this time of turmoil came splendid legends of valor and derring-do, of knights and wizards, of the search for the Holy Grail and the reconquest of Britain. The central figure in these tales is King Arthur.

Not until after the Norman Conquest in the eleventh century were these tales gathered up and set down in writing. By then Arthur's legend had spread across the continent of Europe and had been embroidered beyond recognition. The versions that found their way into the works of such writers as Geoffrey of Monmouth and Sir Thomas Malory were such a rich broth of history and legend and pure unbridled fancy that no one knew whether they contained a word of truth. The impulse of most writers in the Age of Reason was to dismiss the whole concoction as medieval hokum.

But Tennyson's *Idylls of the King* stirred up new interest in the old tales, and scholars began to take a closer look. In this century historians have pored through the old manuscripts and come up with scraps of hard evidence. And archaeologists, sifting the earth at sites where legend says that Arthur and his knights once lived, have unearthed traces of the Britons who lived there in the Dark Ages. From these pinpoints of light we begin to see the outlines of a likely, if not yet proven, lost chapter in English history.

The real Arthur, it is now proposed, was a leader of the British resistance to the Anglo-Saxon invaders in the fifth and sixth centuries A.D. His name, Artorius, suggests that he may originally have been a native commander of Roman forces and may even have had Roman blood.

The earliest contemporary chronicler, a Celtic monk named Gildas, speaks of a Roman-British chieftain named Ambrosius, who rallied the British against the Saxon invaders and who was succeeded by another and greater leader. Curiously Gildas does not name this second commander but refers to him as "The Bear"; the Celtic word for bear is *arth* or *artos*. There are hints that Arthur, although he led the Christianized Britons against the pagan Saxons, dealt roughly with churchmen, possibly commandeering their wealth for his troops. It may be that the monk Gildas could not bring himself to mention his name.

Arthur's name first appears as a historical figure three centuries later in the *Historia Britonum* of the Welsh monk Nennius. There it is told that he fought the enemy in an epic series of twelve battles. The last climactic battle was fought at Mount Badon, which is sometimes thought to be the hill of Bath. In this glorious engagement Arthur inflicted such a crushing defeat on the Saxons that many of them fled across the Channel, and England was saved for forty years of peace.

Readers of these early accounts would never recognize the Arthur of later legend, the chivalric king surrounded by perfect knights. Sir Kei (Kay) and Sir Bedvyr (Bedivere) figure in these accounts, as does Arthur's "second wife," Gwenhyfar (Guinevere), but there is no Lancelot, no Round Table, no quest for the Holy Grail. These were later embellishments by French romancers. We must picture Arthur rather as a rough and ready military commander, using his mobile cavalry force to swoop down from his mountain fastness, striking at the unmounted Saxons—often, it would seem, when they were crossing rivers, for many of the battles take place at fords.

There are Arthur's Stones, Arthur's Seats, Arthur's Caves, and Arthur's Fords scattered up and down the west of England from Cornwall to Scotland. But his stronghold was somewhere in the southwest, in the neighborhood of the Wansdyke, a fifty-mile-long earthwork thought to have been built by Britons for defense against the Saxons. As early as the twelfth century Glastonbury, the seat of a medieval abbey, was identified as the enchanted Isle of Avalon, where Arthur had been buried in secrecy to conceal his remains from the enemy. Today Glastonbury is surrounded by dry land, but in Arthur's time it was indeed an island in the middle of marshes, which were not drained until much later.

After a fire destroyed the abbey in 1184, the monks announced that they had discovered a deep tomb contain-

*King Arthur, carved in stone
by a fifteenth-century sculptor*

ing the skeletons of a tall man and a fair-haired woman. Above it, they said, was a cross bearing the words, "Here lies buried the renowned King Arthur in the Isle of Avalon." It was a most convenient discovery, for it attracted crowds of visitors and brought funds with which to build a larger abbey. The bones were reburied in a marble shrine by King Edward I, but in the sixteenth century the shrine, the bones, and the inscription were all lost in the dissolution of the monasteries by Henry VIII.

Historians have never taken the monks' story at face value, but in recent years archaeologists have uncovered some suggestive bits of evidence. Digging in the ruins of the abbey they found an empty grave which answered the description of the one the monks had found. On Glastonbury Tor, which rises to the east of the abbey, they found fragments of pottery from the Mediterranean, indicating that Glastonbury was an active trading center in the sixth century and a likely seat for a military leader's headquarters.

Not far from Glastonbury is the hill called South Cadbury Castle, which had been used as a fort since Neolithic times, more than four thousand years ago. It was defended against the Roman legions and conquered only after a stiff battle. On the flat summit of the elevation archaeologists have found the remains of extensive buildings that covered the site in the Dark Ages. Could this, as local legend insists, be Arthur's stronghold, Camelot?

The hill is ringed by a series of concentric ramparts of earth and stone, indicating that it was continuously rebuilt and strengthened as a fort. As yet there has been no definitive find—no sword or stone with the name Arturus—that would prove that Cadbury was indeed Camelot. But in the minds of many old people in the west country there is no need for proof. When the archaeologists began their work an old man asked them anxiously if they had come to release Arthur from the hollow mount within which the Once and Future King had been resting all these centuries.

Far left, Camelot as imagined by Gustave Doré; above, South Cadbury Castle, the hill often identified with Camelot; below, Glastonbury Tor, identified with the Isle of Avalon (the monastery tower on top dates from the fifteenth century)

8: The Trail of the Vikings

by GEOFFREY BIBBY

The towering headland of Dyrholaey (background picture) was a landfall for Viking ships sailing to Iceland. Above: This silver coin bearing a Viking ship was minted in 825 at the port of Hedeby on the Baltic coast.

There is no mystery about the Vikings. Except perhaps the greatest mystery of all—why they appeared when they did, and how they managed to make a name for themselves that has rung down the centuries. In one sense there is no "lost world" here to discover; the Vikings were never lost, they never faded into the obscurity of forgotten things. On the contrary, such was the impression they made on their contemporaries that they were remembered long after they had themselves ceased to exist, and there are churches in England where the litany "From the fury of the Danes, Good Lord deliver us" is still used.

This bronze amulet found in Iceland represents Thor, the Norse god of the sky.

On the other hand, the Vikings, though a name to conjure with, were never very much more than a name, even to most of their contemporaries. We know them from the accounts of their enemies, and their victims. And it is only within this century that a picture of the Vikings as they were, and as they saw themselves, has been pieced together.

Even the name is a mystery, of a sort. When the first raids by ship-borne Scandinavians began on the coasts of England and France in the closing years of the eighth century of our era the chroniclers did not call them Vikings, but Danes or Northmen. The Germans called them Ascomanni, "ashmen," probably from the wood of which their oars were made. When Vikings reached the Black Sea and the Byzantine Empire by way of the rivers of eastern Europe, they were called Vaeringer, or Russ, from which the name Russia derives.

They seem to have called themselves Vikings, but more as an occupational description than as a tribal or national name. They were still Danes or Swedes or Norwegians, but if they embarked on a raiding expedition they "went Viking," as they said, and termed themselves Vikings. The origin of the term is unknown; it is probably connected with the word *vik*, meaning "a fiord or firth" (and found in many place names like Fishwick and Berwick, Ipswich and Norwich and Narvik and Schleswig). Whether they called themselves Vikings because they came from bases in the fiords of Scandinavia or because they raided by preference settlements in the fiords and inlets of Europe, nobody knows. But the name was in early use; Adam of Bremen, writing in the eleventh century, talks of "the pirates whom the Danes call Vikings but we Germans call Ashmen," and the Icelandic sagas use the term commonly of ship-borne warriors. Certainly that is what the term originally meant: independent sea raiders in search of booty—freebooters in fact—and the glamour of the Viking name has disguised to some degree the fact that the Scandinavian eruption into world history was often something very different. Often it took the form of long-term trading ventures, often of wide-scale campaigns of conquest, often of voyages of exploration and colonization.

Certain it is that the precariously civilized world of Dark Age Europe had scarcely heard of Scandinavia before the long ships landed and sacked the monastery on the holy island of Lindisfarne off the northeast coast of England in 793. Yet for the next 250 years the Vikings played a dominating role in the history of every country with a seaboard on the Baltic, the North Sea, or the Atlantic—including America.

The reasons for this sudden upsurge of an area previously of no political, military, or economic significance, a distant, poverty-stricken, and sparsely populated corner of Europe, have been the subject of much theorizing. Some would see it as a reaction to the establishment of the Frankish empire of Charlemagne. Charlemagne was the grandson of Charles Martel, who as king of the

Franks had halted the Arab invasion of Europe, by way of Spain, at the battle of Poitiers in 732. Charlemagne succeeded to the Frankish throne in 768, extended his realm until it stretched from the Pyrenees to the Carpathians, and he was crowned Holy Roman Emperor on Christmas Day, A.D. 800. There is evidence that the peoples of Scandinavia, then probably organized in a dozen or so principalities, felt themselves threatened by this power to the south and armed and fortified themselves to meet the threat. Certainly Charlemagne felt it necessary to fortify his northern coasts with a chain of watchtowers, beacons, and garrisons. And when he died in 814—twenty years after the first Viking raid on Lindisfarne—and the dynastic troubles began which were to split up his empire, he left a potentially aggressive foe on his northern frontier.

Another theory would see the origin of the Vikings in the system of land-tenure believed to be in vogue then in Scandinavia. By the laws of primogeniture, farms and estates went to the eldest son. Thus a host of land-hungry younger sons—princes of the court, nobles, and yeomen—could see no other means of making a career for themselves and achieving the wealth and position that chance of birth had denied them than to man a ship and seek their fortune across the seas.

It was the Viking ship, runs a third theory, that made the Vikings inevitable. They were the first—perhaps in all the history of the world—to build a really seaworthy boat. It was broad in the beam yet shallow in draft; it had a long rigid keel but was clinker-built, with overlapping planks sewn to each other with willow withes, allowing the ship to "give" to the waves; it answered well to oars but had a square sail with some of the qualities of the lateen rig. Thus it could sail into the wind, an ability which we now take for granted. These qualities—speed, maneuverability, shallow draft, and good carrying capacity—made it an ideal craft for coastal raiding. Inevitably it was used for that purpose.

Probably all these theories are partially right. As in a good murder mystery, the breakup of Charle-

magne's empire provided the opportunity, the land hunger of the younger sons of Scandinavia provided the motive, and the Viking long ship provided the means, the weapon. There is more to it than that, but let us for the moment leave it there.

Our knowledge of the Viking ship, and indeed our knowledge of the material and artistic wealth of the Vikings, depends very largely on a series of sensational discoveries made in Norway almost a century ago. It was in April 1880 that Nikolas Nikolaysen, the president of the Oslo Antiquarian Society, started digging into a large mound on a farm at Gokstad, almost at the mouth of the Oslo fiord.

Oslo fiord runs in from the Skagerrak, the arm of sea that joins the North Sea to the Baltic, and divides Norway from Denmark. It runs due north for fifty miles to Oslo, Norway's capital, and its shores are the most fertile, and the most storied, regions of the country—to the east the Ostfold, to the west the Vestfold.

The wide valley of the fiord is a Valley of the Kings. Its story is told in the Ynglingasaga, written down in Iceland by Snorri Sturluson in the beginning of the thirteenth century A.D., but based beyond doubt upon sources dating back to the end of the ninth century. The Ynglingasaga is the story of a royal house of Swedish kings who, driven out of Sweden in the second half of the seventh century, settled in the lands around the Oslo fiord. There they carved out small kingdoms and for two hundred years warred and intermarried among themselves in the intervals of raiding far and wide over the seas of northern Europe. The story of these early Vikings is told in circumstantial detail, and it culminates in the fully historical figure of Harald Fairhair, who in 872 established his rule over the whole of Norway at the battle of Hafrsfiord. The Gokstad tumulus at the southern tip of the Vestfold had, for as long as memory could recall, been known as the King's Mound because, it was said, a king had been buried there with all his treasure.

Nikolaysen's excavation was by way of being a "rescue dig." The sons of the farmer on whose land the tumulus lay—fifty yards across and still, despite constant plowing, fifteen feet high—had begun a haphazard shaft from the center of the mound toward the bottom. But Nikolaysen, an experienced excavator of tumuli, knew the dangers of digging downward from the summit, a process which means standing upon the objects for which you are digging and which involves ever increasing difficulty in disposing of the earth removed. He decided to drive a trench in from the side and, quite arbitrarily, began from the south.

Rarely has an excavation given such immediate results. On the second day's digging through a thick layer of blue clay, which rather inexplicably appeared to form the base of the mound, they struck a massive worked beam standing almost vertically in the exact center of the trench. Digging onward on either side of it, they found horizontal planks abutting it, splaying outward toward the sides of their cut. By the end of the day there could be no doubt as to what they

had found. Jutting out from the center of the trench was the prow of a mighty ship.

Nikolaysen recognized at once the significance of the discovery. He was certain that here lay a ship burial of the Viking period. Nikolaysen was already an expert in ship burials. Nearly thirty years earlier a tumulus had been razed for its gravel content at Borre, twenty miles or so to the north, and in it had been found a clinker-built ship over fifty feet long. It had been considerably damaged in the course of the digging, but Nikolaysen himself carried out an excavation of the ruins, discovering the bones of three horses and a dog, as well as quantities of harness, iron axes, a caldron, and a glass drinking vessel. He had also been present when Professor Oluf Rygh excavated a ship burial at Tunö, in the Ostfold, in 1865. There the greater part of the ship had completely rotted away, though a forty-foot length of keel remained. On the deck of the ship the remains of a rectangular plank-built chamber had been found, and in it the skeletons of a man and a horse, the latter still standing, held upright by a packing of clay. These two important discoveries, as well as some

The carved prow of a Viking ship, remarkably preserved after ten centuries, was photographed (opposite page) in 1904 as it emerged from a burial mound at Oseberg in Norway. In the reconstruction drawing above, Norsemen build a similar ship.

hundreds of smaller boat burials found in Norway and Sweden, had prepared Nikolaysen for the possibility of finding a ship beneath the Gokstad tumulus, but there had been nothing previously to suggest that a vessel in such a magnificent state of preservation could be found. For the timber of the Gokstad ship was as sound as when the vessel was laid down.

The next day Nikolaysen began widening his trench to a breadth somewhat greater than he estimated the ship would be. In the following months the broad trench was pushed onward along both sides of the ship, and from these parallel cuts the soil above the ship itself was removed. The excavation went forward rapidly. For two months not a drop of rain fell, and the digging could go on from dawn to dusk, in the long days of the northern midsummer.

The dry weather was not, however, an unmixed blessing. As more and more of the ship was exposed, the wood of its structure tended to dry out and warp. It proved necessary to douse the ship with water once or twice a day and to cover it with spruce branches to slow down evaporation. Even so, some of the wooden objects found in the ship were ruined by being exposed to the air.

As the trenches crept forward along the outside of the ship the spades of the diggers began to turn up animal bones. Altogether the skeletons of twelve horses and six dogs were unearthed, together with iron horseshoes and two dog collars, one of bronze and one of iron.

The ship proved to be nearly eighty feet long and was a magnificent example of the craftsmanship of the Viking shipwrights. Upon the sixty-five-foot keel seventeen frames were erected, and to these, sixteen planks a side were attached clinker fashion. These planks were not nailed in position but were sewn onto the frames with withes. The interstices between the planks were caulked with three-stranded rope of cattle

This snarling beast, forming the top of a wooden post, was found in the buried ship at Oseberg.

hair, laid in position when the ship was built. All the woodwork of the ship was of oak, except the deck planks, which were of pine. A little forward of the center of the ship was a stepped mast, and extreme aft on the starboard side the steering-oar was still in position.

In the third plank down from the gunwale, sixteen oar ports had been cut on each side, all of them closed, when not in use, by swiveling shutters on the inside. Covering these ports on the outside there lay, still in position, thirty-two shields on each thwart, each shield circular and three feet across. They overlapped each other to half their diameter, and the paint with which they had been colored alternately yellow and black could still be seen.

The vessel had been set in a bed dug four feet into the clay that underlies the mound, and had been supported in an upright position by massive horizontal beams. It had then been packed up to the gunwales with blue clay and filled up inside with the same material, topped by a layer of moss and hazel branches. It was the fact that the ship had thus been entirely buried in clay which had resulted in its astonishing degree of preservation. Where the prow and sternpost and, of course, the mast had projected above the clay layer, they were rotted clean away. The upper bulwarks were pressed inward upon the vessel by the weight of the mound above, but otherwise the ship was as sound and apparently even as seaworthy as when it had been buried, probably a full thousand years before.

As clearing progressed toward the northern end, an out-of-place structure appeared abaft the mast. It was a square, tent-shaped room of massive logs, and from the analogy of the Tunö ship Nikolaysen knew that this must be the burial chamber. He was, however, disappointed, though hardly surprised, to see that the chamber showed signs of having been broken open from the stern end. For in the sides of the trench that he had by now cut almost across the mound, he had already noticed a point where a looser filling revealed the outlines of a previous excavation, a shaft dug down from

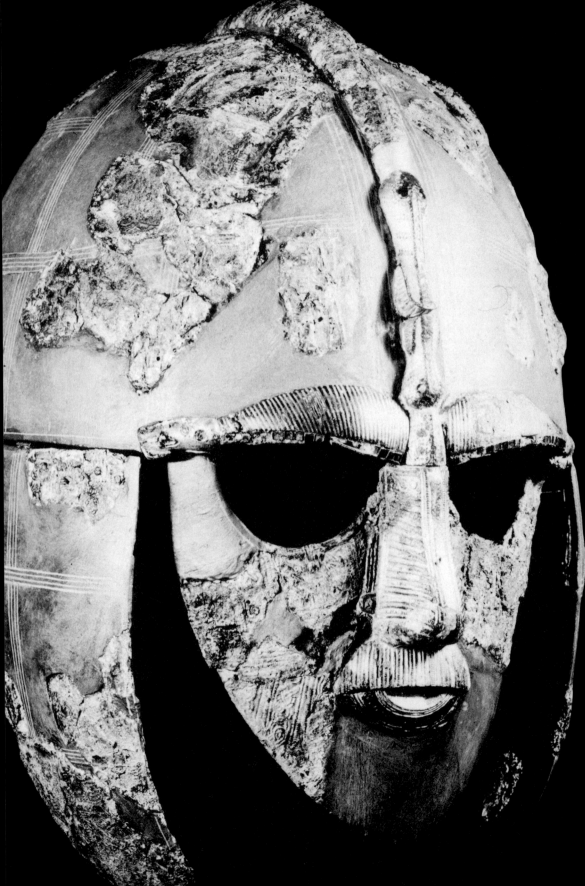

These magnificent accouterments of an Anglo-Saxon warrior chief were buried with his ship in the seventh century at Sutton Hoo, on the east coast of England. The iron helmet on this page is sheathed in bronze with silver and garnet inlay. On the facing page, from top to bottom, are a stylized flying eagle from the front of a shield, the lid of a purse with gold cloisonné decoration, and the shoulder clasp of a cloak. Their owner was probably a king of East Anglia, who lived two centuries before the height of the Viking era but wore similar armor and ornaments.

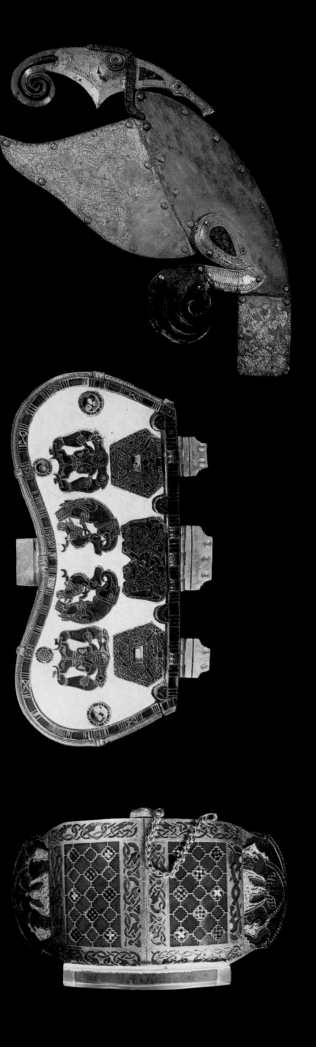

the top of the mound toward the stern of the ship. With little hope of finding anything of value left within the chamber, he ordered the removal of the logs of the roof and began excavating the soil beneath.

As expected, the contents were fragmentary and showed every sign of a thorough ransacking. But enough was found to give an idea of the rich furnishings that must originally have accompanied the burial. The list includes 122 separate items. The majority of them were metal buttons, buckles, and strap terminals, of bronze and lead and silver-gilt. They indicated that originally a very large quantity of clothing, belts, and horse trappings had been deposited in the chamber. Only very little of the textiles that must have formed a large part of the treasure had escaped the hand of time and of the tomb robbers, but a large length of silk damask interwoven with gold thread gave an indication of the lost wealth. Fragments of a wooden bedstead were found, the fittings of several iron-bound chests, and the remains of carved trays, a games cabinet designed to be used as a checkerboard, draughtsmen, and a slashed-leather purse. Among the debris lay the scattered bones of a man, of whom the anatomists could say that he had been well over six feet tall and over fifty years old, and that he had suffered severely from gout, probably to the extent of partial paralysis.

The remainder of the ship gave a rich haul of untouched articles, which suggests that when the ship was buried it was fully equipped and provisioned for a long voyage. Oars and anchor lay ready, a gangplank and three ship's boats were aboard, as well as a tent with richly carved, dragon-headed tent poles. There were barrels and kegs, a copper caldron and an iron caldron with its tripod, cups and bowls and plates of wood, five bedsteads, and a wooden sledge.

An exotic and unexpected discovery was made aft of the burial chamber. There by the steering oar lay, in the bottom of the ship, the bones and feathers of a peacock.

When the excavation was completed the vessel, still sound enough to be moved, was drawn out by

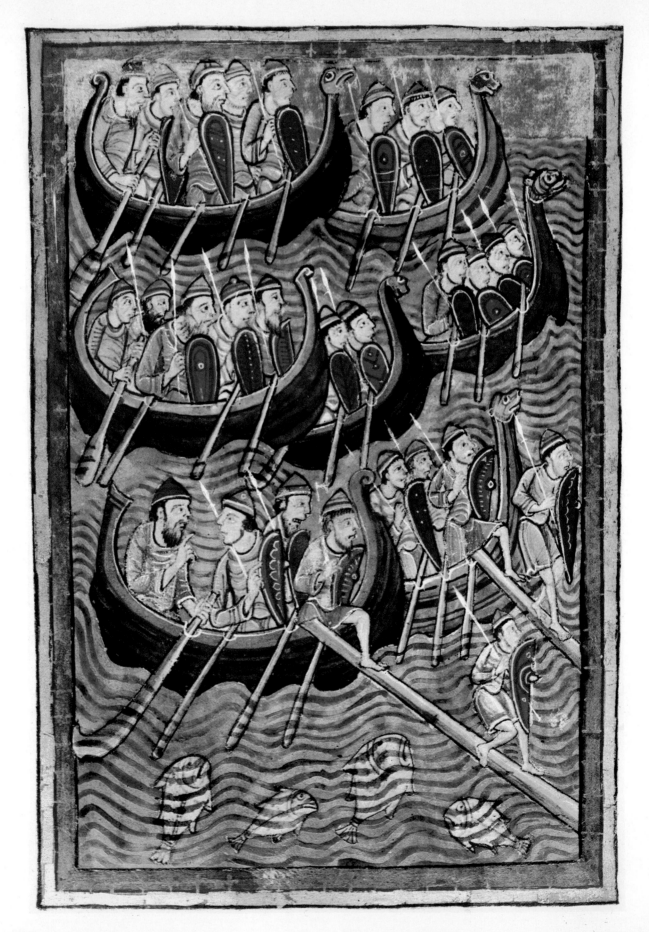

winches from the mound in which it had lain for a thousand years, and transported by barge to Oslo. There for twenty years the Gokstad ship was the showpiece of the university museum. Then it was eclipsed by a discovery of even greater magnificence. In 1904 Professor Gabriel Gustafson, the director of the museum, began the unearthing of a ship of almost the same size from a burial mound at Oseberg, halfway between the first ship discovery at Borre and the second at Gokstad.

Again it was a rescue dig. The farmer who owned the land had been fired by the splendor of the Gokstad discovery to begin his own excavation on his own mound the year before. He had dug down to the mast and to the roof of the burial chamber before he reported what he had done. Gustafson, in cleaning up his excavation, located the sternpost of the ship. It was of oak and intricately carved. Already it appeared that the Oseberg ship was more richly equipped and furnished than the one from Gokstad.

Early in the excavation it was discovered that the burial chamber had been plundered. A large hole in the triangular roof of the chamber showed the way that the grave robbers had taken, and even the massive roof beam, so large that it took fifteen men to lift it, had been broken through. Along the whole length of the ship the trench could be traced which the robbers had dug, and a quantity of objects lay in the bottom of this trench, clearly items that had been taken from the burial chamber and dropped on the way. Among them were the remains of the skeletons of the two occupants of the chamber, one a woman of about thirty and the other a woman of about fifty. Of the first skeleton very little was found, but the other could be practically completely reassembled, the only portions missing being the right hand, the fingers of the left hand, and left upper arm. The missing parts were gruesomely significant. The fingers of both hands must have been loaded with rings, and there had probably been massive gold bracelets on the right wrist and left arm. The robbers had not wasted time on stripping these

Invading Norsemen are illustrated in a twelfth-century English manuscript called The Miracles of Saint Edmund. *In the illumination on the opposite page they approach the shore, through a sea of woeful fish, in cockleshells that the artist meant to represent Viking ships. Above, they storm the ramparts of a town, probably Thetford. The artist was wrong in thinking that they carried pointed shields and fought barefoot; their shields were oval and their feet were clad in leather shoes.*

objects from the dead limbs but had taken them bones and all.

Other items from the chamber found in the robbers' trench included quantities of woolen cloth and silk ribbons and of eiderdown from cushions and quilts; fragments of three carved chests; a little cask full of wild apples; wooden buckets and ladles and dishes, including one dish shaped like a fish; pieces of a wooden saddle and of two carved bedsteads; a wooden walking stick with a handle carved in the likeness of a dog's head; and portions of a loom.

It was found that the robbers' trench had led past the prow of the vessel, and the robbers had ruthlessly cut through the prow to make room for the removal of the treasures from the chamber. Fragments of the dragon's head that had adorned the prow were found scattered among the debris from the chamber. The Oseberg ship had originally had a prow running up to a carved spiral, representing the neck of the snake to which the long ships of the Vikings were often likened by the saga writers. At the top of the spiral was the head of this snake-dragon.

As was to be expected, no objects of precious metal were to be found in the despoiled chamber. The room, seventeen feet square, had been ravaged until scarcely a single object was complete or lay in its original place. But the list of the larger items that the room had held could be made out with fair certainty from the fragments. There had been two beds and quantities of pillows and quilts and blankets. There had been a roll of tapestry and three looms. And the cloth and ropework of a tent or awning were found. Apart from these, the remaining furnishings of the chamber consisted of chests and kegs, iron- or bronze-bound. Only two chests were found complete and unrobbed. One contained a store of wheat and some more wild apples, the other held wooden dishes and cups, iron knives and shears, and a number of what appeared to be kitchen utensils.

Viking trade routes (opposite page) covered a watery empire of oceans and rivers that stretched from Greenland to the Caspian Sea. The drawing below is based on a ship unearthed off the coast of Denmark in 1957. At left is a glob of Baltic amber, one of the low-bulk, high-value stand-bys of Viking commerce.

It was by now obvious that this was the burial place of a woman. Nothing masculine had been found at all, both the skeletons were identified as women, and the presence of the looms clinched the argument. Clearly a lady of wealth and position, almost certainly a queen, was buried here.

The stern of the ship, abaft the chamber, had been untouched by the robbers. It turned out to be fully equipped as a ship's galley. Two iron caldrons and a curiously modern-looking frying pan lay there, and beside them all the equipment for preparing food—wooden troughs, knives and ladles and hatchets, even a complete hand mill for grinding the flour. Nor had the actual provisions been forgotten. Beside the cooking pots lay the complete skeleton of an ox.

The clearing of the vessel aft of the mast produced its complement of oars and tackle and revealed the magnificent carving of the sternpost and gunwales. Attention was now concentrated on the area forward, below the level of the robber trench. It soon became clear not only that the vessel was a state barge but also that it carried the state vehicles for the use of the queen ashore. The whole of the fore part of the ship was covered by a thick blanket of stones, and when these were removed a remarkable assemblage of objects was revealed, broken into thousands of pieces by the weight and angularities of the stones but preserved by them from the corrosive influence of direct contact with the soil. Among the ship's stores, water casks and oars and anchor and gangplank, lay the remains of a four-wheeled cart and four sledges, all a mass of intricate carving, and with their paintwork still vivid. Along the ship's rail were found the skeletons of the ten horses that had drawn the vehicles, two to each of them. They had clearly been poleaxed, as had at least two of the four dogs that lay among them.

The ship was now completely cleared, and the tarpaulins that covered the already excavated

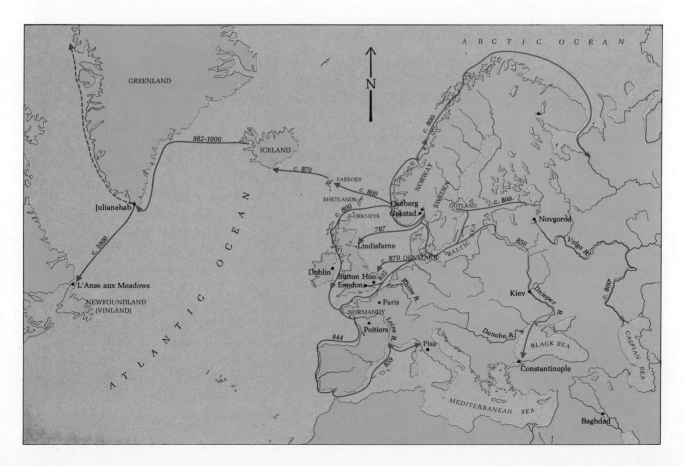

portions could be removed. For the first time the ship could be seen in its entirety.

Seventy feet long from stem to stern it lay, scarcely a man's height from keel to gunwale, though the richly carved prow and sternpost rose twice that height to end in splintered stumps. It had only thirty oars to the Gokstad ship's thirty-two, but it was similar in construction, clinker-built with a massive steering oar on the starboard side.

The robbed burial galleys of the Vestfold kings give almost as unsatisfactory a picture of the wealth that they must once have contained as do the robbed tombs of the pharaohs. A Norwegian Tutankhamen, an unplundered royal burial mound, has not yet been found. But the very gaps in the lists of objects found give us a clear idea of the treasures that rewarded the robbers. No personal jewelry of any sort was found, and while the kitchen utensils were complete, no metal plates or bowls or cups for eating and drinking remained. All of these, we may assume, were of precious metals.

A glimpse of the lost wealth was given in 1939 on the east coast of England. Just before the outbreak of the Second World War, excavation of a mound at Sutton Hoo in Suffolk revealed a ship burial. The ship, though of the same length as those from Gokstad and Oseberg, was of lighter construction, and its contents dated it to around A.D. 660, some two centuries earlier than the Viking ships of the Oslo fiord. It lay in sand, and practically everything perishable had disappeared without a trace. Even the timbers of the ship could be identified only by the rows of iron clinch-nails still in position. But the robber shaft that was traceable in the substance of the mound had not reached the burial chamber, and its wealth lay intact. A helmet of iron, but gilded and bound with silver, a shield ornamented with gold leaf, and a sword with a hilt of gold and a jeweled pommel formed the surviving armament of an Anglo-Saxon king of East Anglia who must have been buried here; his trappings had been held in place by massive gold clasps and buckles, inlaid with garnets and enamel. The solid-gold frame of a purse, ornamented with gold cloisonné work, still contained forty gold coins. And in addition to these more personal effects there were no fewer than ten silver bowls, two large silver dishes, silver spoons and ladles and silver-mounted drinking-horns, seven bronze caldrons, and a large number of silver and gold handles and fitments and pieces of inlay, which must at one time have adorned objects of wood and leather and cloth.

Sutton Hoo is complementary to Oseberg and Gokstad. That which the thieves had spared in the

Vestfold the hand of time had consumed in Suffolk, and that which the thieves had taken in Norway was found intact at Sutton Hoo. We would not go far wrong in assuming a treasure in the Norwegian royal graves at least as magnificent as that of the kinglet of the Suffolk shore.

The kings and queens of the Norwegian ship burials are not unknown. A magnificent process of deduction on the part of Professor Brøgger has identified the Gokstad and Oseberg burials with the relevant periods of the Ynglingasaga, the heroic account of the lives and deaths of the kings of Ostfold and Vestfold. The style of the decoration of the objects found in these two mounds can be dated with great certainty to about A.D. 850. We are concerned therefore with the generation immediately prior to that date.

The central figure of this period, says the Ynglingasaga, was Queen Åsa. As a young maiden, daughter of a king in western Norway, she was sought in marriage by the elderly King Gudröd of Vestfold. The suit was refused, but Gudröd in a surprise attack slew Åsa's father and brother and took the young princess by force. The marriage was short-lived. Åsa bore a son, Halvdan, but before he was a year old Gudröd fell to an assassin's spear. The assassin was Åsa's servant.

The Vestfold kingdom fell to Gudröd's son by a previous marriage, Olav, and Åsa's father's kingdom fell to the infant Halvdan. But when Halvdan became a man, Olav, who was severely stricken with gout, died and was buried in the district of Geirstad (which includes Gokstad) and Halvdan inherited both kingdoms. Åsa made her home with him in Vestfold, and it was to Vestfold that he brought his bride, Ragnhild, whom he, a true son of his father, had taken by force of arms, bringing her home, it is said, in a carved and tented wagon. A year later, just after the birth of Halvdan's son—that Harald Fairhair who was to unite all Norway into a single kingdom—Åsa died, at the age of about fifty, and was buried with great pomp in Vestfold.

There can be little doubt that the skeleton of the gout-paralyzed man that lay in the Gokstad ship is the mortal remains of King Olav Gudrödson. And the probability is high that the Oseberg ship is the last resting place of Queen Åsa, and that hers is the skeleton of the middle-aged woman that was found scattered along the trench dug by the robbers who desecrated her grave.

It is an attractive thought, too, that the carved and painted cart that is the showpiece of the Oseberg collection may well be the selfsame wagon in which King Halvdan brought home his

captured bride, the mother-to-be of the royal line of all Norway.

During the lifetime of Queen Åsa, which must have covered the middle years of the ninth century A.D., the activities of the Vikings had increased in scope and changed in character. And while Harald Fairhair was fighting to unite Norway, a Danish grand army under the sons of Ragnar Lodbrok ("Hairy-breeks") had been campaigning for over seven years in England, had won the greater part of the country, and had just turned against the last surviving opposition, the kingdom of Wessex under a newly crowned king called Alfred. It was now no longer a matter of four or five ships plundering monasteries along the coasts or a dozen ships sacking a market town at the mouth of a river. Organized fleets of hundreds of ships were occupying islands as permanent bases and from them conducting regular campaigns, often hundreds of miles inland.

It was mainly the Danes. They had been well armed and well organized against the threat of Charlemagne, and in the twenty years following the great emperor's death they raided along the coasts of his empire as far as the estuary of the Seine. In 834 they sacked Dorestad on the Rhine, the greatest merchant emporium in northern Europe. And the following year they raided the Thames estuary and established a base on the Isle of Thanet. In 845 the Danish king sent a fleet of several hundred vessels to ravage Hamburg, and another under Ragnar Lodbrok to attack Paris.

In the meantime the Norwegians, too, had been active. While Lodbrok was raiding up the Seine the men of Vestfold (and perhaps even the Gokstad galley) were raiding up the Loire and levying toll on the sea and river commerce of the whole of western France, and the Arabs tell of raids on the coasts of Spain and into the western Mediterranean. It would be the booty of these raids which, some years later, would be buried

At this Viking graveyard at Lindholm Høje, Denmark, burials are marked by stones laid in the shape of ships.

with King Olav and his stepmother, Queen Åsa.

The campaigns of the Norwegians farther north are less well chronicled, but it is clear that in these years they raided around the north of Scotland and found easy prey in the small and ever-warring principalities of Ireland. And here for the first time the Vikings came to stay. Permanent Norwegian settlements—permanent in a way to this day— were established in southwest Scotland and north-west England. Dublin was founded as a Viking town in 839, and there were Viking kings both there and in Limerick.

In 865 the Great Army of the Danes, amassed at their bases on Thanet and Sheppey and in East Anglia, marched north under the sons of Lodbrok in a regular campaign of conquest. They subdued the kingdom of Northumbria, and York in 866. The following year they invaded the kingdom of Mercia and captured Nottingham. The king of Mercia saved his throne by paying a large sum in Danegeld, the first time the Vikings were bought off in this way. In the course of the next century this "racket," exacting payment for not attacking, was developed into a fine art both in England and on the continent, and its results can be seen archaeologically in the vast increase in hoards of Anglo-Saxon and western European coins found in Scandinavia from these years. Anyway, the Great Army moved south, against the kingdom of Wessex, and occupied London in 871. In the following years half the Danish army remained in the north, where it established the Danelaw—the area around the "five boroughs" of Lincoln, Stamford, Leicester, Nottingham, and Derby—which was to remain a center of Danish occupation until the time of William the Conqueror. The other half, from its headquarters at Cambridge, campaigned against Alfred of Wessex but was never able to win a decisive victory and was finally defeated at the battle of Etheldune in 878. But though defeated the Great Army was far from destroyed; it crossed the English Channel, and with reinforcements from Denmark it spread destruction through northern France and Belgium for the next fourteen years.

During all these years events of perhaps even greater moment were taking place farther east. Along the rivers and lakes of eastern Europe Viking ships were creeping south and east through present-day Russia. The story is not easy to piece together, since the written evidence consists of sporadic references in the chronicles of the emperors of Byzantium, short accounts by Arab geographers who met Vikings in the Black Sea and at the mouth of the Volga, and medieval Russian historical manuscripts. But to this can be added a very considerable quantity of archaeological evidence. The routes across eastern Europe, to Lake Ladoga and along the great south-going rivers, the Dnieper, the Don, and the Volga, are dotted with relics of the traffic of this period. In particular, more than three hundred hoards of coins—western European, Byzantine, and especially Arabic—have been found along the river routes, while no fewer than 73,000 silver coins, including 25,000 Islamic, have come to light on the Swedish island of Gotland. Graves containing Viking ornaments and weapons are common, particularly in the north, and boat burials clearly analogous to the ship burials of Norway have been found as far south as Smolensk, while a runic inscription occurs near the mouth of the Dnieper on the Black Sea—and another at the Piraeus at Athens!

It seems to have been from Sweden, and particularly from Gotland, that this eastern Viking movement took its start. It must have been very different from the western expansion. Here there were no wide seas to cross and no rich cities or monasteries to sack. The river routes ran through endless tracts of forest and steppe peopled by pastoral Slavs and nomadic Bulgars and Khazars. But at the other end of the routes lay the wealth of the East, the Byzantine Empire, the caliphate of Baghdad, the Golden Road to Samarkand, and the Silk Road to China. They were too far away for raiding, and from the beginning the main object was trade. Yet it was trade with an unmistakable Viking stamp. The Viking ship was what made it possible. Immensely maneuverable under oars or sail and of incredibly shallow draft, it was as suitable for the wide rivers of southern Russia as for the estuaries of western Europe. And the crews were just as warlike, just as rapacious. Ibn Rustah, an Arab geographer writing in the tenth century, tells us that their main commodities for sale were furs and slaves, and that they captured the slaves in raids upon the Slavs from permanent fortified strongholds on islands in the rivers. "They are courageous in battle," says Ibn Rustah, "but their bravery does not appear on land. They always make their attacks and expeditions from ships."

They appear to have begun to make permanent settlements early in the ninth century, founding first Novgorod and later Kiev. It is possible to regard them as the founders of Russia, the name Russ by which they were known coming probably from the Finnish name for Sweden, Ruotsi; and it is probably from Novgorod, from the "Khaganate of Russ," that ambassadors were sent in 839 to the emperor of Byzantium. Viking ships cannot have been unknown in the Golden Horn at Constantinople, and in the tenth century Vikings were recruited to form the personal bodyguard of the emperor. Harald Hardraade, the king of Norway who was defeated by King Harold of England at Stamford Bridge a fortnight before the Battle of Hastings, was in his youth commander of the bodyguard at Constantinople.

By the end of the ninth century, when Viking raids had been going on with increasing intensity for over a hundred years, the tendency for the invaders to establish settled kingdoms independent of their Scandinavian motherlands was becoming more and more marked. Norwegians had settlements in Scotland and Ireland, Swedes in Russia, and Danes held their Danelaw in central and northern England. In 911 the king of the Franks made a virtue of necessity and granted the dukedom of Normandy to a Norwegian chieftain called Rolf, who had been campaigning for ten years in the north of France.

The most remarkable, and the best known, of the Norwegian colonization projects had begun much earlier, in the time of Queen Åsa of Vestfold, before the middle of the 800's. But it was the uniting of Norway under her grandson, King Harald Fairhair, that gave the real impetus to the exploration of the north Atlantic, and many of the prominent settlers in the Faeroe Islands and Iceland can be regarded as "political refugees" from Norway. Iceland, at least, was probably uninhabited before the Vikings arrived in the 830's, though there is slight evidence that it may have been sighted earlier by Irish monks during the semimythical voyages of Saint Brendan. There are said to have been Irish monks on the Faeroe Islands, and there certainly appear to have been sheep on the islands, since the name means "island of sheep."

The Viking crossing of the Atlantic was no single daring venture of an intrepid explorer, no wild fluke of wind and weather. Compared with the Vikings, it was Christopher Columbus who was the rash and romantic adventurer into the unknown. One hundred seventy years of patient exploration intervened between the landing of the first Norseman in the Faeroe Islands and the landing of Leif the Lucky in Vinland. It is said that Iceland was first sighted by voyagers blown off their course to the Faeroes, but once it was known to exist, regular fleets set off to colonize it. The traditional method was for the ship's captain to throw overboard the pillars supporting his high-seat and to site his home where they were washed ashore. In this way the fertile land between the sea and the steep ice-covered mountains of the interior was gradually settled, and in the course of fifty years, by about 930, all the available land, it is said, was occupied. The great Landnámabók, the Book of Land-taking, compiled in Iceland about 1200, gives the names of four hundred settlers, who with their families and retainers probably represent a population in 930 of over four thousand. The later comers, who continued to stream in, would have to take service with, or buy land from, the settlers already there—or else look farther afield.

Greenland had by then been long known, sighted, and even landed upon, by a man called Gunbjörn, who was blown off his course from

Norway to Iceland. But it was in 982 that Erik the Red, a Norwegian who had been banished from his homeland for complicity in a murder and who had sought refuge in Iceland, was in turn banished from Iceland for a term of three years for another murder. He decided to employ the three years in an exploration of Gunbjörn's land and sailed westward to Greenland. Coasting south along the inhospitable east shore, he rounded the southern tip and explored northward along the much more sheltered and ice-free western coastline, finding several places suitable for settlement. After the three years were past he returned to Iceland, and the following year he set off with twenty-five ships loaded with settlers for the new land. Of these only fourteen successfully completed the voyage, and they established two settlements in the most promising areas, near the present sites of Greenland's two largest towns, Julianehåb and Godthåb.

It was some years later, probably in 992, that Erik the Red's son Leif started out to explore farther west. Again it was not an adventure "into the blue." According to the accounts written down in Iceland between two and three hundred years later, a ship captained by Bjarni Herjulfson had been blown off course on its way from Iceland to Greenland and had three times sighted land southwest of Greenland before reaching Erik's settlement. It is told that Leif bought Bjarni's ship and set off with thirty-five men. They first struck a barren rocky coast and, sailing southward, skirted flat wooded shores followed by long beaches, and finally landed on a grassy area by a river, where they built themselves houses and spent the winter, before returning home. Leif christened the land where he established his winter quarters Vinland. There can be little doubt that Leif and his companions fully intended to establish a permanent colony, as had been done in Greenland and Iceland. At least three other expeditions sailed in the following years to Leif's encampment, one, led by his brother Torvald, spending three winters there and exploring the coasts farther south during the summers. But they met hostile natives with bows and arrows, and Torvald was killed, and the colonizing attempts were abandoned—at least for the time. There is no certainty. No records were compiled in Greenland of voyages from there, and the Icelandic records only tell of such events as were reported back to Iceland.

But the Greenland settlements prospered for another four hundred years, with ships sailing yearly to Norway carrying the seal and polar bear skins, the Greenland falcons, and the walrus and narwhal ivory that were among the prized treasures of the courts of medieval Europe. Greenland had its own bishop from the beginning of the twelfth century. It would be surprising if the Greenland Vikings never again crossed to the lands to the westward, and indeed the bishop of Greenland is said to have traveled to Vinland in 1121, perhaps to visit a congregation there. But in the 1400's ships stopped sailing from Norway to Greenland, and the later fate of the Greenland colonies is unknown. When sailing was resumed on the route in the eighteenth century the settlements were found deserted.

There have naturally been many attempts to find traces of Viking visits and settlements in North America, and a number of apparent relics has been adduced. But the runic stone from Kensington in Minnesota has now been shown to be a nineteenth-century forgery, excavation around the Newport tower in Rhode Island has produced fragments of seventeenth-century clay pipes, and the "Viking grave" from Beardmore in Ontario is rendered suspect by the reported association of the finder with a Norwegian immigrant whose father had owned a collection of Viking antiquities. Attempts to follow the fairly clear descriptions of the coasts given in the Icelandic accounts are made difficult by uncertainties about distances and inaccuracies of direction natural enough in voyages without a compass. The story of Leif's crew gathering wild grapes (an obvious attempt to explain the name Vinland) has been used as evidence pointing to a southerly location, while the statement that at the winter solstice the sun rose at 7:30 A.M. and set at 4:30 P.M. would put the latitude at 41° north, which is the latitude of New York City!

But then in 1960 Helge Ingstad, a Norwegian who had spent years examining the Atlantic coastline of North America and attempting to reconcile its features with saga descriptions, found at L'Anse aux Meadows on the northern tip of Newfoundland traces of a settlement with long turf houses with a central hearth, very similar to the Viking houses of Scandinavia. There were clear signs of ironworking, which ruled out the possibility of the remains being Indian or Eskimo, and radiocarbon dating of charcoal from the hearths gave dates very close to A.D. 1000. There is no doubt at all that L'Anse aux Meadows is a Viking settlement, and a very strong probability that it is the actual site of Leif Erikson's winter quarters.

The windswept house sites off the American coast have little in common with the magnificent ship burials of Oslo fiord, but they show dramatically the capabilities of the men and the ships that for two hundred years sailed forth from the coasts of Scandinavia to terrorize and plunder the world. The Vikings stand at the dawn of the medieval era as the last of the barbarian hordes to ravage civilized Europe, and the first of the explorers who would carry a European way of life to the ends of the earth. Hated and feared in their time, the Vikings have in retrospect acquired a glamour that is not entirely undeserved. For they were at least internally consistent. They cast themselves in a heroic role, and they lived up to it. They dealt in brutality, treachery, and violent death—and they accepted brutality, treachery, and violent death as their own lot, without rancor or reproach.

Their religion mirrored and motivated their lives. The world, both of gods and of men, was doomed from the start. All that a man could do with his life was to feast and to fight; all he could hope for was to die in battle, whereupon, as the chosen of Thor and Odin, he would continue the feasting in the hall of the gods, Valhalla, until the time when everything would go under in the final battle of Ragnarok.

This Viking memorial stone comes from the island of Gotland, off the coast of Sweden. One of hundreds carved from local limestone, it stands more than eleven feet tall. The scenes depict Viking voyages and battles.

IN SEARCH OF . . .
The Tomb of Philip of Macedon

The image of the archaeologist as treasure hunter, digging up the mask of Agamemnon or finding the tomb of Sennacherib, is supposed to be passé. Present-day archaeologists are more often to be found measuring the radioactive carbon in a bit of charcoal to determine its age, or sifting seeds from the soil of ancient campsites to find out what prehistoric men ate. But the romantic spirit of Heinrich Schliemann and Leonard Woolley is not yet dead.

One archaeologist who recently found the golden prize of a lifelong search—or so he firmly believes—is Manolis Andronikos, professor of archaeology at the University of Salonika in Greece. Off and on for forty years Andronikos has been digging at the site of an ancient Macedonian city near the modern village of Vergina. He believes that this place, with its numerous burial mounds and one giant tumulus, was the capital of Macedon in the great days of King Philip II, who conquered Greece, and his son Alexander, who came close to conquering the known world.

Over the years Andronikos dug into many of the smaller mounds in the area, sometimes turning up a clay vase or an iron weapon or a piece of bronze jewelry. But many of the graves had already been looted, probably by barbarian Gallic soldiers during antiquity. Not until 1976 did Andronikos get together the funds and equipment to begin a full-scale probe of the great tumulus. The first season's work yielded some broken bits of gravestones and one marble sculpture of a boy's head, but no tomb. The next year his crew found and opened a small tomb. It

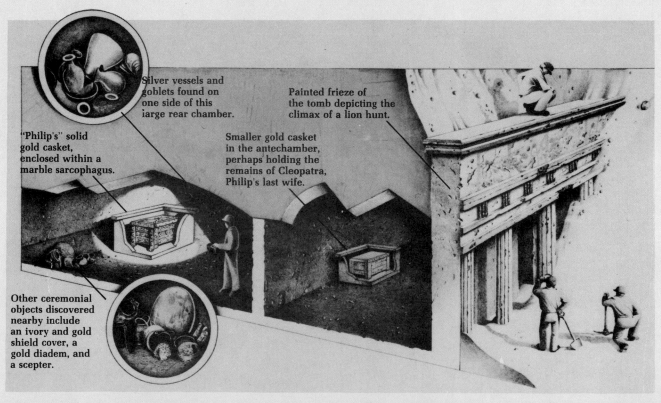

Silver vessels and goblets found on one side of this large rear chamber.

Painted frieze of the tomb depicting the climax of a lion hunt.

"Philip's" solid gold casket, enclosed within a marble sarcophagus.

Smaller gold casket in the antechamber, perhaps holding the remains of Cleopatra, Philip's last wife.

Other ceremonial objects discovered nearby include an ivory and gold shield cover, a gold diadem, and a scepter.

The tomb consists of two chambers, each containing one sarcophagus. Excavators entered from the side, leaving the marble doors unopened for fear the roof of the tomb might collapse.

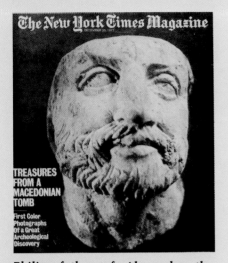

Philip, father of Alexander the Great, may be depicted in this ivory head, found in a Greek tomb. The little carving, less than an inch high, looms large on the cover of The New York Times Magazine.

had been looted but its walls were painted with fine frescoes. Andronikos believes that the Gallic robbers, having looted this tomb, assumed that they had found all the treasure buried in the mound. But further digging uncovered a second, larger tomb, which had not been disturbed. Within it Andronikos found a treasure of precious objects: bronze armor, sword, scepter and golden diadem, silver vessels, and a marble sarcophagus. Within the sarcophagus was a solid gold casket, weighing twenty-four pounds, embossed with a sunburst, a familiar Macedonian symbol. Inside the casket were the bones of a middle-aged man, bearing the burn marks of cremation, and a golden wreath of oak leaves and acorns, as well as traces of the purple cloth in which the bones had been wrapped. To Andronikos these discoveries bore all the signs of a royal burial. But whose?

In his first survey of the tomb's contents Andronikos had noticed five tiny ivory heads, which had apparently been decorations of a wooden bed, long since crumbled to dust. Not until nine days later did he take a closer look at one of the heads; but then, as he wrote: "I could hardly believe my eyes: it was an excellent portrait of Philip." Another head, of a younger man, looked to him like Alexander. That night he took the five heads home, set them up by his bed and gazed at them through most of the night, comparing them with known representations of Philip and Alexander. Recalling that Philip had commissioned a set of family statues that once stood in their own building at Olympia, he guessed that these tiny heads represented the same figures: Philip, Alexander, Philip's parents, and his first wife Olympias, Alexander's mother.

Meanwhile the diggers had found in the anteroom of the tomb a second marble sarcophagus containing a second, smaller golden casket. Among the charred bones were the remains of purple fabric interwoven with gold thread, and a golden diadem of intertwined leaves and flowers. The delicacy of this ornament suggested to Andronikos that the burial had been that of a woman. If so, the natural candidate was Philip's last wife, named Cleopatra. Yet the absence of specifically feminine jewelry also allowed the possibility that the burial was a man's. Who could that have been? It is known that Philip was murdered, probably by conspiracy of his first wife Olympias, who wanted to assure the throne to her own son, Alexander. And it was later related by the Roman historian Justin that Olympias caused the slayer, Pausanias, to be buried in the same tomb with her slain husband. Conceivably the sarcophagus might be his.

Leaving aside this added mystery, was the main tomb really Philip's? The evidence is circumstantial. Among the grave goods are red figure vases which, Andronikos says, were made no later than 320 B.C., and an oil lamp that was made no earlier than 350. The only Macedonian king who died between those years (in 336) was Philip. Moreover, one of the bronze greaves that covered the wearer's legs in battle is shorter than the other—and Philip was lame. The identification of the heads is more subjective; sculptors of that time did not usually strive so much for realistic depiction as for the heroic image.

Andronikos is not the first archaeologist to identify his most dramatic find with the most famous figure of the period. When Schliemann found a golden mask in his excavation of the Royal Grave Circle at Mycenae he was moved to exclaim: "I have looked upon the face of Agamemnon"—whereas it turned out later that the mask and its owner had been buried three centuries before Homer's king. It would be a remarkable stroke of luck, as one of Andronikos's former colleagues pointed out, if the only unlooted royal tomb ever found in Macedonia were indeed that of its most celebrated king. Still, rival archaeologists are at least as strongly tempted to doubt a great discovery as the discoverer is to claim it. As of the moment, Andronikos seems to have persuasive evidence to support his claims, and no one has any evidence to show that the tomb could not indeed have been Philip's.

221

9: The Indian Discovery of America

by ROBERT CLAIBORNE

The ice sheets that covered much of North America (exemplified here by the Nabesna Glacier in the Wrangell Mountains of Alaska) alternately opened and closed the routes of Indian migration from Asia. Above is a "Clovis point" used by early big-game hunters.

One day in 1926 a group of archaeologists from the Colorado Museum of Natural History, led by J. D. Figgins, was digging in a clay bank on the steep side of a gully or arroyo near Folsom, New Mexico. The objects of their dig were some fossil bones that had been partly exposed through erosion by the small, intermittent stream at the bottom of the arroyo. So far as the diggers were concerned, there was nothing very special about these bones, apart from their being fossils. The site itself had been known for years, having first been spotted by a black cowboy, George McJunkin, while searching for some lost cattle. McJunkin had noted that the bones were bigger than cattle bones and were unusually white and chalky; later he casually mentioned his find to an acquaintance in the nearby town of Raton, whom he knew was interested in fossils. The acquaintance in turn eventually made his way to the site, dug out one of the bones, and took it to Figgins in Denver. The latter, a professional paleontologist, confirmed what McJunkin and his amateur fossil-hunter friend had suspected: the bones were indeed not cattle bones but rather those of a species of long-horned bison that had almost certainly been extinct since the close of the last ice age.

Though the animal was already known from other diggings, Figgins decided that the site was worth looking into. Soon after the excavations began, one of the party spotted, in the loose dirt thrown up by their spades, two fragments of flint apparently shaped by human hands. The excavators began working more carefully and were rewarded by finding a third fragment actually imbedded in the clay near one of the fossil rib bones. Back at their laboratory in Denver they discovered that this fragment and one of the others fitted together, forming part of what was clearly a spear point or javelin point (it was too big for an

This shinbone of a caribou, made into a saw-toothed scraper, was found in Yukon Territory. Its radiocarbon date places Indians in North America 27,000 years ago.

arrowhead). Moreover, the point was oddly shaped: its faces, unlike those of other Indian points, were not convex or even flat but shallowly concave or fluted. But the most arresting thing about the discovery was not its size or its shape but its location—leading to the almost inescapable deduction that a weapon had been used by humans in North America to kill an Ice Age animal. The Folsom point and the bones among which it was found—originally spotted, ironically, by a man whose name has all but vanished from archaeological textbooks—were shortly to revolutionize the study of American prehistory. Almost at one stroke they doubled the accepted age of man in the New World and thereby opened up to really scientific scrutiny the questions of how and when America was first discovered.

To understand the significance of this archaeological revolution, however, we must backtrack some four centuries. Speculation about the origin of the native Americans began almost as soon as it became clear that they *were* Americans and not, as Columbus had believed, residents of the East Indies—though the name based on his mistake has clung to them ever since. As early as 1512 the pope declared officially that these "Indians," though not mentioned in the Bible, were nonetheless human beings—and therefore, of course, descendants of Adam and Eve. His Holiness, however, prudently did not try to explain how they had gotten from the Old World's Garden of Eden to the Americas.

In 1590 a Spanish Jesuit, José de Acosta, tackled the problem. "It is not likely," he wrote (as translated by a contemporary), "that there was another Noes Arke, by the which men might be transported into the Indies, and much less any Angell to carie the first men to this new world, holding him by the haire of the head, like to the Prophet Abacuc. . . . I conclude, then, that it is likely the first that came to the Indies was by shipwracke and tempest of wether." De Acosta, however, was shrewd enough to realize that "shipwracke" would hardly explain how *animals* got to America. He therefore guessed that somewhere to the north there must exist a part of America joined to the Old World, or at least "not altogether severed and disjoined."

A generation later an Englishman, Edward Brerewood, narrowed down the problem still further by practicing a primitive form of what would much later be called anthropology. The Indians, he declared, "are not of the Africans progeny"; their color was wrong. Further, "they have no relish or resemblance at all, of the Artes, or learning, or civility [civilization] of Europe." Nor, for that matter, did their cultures resemble those of China, India, or any other civilized region of Asia. All that was left, then, were the "rude" and "barbarous" cultures of the "Tartars"—a term then vaguely denoting the peoples of central and northeastern Asia—which Brerewood believed resembled the native American cultures. The resemblances were mostly imaginary, but Brerewood's shaky reasoning had still led him to a correct conclusion. Like de Acosta, he proposed a land connection or near connection between the Old World and the New, and put it in "that Northeast part of Asia possessed by the Tartars." Something over a century later the explorer Vitus Bering sailed through the strait that now bears his name, where "that Northeast part of Asia" is indeed "disjoined" from America by only about sixty miles of water.

Brerewood's linking of Indians and "Tartars" was unwittingly correct in another way: physical resemblance. In 1811 the great naturalist Alexander von Humboldt noted a "striking analogy between the Americans and the Mongol race," and modern anthropology has fully documented his finding. In neither group do we find either the pinkish-white complexions of Europe or the dark-brown to black tints of Africa, India, and Australasia. The hair of both groups (like that of most other East Asians) is neither wavy nor kinky but straight, coarse, and black, thick on the head (baldness is rare) but sparse on the face and body. Both groups have wide cheekbones, often making the eyes appear somewhat elongated. And both groups possess the curious genetic trait called shovel incisor, referring to the concave inner surfaces of the upper front teeth: it is found in some ninety per cent of both Indians and East Asians, but in only fifteen per cent or less of other peoples.

However, though the similarities between Indians and modern "Tartars" are clear, the differences between them are no less clear. Indians are mostly reddish or yellowish-brown, in contrast with the northeast Asians' yellowish-white. Most of them lack the Mongolian fold that gives the East Asian eye its characteristic "slantiness." And many Indians have the hawk-nosed profile familiar to anyone who has ever seen an old "buffalo nickel," while nearly all East Asians are (by our standards) rather flat-faced. The Indians, in short, do not seem to be descended from people closely resembling modern East Asians but are rather genetic "cousins," stemming from some mutually ancestral stock that eventually produced distinctive branches in East Asia and the Americas.

For at least a century anthropologists have agreed on where the Indians originally came from—Asia—and where they entered America—Alaska, probably in the Bering Strait area. Where they have disagreed and still do—sometimes vituperatively—is on *when* they arrived. And the question of *when* is, as we shall see, closely tied to the question of *how* they got from Siberia to Alaska and from there to the more southerly parts of the Americas.

Until about fifty years ago there was little firm evidence on when the Indians discovered America; opinions on the matter ranged from educated guesses to outright fantasies. The probable record in the latter department is held by a nineteenth-century Argentine professor who, on the basis of a skull that he claimed to be a million years old, declared that the Indians—in fact, the entire human race—had *originated* in the Americas. And, of course, in Argentina. This and other theories only somewhat less fantastic inevitably begot a twentieth-century reaction, in which man's residence in the New World was limited to only a few thousand years. Unfortunately this theory was taken up by one of the most distinguished, influential, and dictatorial scientists of the early twentieth century, the anthropologist Aleš Hrdlička of the Smithsonian Institution.

Hrdlička on at least one occasion dated the first American immigrants at no earlier than some five thousand years ago. He based this estimate on physical anthropology—specifically, on the forms of Indian skulls. These, as he correctly pointed out, were of wholly modern type and therefore—as he quite incorrectly concluded—must date from postglacial times. In vain did other anthropologists point out that equally modern skulls had been dug up in Europe from what were unquestionably Ice Age deposits, and that some of the skulls' owners had embellished the walls of their caves with vivid pictures of Ice Age animals now extinct; Hrdlička brushed away such criticisms. More accurately, he blasted them away, denouncing critics in language more suited to an Old Testament prophet than a scientist. By 1925 his formidable reputation—and even more formidable command of invective— had made him the virtual dictator of American prehistoric studies; few of his colleagues cared to invite denunciation and possible professional suicide by crossing his opinions. Which brings us back to J. D. Figgins and his fluted point.

By the gospel according to Hrdlička, a fluted point or any other human tool mingled with the bones of an ice-age bison was rank heresy—and Figgins's efforts during the following winter to win converts met with little success. Fortunately he was stubborn enough to continue digging the next year, and he found five more broken points of the same pattern; the fifth, almost undamaged, was actually embedded in the clay between two bison ribs (see page 228). Immediately he ordered all work stopped and telegraphed the leading American museums and universities, inviting them to send representatives to view the evidence. He got only three takers, but all three were convinced—

though it took another season of excavation and many more visitors to the site before the bulk of the profession accepted his interpretation.

The Folsom discovery, which apparently put human hunters in New Mexico near the end of the Ice Age, in turn carried even more far-reaching implications. If Indians had been killing bison in New Mexico at the end of the Ice Age, their ancestors must surely have arrived in Alaska at least one or two thousand years earlier—that is, in the latter stages of the Ice Age itself. And this suggested a new notion of how they had got to Alaska from Asia.

Arriving in America a mere five thousand years ago, as Hrdlička had contended, the Indians would have had to cross in boats—as the Eskimos and Aleuts did. Arriving during the Ice Age, however, they could have walked from Asia to America. The formation of the great continental ice sheets had, in effect, removed several million cubic miles of water from the oceans, making them shallower— with their shallowest portions becoming dry land. Some of these uncovered lands had formed natural bridges between one land mass and another, linking Japan and Taiwan with the Asian mainland, Australia with New Guinea—and, in the Bering Strait area, Asia with North America. At its greatest extent, in fact, this last bridge—naturalists now call it Beringia—was nearly a thousand miles wide.

Like other land bridges, Beringia repeatedly appeared and disappeared as the great ice sheets waxed and waned. During its several appearances it served as the route by which many animals reached the Americas, including such now distinctively American species as the musk ox, bighorn sheep, mountain goat, bison, grizzly bear, and skunk. Less distinctive migrants included the caribou (identical with the Eurasian reindeer), the moose (very like the Eurasian elk), and the extinct mammoth, which once inhabited the northern parts of both land masses. Reverse migrations had brought the wolf, fox, and woodchuck from North America to Eurasia. If all these animals had been wandering back and forth across Beringia, human

When the North American ice cap was at its maximum, the land bridge (Beringia) was a thousand miles wide, but migration routes to the south were blocked. Later the bridge was flooded, but migration routes opened.

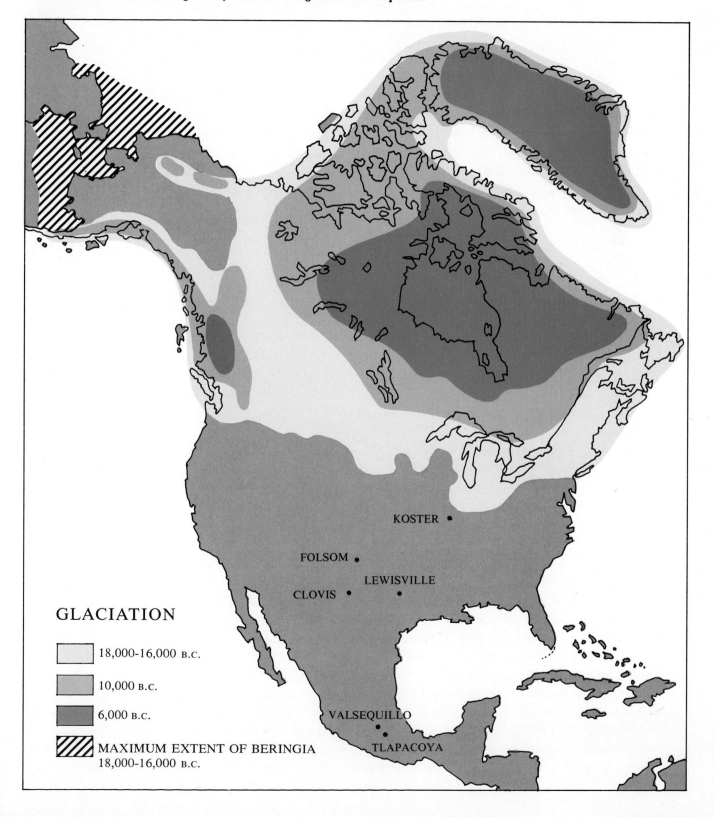

KOSTER •

FOLSOM •

LEWISVILLE
•

CLOVIS •

GLACIATION

18,000–16,000 B.C.

10,000 B.C.

6,000 B.C.

MAXIMUM EXTENT OF BERINGIA
18,000–16,000 B.C.

VALSEQUILLO
•
•
TLAPACOYA

beings could surely have done so—and the animals themselves provided a plausible reason. If the first Americans were big-game hunters, as the makers of the Folsom points clearly were, then there was no reason why their Asian ancestors, ranging ever wider in search of game, could not have reached Beringia, wandered across it into Alaska, and thence south and east to Folsom.

The route of that southward journey became the next point of dispute. Some prehistorians opted for the coastal strip through what is now southern Alaska and British Columbia to the Puget Sound country, and thence, by various routes, to the interior of the continent. However, as Alan L. Bryan of the University of Alberta was to write much later, those who favored the coastal route "have never visited this region of steep-walled fiords, where the bases of mountains often jut directly out of the sea with no beach." Even today, the only practicable surface route between Alaska and, say, Seattle is by boat; a land journey involves a lengthy inland detour that crosses and recrosses the precipitous coastal mountains. During the Ice Age things would have been worse, with much of the coast entirely ice-covered and little game to support human hunters.

The coastal route, in short, could have been traversed only by a maritime people, possessing both boats and the technology to exploit the sea's resources—fish, seal, and whale—as much later inhabitants of the coastal strip did very successfully. But there is no evidence that the first Americans had either boats or such tools as fishhooks and harpoons with which to harvest the sea's bounty. If, like the Folsom people, they were hunters, they would have gone where the game was: not along the coast but into the interior of Alaska. A glance at the map, in fact, reveals a quite plausible migration route: east through the Yukon basin and up its tributaries and thence, by any of several low mountain passes, into the northern Mackenzie Valley, whose extensive lowlands would have provided a highway to the south.

The route was feasible, but the journey would have been a fearsome one. Even today, midwinter

This picture shows the historic find that placed human hunters near Folsom, New Mexico, near the end of the Ice Age. A projectile point made of chipped stone lies embedded between the ribs of a prehistoric bison of a type that became extinct some 10,000 years ago.

temperatures around the Bering Strait average below zero; they would have been lower during an ice age. In the interior, winters would have been still worse: in some places present midwinter temperatures average -20° F and hit -50° F during cold snaps. Summers are reasonably warm but also short—too short to thaw the permanently frozen subsoil (permafrost). As partial compensation, however, the area was then fairly rich in game. Instead of the dense coniferous forest that grows there today, the region was covered during the Ice Age by a mixture of grass and low shrubs, which supported sizable herds of horses, camels, bison, mammoths, and other grazers.

What manner of people made this extraordinary journey? The most obvious thing about them is that they must have had ways of keeping warm during the long winters. They would have lived in wigwamlike huts of skins draped over poles and weighted down with stones or heavy bones at the sides; probably the floors were dug a foot or two into the topsoil for added insulation. These "pit huts" would, of course, have been heated with open fires burning brushwood and, probably, animal bones, some of which contain enough fatty marrow to provide plenty of heat—and smoke. For outdoor work in winter the migrants must have had fitted, windtight garments made of fur sewn with sinews or tough roots, and in the coldest weather, probably outer parkalike coats.

The second obvious point is that they must have lived mainly by hunting. The short summer season would have yielded berries and nutritious roots, eggs from the waterfowl and other birds that nested there in the millions, as they still do, and, along the Beringian shores, seals to be speared or clubbed, and shellfish to be gathered at low tide. But for most of the year plants would have been dormant, with their roots sealed beneath the frozen earth; the shore lines would have been locked beneath tumbled ice floes, and the birds would have flown south: it was hunt or starve. Doubtless many of the immigrants did starve. In years when the hunting was good, they could have lived comfortably enough through the winters with a natural deepfreeze just outside the hut. When the hunting was not good, some of them died; perhaps the old people, as among the much later polar Eskimos, walked out into the arctic night to save their families the burden of feeding them.

We can imagine these first Americans, over a period of generations or centuries, wandering back and forth across Beringia, with a few of the more daring—or perhaps hungrier—bands pressing eastward in search of more game. And eventually, as the ice sheets melted, the land bridge would again have been submerged—meaning that east was the only way to go, at least until the Macken-

zie Valley was reached. From there, the hunters could have moved south quite quickly, and probably did. To be sure, they had no way of knowing that warmer climates and happier hunting grounds lay that way, but there were plenty of natural pointers. Along the lower Mackenzie they would have seen each autumn what they had seen for generations: the sun dipping lower and lower into the south until at last it was visible for no more than an hour or two each day. During the same season they would have watched the clouds of ducks and geese, curlew, plover, and sandpiper heading south, followed by the caribou in their tens of thousands—accompanied, probably, by other migrating game animals, now extinct, whose habits can only be guessed at. It is hardly stretching probability to imagine the hunters deducing that the animals knew something they didn't—and following them south.

But how far south? At the time of the Folsom discoveries most geologists believed what many still do: that during most of the Ice Age the southern part of the Mackenzie basin was blocked by a mile-high wall of ice, formed when the great ice sheets of eastern Canada met and merged with a smaller sheet descending from the Canadian Rockies. Thus, while the ancestors of the Folsom hunters could have crossed Beringia and reached the Mackenzie basin at any time during the Ice Age (the Yukon basin was never ice-covered), they could not have moved very far south until the ice barrier melted. By the loose chronologies of the 1920's, this seemed feasible: the barrier, it seemed, would have melted in time for men to get to Folsom by the presumed date of the findings there. Over the next thirty years, however, other discoveries introduced complications.

During the 1930's it became apparent that "Folsom man" was not the earliest inhabitant of the Americas. In at least two places, points of different patterns were found in deposits beneath other, later layers containing the now familiar Folsom points. The most notable of these were first found near Clovis, New Mexico, less than two hundred

miles from Folsom. They were longer than the Folsom points, cruder, and fluted only at the base (see page 222), but their makers had clearly been skillful hunters. The first Clovis points were found amid bones of the mammoth—an eighteen-foot superelephant tall enough to look into a modern second-story window without stretching. Even more interestingly, it became apparent that the Clovis people, or at any rate their cultural influences, were extraordinarily widespread: Clovis or Clovislike points have turned up from Alaska to Mexico, from California to Massachusetts.

An even more important development occurred during the 1950's with the discovery of a new dating technique using the radioisotope carbon-14. This technique (unlike previous dating methods) is both reasonably accurate and applicable to the last 40,000 years or so—precisely the period that American archaeologists were interested in. Carbon dating put the Folsom people at about 10,500 years ago, the Clovis cultures at about a thousand years earlier. But many geologists then believed that the

opening of the ice barrier did not occur until some 2,000 years *later*. And if this was so, then the ancestors of the Clovis people must have moved through southern Canada before the ice barrier closed—25,000 years ago or even earlier. Most prehistorians found this date impossible to swallow without positive evidence of human presence in America that long ago.

Over the past twenty-odd years that evidence has come in. There is now pretty general agreement that human beings arrived in the New World at least 25,000 years ago and perhaps earlier; how much earlier depends on how much of the evidence you believe, and how you interpret what you do believe. And in this area the "conservative" and "radical" factions in the American archaeological establishment are as contentious as they were in the days of Aleš Hrdlička—though rather more considerate of one another's feelings.

Perhaps the leading figure in the radical camp is Richard S. MacNeish, head of the Robert S. Peabody Foundation for Archaeology in Andover,

Massachusetts. Small and compact, "Scotty" Mac-Neish is a onetime Golden Gloves bantamweight—as his slightly dented nose bears witness—and though the years have taken away some of his speed they have not diminished his pugnacity. He delights in unconventional ideas and behavior (his habit of driving a jeep at full speed along back-country roads near archaeological digs, while gesturing vigorously with both hands, has shaken the nerves of several distinguished colleagues).

But MacNeish is a lot more than a professional *enfant terrible.* His career during the last thirty years has taken him from the Yukon to Mexico to Peru in search of early Americans. In an extensive series of diggings in Mexico's Tehuacán Valley he reconstructed some ten thousand years of prehistory—and incidentally turned up the first traces of the extinct wild plant from which corn is descended. Even his critics admire his energy, which is coupled with an almost uncanny eye for terrain. He appears to operate on the principle of the little boy who, when asked how he had found a lost

Crossing the Bering land bridge, early migrants carry stone-pointed spears to hunt the plentiful herds of animals. The reconstruction was painted for the National Anthropology Museum in Mexico City.

horse, replied, "I thought where I would go if I was a horse, and I went there, and there he was." MacNeish thinks where he would go if he were a prehistoric Indian, and he goes there—and, often enough, finds evidence that the Indians were indeed there before him.

C. Vance Haynes, of the University of Arizona at Tucson, is as cool as MacNeish is ebullient, though his professional career is no less distinguished—much of it devoted to picking holes in the findings of MacNeish (whom he deeply respects) and other archaeological radicals. Haynes describes himself as a professional devil's advocate and naysayer, whose views on prehistory, as he dryly remarks, "aren't the sort of thing that sells papers."

MacNeish puts the discovery of the New World

231

at 70,000 years ago, give or take 30,000—which he cheerfully concedes covers a considerable span of time. Haynes, working from the same evidence, sees the discovery as taking place no more than 25,000 years ago, with man reaching the interior of North America (e.g., the Great Plains) perhaps no more than 12,000 years ago—though he concedes, just as cheerfully, that a new discovery could change these figures radically.

To understand how two equally able experts can reach such different conclusions from the same facts, we must take a look at the facts themselves. We can begin with a date everybody accepts. By 11,000 years ago human beings had reached the Strait of Magellan, where their relics have turned up amid bones of the extinct giant sloth as well as its dung—which has been dated by the radiocarbon technique. Whatever the date of man's arrival in the New World, it must have been early enough for him to travel from Alaska almost to the tip of South America—at least 13,000 miles—and arrive there about 11,000 years ago. This last date is, perhaps, a point against Haynes: a thousand years seems a pretty short time in which to migrate from the Great Plains to the Strait of Magellan. Physically, of course, it was and is perfectly possible to walk the distance in much less than a thousand years. But the journey also involves passing through a whole series of environments—the near desert of northern Mexico, the dense forests of Central America, and several others—each of them with different plant and animal food resources, whose exploitation would have required the development of different techniques and life styles. To accomplish all these innovations and adjustments in a mere thousand years seems, if not impossible, certainly not very probable.

Leaving the Strait of Magellan and moving north into Peru, we find a site whose native name translates as "Flea Cave." Here MacNeish himself has found very crude stone tools along with the bones of extinct animals dating, he says, from at least 22,000 years ago. Haynes is not so sure: the "tools," he says, are so crude that they may be merely bits of stone fallen from the cave roof.

MacNeish, in turn, ripostes that under the microscope the stones show marks of human use.

Moving north again, we come to Tlapacoya and Valsequillo, Mexico, where archaeological sites have been dated at about 22,000 and 23,000 years ago. One of these dates rests on the seemingly conclusive evidence of a tool lying beneath a log dated by the radiocarbon technique—but Haynes, as usual, has doubts. The soil at the site, he says, contains many deep cracks—and the tool could have slipped down through just such a crack.

Once again moving north, we come to some very controversial evidence indeed. The first is from a site near Lewisville, Texas, where simple tools were dated by what looks like charcoal (presumably the debris of a human campfire) at more than 38,000 years ago. MacNeish considers this evidence "reliable"; Haynes points out that the site was not intact but somewhat churned up—it was found during excavations for a dam—and that in any case the "charcoal" may actually be decayed and compacted wood, which would be evidence only that trees were present there that long ago.

The second controversial finding is a number of skulls found near San Diego dated at from 28,000 to 70,000 years ago. The dating, however, is by a new and not necessarily reliable technique, and the modern form of the skulls raises other problems that we shall consider in a moment.

The third finding is less controversial, in the sense that only a few enthusiasts accept it; most archaeologists, including MacNeish, are either skeptics or outright unbelievers. Some years ago, the late Louis S. Leakey, justly famed for his work at Olduvai Gorge in eastern Africa, turned up what he claimed were very crude flint tools at a site in southeastern California; he dated them at perhaps 80,000 years ago. Critics were quick to point out, however, that the "tools" were found amid hundreds of thousands of other pieces of flint, all more or less chipped by natural processes. Given this amount of material to work on, it seems almost certain that the same processes could, quite fortuitously, have formed a few tool-like objects.

Some of the most recent and interesting

evidence on the discovery of America comes from far to the north, in Canada's Yukon Territory. For several years Canadian archaeologists have been systematically searching the region for traces of early man, because it lies directly on the presumed migration route from Siberia to the Mackenzie basin. The search, says Richard E. Morlan of Canada's National Museum of Man, is "rather like looking for a needle in a haystack—and a frozen haystack at that," referring to the permafrost that underlies the area. Nonetheless, the "haystack" turned out to contain apparent traces of early man

Some of the animals that confronted early American man are depicted in this painting at the National Anthropology Museum at Mexico City. At top, from left to right, are a giant ground sloth, a mastodon, a mammoth, and a bear. In the center row are a smaller member of the elephant family (Rhynchotherium), an American Ice Age horse, the North American camel (Camelops), and a bison. In the front row are a saber-toothed cat, a wolf, a giant armadillo, and a small ground sloth.

Spokesmen for two widely different views on the date when humans arrived in the Americas are Richard S. MacNeish (opposite page) and C. Vance Haynes (left). At right is the site of "Flea Cave" in Peru, where MacNeish found crude stone tools (above) along with bones of animals dating at least 22,000 years ago. Haynes thinks the "tools" may be merely bits of stone fallen from the cave roof.

at some fifty sites. These are not the stone tools usually considered the hallmark of primitive man but rather animal bones shaped into tools or otherwise modified by human agency. Hundreds of them show curious spiral fractures produced while the bones were still fresh.

The tools consist of polished and cut bones, and of flakes struck off larger bones, precisely as human toolmakers elsewhere had long been striking them off lumps of flint or other suitable rock. Experiments have shown that such flakes, knocked off while the bone is still fresh, have sharp, tough edges suitable for butchering game. They wear out more quickly than stone flakes—but once the butchering was under way there would be plenty of bone for replacements. Indeed, Morlan describes this technique of, in effect, butchering an animal with its own bones as "the earliest known form of recycling." He also points out that this bone-instead-of-stone technology would have been invaluable in an area where stones are few and, because of the frozen ground, seldom accessible.

Unfortunately, many of these bones lie at the very limits of radiocarbon dating—meaning that

accurate dates require the sacrifice of large quantities of material, which the archaeologists are understandably reluctant to do. Such dates as have been obtained range from 28,000 to more than 42,000 years ago. Spirally fractured bones have been found beneath peat dated at 41,000 years ago, so they are older than that—how much older no one can yet say.

Haynes, of course, has doubts. Spiral fractures, he points out, normally occur in any fresh bone, whether it is broken by the foot of some large animal, a boulder in a stream bed—or a rock wielded by a human hand. He is intrigued by the Yukon findings, as any archaeologist must be, but not yet convinced by them.

If the Yukon discoveries mean what the Canadians think they mean, the Americas were discovered more than 40,000 years ago. How much before? There are powerful reasons for thinking that it could not have been very much earlier. Modern man—technically, *Homo sapiens sapiens*—did not appear on earth much before that: the earliest Old World modern skull dates from 39,000 years ago. Earlier skulls—including *all* those

beyond the 40,000-year range of radiocarbon dating—are uniformly of the Neanderthal or Neanderthaloid type, with more or less pronounced brow ridges, protruding jaws, and rounded rather than pointed chins. In the New World we have a single Californian skull equivocally dated at 70,000 years ago, and it is of completely modern type. If the dating is right, modern man would have reached the New World some 30,000 years before the date of his earliest bones in the Old World! Which is one of several reasons for distrusting the dating. Without new and incontrovertible evidence—say, a Neanderthaloid skull in an undisturbed American site—one cannot reasonably date the discovery of America before 45,000 years ago, give or take a couple of thousand years.

The span of 20,000 years—between the appearance of modern man on earth and the 25,000 years that Haynes and the conservatives will accept—covers a lot of possibilities. And here we run into another complication. The geologists tell us that for a period of some 9,000 years—between about 35,000 and perhaps 26,000 years ago—Beringia was

submerged during a recession of the Ice Age. This would seem to mean that man must have crossed from Asia either near the beginning of the suggested time span (45,000–36,000 years ago) or near the end (no more than 26,000 years ago).

The ice barrier across southern Canada may impose still further limitations—though this, like most other facts about early American prehistory, is now controversial. Both Haynes and MacNeish agree (for a change) that the effects of the barrier have been greatly exaggerated. MacNeish, indeed, claims that the road south was blocked only by a few small tongues of ice, perhaps ten miles wide and one or two hundred feet high—easily enough crossed by any band of hunters with enough initiative to climb to the top and see the open country on the other side.

When, in fact, *was* America discovered? At the moment—as in many other areas of prehistory—one can do no more than strike a balance of probabilities, and which way the balance swings will depend to some extent on one's personal biases. My own suspicion is that 25,000 years ago, which is the most the conservatives will allow, will

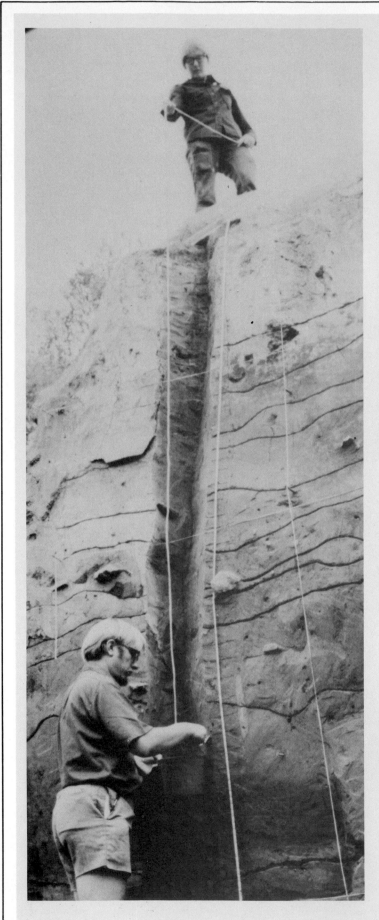

An Illinois Dig

The scientist seen at work in the picture at left is digging snail shells out of the wall of an excavation trench at the so-called Koster site near Kampsville, Illinois. From study of shells (below) found at any level of the clay wall, he can learn something about what the climate was like when that layer of clay was deposited.

Such painstaking field study helps archaeologists to recreate the living conditions of the Indians who occupied the Koster site since the last ice age. This intensive study, under the aegis of Northwestern University, is part of a project to reveal the prehistory of the Illinois River valley. It has offered archaeological field experience for college students for almost ten years.

By the end of the 1978 season the project had uncovered levels of Indian settlement dating back 9,200 years. The site was occupied continuously for some 300 generations, without evidence of any catastrophe, either natural or man-made. Inhabitants of even the earliest settlement were well fed. According to Professor Stuart Struever, director of the project, their diet "approximated a diet that might be designed by a modern nutritionist with present-day knowledge of the nutritional qualities of the various wild food species available to these Indians at the time."

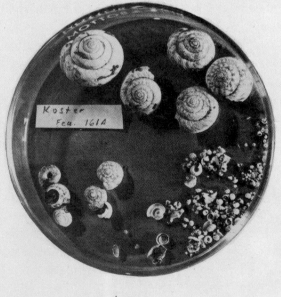

turn out to be too conservative. I believe the discovery occurred between 40,000 and 45,000 years ago, across the earlier land bridge. By around 35,000 years ago, that bridge would have been under water, but any earlier ice barrier across Canada would have melted. With this obstacle out of the way, the multiplying immigrants could easily have reached the present United States-Canadian border by 30,000 years ago, crossed the Mexican border perhaps 25,000 years ago, and made their way through Central America into South America a few thousand years later. Meanwhile, of course, their relatives were spreading over those portions of North America that were not ice-covered. (In theory, the immigrants need not have entered South America via Central America: they—or some of them—could have invented boats and island-hopped from Florida through the Antilles. In fact, all the evidence indicates that the Antilles were not settled until much later—and from the south, not the north.) As to the route or routes they followed from Canada to Mexico, the Great Plains seems the most reasonable guess: it was somewhat moister then and was probably the richest hunting ground in North America. On the routes down through South America we are simply in the dark: the only one that can be excluded is the Pacific coast, a long stretch of which is covered by desert.

Two other controversies on the discovery of America remain to be considered—though not settled! The first centers on the question: Was there one migration or several?

Everybody agrees that there were at least two migrations from the Old World to the New before the Europeans moved in: the Indians and (much later) the Eskimos and Aleuts. These latter peoples speak languages related to some in eastern Siberia. Moreover, they are physically almost indistinguishable from modern East Asians: most Eskimos, appropriately dressed, would attract no attention in Tokyo or Peking.

Many anthropologists believe there was at least one other migration—that of the Indians speaking the Athapascan or Na-Dene languages. Most of these tribes inhabit the forested regions of west-central Canada and the adjacent parts of Alaska, with outlying groups along the northwest coast and in the U.S. Southwest (the Navaho and Apache). Most Athapascans look almost as much like Eskimos as they do like Indians, and their blood groups, too, resemble those of the Eskimos—notably, in the relatively high proportion of group A (other Indians are overwhelmingly group O).

Haynes and some other prehistorians see a fourth migration—that of the people (or peoples) we know as the Clovis hunters. These people, from the archaeological record, appeared quite suddenly (presumably, just after the second ice barrier melted). Their culture and tool kits, says Haynes, have no roots in the New World but show clear similarities to contemporary hunting cultures in Siberia. MacNeish, as one would expect, disagrees. He finds the evidence for Haynes's "Clovis migration" inadequate but sees a whole series of other migrations or "infiltrations"; indeed, he describes the Bering Strait area as a corridor—whether of land or water—over which people and ideas moved back and forth almost continuously between the Old World and the New.

Again one must balance the probabilities, and for me the balance favors the minimum feasible number of migrations—the first Indians and the Eskimos certainly, the Athapascans probably, the other hypothetical migrations probably not. My main reason is that the physical characteristics of the Indians themselves show far less variation than we find among the inhabitants of any other comparable land mass. While it is by no means true that (as many earlier travelers claimed) "he who has seen one Indian has seen all," they are far more alike than the peoples of Asia—even of East Asia—or Africa. The simplest explanation is that all of them, probably excepting the Athapascans, are descended from a few "first families," genetically very homogeneous and therefore possessing only a limited potential for future variation.

Further evidence on this point comes if we compare the inhabitants of the Americas with those of Australasia—the great arc of islands that extends southeast from the Asian mainland through Indonesia, New Guinea, and Australia to Tasmania. Both regions are geographical "sacks," closed at the bottom (Tasmania and Tierra del Fuego) but open at the top (Indonesia and Alaska) to migration from the Asian mainland. In any such situation, one would expect to find the earliest migrants at the bottom of the sack, with late immigrants forming a series of layers above them. Moreover, if the various migrations occurred over a protracted period, one would expect to find physical differences among the various layers.

In Australasia this is just what we do find. The extinct Tasmanians (they were wiped out by Europeans during the nineteenth century) differed physically from the Australian aborigines, who in turn differ from the Papuans of New Guinea, who in turn differ even more markedly from the Indonesians to the west. In the Americas, we find only three such layers: the Eskimos and Aleuts at the top, then the Athapascans, with the bottom layer including all the rest of the native Americans in both North and South America; there are no clear physical differences between the Indians of Tierra del Fuego and those of the Great Plains. Which again suggests that this "layer" represents the descendants of a single migration or, at most, a few migrations bunched quite closely in time.

This view is consistent with everything we know or can imagine about the problems of survival in the Alaskan and Canadian Arctic with the technologies of 45,000—or even 25,000—years ago. Leaving aside the ice barrier question, the arctic climate and terrain would themselves have provided a barrier whose crossing few people would have attempted—and even fewer survived. And in fact, from all the evidence, *Homo sapiens* remained a very rare animal in the Americas until Clovis times, a mere 11,500 years ago; considering merely the known number of human relics, one would have to conclude that before that time there were more people in southwestern France alone than in the entire New World. This is, of course, an exaggeration: archaeologists have explored France far more intensively than the Americas. But making every allowance for that, there still seem to have been few people in America before 11,500 years ago—and the likeliest explanation is that very few ever got here in the first place.

The last controversial question is the effect of early Americans on the untouched resources of their new habitat. A common belief nowadays—composed in equal parts of white guilt and eighteenth-century "noble savage" mythology—is that the native Americans were intuitive ecologists, living in perpetual harmony with their environment. Now, there can be no doubt that the Indians, at least during the periods we have any good evidence for, disrupted the natural environment in most places far less than their European successors did, but the most likely reason for this is also the most obvious one: there were far fewer of them. The population of the Americas before Columbus has been estimated at perhaps 30,000,000; outside the densely inhabited areas of Middle America, probably a third of that figure. Even the larger number is only a little over a twentieth of the present population—and one person, other things being equal, is bound to do far less damage to the environment than twenty.

Early in the 1960's Paul S. Martin of the University of Arizona attacked the whole notion of primitive man as a pioneer ecologist. Rather, said Martin, he was a "superpredator," responsible for the extinction of dozens of other species. In the Americas specifically (according to Martin), early man's "prehistoric overkill" wiped out most of the indigenous large animals, including the mammoth, mastodon, camel, native horse, ground sloth, and a dozen less well-known species.

Martin's argument is complicated but rests essentially on two pillars. The first is that the extinctions coincide with the appearance of modern man, or at least modern man specializing in big-game hunting—earliest in Africa and southern Asia, somewhat later in Europe, still later in Australia, and last of all (some 11,500 years ago) in the Americas. The second part of his argument is that the only other likely explanation—the sharp change in climate as the last ice age ended—is not plausible: if the end of an ice age can produce mass extinctions, why didn't these occur at the ends of earlier ice ages, of which there were at least three?

So far as Australia is concerned, new archaeological findings have thrown grave doubt on Martin's theory. It now appears certain that man arrived in that continent at least 35,000 years ago (some Australian archaeologists say 50,000), which was more than 20,000 years *before* the extinctions that Martin ascribes to human overkill. But in any case the whole argument is purely circumstantial: human beings must have caused the extinctions because they were there—and because we can't think of any other explanation. Before we convict our species of this major ecological crime, we need more evidence—in the classic police tradition: opportunity, means, and motive.

Early Americans certainly had the opportunity, in the sense that they were in the neighborhood. But were they present at the scene of the crime? The answer is, not often. For the majority of extinct species, we have no evidence that they were ever hunted by early man; for most of the rest, no evidence that they were hunted often or in quantity. The most striking case is that of the mastodon, related to the mammoth but somewhat smaller—though its five-foot tusks made it a formidable opponent. Mastodon bones and teeth have been found in hundreds of places in the northern and eastern parts of the United States— more than 150 in southern Michigan alone—yet *not one* of the beasts, so far as we can tell, was killed by man. Martin explains the lack of kill sites for this and other species on the grounds that early men were few (but if they were so few, how did they kill so many?) and also that the process was so rapid, in his view requiring only a thousand years or so. The best one can say about this is that a theory which can be "proved" equally well by evidence or by the lack of evidence must have some holes in it.

If opportunity is dubious, means is no less so.

The Clovis and Folsom peoples—who are the "overkillers" Martin is talking about—were certainly skilled hunters, but were they really that skilled? Their spears or javelins were deadly enough to kill mammoth (Clovis) and giant buffalo (Folsom) but hardly good enough to kill these formidable beasts en masse, at least without very special techniques.

As it happens, some of these early Indians did kill bison (and possibly mammoth) en masse by stampeding them into deep gullies or over cliffs: one site in Colorado contains the remains of some two hundred bison killed in just such a way (see page 241). Unfortunately for Martin's theory, however, modern Indians were still using these techniques to kill modern bison by the hundreds in 1805, when Lewis and Clark passed along the upper Missouri—at which time there were still an estimated 30 million bison in North America.

The only extinctions or near extinctions that actually have been observed in North America were achieved not by Indians but by whites, using firearms and hunting for the market. The passenger pigeon, flocks of which once darkened the heavens, was wiped out during the nineteenth century by market gunners—helped along by lumbermen who cut down the beech forests whose nuts were one of the bird's main food resources. The bison was almost wiped out during the same period by hunters with repeating rifles and pistols—partly to meet the demand for hides, and partly to wipe out the Indians who depended on the herds for food.

The theory of extinction by mass killing also conflicts with a basic ecological principle governing relationships between predators (whether animals or primitive humans) and their prey: in colloquial language, "You've got to find 'em before you kill 'em." In more sedate terms, this means that the rarer a prey species becomes, the harder the predator must work simply to locate it—and must therefore shift to some other species or starve to death while tracking down its preferred victim. Any primitive American would have walked ten miles for a camel—or a horse, or a mammoth. But

walking a hundred miles to find an almost extinct mammoth is a project with little appeal to anyone who cares about eating regularly. The large economy size, in meat or anything else, has always had its appeal—but not if you have to spend days or weeks shopping for it.

Turning finally to motive, the evidence is even less convincing. The only plausible motive for hunting down and attacking a large and dangerous animal, with only primitive weapons, is to eat it—meaning that so long as the meat holds out, the hunters will hunt less energetically or not at all. Moreover, to eat the animal you must first skin and

butcher it, which takes time. And if you have a reasonable amount of foresight, you will also slice up and dry some of the meat, in case your next kill proves hard to find—which takes more time. Finally, if you are human, you will want to take still more time for making love, playing with your kids, worshiping your gods, gambling, and engaging in sports—all of which the Indians of historic times devoted considerable effort to, so long as food was plentiful. Being a superpredator is almost a full-time job—as well as a risky one.

Martin, however, ignores these considerations, insisting that our species typically "kills for more than food." In effect, he is saying that the Clovis and Folsom hunters systematically killed off the ten-foot mastodon and the thirteen-foot mammoth, not to mention the long-horned bison, for kicks ("the excitement of the chase and the killing passion"). And there is simply no known primitive people that has ever behaved in this way.

Some tribes do kill—occasionally—"for more than food." A youth of the African Masai, for example, is (or was) expected to kill one lion single-handedly to demonstrate his manhood. But neither the Masai nor any other primitive people has ever made a habit of repeatedly attacking lions or other dangerous beasts for kicks, machismo, or any other reason: there are plenty of easier and safer ways of getting one's kicks—or, for that matter, demonstrating one's machismo. If the Clovis people had gone chasing after mammoths for the sheer pleasure of the hunt, the odds are pretty good that they, not the mammoth, would have become extinct.

Taking opportunity, means, and motive together, then, I do not think that any jury would hesitate to vote the Indians not guilty of the crime of overkill. They may have been accessories in some extinctions of 10,000 years ago, perhaps giving the *coup de grâce* to certain species which climatic change or other causes had already placed on the endangered list. But as the major cause of extinction they just don't fit: they probably could not have killed on that scale if they had tried—and they would have been fools to try.

The native Americans, whenever and however they reached this continent, and whatever they did when they got here, were not fools. Fools could not have made the journey through the arctic wastes of Beringia, Alaska, and the Yukon. Fools could not have successfully populated two great continents—in the process evolving dozens of different life styles to cope with dozens of different environments, from the arctic tundra to the southwestern desert to the dense rain forests of the Amazon. Nor, for that matter, could fools have survived the murderous impact of European civilization, as the native Americans survive today.

One method the Indians used to kill bison for food was to stampede them over a cliff or into a deep arroyo. In the reconstruction scene on the opposite page the animals are being driven into an arroyo, where they die from the fall or from being trampled by the herd. After the kill the hunters cut off the meat and discarded the bones. The long row of bones in the picture above was unearthed at a site in Colorado, where the hunters had dumped them in a narrow draw some 8,500 years ago. Indians were using the same technique of killing bison when white men reached the Plains.

IN SEARCH OF . . .
The Cardiff Giant

Archaeology has always been an inviting field for hoaxers. One of the most engaging, if least convincing, fakes was the Cardiff Giant, whose story was told in AMERICAN HERITAGE by Stephen W. Sears.

One morning in early November of the year 1868 three men appeared at the railroad depot in Union, New York, just outside Binghamton. The most imposing of the trio, a tall, heavily bearded figure in his mid-forties, dressed in funereal black, identified himself to the station agent as George Hull and explained that he wanted to collect a shipment being held for him. After the necessary formalities the visitors carefully levered a heavy, iron-strapped wooden box almost a dozen feet long into their wagon and set off in a northerly direction.

Their journey was a slow and circuitous one, for they were at pains to avoid settled areas. It took them five days to travel sixty miles as the crow flies. At stopovers curious farmers or tavern loungers were told, variously, that the big crate contained castings, a tobacco press, or a monument to fallen heroes of the late war. Finally, on the night of November 9 in a pounding rainstorm, they pulled up at the farm of Hull's brother-in-law, William C. Newell, near Cardiff, a village twelve miles south of Syracuse. The box was unloaded behind Newell's barn and covered over with straw. Hull and his two helpers left the next morning.

Two weeks later Hull returned. He and Newell dug a pit five feet deep in a low, marshy area between the barn and nearby Onondaga Creek. The crate was opened to reveal an enormous stone figure, which with the aid of block and tackle they buried in the pit, planting the site in clover.

By trade a cigar maker in Binghamton, Hull was a man of unbridled imagination whose reach for the main chance had so far always fallen short. A variety of inventions had brought him disappointing profits, and certain of his tobacco dealings had brought him only trouble with the internal-revenue laws. A plunge into the study of natural sciences had led him to alchemy experiments, with predictable results. Never before, however, had any scheme so engaged his full powers of creativity as this one.

In 1866 while visiting another brother-in-law in Ackley, Iowa, he had become involved in a heated discussion with a visiting revivalist preacher, one Reverend Turk. The debate got around to the biblical reference "There were giants in the earth in those days" (Genesis 6:4), which the preacher insisted on interpreting literally in the face of Hull's scoffing. Then the flash of inspiration: suddenly, Hull later related, he

The Cardiff Giant in his final resting place at the Farmers' Museum in Cooperstown, New York

"thought of making a stone, and passing it off as a petrified man."

The inspiration fermented slowly. Two years later, in June, 1868, Hull returned to Iowa, to the gypsum quarries at Fort Dodge. He engaged a quarryman to cut him a block twelve feet by four feet by two feet for what Hull described as a piece of patriotic statuary. The block was soon on its way to 940 North Clark Street in Chicago.

The North Clark Street address was the establishment of a journeyman stonecutter named Edward Burghardt, to whom Hull had entrusted the task of (so to speak) bringing his petrified man to life. To ensure security Burghardt and his two assistants, Fred Mohrmann and Henry Salle, did the carving in off hours and on Sundays.

Through the summer months the sculptors chiseled away. Hull, who supervised every detail, ordained that his biblical Giant assume a supine position, turned slightly to the right with the left leg drawn up. The left arm extended straight along the side and somewhat underneath the body, while the right hand clutched the stomach. The over-all impression of this posture was of an agonizing death—perhaps from a stomachache. In striking contrast were the Giant's features: regular, composed, with even the hint of a smile. An anguished facial expression may well have been beyond the limited skill of the carvers; or possibly Hull, who unblushingly served as the model, was too pleased with his scheme to put on a suitable face. In any event, the final effect was intriguingly mysterious.

Hull's study of paleontology had led him to conclude that hair did not petrify, so the Giant was bald and clean-shaven. Nor, he decided, should there be any traces of clothing. (The Giant was a giant in every respect, requiring the attachment of a sizable fig leaf in the woodcut illustrations that later appeared in newspapers and pamphlets.) The striations in the gypsum produced a nice effect of veins and musculature, and Hull added skin pores by hammering with a mallet faced with darning needles. The underside of the figure was grooved by scouring with wet sand to imitate the erosive effects of ground water. After some experimentation a suitably aged look was induced with sulphuric acid.

The finished Giant was ten feet four and one-half inches tall and weighed in at a fraction under three thousand pounds. His shoulders were three feet across and his feet twenty-one inches long. He would have taken a size 37 collar. The stone man was crated up and shipped to the Union depot near Binghamton. After the November burial on the Newell farm Hull returned to the prosaic business of making cigars, giving the Giant time to settle comfortably in his grave. The undertaking had thus far cost him twenty-six hundred dollars; the best investment of his life.

In October, 1869, Hull passed Newell the word to begin Operation Discovery. Newell hired two local handymen, Gideon Emmons and Henry Nichols, to dig a well for him. He carefully specified the spot, some twenty feet behind his barn, and on Saturday, October 16, Emmons and Nichols set to work. Three feet down their shovels struck what appeared to be a large stone foot. With rising excitement they soon uncovered the rest of the Giant. "Jerusalem, Nichols, it's a big Injun!" exclaimed Emmons.

The word that something was up at "Stub" Newell's place spread at a rate possible only in a small town. That day and the next, reported the Syracuse *Journal*, "men left their work, women caught up their babies, and children in numbers, all hurried to the scene where the interest of that little community centered." Speculation was intense. Some, like well digger Emmons, recalled the Onondaga tribal legend of a race of great stone men that had once stalked the valley. Among the faithful the reference in Genesis to giants in the earth was explanation enough. Whatever his origin, all agreed, the Cardiff Giant was a sensational find.

By Monday a tent had been erected over the pit, and tickets of admission cost fifty cents. The spectators were herded into the tent, where an "exhibitor" delivered a spiel on the Giant's vital statistics and discovery and the speculations about his pedigree. "An air of great solemnity pervaded the place," a witness recalled; "visitors hardly spoke above a whisper." After fifteen minutes the crowd was herded to the exit to make room for the next group of gawkers.

As the Syracuse papers spread the news Newell's business grew to land-office proportions. The roads to Cardiff were jammed with buggies, rude farm wagons, and special stages from Syracuse that carried passengers to the scene for a dollar a head. Weekday attendance was in the hundreds, and on Saturdays and Sundays the daily draw was as much as twenty-six hundred. Crude eateries sprang up near the site, advertising "Warm Meals, Oysters and Oats." Taverns and hotels in Cardiff and the surrounding towns, bearing such freshly painted signs as "The Giant Saloon" and "Goliath House," were filled to the rafters.

The gullible, through ignorance or a pathetic willingness to believe anything delivered in high-flown terms by an "authority," were the sort who had made P. T. Barnum wealthy. Among the more sophisticated who flocked to see the Giant were amateur scientists inspired by Darwin's recent evolutionary theory to dabble in geology and paleontology. Local tales of past findings of strange fossil forms and oversized skeletons and human remains turned "hard as stone" were trundled out to buttress the arguments of the "petrifactionists."

A local lecturer on scientific matters, Dr. John F. Boynton, was quick to point out that no evidence existed for the petrifaction of flesh. The Giant was therefore not a petrified human, from biblical days or any other. He was, however, a figure of nearly equal interest. The Cardiff Giant, Dr. Boynton theorized, was a magnificent statue, carved some 250 years before by a French Jesuit priest to awe the local Indians. "The chin is magnificent and generous," Dr. Boynton wrote; "the eyebrow, or superciliary ridge, is well arched; the mouth is pleasant; the brow and forehead are noble." The figure was definitely "the Napoleonic type," bearing a striking resemblance to both George Washington and former New York Governor De Witt Clinton.

The Reverend S. R. Calthrop of Syracuse embraced the Boynton statue theory and offered his own embellishment. The unknown French sculptor, he announced, was a man of "noble original powers . . . someone with a righteous soul sighing over the lost civilization of Europe, weary of swamp and forest and fort, who, finding this block by the side of the stream, solaced the weary days of exile with pouring out his thought upon the stone." The Giant, the Reverend Mr. Calthrop concluded, represented a heroic Northman shot through the back by a poisoned Indian arrow.

The statue theory received important reinforcement from Professor James Hall, New York State's geologist and a recognized authority on paleontology. After a fifteen-minute examination (which was all a no doubt nervous Stub Newell would allow) Hall agreed that the figure was a statue of some antiquity, "the most remarkable object yet brought to light in this country."

The petrifactionists hastened to fill the newspaper columns with denunciations of the Boynton-Hall statue theory. The Giant had no pedestal or base; who ever heard, they asked, of a statue of a reclining figure contorted in agony? His exquisite naturalness was beyond the sculptor's art; he could be nothing except a petrified man. In rebuttal the statuists dismissed the contention that flesh petrified as scientifically unfounded and pointed out that close study of the body's striations revealed definite patterns that proved it had been carved from a single block.

The beauty of this heated debate, from the standpoint of Hull and Newell, was that it quite obscured more skeptical speculations on the

Giant's origin. It was also very good for business.

A week after the discovery a five-man syndicate of local businessmen paid thirty thousand dollars to Newell—Hull remained in the background, pulling the strings—for a three-quarter interest in the Giant. Heading the syndicate was a shrewd, dryly humorous banker and horse trader named David Hannum, who would achieve a fame of sorts as the model for the title character in the best-selling novel *David Harum* by Edward Noyes Westcott. On November 5, 1869, Hannum had the Giant disinterred and shipped to Syracuse.

In this new setting the Giant was a bigger hit than ever. The New York Central added a special stop so passengers could make a quick inspection of "the wonder of the age."

However, Hull's hoax was now starting to come unraveled. Skeptical reporters were asking hard questions. One local paper ran the headline "Scientific, Official Report of the recent Scientific Examination of the Stone Giant" over a column that was entirely blank. More devastating

The Giant in the pit where he was "discovered" at Cardiff, New York

244

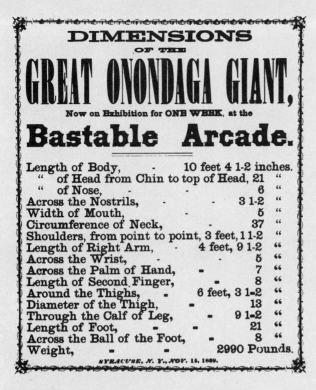

DIMENSIONS
OF THE
GREAT ONONDAGA GIANT,
Now on Exhibition for ONE WEEK, at the
Bastable Arcade.

Length of Body,	10 feet 4 1-2 inches.
" of Head from Chin to top of Head,	21 "
" of Nose,	6 "
Across the Nostrils,	3 1-2 "
Width of Mouth,	5 "
Circumference of Neck,	37 "
Shoulders, from point to point,	3 feet, 1 1-2 "
Length of Right Arm,	4 feet, 9 1-2 "
Across the Wrist,	5 "
Across the Palm of Hand,	7 "
Length of Second Finger,	8 "
Around the Thighs,	6 feet, 3 1-2 "
Diameter of the Thigh,	13 "
Through the Calf of Leg,	9 1-2 "
Length of Foot,	21 "
Across the Ball of the Foot,	8 "
Weight,	2990 Pounds.

SYRACUSE, N. Y., NOV. 15, 1869.

Broadside for the Syracuse exhibition

was the report of the brilliant Yale paleontologist Othniel C. Marsh, published November 25. After inspecting the Giant, Marsh was blunt and to the point: "It is of very recent origin, and a most decided humbug." He pointed out fresh tool marks and smoothly polished surfaces, both of which would have been roughened by lengthy exposure in the earth.

The clincher was the story, leaked out of the Onondaga County Bank, that Stub Newell had withdrawn a sizable sum from his account in the form of a draft drawn to one George Hull. This jogged memories. Local farmers remembered Hull with the wagon carrying the great iron-bound box, seen on the roads south of Cardiff the year before. Fort Dodge quarrymen recalled Hull's purchase of an outsized block of Iowa gypsum. Tracked down in Chicago, the stone cutters Mohrmann and Salle confessed their role in the hoax. By then

Hull had seen that the jig was up, and early in December he admitted the whole story.

Nevertheless, Hannum and his syndicate pressed on undaunted. On December 20 the Giant went on display at the Apollo Hall at Broadway and Twenty-eighth Street in New York City under a banner proclaiming "Genuine. CARDIFF GIANT. Original. Taller than Goliath Whom David Slew."

In New York, however, the Cardiff Giant came up against stiff competition from the Barnum Giant. The famous showman, balked in his effort to lease the stone man for sixty thousand dollars, promptly had a replica carved and put on display at Wood's Museum, two blocks from the Apollo. The fake fake outpulled the real fake, proving again that no one could outhumbug the old master. In February, 1870, the syndicate moved the Giant to Boston. This time

he had the town to himself, and he drew well. Ralph Waldo Emerson was reported to have called him "very wonderful and undoubtedly ancient."

But Boston was his last hurrah. The bubble had burst. After touring New England and Pennsylvania with indifferent success for several years, the Giant was put into storage in a barn in Fitchburg, Massachusetts. Except for an appearance at the Pan-American Exposition in Buffalo in 1901, there he gathered dust for three decades.

In 1913 he was purchased for a reported ten thousand dollars and taken back to Fort Dodge, Iowa, the place of his birth. There followed various appearances at state fairs in Iowa and New York. In the 1930's he was rescued from a bankrupt carnival in Texas by publisher Gardner Cowles, whose Iowa boyhood near Fort Dodge had been enriched by tales of the hoax. Cowles installed him as a conversation piece in the rumpus room of his Des Moines home.

During his stay in Des Moines the Giant suffered the indignity of having his manhood chipped by Cowles's prankish, hammer-wielding young son and some of his friends, but after Cowles went to "considerable trouble" he was at least partially restored.

In 1948, thanks to the efforts of Stephen C. Clark and Louis C. Jones of the New York State Historical Association, the Giant found a permanent home at the Farmers' Museum in Cooperstown. Today he rests peacefully under a shed roof in a reconstructed crossroads village that is not unlike the Cardiff of a century ago. And like those who once thronged to Cardiff, today's visitor must still buy a ticket of admission in order to view the great stone man with the faint smile.

—Stephen W. Sears

10: The Lost Cities of the Incas

by JOHN HEMMING

The Bolivian altiplano, a plateau in the Andes (background picture), was part of the Inca empire. At left, an Inca noble.

The llama, represented by this silver statuette, was the pack animal of the Incas.

On the morning of July 24, 1911, a young Yale graduate named Hiram Bingham crept across the raging waters of Peru's Urubamba River on a slippery log bridge. A local farmer called Arteaga had told him that the steep forested mountain on the far bank contained Inca ruins. It sounded improbable, and Bingham's American companions decided not to accompany him in following up this tenuous lead. Bingham felt that he must investigate, for he was leading an expedition whose objective was to find Inca sites. He had seen his first ruins of that great empire during a visit to Peru two years before; and his enthusiastic stories about them at a class reunion had encouraged his friends to support the Yale Peruvian Expedition. So Hiram Bingham toiled up the slopes on the far bank of the Urubamba. He and his two Peruvian companions paused for lunch in a jungle clearing two thousand feet above the swirling river. Bingham was unenthusiastic about the prospect of more climbing in the humid afternoon heat. But just around a promontory he came upon his first sight of a magnificent flight of stone agricultural terraces. These had been partially cleared for farming by some local Indians, but they were clearly the work of a more advanced civilization. There were a hundred terraces, climbing for

almost a thousand feet up the hillside.

It was in the deep jungle above the terraces that Bingham made his breathtaking discovery. There, amid the dark trees, creepers, mosses, and undergrowth, he saw building after building, a holy cave, and a three-sided temple whose granite blocks were cut with the beauty and precision of the finest buildings of the Inca empire. Bingham left an unforgettable account of his excitement that afternoon. The young American had the dreamlike experience of finding archaeological wonders. He pushed through the snake-infested jungle, seeing each successive treasure of the lost city on its sharp forested ridge. On his first attempt he had discovered Machu Picchu, the most spectacular ruin in South America.

The ruins of Machu Picchu are remarkable in many ways. The physical location is stupendous: the city is perched on a promontory thousands of feet above a hairpin bend of the Urubamba River. At the end of the ridge, the sugar-loaf peak of Huayna Picchu rises like the horn of a rhinoceros. Mist-shrouded mountains and jungle valleys enclose the site in all directions. The mysterious, beautiful ruins are linked to one another by a network of hundreds of flights of stone staircases.

There are many unusual features in the town itself. Its buildings were clearly designed for different social groups: superbly cut ashlars in the palaces reserved for the ruling Inca and his entourage; spacious quadrangles and high houses for the nobility; and rougher rectangular houses of fieldstone set in clay mortar for the ordinary people. Agricultural terraces march in tiers up the steep hillsides—indicating perhaps that Machu Picchu was a center for growing special produce for the Inca court in the capital city, Cuzco. The crop may have been coca, for the leaves of this bush are a mild narcotic whose use was a privilege reserved for the Inca nobility. But Machu Picchu was also a religious center. The site has an unusual number of holy places: caves, tombs, temples, outcrops of rock shaped into sacrificial altars, and a cascade of stone baths possibly used for ritual ablutions.

Bingham knew that when the Inca ruler Manco

fled from the Spanish conquerors in 1536 he led his followers into this remote country, where the eastern ridges of the Andes fall away into the Amazon jungle. There he had finally built a new capital called Vilcabamba, where he and his successors had ruled in independence until 1572. Bingham concluded that he had found this last imperial city, but in that belief he was wrong. The identification of the true Vilcabamba, as we shall see, was not made until half a century later, by another American explorer. Machu Picchu was built before the Spanish invasion, and its remarkable preservation is due in large part to the fact that it escaped the notice of the Spaniards for four centuries after the fall of the Inca empire.

Almost all the rest of the empire had fallen swiftly to the Spaniards' devastating conquest. A ship of the conquistador Francisco Pizarro first sighted the northern coast of the Inca empire in 1528. Pizarro himself returned with less than two hundred men in 1532 and boldly marched into this unknown empire, a civilization that had evolved in isolation from the rest of the world during the preceding millennia. The discoverers and conquerors of the Inca empire were the same men. The first Europeans to see the splendors of Inca society, the chroniclers who recorded these new marvels, were the conquistadors themselves. The thrill of first discovery belonged to the very soldiers who were about to conquer, pillage, and enslave Peru.

The first of the Incas' many achievements that impressed the conquerors was their system of roads and bridges. The Incas excelled as engineers, soldiers, and administrators. Francisco Pizarro's brother Hernando declared that "the mountain road really is something worth seeing. Such magnificent roads can be seen nowhere in Christendom, in country as rough as this. Almost all of them are paved." The Incas were by origin a mountain tribe, a people physically evolved to live at high altitudes. Their main highway therefore ran along the spine of the Andes, linking the capital city, Cuzco, with the northern capital,

Quito, and the southern outposts in Chile, a distance of about 2,500 miles. A parallel highway ran along the narrow desert plain between the high Andes and the Pacific Ocean, and many lateral roads climbed into the mountains to link the two great arterial highways.

Although paved, the Incas' highways were built only for human beings and trains of pack llamas. There were no other beasts of burden native to South America, and with no animal strong enough to pull vehicles, the Incas found no need for wheels rotating on axles. Since they had no wheeled traffic, Inca road builders could use steps, curving suspension bridges, and narrow tunnels or causeways. They were thus able to drive their road network through the vertiginous world of the Andes, a land where mountains are deeply cut by fierce rivers plunging toward the Amazon. One conquistador marveled that during the invasion

we had to climb another stupendous mountainside. Looking up at it from below, it seemed impossible for birds to scale it by flying through the air, let alone men on horseback climbing by land. But the road was made less exhausting by climbing in zigzags rather than in a straight line. Most of it consisted of large stone steps.

Inca roads frequently had to cross mountain rivers. The first discoverers were impressed—and frightened—by the native suspension bridges. One of them explained how these were built:

At a point where the rivers are narrowest and most terrifying, and their waters most compressed, they make a great stone foundation on either bank. Thick wooden beams are laid across this stonework, and they fasten across the river cables of thick osier, made like anchor ropes. . . . When half a dozen of these have been joined and laid across the river, to the width of a cart, they are interwoven with strong hemp and reinforced with sticks. . . . When this is done, they place edges on either side like the sideboards of an oxcart.

Pizarro's secretary, Pedro Sancho, recalled his own fear at crossing such a bridge.

To someone unaccustomed to it, the crossing appears dangerous because the bridge sags with its long span . . . so that one is continually going down until reaching the middle, and from there one climbs to the far bank.

The massive walls of the fortress of Sacsahuaman at Cuzco exhibit the Inca genius for masonry. The huge stones were quarried and shaped with stone tools and moved without the help of wheels or draft animals. So closely are the stones interlocked that a knife will not slip between the joints. The irregular pattern of the walls has made them proof against earthquakes.

When the bridge is being crossed it trembles very much—all of which goes to the head of someone unaccustomed to it!

He was worried that the Spanish horses might not cross these swaying bridges.

It seemed impossible to make the horses, which weigh so much and are such timorous and excitable creatures, cross something suspended in midair. . . . Although they refused at first, once they were placed on it their fear apparently calmed them, and they crossed one behind the other.

The Spanish discoverers were also impressed by the efficiency with which the Incas organized movement along their highways. There was a system of imperial relay runners called *chasquis*. Each community along the road had to provide runners, who waited for a royal dispatch and then raced with it to the next relay. It was said that the Inca court at Cuzco received fresh fish from the Pacific: *chasqui* runners carried it for hundreds of miles over the main chain of the Andes in a couple of days. The Incas had post houses at regular intervals along the roads. These *tambos* consisted of a few enclosures of lodgings for royal officials: archaeologists are still surveying and excavating well-preserved *tambos* in many parts of Peru.

Far more important were the provincial capitals. It was through these cities that the Incas imposed their colonial rule on subject tribes in their vast empire. Each city was carefully laid out by official Inca architects and planners, and each contained the same official buildings. There was always a magnificent central square, in which the populace would gather for the periodic festivals of the Inca religious calendar. In the center of this plaza there was a stone-flanked platform, an *usnu*, which was evidently used by the imperial and ecclesiastical authorities when they presided over ceremonies in the square. On one side of the square there would be one or two long rectangular buildings, great assembly halls with pitched thatch roofs. These *kallanka* halls had many openings onto the square. They apparently served to house assemblies when Andean rains drenched the plaza.

Pizarro's invaders marched into the mountains in 1532 and confronted the Inca emperor, Atahualpa, at the provincial capital Cajamarca in the north-central Andes. Within a day of their arrival they took the audacious, even foolhardy decision to try to capture the Inca ruler. There were less than 170 Spaniards with a few dozen horses. They reckoned that the Inca's army encamped nearby numbered more than eighty thousand men, and "so many tents were visible that we were truly filled with great apprehension." The town's square filled with thousands of native courtiers, officials, priests, and soldiers—all unarmed for Atahualpa's ceremonial meeting with the unknown arrivals from an alien culture. Pizarro's young cousin Pedro recalled: "I saw many Spaniards urinate without noticing it, out of pure terror." Despite their fear, the Spaniards decided to exploit the advantage of surprise by launching an unprovoked and totally unexpected attack.

Pizarro used the Inca buildings to help his murderous plan. He installed some small cannon on the *usnu* platform. He concealed his men in the *kallanka* halls, whose twenty doors gave quick access to the square, "almost as if they had been built for [our] purpose." At a prearranged signal, the guns were fired and the concealed horsemen charged out of hiding. There was no escape for the unarmed natives packed tightly into the square. They panicked. Some were trampled to death in the confusion. Thousands were butchered by the Spaniards' sharp swords, lances, and battle axes. Atahualpa was dragged from his litter after the nobles carrying him had been killed. One conquistador exulted that "in the space of two hours all those troops were annihilated. . . . That day, six or seven thousand Indians lay dead on the plain, and many more had their arms cut off or other wounds." Wrote another, "It was extraordinary to see so great a ruler captured in so short a time, when he had come with such might." It has been said that the conquest of Peru began with this checkmate: the capture of the ruling Inca.

The captive Inca soon realized that the invaders were obsessed with gold and silver. Reasoning that he could obtain his freedom through a ransom of

Hiram Bingham discovered the lost Inca city of Machu Picchu in 1911. His later career included service as governor of Connecticut and as a United States senator.

OVERLEAF: *A modern photograph shows Machu Picchu as it looks today, cleared of the forest that covered the site when Bingham found it.*

This kero or wooden cup is carved and painted to represent an Inca nobleman; he wears a turban and a pair of the ear plugs that caused the Spanish to call the upper-class Incas Orejones ("Big Ears").

these precious metals, he made a famous offer to fill a chamber, once with gold and twice with silver. Llama trains made their way across the Andean trails to Cajamarca, where the Inca was imprisoned. They brought tons of magnificent gold and silver objects, masterpieces of the Incas' metalworkers. There were figurines of men, animals, and birds; beakers; jewelry; gold altars; great urns; and seven hundred gold plates that had once clad the walls of the temple of the sun in Cuzco. All these lovely objects were ruthlessly crushed and melted down by the philistine conquerors. A few of the most splendid pieces were sent to Spain; but the king ordered that they too must be destroyed and turned into Spanish coin.

Atahualpa's ransom was probably the richest ever paid; but it was in vain. Within a few weeks of its completion, on July 26, 1533, the Inca was garroted in the square of Cajamarca. The Spaniards claimed that he had been secretly organizing an army to attack them; in fact, the Inca generals did not dare attack Cajamarca while their ruler was held as a hostage there. But he was executed for mere expediency. Pizarro's men had by now been joined by reinforcements, and they were determined on permanent occupation of the great empire they had discovered. They could not release Atahualpa and were frightened even to have him with them as they carried their invasion deeper into his realm.

Pizarro's experiences with the captive Atahualpa taught the Spaniards about the government and organization of the kingdom they were invading. They found that the Inca was an absolute monarch whose authority was unquestioned. The Inca's prestige was enhanced by a claim that he was the son of the sun, with which he was supposed to be in constant communication. This identification with the most powerful influence on men's lives meant that the Inca was worshiped during his lifetime—in the manner of Egyptian pharaohs or Japanese emperors. Pedro Pizarro observed the rituals that surrounded Atahualpa, even when he was a captive of the Spaniards. When he ate,

he was seated on a small wooden throne . . . of very lovely reddish wood that was always kept covered with a delicate rug. . . . The ladies brought his meal and placed it before him on tender thin green rushes. . . . He pointed to whatever he fancied and it was brought. One of the ladies took it and held it in her hand while he ate. He was eating in this manner one day when I was present. A slice of food was being lifted to his mouth when a drop fell onto the clothing he was wearing. Giving his hand to the Indian lady, he rose and went into his chamber to change his dress and returned wearing a dark brown tunic and cloak. I approached him and felt the cloak, which was softer than silk. I said to him, "Inca, of what is a robe as soft as this made?" He explained that it was from the skins of [vampire] bats that fly by night . . . and bite the natives.

Everything touched by the semidivine Inca was later burned. Another conquistador noted that

he did not spit on the ground when he expectorated: a woman held out her hand and he spat into it. The women removed any hairs that fell onto his clothing and ate them. We asked why he did that when he spat, [and learned that] he did it out of majesty. But with the hairs he did it because he was very frightened of sorcery: he ordered them to eat the hairs to avoid being bewitched.

Anyone seeking an audience with the Inca—even powerful generals or provincial administrators—entered his presence barefoot, bowed down and carrying a token load.

Although the Inca had a harem of many women, his most honored wife was his full sister. Only the son of this incestuous union was considered to be of sufficiently pure blood to succeed as Inca. Remarkably, the royal family produced a series of outstanding rulers despite this inbreeding.

The Incas were an insignificant mountain tribe that had expanded with explosive force in the century before Pizarro's invasion. Successive Inca rulers and military commanders had led the tribe's warriors in wars of conquest that rivaled those of Alexander the Great. The roads that so impressed the Spaniards were then built to unite the empire and provide fast lines of communication for its armies. Provincial towns like Cajamarca were not walled or fortified: the Incas evidently relied more

The cycle of Inca agricultural life as depicted by a Spanish artist: At left, nobles open the season by breaking earth with gold-tipped spades; in center panels, farmers harvest corn and dig potatoes; at right, the corn is stored in government granaries.

on the mobility, discipline, and efficiency of their armies than on static defenses that could be turned against them by rebellious subject tribes.

The Incas also learned many of the techniques that have been used elsewhere by other colonial powers. They left the chiefs of assimilated tribes with outward pomp but no real power. The sons of such chiefs were taken to Cuzco for education, and idols or totems of their tribes were taken to the capital as a mark of respect—but also as hostages for the tribe's good behavior. Pockets of Inca tribesmen were planted in conquered areas to form a loyal nucleus in case of revolt. The Incas' language, Quechua, was imposed throughout the empire, as was the official religion of worship of the sun, the Inca, and the creator god Viracocha.

At the time of the Spaniards' arrival, the Inca empire was still expanding—into what is now southern Colombia in the north, against the Araucanians of southern Chile, and into the forested eastern foothills of the Andes. Conquered chiefs were still being supplanted by a pyramidical hierarchy of Inca officials. New roads, storehouses, *tambo* inns, provincial cities, and royal palaces were being built throughout the vast empire. The deification and glorification of the Inca were carefully cultivated as props of this new empire. The Incas devised a calendar of ceremonies to cele-

brate the seasons and the stages in the agricultural and astronomical year. Plowing could begin throughout the empire only after the Inca himself had turned the first sod of earth in a ceremony near Cuzco. Similarly, the initiation rites of sons of the nobility were co-ordinated from Cuzco, and marriage ceremonies in each village were organized by visiting officials.

As Pizarro's band of invaders marched toward Cuzco along the Inca highway, they became aware of tensions within the Inca state. They had the extraordinary good fortune to reach Peru in the midst of a civil war between Atahualpa and his half-brother Huascar. The two princes were disputing the succession to the Inca throne, and when Pizarro captured him, Atahualpa's armies had just defeated those of his opponent. The Europeans had no difficulty in exploiting this fierce internal rift. As they advanced south after executing Atahualpa, they found themselves welcomed by followers of Huascar's faction. The Inca royal family was too myopically obsessed with the passions of its civil war to recognize that the Spaniards represented a threat to their very civilization.

Another structural weakness helped the invaders. The Inca empire was still so new that many powerful tribes had been only half assimilated into it. These tribes also welcomed the Europeans, as a

On these terraced mountainsides, at an elevation of 11,000 feet, the Incas grew corn. On the steepest slopes each narrow terrace was supported by a fifteen-foot rock wall. Stones jutting from the walls served as steps from one terrace to the next.

means of throwing off the yoke of Inca rule.

Atahualpa's armies did try to stop the Spaniards' advance. They destroyed bridges and burned stores of food along the invasion route. They attacked the Spanish column and sought to stop it in a number of pitched battles. But the Incas were no match for Spaniards on the battlefield. Spanish soldiers were the best in Europe in their day, and those who crossed to the newly discovered Americas were the toughest of young desperadoes. They came armed with fine weapons—razor-sharp swords, steel helmets, chain mail, crossbows, and a few cumbersome firearms. But their greatest advantage came from their horses, animals quite unknown in South America. Horses were the tanks of the conquest, and the Spaniards owed everything to them. On the march their horses gave them a mobility that continually took the natives by surprise. Even when the Indians had posted pickets, the Spanish cavalry could ride past them faster than the sentries could run back to warn of danger. In battle a mounted man has an overwhelming advantage over a man on foot, using his horse as a weapon to ride down the enemy, maneuvering more rapidly, continually striking downward from his greater height. The strange animals also gave their owners a immense psychological advantage.

Atahualpa's nephew, later to become the Inca Titu Cusi Yupanqui, wrote of the awe felt by his people in the face of the strangers:

They seemed like gods . . . partly because they were very different from us in clothing and appearance, and also because we saw that they rode on enormous animals that had feet of silver. . . . We called them gods because of their magnificent appearance and physique, because of the great differences between them—some had black beards and others red ones . . . and also because they possessed "thunders" . . . we said this to describe the arquebuses which we thought to be thunder from heaven.

But the conquistadors knew that it was their horses that filled the Indians with dread.

They thought more of killing one of these animals that persecuted them so than they did of killing ten men. They always placed the horses' heads afterward somewhere that the Christians could see them, decked in flowers and branches as a sign of victory.

The conquistadors thus had little difficulty in marching and fighting along the Inca highways, deep into the Andes, toward the legendary city of Cuzco. Their reward came on the morning of November 15, 1533, when the weary invaders marched or rode two abreast into the streets of the capital. All of Cuzco's monumental buildings were clustered on a tongue of high ground projecting into the valley between two small streams. The swift mountain water of these streams added to the

257

clean, almost austere character of the Inca city, and the channels of the two rivers were elegantly lined with flagstones. One stream's culvert crossed the great central square in which the Incas held their magnificent, often drunken, festivities. When Pizarro's men marched into this square they savored a supreme moment, the final triumph of successful explorers and conquerors. They described their prize to their king with pride: "This city is the greatest and finest ever seen in this country or anywhere in the [Americas]. We can assure Your Majesty that it is so beautiful and has such fine buildings that it would be remarkable even in Spain!"

The central square of Cuzco was flanked by the Incas' monumental buildings. Each ruler built himself a palace during his reign, and after his death his clan preserved the palace as his spiritual resting place. It was filled with his furnishings, and the dead Inca's mummified body still presided over the building. The Incas were too confident of the security of their empire and the honesty of its citizens to have hidden their dead kings' possessions. There is thus no hope of the discovery of a Tutankhamen's tomb in Peru. Instead, the palaces provided billets and loot for the officers and men of Pizarro's small army.

These royal palaces were built of masonry for which the Incas are justly famous. The outer surface of each stone bulges slightly, so that the joints appear countersunk and there is a dazzling play of light and shadow over the wall's surface. The blocks fit into one another with uncanny precision, the product of weeks of patient grinding by dedicated masons. Successive courses of stone blocks are smaller, for visual effect, and the walls taper and lean slightly inward to correct optical illusion. The royal palaces were compounds, with chambers ranged around courtyards in imitation of the llama corrals of Andean village houses. Many palaces also had great assembly halls, similar to the *kallankas* in Inca provincial centers.

The Incas conceived the center of Cuzco as a crouching jaguar or puma. The district where the two streams met was called the puma's tail; the great square was his heart; nearby was Coricancha ("the golden enclosure"), the most holy temple of the sun, and also the convent of *mamaconas* and *acllas*, virgins dedicated to the service of the Inca and his religion. The puma's head was a hill or cliff rearing above the city. This crag of Sacsahuaman was fortified with the most spectacular of all the Incas' magnificent masonry. Three gigantic terrace walls enclosed the side of the hill away from the city. They were built in great zigzags, to expose an attacker to flanking fire; and these angled walls formed the puma's teeth.

When the Incas built terrace walls they fitted stone blocks in irregular or polygonal shapes. In the agricultural terraces of Machu Picchu and many other hillsides, the stones were roughly shaped to fit into one another. But at the royal fortress of Sacsahuaman gigantic blocks were locked together with joints so tight that a knife still cannot be inserted between them. The chronicler Bernabé Cobo marveled:

Although they are not cut straight, they are nevertheless tightly jointed to one another. One can imagine the amount of work involved in making them interlock in the way we see . . . If the top of one stone has a salient corner, there is a corresponding groove or cavity in the stone above to fit it exactly. . . . To make the stones interlock it must have been necessary to remove and replace them repeatedly to test them. And with stones as large as these, it becomes clear how many people and how much suffering must have been involved.

Cobo did not exaggerate—for the mighty stones of Sacsahuaman are possibly the biggest ever incorporated into any human structure. One huge block is 28 feet high and reckoned to weigh 361 tons.

The Spanish discoverers were baffled to explain how such immense stones were moved from their quarries some miles away across the mountains. Everything had to be done by human muscle in a land with no domestic animals larger than the delicate and stubborn llamas. There was no mystery about it. The Incas simply applied thousands of patient laborers and skilled artisans to these herculean tasks. Later interrogations of aged

This Inca boy, wrapped in a llama-wool tunic, his face painted red with yellow stripes, was a sacrifice to the sun. His body was discovered in 1954 on a mountaintop within sight of Santiago, the capital of modern Chile. Beneath the tunic, the body had been preserved for five hundred years in the ever-freezing climate.

At his feet is a bag of coca leaves, which may have been administered as a narcotic to numb him against the pain of freezing to death. Other pouches contain nail parings and baby teeth, so that he would not have to search for them in the afterworld. The boy is preserved still, in a refrigerated showcase at the museum of Santiago.

The Incas worshiped at huacas, or holy places, throughout the Inca empire. In the schematic diagram at top left, Gary Vescelius, an Inca scholar, has plotted the location of such shrines along lines radiating from the Temple of the Sun at Cuzco. Each chain of identical dots, he believes, corresponds to the waxing, full, or waning phase of a lunar month. Each line of shrines was tended by a single kinship group.

259

Gold and silver were royal metals, owned by the Inca emperor and used mainly for the decoration of temples, palaces, and noble persons. Not much of the Inca goldwork escaped the Spaniards, who melted it down for bullion. Most of the best pre-Columbian pieces that still exist came from tombs of earlier cultures, especially the Chimu and Mochica, and were not discovered until after the conquest.

At left is a sixteen-inch Chimu ceremonial knife with a copper blade and a handle in the shape of a man or god made of gold with turquoise inlays. The three-inch Mochica ear disk above, adorned with a warrior, combines turquoise, gold, and shell. On the opposite page, left to right, are a Mochica vessel for coca leaves, made of hammered gold in the form of a hide (fourteen inches long); a Chimu hollow arm and hand of beaten gold (life size); and an Inca statue of electrum, the gold and silver alloy (six inches tall).

Indians revealed that each village and district of the empire had to send levies of men to work on "the houses of the Inca" for months or years at a time. These labor levies went willingly, as proud of their work for the divine Inca as were the builders of cathedrals in Europe at that same time.

The Incas excelled at organization. They were not particularly artistic—far less so than many of the Peruvian cultures that preceded them—but their military and engineering triumphs stemmed from an ability to harness their subjects. An absolute monarchy at the top, the Inca state was totalitarian, highly regimented, and communistic at its base. Much of the land was owned by the state, along with llama cattle, and was farmed collectively for the community as a whole. There was a decimal system of control, with overseers of ten, a hundred, a thousand, and up to ten thousand people. Each age group had its allotted tasks, and young couples were even paired off for marriage by state officials. Girls were selected to work for the Inca or his religion, and the most beautiful served the Inca himself or his high officials. Men went to serve the state or its armies. There was no place for nonconformists; any citizens who broke the simple laws were rigorously punished. The result was an austere and unimaginative state but a contented society nonetheless.

Much of the people's produce was taken by the state, but a proportion was stored against a possible drought or famine. The Spanish invaders marveled at such efficiency. They found tidy rows of stone storehouses along the highways, ready to feed passing armies. When they reached Cuzco they were amazed to see

storehouses full of cloaks, wool, weapons, metal, cloth, and all the other goods that are grown or manufactured in this country. There are shields, leather bucklers, beams for roofing the houses, knives and other tools, and sandals and breastplates to equip the soldiers. All was in such vast quantities that it is hard to imagine how the natives can ever have paid such immense tribute of so many items.

Pedro Pizarro was particularly impressed by the materials stored to make the Inca's superb fabrics:

There were vast numbers of storehouses . . . filled with very delicate cloth and with other coarser cloths; and stores of stools, of foodstuffs, or of coca. There were deposits of iridescent feathers, some looking like fine gold and others of a shining golden-green color. These are the feathers of . . . hummingbirds. Quantities of them are threaded together on fine thread and skillfully attached to agave fibers to form pieces of cloth over a span in length.

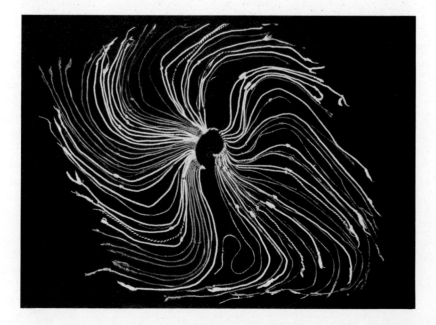

In the scene on the opposite page the Inca ruler listens to the reading of a quipu. In the absence of writing, the Incas kept records by such knotted strings (right). The size, color, and configuration of the knots recorded information on taxes, population, crop yields.

Once they were in control of Peru, the Spaniards sought to turn the Inca system of tribute to their own advantage. They divided the empire among some five hundred conquistadors, each of whom received tribute from thousands of natives living within a designated area known as an *encomienda*. The mass of Peruvian natives found that they had exchanged an Inca master for a Spanish one; but they lost heavily on the exchange. One Spanish administrator admitted that "the natives are forced to pay far more tribute than during the Inca era."

Peruvian men were forced to labor unremittingly and were often insulted or punished barbarously by their new masters. Many were forced to work in mines, under conditions of inhuman hardship, or to grow the narcotic coca in forest regions that destroyed their health. There was an appalling decline in population caused by imported diseases, starvation provoked by the collapse of Inca social systems, and cultural shock that led to disintegration of family life and a consequent decline in the birth rate. Valleys that had contained thousands of prosperous farmers when the Spaniards arrived were reduced to a few hundred ragged survivors within a generation.

The gulf between colonial rulers and conquered natives was enormous. Apart from supplanting the Incas as political masters, the Spaniards were also determined to destroy preconquest religious beliefs and replace them with Christianity. The two races were fundamentally incompatible. Miguel Agia, a contemporary official, wrote that

the Spaniard and Indian are diametrically opposed. The Indian is by nature without greed and the Spaniard is extremely greedy, the Indian phlegmatic and the Spaniard excitable, the Indian humble and the Spaniard arrogant, the Indian deliberate in all he does and the Spaniard quick in all he wants, the one liking to order and the other hating to serve.

One stretch of the royal road crosses Chile's Atacama Desert. Messages were carried on Inca highways by couriers running in short relays at breakneck speed. They maintained the almost incredible pace of 250 miles a day, faster than the speed of mounted couriers on the famous Roman roads.

Immediately after occupying and looting Cuzco, Pizarro tried to install a puppet Inca to help him rule the empire. He chose a prince called Manco Inca, a half-brother of Atahualpa from the side of the family opposed to him in the civil war. Manco tried to rule alongside the intolerable strangers. But in little over a year he decided that he must try to shake off this terrible invasion. He secretly mobilized his people in a great rebellion. Thousands of Inca levies besieged Cuzco and nearly destroyed its beleaguered Spanish garrison. Other native troops attacked Pizarro's new coastal city, Lima, and killed all isolated Spaniards in other parts of the country. The rebellion lasted for a year, 1535–36; but it was finally defeated by the stubborn resistance of the Spaniards in Cuzco and Lima, and by the arrival of shiploads of reinforcements from other Spanish colonies. With the collapse of his rebellion, Manco Inca retreated to the wild forested hills north of Cuzco. He established himself in the valleys beyond Machu Picchu, in rugged country covered by the beginning of the endless Amazon jungles.

Manco Inca's first refuge was a place called Vitcos. He set up a court there, a valiant but pathetic replica of the splendor of Cuzco, where his family had ruled in undisturbed majesty only a decade earlier. Vitcos lay on a tributary of the Urubamba River, one of the main branches of the upper Amazon. Near Cuzco this river flows through open upland country, the homeland of the Inca. It then enters a gorge of granite and abruptly changes character. The river itself becomes a thundering torrent, and the climate becomes tropical, with heavy rains, electric storms, and clammy mists shrouding the steep green hillsides. Below the gorge there are tropical insects, snakes, lianas, and a never-ending carpet of trees and matted undergrowth.

Manco Inca was not allowed to rule his remote retreat in tranquility. A Spanish raid in 1537 reached Vitcos and came within a few minutes of catching the Inca himself. Manco lost his llamas and other possessions; his wives and even his son

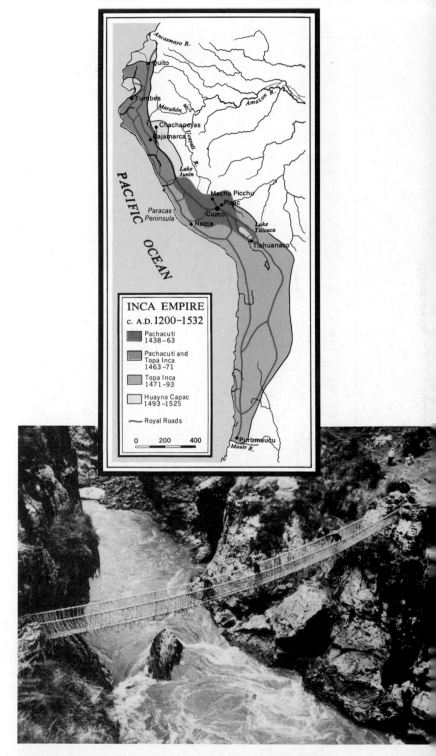

The Inca road system, with its two great mountain and coastal highways and many offshoots, extended for more than 2,500 miles from north to south. The straw suspension bridge above, made with 22,000 feet of handmade rope, carries one branch of the royal road across the Apurímac River.

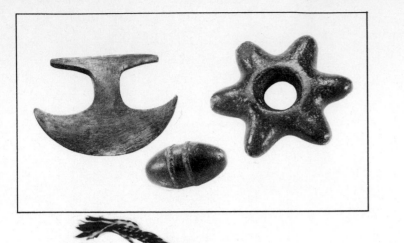

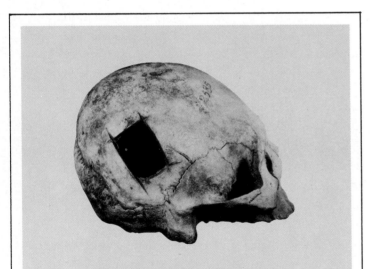

Shown here are some of the weapons that enabled the Incas to conquer their empire. In close combat they used the axhead and the star-shaped mace (in box at left), attached to wooden handles. The woven slings below were used to hurl missiles (such as the slotted stone at left) at distant enemies. Such weapons, along with spears, clubs, and shields, appear in the drawings from a Spanish manuscript, opposite.

INCA TREPANNING

The fearful head wounds inflicted by enemies who used weapons like their own may have led the Incas to pioneer in skull surgery. To relieve pressure on the brain they learned to cut away parts of the skull in the operation of trepanning. Examination of the skull above shows that its owner survived the operation at least long enough for the bones to begin knitting together.

The efficacy of Inca medical tools was tested in 1953 when some Peruvian doctors, carried away by scientific curiosity, used a set to operate on a modern brain patient. He recovered nicely.

were taken prisoner by the Spaniards. He decided that Vitcos was too exposed. He moved his court farther north, deeper into the Amazon forests, down to tropical lowlands thousands of feet below the normal habitat of the Incas. His new capital was called Vilcabamba. But even there he was not safe. In 1539 Gonzalo Pizarro, youngest brother of the conquistador Francisco Pizarro, led an expedition past Vitcos and down the jungle valleys to Vilcabamba itself. Once again Manco only just escaped capture, although his men fought hard to defend their new territory. The Spaniards now wearied of trying to catch the elusive Inca. Manco was left alone to develop his tiny neo-Inca state.

The Spaniards themselves were in disarray, quarreling over the prize they had conquered. Pizarro's original partner, Diego de Almagro, was killed during a civil war over who should govern the city of Cuzco. Then, in 1541, Almagro's son led a gang that assassinated Francisco Pizarro and seized control of Peru. A royal army reconquered Peru from the Almagran rebels, and in 1542 a group of defeated rebels sought refuge with Manco Inca in Vilcabamba. The Inca magnanimously received these Spanish fugitives, who lived with him for a few years, enjoying his hospitality and training his men in European fighting skills. He should never have trusted any Spaniard, for in

1545 Manco's guests repaid his hospitality by murdering him and trying to escape back to Spanish-occupied Peru.

The Inca state did not cease with Manco's murder. His three sons ruled there successively until 1572, when a large Spanish expedition again invaded. It reached Vitcos and then Vilcabamba in the low jungles beyond. Manco's son Tupac Amaru was now Inca, and he tried to escape among tribes of the deep forest. But Tupac Amaru was caught, led back to Cuzco, and executed in the main square amid a vast crowd of lamenting natives. His death marked the end of Inca rule over any part of Peru.

The Spaniards occupied Vilcabamba for a time after the defeat of Tupac Amaru. But this remote and difficult region held few attractions, and it was eventually abandoned by all but a few isolated farmers. People traveling to Vilcabamba used to take a trail around the mountains on the east bank of the Urubamba and then recross the river to the valley of Vitcos. This route meant that travelers avoided the gorge of the Urubamba; but it also meant that none discovered the ruins of Machu Picchu, which were perched among the forests far above that stretch of the river. It was only at the beginning of this century that a trail

was blasted through the Urubamba canyon in order to gain access to the wild rubber trees in the forests beyond. This new trail was the one used by Hiram Bingham on his expedition in 1911, and it enabled him to discover the famous ruin of the city forgotten since Inca times.

Bingham was not only tough and determined, he was also extraordinarily lucky. A few weeks after finding Machu Picchu, Bingham's expedition entered the valley of Vitcos and found more Inca ruins. Bingham was able to identify his new find as Manco Inca's residence of Vitcos. Nearby was a neighboring shrine known as Yurak Rumi, "the White Rock," a great outcrop carved in unmistakable Inca style. These places had been described by missionaries and envoys who penetrated the kingdom of Vilcabamba when Manco's sons were ruling there. Bingham had undoubtedly discovered Vitcos.

Not content with this second spectacular discovery, Bingham pushed on, over the hills of Pampaconas and into the valley of the Pampaconas or Concevidayos River in the jungles below. It was a daring venture, for local people warned the American explorers that the tribes of this valley were hostile. They also said that there were ancient ruins in its forests, at a place called Espíritu Pampa ("Plain of the Spirits"), but that these were haunted and dangerous. Bingham persisted and was rewarded, after a few days of hard going along abandoned trails, by discovering some more ruins overgrown by dense jungle. Bingham's guide and porters were restless, so that he had time only for a cursory reconnaissance. He noted that these ruins of Espíritu Pampa were clearly of Inca origin. But he was mystified to find a series of crude curved Spanish roofing tiles embedded in the litter of the forest floor.

Bingham's remarkable discoveries of 1911 were followed up by large expeditions from Yale University in 1912 and 1915. Machu Picchu was cleared of some vegetation, but there were no further dramatic discoveries. More clearing and restoration were done by Peruvian archaeologists in the 1930's, and Machu Picchu began to be an attraction for adventurous travelers. In time a railway was built down the Urubamba Valley; a road now climbs in hairpins from the railway to the lost city.

Chronicle sources stated that Manco's final refuge of Vilcabamba lay two days' march from his first retreat, Vitcos. After Bingham had discovered and identified Vitcos, he sought to prove that Machu Picchu was in fact Vilcabamba. The two places were approximately two days apart; but the difficult country between them did not correspond to clues left by sixteenth-century visitors to the Inca state. Not everyone was satisfied with Bingham's identification of Machu Picchu as Vilcabamba. In July 1964 another American explorer, Gene Savoy, decided to investigate the ruins of Espíritu Pampa that Bingham had seen so briefly fifty-three years before. Savoy found that the ruins were more extensive and important than Bingham had realized. In the gloom of the forest, covered by dense undergrowth, Savoy's team discovered the foundations of a hall with twenty-four doors and a "sunken palace" nearly three hundred feet long, as well as the remains of many smaller buildings. Savoy also noted the same Spanish roofing tiles that had surprised Hiram Bingham: both explorers

assumed that the site must at some time have been occupied by Spanish settlers. Savoy proclaimed his discovery the lost city of Vilcabamba.

A careful study of every source describing the neo-Inca state of Vilcabamba has led me to agree with Gene Savoy. In my book *The Conquest of the Incas* I showed how every place mentioned in the chronicles could be identified by modern locations on the trail between Vitcos and Espíritu Pampa. Two important sources that eluded Bingham and Savoy described the Spanish entry into Vilcabamba itself in June 1572. These said that Manco's town was built largely of cedar wood on stone foundations. It was set on fire by its inhabitants as the Spaniards entered—this fire is confirmed by a layer of ash noticed by both Bingham and Savoy. The Spanish sources described Vilcabamba as lying in hot, humid country and in a broad valley—a description that could hardly fit Machu Picchu on its knife-edge ridge. But to me the conclusive proof lies in a passage in the chronicles of Martín de Murúa. Writing about Vilcabamba soon after 1572, Murúa said that "the Incas had a palace on different levels, covered in roof tiles." Before the conquest, the Incas invariably used thatch for their roofs. There are no roof tiles at Machu Picchu, and none have been found in any other Inca ruin. I am therefore convinced that the person who rediscovered and correctly identified Manco Inca's last refuge of Vilcabamba was Gene Savoy.

Murúa said that at Vilcabamba "the Incas enjoyed scarcely less of the luxuries, greatness, and splendor of Cuzco in that distant land of exile. For the Indians brought whatever they could get from outside for their contentment and pleasure. And they enjoyed life there." The Spaniards, time, and the jungle have all dealt more harshly with Vilcabamba than they have with Machu Picchu. Today the ruins are too badly destroyed, too overgrown, and too remote to be worth excavating. But they still recall a brief time when this city was the last independent vestige of the once great Inca empire.

The portrait of Atahualpa (below) and the engraving of his execution (right) are both based on imagination. The Inca emperor was not killed by his own Indians but was treacherously seized, held for an enormous gold ransom, and then garroted slowly by Spanish soldiers acting on Pizarro's order.

The Stones of Tiahuanaco

The weeping god

The ruins of Tiahuanaco lie on the Bolivian altiplano, the high plateau of the Andes, just south of Lake Titicaca. The site is higher than that of the Inca capital at Cuzco, higher even than the Tibetan capital of Lhasa. The altiplano is a bleak land where the Indians have developed outsize lungs to breathe the thin air and chew wads of coca leaves to numb themselves against the cold winds and the hard labor of their lives. It seems a harsh, unlikely place for an ancient culture to arise.

Face carved on a pillar

The Gateway of the Sun

But here on the roof of the Americas, half buried and scattered over fifty acres, are thousands of huge stones that once made up the temples and plazas of a ceremonial city. In recent years a few great columns, carved with stiff, expressionless faces, have been set up again in the spots where they fell. A monumental portal called the Gateway of the Sun, cut from a single block of stone, has been rescued from imminent collapse. It bears the face of a deity, perhaps the creator god Viracocha, with staring eyes from which tears appear to be flowing down his cheeks. The weeping god is found wherever the Tiahuanaco culture reached.

Tiahuanaco flourished and fell before the Incas emerged from tribal obscurity. Its people developed distinctive designs in pottery and textiles, including images of the weeping god and his attendant symbols, the condor and the puma. But they had no writing and left no records, unless the curious markings on the statues have a meaning that no one has yet been able to decipher. The Tiahuanacans were ignored by the Incas, who assiduously propagated the idea that history began with their own civilization.

All that is left are the legends still told by the Indians of the high Andes. One legend says that long ago the people then living on the earth were destroyed for their sins by a great flood. A god then rose from an island in Lake Titicaca and created the sun, the moon, and the stars, and prototypes of different peoples, each distinguished by details of costume. Another myth tells of a long period of darkness; when at last the sun rose, a tall, bearded white man appeared from the south. He gave life to man and animals, called forth streams from the rock, preached a religion of love and charity, and traveled northward, working more miracles as he went. These strangely biblical traditions were related by the Indians to the first Spaniards who reached their land.

Modern mythmakers such as Erich von Daniken have a different version of the beginnings of Tiahuanaco. They say that no earthlings of the time could have moved the huge stones—some of them weighing up to 100 tons—from which the city was built. They see in the face on the carved pillar on the opposite page the image of an alien visitor, possibly wearing a spaceman's goggles and mask. They speculate that Tiahuanaco was a colony built by voyagers from another planet, who taught the local Indians the art of massive building that they in turn handed down to the Incas.

Archaeologists have dispelled some of the mystery. They have found that the lowest levels of settlement at the site go back to 200 B.C. and that most of the great stone buildings were built between A.D. 200 and 500. They have found the characteristic designs of pottery and textiles that originated at Tiahuanaco scattered over a vast area of modern Bolivia, Peru, Ecuador, and Chile. They surmise that the Tiahuanacans were crusaders and warriors who were capable of conquering an empire in the name of the weeping god but who never developed, as the Incas did, the administrative skills needed to hold an empire together. It collapsed around A.D. 1000.

The scientists have located the source of the great stones, some of them in quarries as far away as 200 miles, others beyond mountains on a peninsula in the lake. One theory holds that the builders brought them to the lake shore and loaded them on rafts at a time of low water; in the spring when the water rose, the rafts were floated across the lake and unloaded after the waters fell again. In any case, it would not have been impossible for large gangs of men to drag the stones on sledges overland for miles and erect them by means of ramps or ropes, as the builders of Stonehenge did.

Beyond these bare material findings, the record is silent. Who the builders were, what they believed, why their god wept—all these are mysteries not likely to be solved.

An Anthology of the Accounts of
TRAVELERS in ANTIQUE LANDS

On the way to Machu Picchu in 1912 Hiram Bingham and his party follow a cliffside trail along the Urubamba.

AGATHA CHRISTIE ON A DIG IN SYRIA

Agatha Christie (1890–1976) was already well known as the creator of Hercule Poirot when she married the archaeologist Max Mallowan in 1930. She spent several seasons in Syria with Mallowan, who was excavating tells—mounds of earth that cover ancient settlements—in search of the remains of Assyrian and prehistoric civilizations. She took time out from her prodigious production of mysteries to write Come, Tell Me How You Live, *in which she describes life on a dig.*

A-SITTING ON A TELL
(With apologies to Lewis Carroll)

I'll tell you everything I can
    If you will listen well:
I met an erudite young man
    A-sitting on a Tell.
"Who are you, sir?" to him I said,
    "For what is it you look?"
His answer trickled through my
    head
    Like bloodstains in a book.

He said: "I look for aged pots
    Of prehistoric days,
And then I measure them in lots
    And lots of different ways.
And then (like you) I start to write,
    My words are twice as long
As yours, and far more erudite.
    They prove my colleagues
        wrong!"

But I was thinking of a plan
    To kill a millionaire
And hide the body in a van
    Or some large Frigidaire.
So, having no reply to give,
    And feeling rather shy,
I cried: "Come, tell me how you
    live!
    And when, and where, and
        why?"

His accents mild were full of wit:

"Five thousand years ago
Is really, when I think of it,
    The choicest Age I know.
And once you learn to scorn A.D.
    And you have got the knack,
Then you could come and dig with
    me
    And never wander back."

At Meyadin *le camping* begins. A chair is set up for me, and I sit in it grandly in the midst of a large courtyard, or khan; whilst Max, Mac, Aristide, Hamoudi, and Abdullah struggle to set up our tents.

There is no doubt that I have the best of it. It is a richly entertaining spectacle. There is a strong desert wind blowing which does not help, and everybody is raw to the job. Appeals to the compassion and mercy of God rise from Abdullah, demands to be assisted by the saints from Armenian Aristide, wild yells of encouragement and laughter are offered by Hamoudi, furious imprecations come from Max. . . .

At last all is ready. The tents look a little drunken, a little out of true, but they have arisen. We all unite in cursing the cook, who, instead of starting to prepare a meal, has been enjoying the spectacle. However, we have some useful tins, which are opened, tea is made, and now, as the sun sinks and the wind drops and a sudden chill arises, we go to bed. It is my first experience of struggling into a sleeping-bag. It takes the united efforts of Max and myself, but, once inside, I am enchantingly comfortable. I always take abroad with me one really good soft down pillow—to me it makes all the difference between comfort and misery.

I say happily to Max: "I think I like sleeping in a tent!"

. . . I wake to find it is five a.m.—sunrise, and time to get up and start a new day.

The mounds in the immediate neighborhood of Meyadin prove unattractive.

"Roman!" murmurs Max disgustedly. It is his last word of contempt. Stifling any lingering feeling I may have that the Romans were an interesting people, I echo his tone, and say "Roman," and cast down a fragment of the despised pottery. "Min Ziman . . . er Rum," says Hamoudi . . .

"I told you," said Max, "that the Habur was the place! Tells all along it on either side.". . .

Life now becomes hurried and hectic. Examination of Tells is daily more zealous. . . . All digging is a gamble—among seventy Tells all occupied at the same period, who is to say which one holds a building, or a deposit of tablets, or a collection of objects of special interest? A small Tell offers as good prospects as a large Tell, since the more important towns are the more likely to have been looted and destroyed in the far-distant past. Luck is the predominant factor. How often has a site been painstakingly and correctly dug, season after season, with interesting but not spectacular results, and then a shift of a few feet, and suddenly a unique find comes to light. The one real consolation is that whichever Tell we select, we are bound to find *something*. . . .

The system is a simple one. The men are organised into gangs. Men with any previous experience of digging, and men who seem intelligent and quick to learn, are chosen as pickmen. Men, boys, and children are paid the same wage. Over and above that there is (dear to the Eastern heart) bakshish. That is to say, a small cash payment on each object found.

The pickman of each gang has the best chance of finding objects. When his square of ground has been traced out to him, he starts upon it with a pick. After him comes the spademan. With his spade he shovels the earth into baskets, which three or four "basket-boys" then carry away to a spot appointed as dump. As they turn the earth out, they sort through it for any likely object missed by the Qasmagi and the spademan, and since they are often little boys with sharp eyes, not infrequently some small amulet or bead gives them a good reward. Their finds they tie up in a corner of their ragged draperies to be produced at the end of the day. Occasionally they appeal to Max with an object, and upon his reply, "... keep it, or Shiluh, remove it," its fate is decided. This applies to small objects—amulets, fragments of pottery, beads, etc. When a group of pots in position, or the bones of a burial, or traces of mud-brick walls are found, then the foreman in charge calls for Max, and things proceed with due care. Max or Mac scrape carefully round the group of pots—or the dagger, or whatever the find is—with a knife, clearing the earth away, blowing away loose dust. Then the find is photographed before being removed, and roughly drawn in a notebook. . . .

Having arrived on the mound at half-past six, a halt is called for breakfast at eight-thirty. We eat hard-boiled eggs and flaps of Arab bread, and Michel (the chauffeur) produces hot tea, which we drink from enamel mugs, sitting on the top of the mound, the sun just pleasantly warm, and the morning shadows making the landscape incredibly lovely, with the blue Turkish hills to the north, and all around tiny springing flowers of scarlet and yellow. The air is wonderfully sweet. It is one of those moments when it is good to be alive. . . .

The foremen blow their whistles. Back to work. I wander slowly round the mound, pausing from time to time at various parts of the work. One is always hoping to be on the spot just when an interesting find turns up. Of course, one never is! After leaning hopefully on my shooting-stick for twenty minutes watch-

ing Mohammed Hassan and his gang, I move on to 'Isa Daoud, to learn later that the find of the day—a lovely pot of incised ware—was found just after I had moved my pitch. . . .

Every now and then during the morning, as Max comes round, a spurt of entirely fictitious energy is shown. Everyone shouts "Yallah!"

yells, sings, dances. The basket-boys rush panting to and from the dump, tossing their empty baskets in the air and yelling and laughing. Then it all dies down again, and things go even more slowly than before.

The foremen keep up a series of encouraging cries of "Yallah!" and a kind of formula of sarcasm, which has presumably become quite meaningless by constant repetition.

"Are you old women, the way you move? Surely you are not men? What slowness! Like broken-down cows!" etc. etc. . . .

At about four o'clock Max starts going round the gangs and bakshishing the men. As he comes to each one, they stop, line up roughly, and produce the small finds of the day. One of the more enterprising of the basket-boys has cleaned his acquisitions with spit!

Opening his immense book, Max starts operations.

"Qasmagi?" (Pickman)

"Hassan Mohammed."

What has Hassan Mohammed got? Half a large broken pot, many fragments of pottery, a bone knife, a scrap or two of copper.

Max turns the collection over,

flings away ruthlessly what is rubbish—usually those things which have inflamed the pickman's highest hopes—puts bone implements in one of the small boxes that Michel carries, beads in another. Fragments of pottery go in one of the big baskets that a small boy carries.

Max announces the price: twopence ha'penny, or possibly fourpence, and writes it down in the book. Hassan Mohammed repeats the sum, storing it away in his capacious memory. . . .

Max goes on to the next man.

"Your name?"

"Ahmad Mohammed."

Ahmad Mohammed has not very much. Strictly speaking he has nothing at all that we want; but encouragement must be given, however small, so Max selects a few sherds and throws them into the basket and announces a couple of farthings.

Next come the basket-boys. Ibrahim Daoud has an exciting-looking object, which is only, alas, a fragment of an incised Arab pipe-stem! But now comes little Abdul Jehar, proffering doubtfully some tiny beads, and another object that Max snatches at with approval. A cylinder seal, intact, and of a good period —a really good find. Little Abdul is commended, and five francs is written down to his name. A murmur of excitement breaks out.

There is no doubt that to the workmen, gamblers all by nature, the uncertainty of the business is its principal attraction. . . .

Once, when we were digging near Mosul, our old foreman came to Max in great excitement.

"You must take your Khatūn to Mosul to-morrow. There is a great event. There is to be a *hanging*—a woman! Your Khatūn will enjoy it very much! She must on no account miss it!"

My indifference, and, indeed, repugnance, to this treat stupefied him.

"But it is a *woman*," he insisted. "Very seldom do we have the hanging of a woman. It is a Kurdish woman who has poisoned three husbands! Surely—surely the Khatūn would not like to miss *that!*"

Work on the mound has been proceeding satisfactorily—the entire lower half has turned out to be prehistoric. We have been digging on one portion of the mound a "deep cut" from the top to virgin soil. This has given us fifteen layers of successive occupations. Of these the lower ten are prehistoric. . . . There are, as always, some Roman and Islamic graves which are purely intrusive. We always call them Roman to the men to spare any Moslem susceptibilities, but the men themselves are an irreverent lot. "It is *your* grandfather we are digging up, Abdul!" "No, it is yours, Daoud!" They laugh and joke freely.

We have found many interesting carved animal amulets, all of a fairly well-known type, but now suddenly some very curious figures begin to be produced. A small blackened bear, a lion's head, and finally, a queer primitive human figure. Max has had his suspicions of them, but the human figure is too much. We have got a forger at work.

"And he's quite a clever fellow, too," says Max, turning the bear round appreciatively. "Nice bit of work."

Detective work proceeds. The objects turn up in one corner of the dig and are usually found by one or another of two brothers. . . .

On pay-day comes the big exposure! Max displays the exhibits, makes an impassioned speech of condemnation, denounces them as trickery, and publicly destroys them (though he has kept the bear as a curiosity). The men who have produced them are sacked, and depart quite cheerfully, though loudly proclaiming their innocence.

The next day the men are chuckling on the dig.

"The Khwaja knows," they say. "He is very learned in antiquities. You cannot deceive his eyes.". . .

And now, packing up once more—days of it! Crate after crate filled and fastened down and stenciled.

Then come the preparations for our own departure. We are going from Hasetshe by a little-used track through complete wilderness to the city of Raqqa on the Euphrates, and crossing the Euphrates there.

"And we shall be able," says Max, to have a look at the Balikh!"

He says the word Balikh in the way he used to say Jaghjagha, and I perceive that he is forming plans to have just a little fun in the Balikh region before he finally leaves off digging in Syria.

"The Balikh?" I say innocently.

"Whacking great Tells all along it," says Max reverently.

D. H. LAWRENCE AMONG THE ETRUSCAN TOMBS

From 1926 to 1928 the novelist D. H. Lawrence (1885–1930) resided in Italy and found himself deeply impressed by Etruscan art. This description of a torchlit visit to a tomb is from Etruscan Places, *first published two years after his death.*

WE arranged for the guide to take us to the painted tombs, which are the real fame of Tarquinia. After lunch we set out, climbing to the top of the town, and passing through the southwest gate, on the level hill-crest. Looking back, the wall of the town, medieval, with a bit of more ancient black wall lower down, stands blank. Just outside the gate are one or two forlorn new houses, then ahead, the long, running table-land of the hill, with the white high-way dipping and going on to Viterbo.

"All this hill in front," said the guide "is tombs! All tombs! The city of the dead."

We walk across the wild bit of hilltop, where the stones crop out, and the first rock-rose flutters, and the asphodels stick up. This is the necropolis. Once it had many a tumulus, and streets of tombs. Now there is no sign of any tombs: no tumulus, nothing but the rough bare hill-crest, with stones and short grass and flowers, the sea gleaming away to the right, under the sun, and the soft land inland glowing very green and pure.

But we see a little bit of wall, built perhaps to cover a water-trough. Our guide goes straight towards it. He is a fat, good-natured young man, who doesn't look as if he would be interested in tombs. We are mistaken, however. He knows a good deal, and has a quick, sensitive interest, absolutely unobtrusive, and turns out to be as pleasant a companion for such a visit as one could wish to have.

The bit of wall we see is a little hood of masonry with an iron gate, covering a little flight of steps leading down into the ground. One comes upon it all at once, in the rough nothingness of the hillside. The guide kneels down to light his acetylene lamp, and his old terrier lies down resignedly in the sun, in the breeze which rushes persistently from the southwest, over these long, exposed hilltops.

The lamp begins to shine and smell, then to shine without smelling: the guide opens the iron gate, and we descend the steep steps down into the tomb. It seems a dark little hole underground: a dark little hole, after the sun of the upper world! But the guide's lamp begins to flare up, and we find ourselves in a little chamber in the rock, just a small, bare little cell of a room that some anchorite might have lived in. It is so small and bare and familiar, quite unlike the rather splendid spacious tombs of Cerveteri.

But the lamp flares bright, we get used to the change of light, and see the paintings on the little walls. It is the Tomb of Hunting and Fishing, so called from the pictures on the walls, and it is supposed to date from the sixth century B.C. It is very badly damaged, pieces of the wall have fallen away, damp has eaten into the colours, nothing seems to be left. Yet in the dimness we perceive flights of birds flying through the haze, with the draught of life still in their wings. And as we take heart and look closer we see the little room is frescoed all around with hazy sky and sea, with birds flying and fishes leaping, and little men hunting, fishing, rowing in boats. The lower part of the wall is all a blue-green sea with a silhouette surface that ripples all around the room. From the sea rises a tall rock, off which a naked man, shadowy but still distinct, is beautifully and cleanly diving into the sea, while a companion climbs up the rocks after him, and on the water a boat waits with rested oars in it, three men watching the diver, the middle man standing up naked, holding out his arms. Meanwhile a great dolphin leaps behind the boat, a flight of birds soars upwards to pass the rock, in the clear air. Above all, from the bands of colour that border the wall at the top hang the regular loops of garlands, garlands of flowers and leaves and buds and berries, garlands which belong to maidens and to women, and which represent the flowery circle of the female life and sex. The top border of the wall is formed of horizontal stripes or ribands of colour that go all round the room, red and black and dull gold and blue and primrose, and these are the colours that occur invariably.

At the end of the room, where there is a recess in the wall, is painted another rock rising from the sea, and on it a man with a sling is taking aim at the birds which rise scattering this way and that. A boat with a big paddle oar is holding off from the rock, a naked man amidships is giving a queer salute to the slinger, a man kneels over the bows with his back to the others, and is letting down a net. The prow of the boat has a beautifully painted eye, so the vessel shall see where it is going. In Syracuse you will see many a two-eyed boat to-day come swimming in to quay. One dolphin is diving down into the sea, one is leaping out. The birds fly, and the garlands hang from the border.

It is all small and gay and quick with life, spontaneous as only young life can be. If only it were not so much damaged, one would be happy, because here is the real Etruscan liveliness and naturalness. It is not impressive or grand. But if you are content with just a sense of the quick ripple of life, then here it is.

The little tomb is empty, save for its shadowy paintings. It has no bed of rock around it: only a deep niche for holding vases, perhaps vases of

precious things. The sarcophagus stood on the floor, perhaps under the slinger on the end wall. And it stood alone, for this is an individual tomb, for one person only, as is usual in the older tombs of this necropolis.

In the gable triangle of the end wall, above the slinger and the boat, the space is filled in with one of the frequent Etruscan banqueting scenes of the dead. The dead man, sadly obliterated, reclines upon his banqueting couch with his flat wine-dish in his hand, resting on his elbow, and beside him, also half risen, reclines a handsome and jewelled lady in fine robes, apparently resting her left hand upon the naked breast of the man, and in her right holding up to him the garland—the garland of the female festive offering. Behind the man stands a naked slave-boy, perhaps with music, while another naked slave is just filling a wine-jug from a handsome amphora or wine-jar at the side. On the woman's side stands a maiden, apparently playing the flute: for a woman was supposed to play the flute at classic funerals; and beyond sit two maidens with garlands, one turning round to watch the banqueting pair, the other with her back to it all. Beyond the maidens in the corner are more garlands, and two birds, perhaps doves.

The scene is natural as life, and yet it has a heavy archaic fullness of meaning. It is the death-banquet; and at the same time it is the dead man banqueting in the underworld; for the underworld of the Etruscans was a gay place. While the living feasted out of doors, at the tomb of the dead, the dead himself feasted in like manner, with a lady to offer him garlands and slaves to bring him wine, away in the underworld. For the life on earth was so good, the life below could but be a continuance of it.

This profound belief in life, acceptance of life, seems characteristic of the Etruscans. It is still vivid in the painted tombs. There is a certain dance and glamour in all the movements, even in those of the naked slave-men. They are by no means downtrodden menials, let later Romans say what they will. The slaves in the tombs are surging with full life.

We come up the steps into the upper world, the sea-breeze and the sun. The old dog shambles to his feet, the guide blows out his lamp and locks the gate, and we set off again.

THOMAS LEGH, LOST IN AN EGYPTIAN CAVE

In 1813 a young English baron named Thomas Legh (1793–1857) set off on a tour of the Middle East that took him through Turkey, Palestine, and Egypt, then controlled by the Ottoman Empire. He chronicled his hair-raising adventures in A Narrative of a Journey in Egypt and the Country Beyond the Cataracts, *from which an excerpt appears below. Legh returned to the Continent in 1815 in time to volunteer as a dispatch carrier at the Battle of Waterloo. His later life in England was much more settled, and to recall the flavor of the East he named new streets in his native Warrington after Egypt, Cairo, Suez, and Palmyra.*

Before our arrival at Miniet [in Egypt] we halted at Manfalout, to examine some mummy pits, of which we had heard an extraordinary account from a Greek we had met at Thebes. He informed us he had been sent by Suliman the Cacheff of Manfalout with a detachment of Arnout soldiers, against the inhabitants of the village of Amabdi. . . . On the approach of the soldiers of the Cacheff, the greater part of the inhabitants of Amabdi fled into the Desert; some few, however, were observed to disappear under ground, and conceal themselves in a pit, distant about an hour from the village. Demetrius, the Greek emissary of Suliman, with a part of the Arnout detachment, pursued them, and descended the pit in which they had taken refuge. At the bottom they observed fragments of the mummies of crocodiles, scattered about, but the fugitives were nowhere to be seen. From what he observed, there was no doubt the pit communicated with lateral galleries of unknown extent, where were probably deposited the crocodile mummies, the fragments of which the Greek had seen at the mouth of the excavation. The soldiers of the Cacheff returned without venturing to explore further the hiding-places of the Arab fugitives; but the story of Demetrius raised in us a curiosity to prosecute his discovery, and ascertain its extent and accuracy. With this intention we continued our voyage down the Nile and halted at Manfalout situated on the left bank of the river, for the purpose of making preparation for a journey to Amabdi. Our party consisted of my friend Mr. Smelt and an American of the name of Barthow, who had traded many years in the Red Sea, spoke Arabic extremely well, and whom we had engaged as a dragoman at Cairo, when we first began our travels in Upper Egypt. We took with us, besides, an Abyssinian merchant, of the name of Fadlallah, and three of our boat's crew who were Barâbras, whom we had brought with us from the Cataracts. Having provided ourselves with asses and torches, we crossed the ferry of Manfalout, at five on the morning of the 30th March. We wandered about till nine o'clock in search of the village of Amabdi, near which we at length found four Arabs employed in cutting wood. They appeared at first unwilling to give us any information about the object of our search, and we observed them consulting together, and overheard them muttering something about danger, and thought we heard the expression, "If one must die,—all must die."

We were bent on going, and the Arabs at last undertook to be our guides for a reward of twenty-five piastres. After an hour's march in the Desert, we arrived at the spot, which we found to be a pit or circular hole of ten feet in diameter, and about eighteen feet deep. We descended without difficulty, and the Arabs began to strip, and proposed to us to do the same: we partly followed their example, but kept on our trowsers and shirts. I had by me a brace of pocket pistols, which I concealed in my trowsers, to be prepared against any treacherous attempt of our guides. It was now decided that three of the four Arabs should go with us, while the other remained on the outside of the cavern. The Abyssinian merchant declined going any farther. The sailors remained also on the outside to take care of our clothes. We formed therefore a party of six; each was to be preceded by a guide—our torches were lighted—one of the Arabs led the way,—and I followed him. We crept for seven or eight yards through an opening at the bottom of the pit, which was partly choked up with the drifted sand of the desert, and found ourselves in a large chamber. . . .

This was probably the place into which the Greek, Demetrius, had penetrated, and here we observed what he had described, the fragments of the mummies of crocodiles. We saw also great numbers of bats flying about, and hanging from the roof of the chamber. Whilst holding up my torch to examine the vault, I accidentally scorched one of them. I mention this trivial circumstance, because afterwards it gave occasion to a most ridiculous, though to us very important discussion. So far the story of the Greek was true, and it remained only to explore the galleries where the Arabs had formerly taken refuge, and where, without doubt, were deposited the mummies we were searching for. We had all of us torches, and our guides insisted upon our placing ourselves in such a way, that an Arab was before each of us. Though there appeared something mysterious in this order of march, we did not dispute with them, but proceeded. We now entered a low gallery, in which we continued for more than an hour, stooping or creeping as was necessary, and following its windings, till at last it opened into a large chamber, which, after some time, we recognized as the one we had first entered, and from which we had set out. Our conductors, however, denied that it was the same, but on our persisting in the assertion, agreed at last that it was, and confessed they had missed their way the first time, but if we would make another attempt they would undertake to conduct us to the mummies. Our curiosity was still unsatisfied; we had been wandering for more than an hour in low subterranean passages, and felt considerably fatigued by the irksomeness of the posture in which we had been obliged to move, and the heat of our torches in those narrow and low galleries. But the Arabs spoke so confidently of succeeding in this second trial, that we were induced once more to attend them. We found the opening of the chamber which we now approached guarded by a trench of unknown depth, and wide enough to require a good leap. The first Arab jumped the ditch, and we all followed him. The passage we entered was extremely small, and so low in some places as to oblige us to crawl flat on the ground, and almost always on our hands and knees. The intricacies of its windings resembled a labyrinth, and it terminated at length in a chamber much smaller than that which we had left, but, like it, containing nothing to satisfy our curiosity. . . .

The Arab whom I followed, and who led the way, now entered another gallery, and we all continued to move in the same manner as before, each preceded by a guide. We had not gone far before the heat became excessive;—for my own part I found my breathing extremely difficult, my head began to ache most violently, and I had a most distressing sensation of fulness about the heart.

We felt we had gone too far, and yet were almost deprived of the power of returning. At this moment the torch of the first Arab went out: I was close to him, and saw him fall on his side; he uttered a groan—his legs were strongly convulsed, and I heard a rattling noise in his throat—he was dead. The Arab behind me, seeing the torch of his companion extinguished, and conceiving he had stumbled, past me, advanced to his assistance, and stooped. I observed him appear faint, totter, and fall in a moment—he also was dead. The third Arab came forward, and made an effort to approach the bodies, but stopped short. We looked at each other in silent horror. The danger increased every instant; our torches burnt faintly; our breathing became more difficult; our knees tottered under us, and we felt our strength nearly gone.

There was no time to be lost—the American, Barthow, cried to us to "take courage," and we began to move back as fast as we could. We heard the remaining Arab shouting after us, calling us Caffres, imploring our assistance, and upbraiding us with deserting him. But we were obliged to leave him to his fate, expecting every moment to share it with him. The windings of the passages through which we had come increased the difficulty of our escape; we might take a wrong turn, and never reach the great chamber we had first entered. Even supposing we took the shortest road, it was but too probable our strength would fail us before we arrived. We had each of us separately and unknown to one another observed attentively the different shapes of the stones which projected into the galleries we had passed, so that each had an imper-fect clue to the labyrinth we had now to retrace. We compared notes, and only on one occasion had a dispute, the American differing from my friend and myself; in this dilemma we were determined by the majority, and fortunately were right. Exhausted with fatigue and terror, we reached the edge of the deep trench which remained to be crossed before we got into the great chamber. Mustering all my strength, I leaped, and was followed by the American. Smelt stood on the brink, ready to drop with fatigue. He called to us "for God's sake to help him over the fosse, or at least to stop, if only for five minutes, to allow him time to recover his strength." It was impossible—to stay was death, and we could not resist the desire to push on and gain the open air. We encouraged him to summon all his force, and he cleared the trench. When we reached the open air it was one o'clock, and the heat in the sun about 160°. Our sailors, who were waiting for us, had luckily a *bardak* full of water, which they sprinkled upon us, but though a little refreshed, it was not possible to climb the sides of the pit; they unfolded their turbans, and slinging them round our bodies, drew us to the top. Our appearance alone without our guides naturally astonished the Arab who had remained at the entrance of the cavern; and he anxiously inquired for his *hahabebas*, or friends. To have confessed they were dead would have excited suspicion, he would have supposed we had murdered them, and have alarmed the inhabitants of Amabdi, to pursue us and revenge the death of their friends. We replied therefore they were coming, and were employed in bringing out the mummies we had found. . . .

We lost no time in mounting our asses, re-crossed the desert, and passed hastily by the village to regain the ferry of Manfalout. . . .

At length it was resolved we should return to Manfalout, and claim the assistance of the Cacheff, or endeavour to convince the Arabs of our innocence. We quickly reached the town, and had no sooner stepped on shore than we were assailed by three women, and five or six children—they were all naked and smeared with mud. We were informed that they were the wives and children of the men who had perished, and the state in which they exhibited themselves was according to the custom of mourning amongst them. As we were armed, we reached without much obstruction the house of the Cacheff, whom we now found surrounded by more than four hundred Arabs, and amongst them the Shekh of the village of Amabdi. Making our way through the crowd, we luckily recognized the person of the Arab whom we had left and supposed to have died with his companions in the cavern. His appearance was most wretched, he was not able to stand, and was supported by two of his friends. We afterwards found he had escaped by the light of Mr. Smelt's torch, when he was obliged to remain for a short time to recover his strength at the edge of the trench. Our dragoman related our story again, and called upon the survivor to confirm the truth of it, but in vain; on the contrary he maintained we had taken him and his companions by force, and compelled them to conduct us to the place. In his falsehood he was supported by the Arab who had remained on the outside of the cavern, and whom we now saw for the first time among the crowd. In our defence we replied it was not possible we could have used any means of compulsion, as we were unarmed. This we boldly asserted, as the brace of pistols I had with me was never produced. Besides, we recalled to his memory that on our way thither one of the guides who

had died, had replenished our *bardak* with water from a well near Amabdi.—This proved that we had gone amicably together.

The Cacheff, who continued to treat us haughtily in public, commanded the Arab to explain the means by which the infidels (who he confessed were without arms) had killed his companions. He replied, *by magic*, for he had seen me burning something on our first entrance into the great chamber. This was the bat I had accidentally scorched. Our cause now began to wear a better complexion: part of the crowd, who treated the idea of magic with contempt, believed us innocent, and the rest probably dreaded the imaginary powers with which we had been invested. Emboldened by this change of sentiment in our favour, our dragoman assumed a lofty tone, and peremptorily insisted on our being sent, together with our two accusers and the Shekh of Amabdi, to Siout to Ibrahim Bey, the son of the Pacha of Cairo, and the Governor of Upper Egypt. The reputation of this man for cruelty was so great, that his very name excited terror in the assembly. It was now our turn to threaten, and we talked of the alliance of our King with the Pacha of Cairo, and the consequence of ill-treating any one protected by his fehrman. This had its effect, and the Cacheff, having consulted for some time with the Shekh, suggested an accommodation by money. This proposal we at first affected to reject with disdain, as it would in some manner be an acknowledgment of our guilt, though we were secretly anxious to terminate the affair at any rate. Our dragoman was sent to negociate with the Cacheff, and it was finally agreed we should pay twelve piastres or two Spanish dollars to each of the women, and the same sum we offered as a present to the Shekh of the village. All animosity seemed now to have ceased, and

we were permitted quietly to return to our vessel, and continue our voyage.

LAWRENCE DURRELL AT A ROMAN IMPERIAL VILLA

The English novelist and poet Lawrence Durrell (born in 1912 in India) is best known for The Alexandria Quartet. *In 1977 he published* The Sicilian Carousel, *a description of his experiences in Sicily in the company of a busload of average tourists.*

Piazza Armerina is a pretty and lively little hill town, boasting of more than one baroque church, a cathedral and a castle, and several other sites of note in the immediate environs. But it is quite impossible to convey that elusive quality, charm, in writing—or even in photography which so often deludes one with its faked images and selected angles. The little town had charm, though of course its monuments could not compare in importance to many another Sicilian town. Yes . . . I found myself thinking that it would be pleasant to spend a month there finishing a book. The walking seemed wonderful among these green and flourishing foothills. But the glimpse we had of it was regrettably brief; having signalled our presence to the hotel where we were to have lunch we set off at once to cover the six or so kilometres which separated us from the Imperial Villa—a kind of summer hideout built for some half-forgotten Roman Emperor. What is intriguing is that almost no ascription ever made about a Sicilian site or monument is ever more than tentative: . . . "It has been surmised that this hunting lodge could have belonged to the Emperor Maximianus Heraclius who shared his Emperorship with Diocletian." The site they chose for the Imperial Villa is almost oppressively hidden away; it makes one conjecture why in such a landscape one should plank down a large and spacious building in the middle of a network of shallow ravines heavily wooded, and obviously awash in winter with mountain streams. Instead of planting it on a commanding hillock which (always a problem in hill architecture) drained well during the rains. There was something rather unhealthy and secretive in the choice of a site, and it must be infernally hot in August as a place to live in. It buzzed with insects and butterflies. We arrived in a cleared space where, together with a dozen or so other buses, we dropped anchor and traipsed off down the winding walks to the villa, marvelling at the sultriness and the oppressive heat—so different from the Attic valleys we had traversed with all their brilliant cornfields.

We came at last to a clearing where an absolute monstrosity greeted our eyes—a straggling building in dirty white plastic which suggested the demesne of a mad market gardener who was specialising in asparagus. I could not believe my eyes. None of us could. We stood there mumchance and swallowing, wondering what the devil this construction was. Roberto, blushing and apologetic, told us.

So precious were the recently uncovered mosaics and so great the risk that they would be eaten into by the climate that someone had had the brilliant idea of covering them in this grotesque plastic housing through which a series of carefully arranged plankwalks and duckboards allowed the curious to walk around the villa. It was a groan-making thing to do and only an archaeologist could have thought of it. Moreover the mosaics, so interesting historically that one is glad to

have made the effort to see them, are of a dullness extraordinary. But then the sort of people who build villas for Governors are for the most part interior decorators with a sense of grandiose banality, a sense of the expensively commonplace. Of such provenance is the Imperial Villa, though of course the number and clarity of the decorations merit interest despite their poor sense of plastic power. Historians must be interested in these elaborate hunting-scenes, the warfare of Gods, and the faintly lecherous love scene which ends in a rather ordinary aesthetic experience. And all this in a white plastic housing which turned us all the colour of wax. Was this the pleasure dome of an Emperor, or was it perhaps (an intelligent suggestion by Christopher Kininmonth) more the millionaire's hideaway, constructed for the rich man who purveyed animals for the Roman arenas? The frescoes of animals are so numerous and their variety so great that it makes one pause and wonder. But as usual there is no proof of anything.

Dutifully we prowled the duckboards while Beddoes, who had culled a whole lot of Latin words from the Blue Guide, made up a sort of prose poem from fragments of it which he murmured aloud to himself in a vibrant tone of voice. Thus:

And so we enter the Atrium
By its purely polygonal court
To the left lies the Great Latrine
Ladies and Gents, the Great Latrine
For those who are taken short
But the marble seats are lost
Yet ahead of us is the Aediculum
Giving access to the Thermae
The vestibule can be viewed from
    the Peristyle
Do not smile.
Next comes the frigidarium
With its apodyteria
Leading onwards with increasing
    hysteria
To the Alepterion

Between tepidarium and calidarium
Whence into a court where the
    Lesser Latrine
Waits for those who have not yet
    been
In construction sumptuous
As befitted the Imperial Purple

But here the Muse punished him and he wobbled off a duckboard and all but plunged down upon one of the more precious tessellations, to the intense annoyance of Roberto and the collective disapproval of the Carousel. The dentist's lady seemed particularly shocked and enraged and flounced about to register her disapproval. "That guy is sacrilegious," she told her companion with a venomous look at Beddoes who seemed only a very little repentant.

JOHN L. STEPHENS VS. THE TEMPLE OF DENDERA

John Lloyd Stephens (1805–1852), a New York lawyer who retired from the bar at the age of twenty-nine in order to travel, is best known today for his discovery and purchase of a Mayan city in Mexico (see page 78). Stephens also journeyed to the Middle East and published Incidents of Travel in Egypt, Arabia Petraea, and the Holy Land *in 1837. The incident below typifies the casual attitude toward ancient monuments that many travelers had in Stephens's time. The temple of Dendera, incidentally, is not to be confused with the smaller temple of Dendur, which is now at New York's Metropolitan Museum of Art.*

Sunday, January 18. At eight o'clock in the morning we arrived at Qena, where, leaving my boat and crew to make a few additions to our stock, Paul and I crossed over in a sort of ferryboat to Dendera.

The temple of Dendera is one of the finest specimens of the arts in Egypt, and the best preserved of any on the Nile. It stands about a mile from the river, on the edge of the desert, and, coming up, may be seen at a great distance. The temples of the Egyptians, like the chapels in Catholic countries, in many instances stand in such positions as to arrest the attention of the passer-by; and the Egyptian boatman, long before he reached it, might see the open doors of the temple of Dendera, reminding him of his duty to the gods of his country. I shall not attempt any description of this beautiful temple; its great dimensions, its magnificent propylon or gateway, portico, and columns; the sculptured figures on the walls; the spirit of the devices, and their admirable execution; the winged globe and the sacred vulture, the hawk and the ibis, Isis, Osiris, and Horus, gods, goddesses, priests, and women; harps, altars, and people clapping their hands, and the whole interior covered with hieroglyphics and paintings, in some places, after a lapse of more than two thousand years, in colors fresh as if but the work of yesterday.

. . . The temple is more than half-buried in the sand. For many years it has formed the nucleus of a village. The Arabs have built their huts within and around it, range upon range, until they reached and almost covered the tops of the temple. Last year, for what cause I know not, they left their huts in a body, and the village, which for many years had existed there, is now entirely deserted. The ruined huts still remain around the columns and against the broken walls. On the very top is a chamber, beautifully sculptured, and formed for other uses, now blackened with smoke, and the polished floors strewed with fragments of pottery and culinary vessels.

Nor is this the worst affliction of

the traveler at Dendera. He sees there other ruins, more lamentable than the encroachments of the desert and the burial in the sand, worse than the building and ruin of successive Arab villages; he sees wanton destruction by the barbarous hand of man. The beautiful columns, upon which the skillful and industrious Egyptian artist had labored with his chisel for months, and perhaps for years, which were then looked upon with religious reverence, and ever since with admiration, have been dashed into a thousand pieces, to build bridges and forts for the great modern reformer.

It is strange how the organ of mischief develops itself when it has something to work upon. I sat down upon the sculptured fragments of a column, which perhaps at this moment forms the abutment of some bridge, and looking at the wreck around me, even while admiring and almost reverencing the noble ruin, began breaking off the beautifully chiseled figure of a hawk, and, perhaps in ten minutes, had demolished the work of a year. I felt that I was doing wrong, but excused myself by the plea that I was destroying to preserve, and saving that precious fragment from the ruin to which it was doomed, to show at home as a specimen of the skill of the Old World. So far I did well enough; but I went farther. I was looking intently, though almost unconsciously, at a pigeon on the head of Isis, the capital

of one of the front columns of the temple. It was a beautiful shot; it could not have been finer if the temple had been built expressly to shoot pigeons from. I fired: the shot went smack into the beautifully sculptured face of the goddess, and put out one of her eyes; the pigeon fell at the foot of the column, and while the goddess seemed to weep over her fallen state, and to reproach me for this renewed insult to herself and to the arts, I picked up the bird and returned to my boat.

CHATEAUBRIAND IN SEARCH OF SPARTA

Called "by far the greatest French writer of his age" by one critic, Vicomte François René de Chateaubriand (1768–1848) visited Greece in 1806 and sought to locate the ruins of ancient Sparta (or as it is sometimes called, Lacedaemon). The locale of that city was a matter of some debate at the time among scholars, but the poet's interest in the city of Leonidas was more romantic than academic.

Those who have read the Introduction to these Travels, will have seen that I spared no pains to obtain all the information possible relative to Sparta. I have traced the history of that city from the Romans till the present day; I have mentioned the travellers and the books that have treated of modern Lacedaemon, but unfortunately their accounts are so vague, that they have given rise to contradictory opinions.

Persuaded, by an error of my early studies, that Misitra was Sparta, I began with the excursion to Amyclae, with a view to finish, first, with all that was not Lacedaemon, so that I might afterwards bestow on the latter my undivided attention. Judge then of my embarrassment, when, from the top of the castle of Misitra, I persisted in the attempt to discover the city of Lycurgus, in a town absolutely modern, whose architecture exhibited nothing but a confused mixture of the Oriental manner, and of the Gothic, Greek, and Italian styles, without one poor little antique ruin to make amends. Had but ancient Sparta, like ancient Rome, raised her disfigured head from amidst these new and incongruous monuments! But no—Sparta was overthrown in the dust, buried in the tomb of ages, trodden under foot by Turks, dead, and not a vestige of her existence left behind.

Such were now my reflections. My cicerone scarcely knew a few words of Italian and English. To make him understand me the better, I attempted some sentences in modern Greek; I scrawled with a pencil a few words of ancient Greek; I talked Italian and English, and jumbled French along with them all.—Joseph endeavoured to explain, but he only increased the confusion; the janissary and the guide (a kind of half negro Jew,) gave their opinion in Turkish, and made matters still worse.—We all spoke at once, we bawled, we gesticulated; with our different dresses, languages, and physiognomy, we looked like an assembly of demons, perched, at sunset, on the summit of these ruins.

This Misitra, said I to the cicerone, is Lacedaemon; is it not?

Signor? Lacedaemon? What did you say?—rejoined he.

Is not this Lacedaemon or Sparta?

Sparta? What do you mean?

I ask you if Misitra is Sparta?

I don't understand you.

What, you a Greek, you a Lacedaemonian, and not know the name of Sparta?

Sparta? Oh yes! Great republic; celebrated Lycurgus.

Is Misitra then Lacedaemon?

The Greek nodded in affirmation. I was overjoyed.

Now, I resumed, explain to me what I see. What part of the town is that? I pointed at the same time to the quarter before me a little to the right.

Mesochorion, answered he.

That I know perfectly well; but what part of Lacedaemon was it?

Lacedaemon? I don't know.

I was beside myself.

At least show me the river, cried I, and repeated: Potamos, Potamos.

My Greek pointed to the stream called the Jews' River.

What! is that the Eurotas? Impossible! Tell me where is the Vasilipotamos?

The cicerone after many gestures, pointed to the right towards Amyclae.

I was once more involved in all my perplexities. I pronounced the name of Iri, on which my Spartan pointed to the left, in the opposite direction to Amyclae.

It was natural to conclude from this, that there were two rivers; the one on the right, the Vasilipotamos, the other on the left, the Iri; and that neither of these rivers flowed through Misitra. . . .

But then, said I to myself, where can be the Eurotas? It is clear that it does not pass through Misitra. Misitra therefore is not Sparta, unless the river has changed its course and removed to a distance from the town, which is by no means probable. Where, then, is Sparta? Have I come so far without being able to discover it? Must I return without beholding its ruins? I was heartily vexed. As I was going down from the castle, the Greek exclaimed: "Your lordship perhaps means Palaeochori!" At the mention of this name, I . . . cried out in my turn: "Yes, Palaeochori! The old city! Where is that? Where is Palaeochori?" "Yonder, at Magoula," said the cicerone, pointing to a white

cottage with some trees about it, at a considerable distance in the valley.

Tears came into my eyes when I fixed them on this miserable hut, erected on the forsaken site of one of the most renowned cities of the universe, now the only object that marks the spot where Sparta flourished, the solitary habitation of a goatherd whose whole wealth consists in the grass that grows upon the graves of Agis and Leonidas. . . .

On the 18th, half an hour before day-light, I mounted my horse with the janissary, and set off at full gallop for Lacedaemon.

We had proceeded at that pace for an hour along a road running direct south-west, when at break of day, I perceived some ruins and a long wall of antique construction: my heart began to palpitate. The janissary turning towards me pointed with his whip to a whitish cottage on the right, and exclaimed with a look of satisfaction, "Palaeochori!" I made up towards the principal ruin which I perceived upon an eminence. On turning this eminence by the northwest for the purpose of ascending it, I was suddenly struck with the sight of a vast ruin of semicircular form which I instantly recognized as an ancient theatre. I am not able to describe the confused feelings which overpowered me. The hill at the foot of which I stood, was consequently the hill of the citadel of Sparta, since the theatre was contiguous to the citadel; the ruin which I beheld upon that hill was of course the temple of Minerva Chalcioecos, since that temple was in the citadel, and the fragments of the long wall which I had passed lower down must have formed part of the quarter of the Cynosuri, since that quarter was to the north of the city. Sparta was then before me; and its theatre to which my good fortune conducted me on my first arrival, gave me immediately the positions of all the quarters and edifices. I alighted, and ran all the way up the hill of the citadel.

Just as I reached the top, the sun was rising behind the hills of Manelaion. What a magnificent spectacle! but how melancholy! The solitary stream of the Eurotas running beneath the remains of the bridge Babyx; ruins on every side, and not a creature to be seen among them. I stood motionless, in a kind of stupor, at the contemplation of this scene. A mixture of admiration and grief, checked the current on my thoughts and fixed me to the spot; profound silence reigned around me. Determined, at least, to make echo speak in a spot where the human voice is no longer heard, I shouted with all my might, "Leonidas! Leonidas!" No ruin repeated this great name, and Sparta herself seemed to have forgotten her hero.

LADY HESTER DESTROYS A STATUE

The adjective "eccentric" suits no one better than Lady Hester Lucy Stanhope (1776–1839), who turned her back on a leisured life in England to become a self-styled oriental queen. In her twenties Lady Hester was the trusted adviser of her uncle, William Pitt the Younger, who said of her, "If she were resolved to cheat the devil she could do it." She left England in 1810 with an entourage that included Dr. Charles Lewis Meryon, who wrote The Travels of Lady Hester Stanhope. *In this excerpt Meryon recounts Lady Hester's hunt for gold in the ruins of Ascalon in what was then Syria. When her workmen turned up a statue at the site Lady Hester ordered it destroyed—a logical step, in her view, because her letter of permission from the Porte (the Ottoman court) allowed digging only for*

gold, not art works. In 1814 Lady Hester took up residence in a ruined convent on Mount Lebanon with a suite of thirty servants. She remained there until her death.

In the preceding year, her ladyship, during her illness, had upon several occasions hinted at the existence of hidden treasures, a clue to which she had by some means become possessed of; . . . as I was to assist in the management of the business, she gave me a history of it, as follows:—

A manuscript was put into her hands, said to have been surreptitiously copied by a monk, from the records of a Frank [European] monastery in Syria, and found among his papers after his decease. It was written in Italian, and disclosed the repositories of immense hoards of money, buried in the cities of Ascalon, Awgy, and Sidon, in certain spots therein mentioned. . . .

The very day of our arrival [at Ascalon], a gang was immediately set to work: and I shall now proceed to detail, day by day, what the excavations brought to light. As a beginning, nothing more was done than just to remove the surface of the ground.

April 2nd. After digging down three or four feet, some foundations were laid open, running east and west. On removing the earth between them nothing was found but mould and loose stones, with two or three human bones. Three fragments of marble shafts of pillars were bared and a Corinthian capital. There were appearances showing that the ground had been disturbed at some former period, particularly in the south-east corner, where there was a ditch of a very recent date, which (it was whispered by the peasants) had been made by Mohammed Aga [a local government official].

On the 3rd day, the excavations were continued along the south wall. The men worked with great animation. The idea of discovering im-

mense heaps of gold seemed to have an effect upon them, although they could not hope for a share in it. On this day there was a great fall of rain and hail, and the weather was so tempestuous as much to impede the labourers. A pipe and tabor were therefore brought, to the tune of which they worked, sung, and danced. Cross foundations were met with, running east and west, seeming to have served for the support of rows of pedestals. About fifteen feet from the centre of the south wall were discovered several large fragments of granite columns.

On the 4th day the work was continued nearly in the same direction. At three in the afternoon, the

workmen struck upon a mutilated statue. I was immediately called, and felt exultation at the sight of a relic of antiquity, which I thought might give celebrity to our labours. The soil around it being removed, it was drawn up by ropes, without damage. There were at the same spot some imperfect remains of the pedestal on which it had stood. The depth of the mould and rubbish which lay over the statue was six or eight feet.

On examination, it proved to be a marble statue of colossal dimensions and of good execution. It was headless, and had lost an arm and a leg;

but was not otherwise disfigured. It seemed to have represented a deified king: for the shoulders were ornamented with the insignia of the thunderbolt, and the breast with the Medusa's head. There was every reason to believe that, in the changes of masters which Ascalon had undergone, the place in which we were now digging had originally been a heathen temple, afterwards a church, and then a mosque. The statue probably belonged to the age of the successors of Alexander, or it might be that of Herod himself. The statue, from the acromion to the heel, was six feet nine inches.

I made a pen sketch of the statue, and represented to Lady Hester that her labours, if productive of no golden treasures, had brought to light one more valuable in the eyes of the lovers of the fine arts, and that future travellers would come to visit the ruins of Ascalon, rendered memorable by the enterprise of a woman, who, though digging for gold, yet rescued the remains of antiquity from oblivion. What was my astonishment, when she answered—"This may be all true; but it is my intention to break the statue, and have it thrown into the sea, precisely in order that such a report may not get abroad, and I lose with the Porte all the merit of my disinterestedness."

When I heard what her intentions were, I made use of every argument in my power to dissuade her from it; telling her that the apparent vandalism of such an act could never be wiped away in the eyes of virtuosi, and would be the less excusable, as I was not aware that the Turks had either claimed the statue or had forbidden its preservation. It was true, that, whilst sketching it, the people had expressed their surmises at what I could find to admire in a broken image; and I heard some of them conjecture that it might be a deity of the Franks, as it had been of the Romans and Greeks. But no idle

notions, I insisted, ought to have weight on her mind; and I begged hard that, if she could not with decency carry it away, she would at least leave it for others to look at. She replied, "Malicious people may say I came to search for antiquities for my country, and not for treasures for the Porte: so, go this instant; take with you half a dozen stout fellows, and break it in a thousand pieces!" Her resolution was not a thing of the moment: she had reflected on it two days; and knowing her unalterable determination on such occasions, I went and did as she desired. When Mohammed Aga saw what had been done, he could not conceal his vexation: for it is probable that Lady Hester had read what was passing in his mind, and had thus prevented many an insinuation against her. Indeed, reports were afterwards circulated that the chest of the statue was found full of gold—half of which was given to the pasha, and the other half kept by Lady Hester. In England, where her motives were unknown, people naturally have decried her conduct, although it is plain that her strict integrity ought to prove her justification.

On the 9th, when the granite pillars were removed, a work of no trifling magnitude, considering the means by which it was effected, the troughs were found empty. The disappointment was very great: and, the more so, as the excavation of the four following days produced nothing but two granite columns at the North West angle, six or eight feet below the surface, a white marble pedestal, some bones of animals, and two earthenware lamps. A small excavation was likewise made in one of the towers of the East wall of the city. With respect to the area of the mosque, almost all of it had been turned up. The North foundation wall had been traced throughout its whole length; and, in that direction, the shafts of two small marble

pillars, about six feet in length, and with rude capitals, had been the only reward. Other masses had been broken up, to see if they had concealed anything. But, when every research was fruitless, the closing hand was, by Lady Hester's consent, put to our labours on the 14th of April, being a fortnight from the commencement. The conclusion that her ladyship came to was, that when Gezzàr Pasha embellished the city of Acre, by digging for marble and other materials in the ruins of Ascalon, he was fortunate enough to discover the treasure. That Gezzàr enriched his coffers by wealth so got was generally affirmed: and it is probable that his pretended mania for building was no more than a cloak to conceal this real motive for excavating. Thus ended this most interesting experiment; which failed in its primary object, but had the desirable effect of establishing Lady Hester's popularity throughout Syria, and of confirming the belief, already grown up, that she was a person of some consideration, even in the eyes of the Sublime Porte.

H. V. MORTON
AMID THE RUINS
OF BABYLON

H. V. Morton (born 1892), a British journalist and travel writer, is the author of over thirty books. In this excerpt from his Through Lands of the Bible *Morton describes a visit in the mid-1930's to the remains of once-proud Babylon.*

Among the most incongruous acts of my life is the journey I made in a taxi-cab to Babylon. The Baghdad owner-driver, unaware of a conflict in association between his cab and Babylon, often pulls up at the kerb and suggests that you might like to take a taxi there at a specially cut price.

The ruins are sixty miles south of Baghdad, and the journey takes three to four hours. The road begins well enough, but soon becomes rough and uneven. I knew we were drawing near when we crossed a single railway track running over the sand, and I saw a notice-board bearing, in English and Arabic, the words: "Babylon Halt."

I have read books which have described the humiliations visited by Time upon the once mightiest city in the world, but this notice-board translated them into the idiom of our own civilization. That "the glory of kingdoms, the beauty of the Chaldee's excellency" should be known as a "halt," a place which even local trains pass with a derisive whistle, seemed to me as bitter as anything prophesied by Isaiah.

On every side I saw sandy mounds lying in the sunlight: some large enough to be called hills, others low ridges, and still more the merest uneasy risings and fallings of the earth. But for miles around the earth was blasted and unhappy with the memory of Babylon. So this was the city whose Hanging Gardens were among the Seven Wonders of the World. Four-horse chariots could pass on its walls; on one altar alone a thousand talents' worth of incense was burned every year.

I climbed a sandy hill in which are embedded the impressive remains discovered by German archaeologists from 1899 to 1917. I found it difficult to understand them, for I saw acre upon acre of brown mud brick walls, broken vaulting, and the lower stories and cellars of buildings lying in such confusion that only a trained architect could sort them out with any certainty. Palace and hovel, wall and roadway, are equally humbled in this post mortem. But one section of the ruins still stands in unmistakable splendour: the great

Ishtar Gate of Babylon built by Nebuchadnezzar. Its towers rise to a height of forty feet, and its mud bricks bear the impression in high relief of a hundred and fifty-two animals, almost life size, alternate rows of bulls and dragons, once brilliantly enamelled, but now bared to the mud from which they were moulded.

What a fortunate discovery this was! Nothing looks drearier than

mud bricks all the same shape, dull in colour, crumbling and already returning to the dust whence they came. Even uncarved stone has a quality and a beauty which are absent from mud. And as I looked at those acres covered with Babylonian bricks, I wondered if the buildings in this land were really as beautiful as we have been told they were. But the survival of the bulls and the dragons on the Ishtar Gate leaves no doubt. The bulls stride forward with the grace and spirit of young horses, clipped like French poodles. Their hair from head to tail along the back, round the jaw, under the belly, down the chest, and curving round the haunches, was arranged in fringes of tight little curls, in which jewels or beads may have been tied. What superb animals they are; not massive and heavy like the Egyptian Apis,

nor fantastic and half-human like the Assyrian bull, but proud, vigorous young creatures, striding forward into the morning and capable of taking a five-barred gate.

Their companions, the dragons or "sirrush," are equally well done, but they are not so appealing because they represent no known animal. They may have been put there to frighten Medes and Persians. The "sirrush" is really a compromise between a serpent, a lynx, and an eagle: the head, body, and tail are those of a scaly snake, the forelegs are those of a lynx, and the hind legs, which end in talons, might be those of any large bird of prey.

The "sirrush" is pictured on many other Babylonian works of art. Professor Koldewey, who discovered the Ishtar Gate, thinks it possible that the priests kept some strange reptilian creature in the darkness of a temple and exhibited it as a living "sirrush." If this is so, it lends colour to the story of Daniel and the Dragon, which appears in many forms but is not printed in the *Book of Daniel*. The story is that Daniel refused to worship a dragon in Babylon and offered to slay the creature single-handed. He was therefore placed in the animal's den, presumably in the belief that he would never emerge from it; but he took with him a potent pill, composed chiefly of hair and bitumen, which he persuaded the dragon to swallow. The poor "sirrush" then died; some accounts say that it blew up.

From the top of the mound you look down over the basements and the brick vaulting of Nebuchadnezzar's Palace. And how hard it is to realize that those incoherent masses of building material near by are all that remain of the Hanging Gardens, or that the mark like the shadow of a broad road losing itself round Babylon is the line of the mighty walls which once astonished all who saw them.

The flat country stretches to the sky, featureless, bare, and arid, except to the west, where the Euphrates flows in a narrow belt of palm-trees. You see no river, but you see this line of foliage running for miles, like a green snake on the sand. Even the "waters of Babylon" have deserted the city, for in ancient times the river ran along the west side of the Kasr, bringing with it the happy sound of water and the scent of flowers. As if obeying a command that no touch of life should remain anywhere near Babylon, the Euphrates has carved a new channel for itself and has departed. . . .

While I stood on the summit of the ruins, an Arab approached and told me that he had worked there with Professor Koldewey. His name was Umran Hamed, "the guide of Babylon." He was a good fellow, and he had absorbed a quantity of accurate information from the German archaeologists, which he was tireless in imparting. We walked about the ruins and he pointed out many things which I should have missed without him.

He showed me the vestiges of three wells in the foundations of the Hanging Gardens and a chamber which he said was a "refrigerator." As he had just confused the word partridge with cartridge, I wondered whether he had got this right.

"Yes; where food was kept cold in snow," he said earnestly.

"Have you ever seen a refrigerator?"

"No, sir," he replied, "but I have heard the Germans talking."

So if Umran overheard correctly, perhaps the lower stages of the Hanging Gardens were stored with cold foods, iced sherbets, and other cool things for the Median princess for whose pleasure Nebuchadnezzar made those gardens. It is believed that in the flatness of Babylonia she became homesick for her native mountains, just as the Jews must have done, and to please her the King ordered the construction of an artificial mountain terraced with gardens. The word "hanging" is not a good description of these gardens. The Greek word is *kremastos,* which was used in ancient Greek for a man hanged, and is used in modern Greek for a suspension bridge.

It is certain that the Hanging Gardens were as solidly anchored to the earth as a pyramid. Like everything else in Babylonia, they were built of mud brick and constructed like a pyramid, or ziggurat, rather like the Mappin Terraces at the Zoo. Water was pumped up from the wells in the foundations to irrigate the gardens. Each series of terraces was planted with trees and flowers, and artificial water-courses may have run musically here and there. In this lovely botanical garden the princess wandered—longing, perhaps, for a piece of real rock. One hopes that Nebuchadnezzar's manly attempt to compensate a lady for a change of scenery was a success. No man, certainly, could have done more; but history, and even the lives of humble men, suggest that such gigantic gestures are not always the most acceptable. Perhaps beneath the troubled bones of Babylon there lies a tablet which records how the maid of the mountains received this proof of the King's affection, when, after many months of laborious rock-gardening, Nebuchadnezzar led her forth.

"Do you call that a garden? Why, it isn't even a hill!"

I asked Umran what he thought the Hanging Gardens were like. He smiled rapturously and replied:

"Like the gardens of Paradise."

He led me to a convulsion in the earth as you see behind a scaffolding in the City of London when a large building has been pulled down. It was the site of the great ziggurat of Babylon, the temple tower called E-temen-an-ki, which archaeologists say was the traditional Tower of Babel. It was evidently a ziggurat of typical Babylonian form, rising by a series of stages sufficiently high above the dusty plain to give astronomers an uninterrupted view of the sky. On the topmost stage was a temple, which Herodotus said contained only a table and a couch which was occupied at night by a single woman chosen by the deity out of all the women in the land. It has been proved by inscriptions that this temple and its high tower go back to the first age of Babylon, and that it was reconstructed from time to time by various kings.

We came to a series of broken arches which once supported the banqueting-hall of Nebuchadnezzar. This was the hall where, according to the *Book of Daniel,* Belshazzar saw the writing on the wall.

And as we wandered over the lonely mounds, silent except for the hum of the wild bee and the hornet, I thought how literally Isaiah's prophecy of the fall of Babylon has been fulfilled. It is, indeed, overthrown as God overthrew Sodom and Gomorrah.

"It shall never be inhabited, neither shall it be dwelt in from generation to generation: neither shall the Arabian pitch tent there; neither shall the shepherds make their fold there. But wild beasts of the desert shall lie there; and their houses shall be full of doleful creatures: and owls shall dwell there, and satyrs shall dance there. And the wild beasts of the islands shall cry in their desolate houses, and dragons in their pleasant palaces. . . ."

The "broad walls" of Babylon have been "utterly broken," as Jeremiah prophesied; her gates have been "burned with fire"; the city has indeed become "an astonishment" and "an hissing without an inhabitant." The words of Jeremiah have become literally true; the city is in "heaps." What word better describes this awful desolation: "And Babylon shall become heaps."

... I left Babylon, its lonely, silent mounds, its cavernous ruins, and its dusty, chocolate bricks, with the thought that though the prophets may not have seen the expected desolation of this city, still their words came true; for time is always on the side of prophets.

REX WARNER AT THE CITADEL OF MYCENAE

Rex Warner (born 1905) is a noted scholar, author, and translator of Greek and Roman classics. Here he describes his visit to Mycenae, where "the bloody legend of the house of Atreus" was played out some thirty centuries ago.

Here, as so often in Greece, the turning of a corner reveals something new and unexpected. A few steps from the place where the road stops will bring one suddenly to the entrance of the Acropolis, a porch built of massive blocks of stone above which stand the famous lions which gave the gate its name. The impression is immediate and overpowering. Here is a place of colossal strength, the remains of the most ancient civilization in Europe, something to which we are irrevocably connected, yet something different from the paths of what progress we have made and, in its difference, somehow sinister, cruel, violent and overwhelming. The walls are built for magnificence as well as for defence, and the sheer size of the blocks of stone is an aspect of this magnificence. The fortresses of Eleutherae and of Aegosthena, in spite of their strength, have a kind of grace, even a humanity, about them. But

Mycenaean architecture strikes one as being, in its size and overloading of weight, somehow devilish. It is not that it is stiff and massive and geometrical like the monuments of Egypt. This people, with all their display of overwhelming power, were also capable of an almost sensual delicacy in their art. Rather, perhaps, one is inclined to feel that the splendour actually achieved was something accidental, that these architects were not in the least interested in what among us are the accepted standards of taste. So the most perfect examples of their work, the great bee-hive tombs, were designed, if for any eyes at all, then for the eyes of the dead and of a funeral cortege.

To the right of the entrance, below the Acropolis itself, is what is assumed to be the royal cemetery, excavated by Schliemann in 1876, where, according to popular tradition, were buried the bodies of Atreus, Agamemnon and Cassandra. Past this circular pit in the ground one ascends to the summit of the hill and on the way can amuse oneself with the conjectures or certainties of archaeological guides as to the precise positions of the various parts of the great palace of the Atridae. Here one may imagine Cassandra standing in terror at her second sight, the visions of slaughtered children and of further slaughter still to come. Here perhaps was the bath where Agamemnon was murdered; here the chamber where Clytemnestra and Aegisthus enjoyed their guilty loves; here Orestes revealed himself as an avenger and here first became aware of the pursuing presence of the Erinyes. Far more than this may be imagined on this grey rock which, in the spring, is scarlet with anemones and which, even then, has a grim aspect as though the very scarlet of the flowers was the stain of blood.

I have seen it at all seasons and even in the sunniest weather when

the air is full of the murmurs of insects, a sound interrupted continually by the distant noise of goat bells, when light drenches the two great hills between which the citadel of Mycenae stands above its steep gorges, when the grey of these mountains seems white and blazing against the blue sky and when, if one looks out to the plain of Argos below and the sea beyond, one will be surveying a view whose calm, flat and various extent must soothe and fascinate the eye—even then this small but immensely powerful rock seems to crouch, alert and instinct with a different kind of life, between mountains that are savage, dominating from its small stature the whole rich plain with a kind of domination that is certain, uncanny and ferocious, like that exercised by a weasel over a rabbit.

I have stood here too in grey and rainy weather when skeins of mist have hung in the gorges and blanketed the two peaks behind. In such conditions, perhaps, this ancient fastness might be expected to wear a desolate and a Gothic air. But it is not precisely so. Nothing here can be imagined of the romantic or the picturesque. Desolate, certainly, and haunted the place may seem, but with a quality that recalls nothing medieval. . . .

As one walks round the summit of the citadel or descends on the further side, admiring the great bastions built above the sheer descent into the gorge, the Cyclopean architecture of the passage that leads down to the hidden well, everything will confirm one's first impressions. And it is difficult indeed to understand why this place should have an impact on the mind which is as powerful as that made by Delphi, though so extremely different. In Delphi one feels the presence of God or of some sublimity which appears divine; but mysterious and unaccountable as is the full force of this feeling, there are certain geographical features—the tremendous rocks, the high mountain air, the richness and profusion of that stream of olives—which can easily be associated with ideas of sublimity and holiness. At Mycenae one's impressions can be, as I have said, opposite of what might be expected. There is no vast extent even of the ruined walls; there is nothing remarkable in the foundations of the courts of palaces; the hill itself, though immensely strong, is not high; nor is it in the least conspicuous, being folded away between two much higher mountains. Yet, of all places, this one pre-eminently, savagely and masterfully exists, so that the whole smiling landscape down to the sea seems to be within its clutches.

ELEANOR CLARK AT HADRIAN'S VILLA

Eleanor Clark, the wife of Robert Penn Warren, is a frequent visitor to Europe. She won the National Book Award in 1965 for The Oysters of Locmariaquer, *which recounts her experiences in Brittany. She is also the author of two novels. The following passage from* Rome and a Villa *describes a walk in the ruins of the villa that the emperor Hadrian built at Tivoli in the second century* A.D.

At Hadrian's Villa the garden is the house, and it is a pity not to know what growing things there were in it. The right kind of literature did not exist to record that, or whether the Romans counted plants for much among their luxuries; it hardly seems so, they had too much nature in themselves to become fanatical over its vegetable refinements as Anglo-Saxons do; the point was always decoration. But they must have noticed the rarer possibili-

ties for that sometimes, or perhaps Hadrian the aesthete might have been the one to think of it; perhaps the flowers here were as exotic as the stones, orchids big as pumpkins and various as African marbles, little botanical delicacies and live aphrodisiacs from the East, each court and banquet hall having its own schemes of plant color and perfume, as it had its fantasy in water.

In this house you would have lived with water, not gone out to see it, except as the outside is part of the conception of the house itself. There must have been a sound of it almost everywhere; you would have moved from room to room, taking various kinds of spaces as rooms, through the flash of crystal and the pull of narcissism, among thousand-faced mobiles or clear shallows where perhaps fish from the Indian Ocean moved in stigmatic flickers of turquoise, silver and pomegranate. Versailles could never have been so bright or so profound. And it seems the imagination was as inexhaustible as the medium; it needed only more space, more time to produce still other poems in water.

The most ambitious were the big nymphaea—three or four of them, one in the heart of the palace, a whole liquid salon, whose bottom-most basin still shows some of its ancient coating of sky-blue paint. One or two of the others may have somewhat resembled the Fountain of Trevi, though the fake boulders of the baroque are hardly in character for Hadrian; nor is the grotto idea, so dear to the Madonna-ridden Italian heart and chronic in Renaissance landscaping; a dripping through moss is not his style. He had a few such places, you can see them, but on the whole these waterworks, though accommodating nymphs, must have had more of a formal elegance, and one imagines running surfaces more in the style of fluted columns; with all the varieties of

cross-motion, however, playing over and around the dolphins and tritons and sea centaurs and marine divinities that are part of the game and its suggestion. Some of the other arrangements are very quiet in their extravagance. There will be a small canal lined with marble, a sudden pool-lit corner; down below the Stadium, near the Pecile, there is a shallow garden basin of sedate geometric design and with a curious illusion of great distance across it, where the boy with the dolphin might have stood; and the four-leaf clover end of the Golden Court has niches at the four corners free for fountains, but surely there only a falling, not a shooting or spraying up of water, probably with goddesses shining above, clear and single at the summit of motion, like Brancusi's bird: this is where one should have seen the Capitoline Venus, though it happens she belonged to somebody else, but some other product of Athens or Aphrodisias was surely here. In the banquet hall too, most fittingly, there is a mystery of water, perhaps separated from the diners by glass: one side or end of the triclinium seems to have been all fountain, which if the meal dragged on after dark must have played like sprayed neon in the light of the high candelabras. Then strangely named Maritime Theatre, and the long canal of Canopus. These and dozens more, big and little, roofed or under the sky, without counting the baths.

Aside from the glory of it, what a pensiveness there must have been around the house from all this water: nothing lazy, but the repose of spaciousness that even one little garden pool can give, or a brook going past the house, and that the whole area has, its one and sufficient fortune, from the waterfall at Tivoli. Nothing else permits such voyages of the spirit, nothing gives such largesse of suggestion and of time present and past.

Unflagging in spirit if not in body, a portly tourist of the nineteenth century is helped up a pyramid.

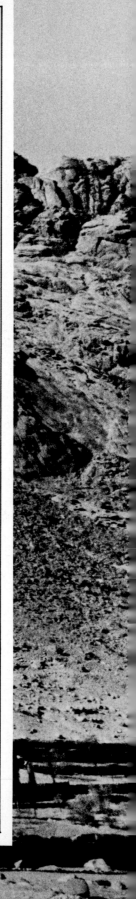

11: The Survival of Records

by GILBERT HIGHET

In the monastery of Saint Catherine at the foot of Mount Sinai (background picture), a German scholar found one of the two oldest Bibles in the world. The limestone tablet above, from Kish in Iraq, c. 3500 B.C., is the oldest example of picture writing yet discovered.

The written records that we possess of ancient times have come down to us through a gantlet of perils, both natural and man-made. They have survived war, fire, weather, natural calamities, and neglect, as well as willful destruction by barbarians and fanatics. The late Gilbert Highet, a renowned classical scholar, was keenly aware both of what has been lost and of what has survived. We take this chapter from an article that he wrote for HORIZON magazine in 1962. At left is the oldest piece of Latin writing in existence, inscribed on a four-and-one-half-inch gold pin of the seventh century B.C. It reads: "Marius made me for Numerius."

The other day I met a friend of mine, an author who is successful and ambitious. Asking him about his work, I found him profoundly depressed. In a few years, he said somberly, there won't be any books. They will all be destroyed, and there will be nobody left to read them. It is difficult to argue with anyone who thinks he foresees the end of civilization; but I tried to console him. Mankind has endeavored to kill itself off before this, and its books have nearly all been destroyed. Yet as long as there was someone who wanted to read, books and records have been saved.

Nevertheless, it still strikes me with amazement when I open a book of speeches by Demosthenes and begin to hear the voice, the very syllables and cadences, of a man who died some twenty-three centuries ago. Surely it is almost miraculous that we can take up the *Aeneid* of Vergil, printed by machinery that would have astonished Vergil himself, on a material he had never seen, in a format he could scarcely have imagined, and after two millennia find that, undimmed by time and change, his poetry still sings, his mystical visions still transport us as they did his first readers, and the subtleties of his poetic architecture still hold secrets only half-discovered.

The miracle of the preservation of thought through marks on a smooth surface is commemorated every week by one of the most impressive little religious ceremonies in the world. Every Sabbath in every Jewish synagogue, a handwritten copy of the Torah, the first five books of the Bible, is taken out of its place. After a reading, the book is carried through the congregation before it is returned to the ark, and every pious Jew kisses it. It is always handwritten with a quill pen. It is always in the form of a parchment roll. Its text is always exactly the same as that of its predecessor, from which it was copied: the very letters are counted so that they may never vary by a jot, any more than the law of God Almighty can vary. By doing homage to the book in this way, the Jews express their devotion to the name of the Creator contained in the Torah; but they also, by implication, express reverence for one of man's greatest inventions—the written book.

The Jews, like the Moslems, have always carried their sacred writings with them: the book and the people have sustained each other. But among the Greek and Latin classics there are no such sacred books: the nations for whom they were written have disappeared; their very languages have assumed new shapes and sounds—remote, although not wholly different from the original tongues. How have the great books of the past survived through so many centuries?

First, we must sadly admit that many, very many, of them have been lost. In Greece and the Greek-speaking world, and later in the Roman world, there were many libraries and many hundreds of thousands of books. Literacy was more widespread in the second century of our era than it was in the eighteenth. The walls of Pompeii, covered with public announcements and private scribbles in three languages (Latin, Greek, and Oscan), show how natural and commonplace was the use of writing then. Nearly all townsfolk could read, freemen and slaves alike. Only on the farms and ranches were many people illiterate. In Egypt excavators now dig up large private book collections buried under the sand near villages where today few of the fellahin own a single book, or could read it if they did.

Although some authors of antiquity composed only a few works, to which they gave all their life's energy, there were many who produced an amazing number of them. The comedian Aristophanes left fifty-four plays. Aeschylus, first of the great tragic dramatists, wrote at least eighty. Livy's history of Rome ran into one hundred and forty-two volumes; and such polygraphs were not exceptional. But of many of the most famous authors we have only a few scanty though precious relics. It is as though we had the titles of all Shakespeare's plays, with some fragments quoted from most of them, but possessed complete only *Hamlet, Henry V, A Midsummer-Night's Dream,* and *As You Like It.* Of Aristophanes' half a hundred comedies, we have just eleven. Of Aeschylus's four score plays, only seven survive. We have a summary of virtually all of Livy's Roman history, so that we know what he covered in each volume, but only thirty-five of his one hundred and forty-two volumes remain. And while these great writers have survived in however meager a proportion, dozens of others have vanished almost without a trace. Aristophanes was only one of a large school of competing comic dramatists. From quotations and allusions, we know the names of about a hundred and seventy poets of the "Old Comedy" (the group to which Aristophanes belonged) with 1,483 titles of their plays. Except Aristophanes, not one survives. Where is his great rival, boozy old Cratinus? Where is the energetic Eupolis, whom Horace linked with the other two in a gay triad? Gone, except for a few jokes, some famous passages preserved in quotation, and many play titles. It is delightful to look through the titles and reflect how much fun the Athenians had in the fifth century before Christ; it is painful to remember how much of it has vanished.

But not all. It would scarcely be worth studying classical literature if it were a heap of insignificant debris. It is not. It is like a city which has been bombed and partially burned, so that whole sections are in ruins and some streets with their houses are irrecoverable; but at its heart many of the most important and beautiful public buildings stand unscathed, full of statues and pictures and memories, while others, although damaged, retain a noble tower or one magnificent wing. The two epics of Homer (or of the two Homers) are safe. All Vergil's poetry is intact. The works of Plato are complete and have even acquired some "Platonic" forgeries in the meantime. We have all that Horace ever published. We can read virtually all of Lucretius and Terence and Catullus in Latin, virtually all of Demosthenes and Thucydides and Herodotus in Greek, and virtually all of a few other first-rate writers in either tongue. Furthermore, we have the complete works of a number of authors who, although not "classics" either in their own time or now, are amusing, shocking, informative, or creatively eccentric. We do not have too many of the classical books from Greece and Rome, but we have much of the best.

The great books of Greece and Rome were written down between 800 B.C. and A.D. 450. They were first printed and disseminated to many modern readers between A.D. 1450 and 1550. Once printed, they were likely to survive because they were so good or because there were now so many copies of them (duplication means preservation). But between the distant centuries when the classics were composed and the comparatively recent centuries when they were reproduced by the man with the machine, grave obstacles and recurrent perils often threatened to obliterate them.

First came the danger that haunts us all. Anyone born since 1900 has grown up with it always in his mind. It is the great destroyer, the waster, the terrible simplifier—war. It is always more violent than we expect. It is capricious. In the conflict of human wills, deliberation and choice and purposive action are often sacrificed to sheer destructive energy. When the Crusaders were sacking Constantinople in 1204, a drunken sailor was seen tearing up the sacred books of the Hagia Sophia.

King Matthias Corvinus of Hungary (1440–1490) had collected a magnificent library of manuscripts, some written for him by Italian calligraphers and some bought by his agents in Greece and Asia Minor. Part of it was captured by the Turks in 1541 during their advance into central Europe and some specimens were sent back to Istanbul. The others were left in storage, damaged by fire and carelessness, recaptured in 1688, and divided up among the conquerors. And yet a few manuscripts of the original library still remained together—at least until the end of the nineteenth century—in the Grand Seraglio at Istanbul, after the drums and tramplings of four centuries.

The most famous of all libraries in ancient times was the collection at Alexandria. In the Western world it was the first large public library; it was the cradle of literary scholarship and of responsible publishing; it was part of the earliest university. In one form or another it seems to have lived for seven hundred years, although many doubtful legends have grown up around it, and its destruction is wrapped in silence almost total.

The library, along with the Home of the Muses (or Museum), was founded by Ptolemy I, Alexander the Great's marshal and his successor as king of Egypt. Its administrators strove to have the best, the most authoritative, copies of all important books, collated and catalogued with utmost care. After two hundred and fifty years it was burned during Julius Caesar's difficult struggle to displace the twelfth Ptolemy and set up his own mistress Cleopatra as monarch. Mark Antony, who succeeded Caesar both as the real ruler of Egypt and as Cleopatra's lover, gave her as a replacement two hundred thousand books from the rival library of Pergamum in Asia Minor; these were stored in the sanctuary of Serapis, and this new library survived until the Empire went Christian. (Tertullian says that the original manuscript of the Hebrew Scriptures translated into Greek, the Septuagint, was one of its treasures.) Then the pagan sanctuaries were turned into churches, and

Christians and pagans fought a cultural and religious war in the streets. In A.D. 414 the Christian historian Orosius wrote that the stacks of the great library "were emptied by our own men in our own time." If anything survived for the Caliph Omar to condemn as fuel to heat the public baths in A.D. 640 (according to a late legend), it was only a group of departmental libraries.

The imperial library of Constantinople, in an even more turbulent city, had still more drastic adventures. Its founder, the Emperor Constantine, intended it to contain both Christian and pagan works and caused fine copies of rare books to be made on durable vellum. Revolt, civil strife, and invasion struck the library again and again, but it was constantly restored by the Greek passion for culture. A rebellion and a fire in the fifth century A.D. destroyed it, with over a hundred thousand books, including one monstrous object, a copy of Homer's two epics written in gold letters on a snake's gut one hundred twenty feet long. Three of the most famous Greek statues perished in the same blaze. Rebuilt, refilled, reopened, the library was closed again for almost a century during the religious conflict over the worship of images and holy pictures. It was burned and looted, at least in part, by the Fourth Crusaders in 1203–4. Restored once again, it was still in existence when Constantinople fell to the Turks in 1453. The Archbishop of Kiev, an eyewitness of the invasion, said that more than 120,000 books were destroyed. And yet many precious manuscripts survived in private collections. Lost in the outbuildings or substructures of some old mosque, some deserted church or forgotten barracks, there still may lie, in sealed jars or dust-covered chests, priceless relics of the classical past, more precious than the Hebrew manuscripts found not long ago in the Genizah, or storeroom, of a synagogue near Cairo.

The invading barbarians from the North, after many attacks, at last split the Greco-Roman world into two parts, an eastern and a western realm. In the west, those who were the heirs of the Roman Empire spoke Latin and tried to teach it to their conquerors. In the east, the language was Greek.

For some centuries the civilized Mediterranean world had been bilingual by practice and by sympathy; but after A.D. 500 or so, nobody in the west could speak or write Greek and nobody in the east could speak or write Latin. Now and then one still hears stories about Irish monks who alone were able to keep the knowledge of Greek alive in the west. Laudable, if true; but unfortunately false. An occasional scribe might copy out an occasional Greek word during the Dark Ages in the west, but the tradition of reading, understanding, and transmitting the Greek tongue—although it was the language in which the Gospels and the Acts and the Epistles were written—virtually died out (with the exception of a few lonely geniuses such as Grosseteste and Erigena) for a thousand years.

The second danger that confronted the Greek and Roman classics was not violent destruction but peaceful change. Nowadays it is almost impossible to purchase the piano works of Alexander Scriabin or to find scores of the music of Lully. Scriabin died in 1915; most of his music has been allowed to go out of print. Much of Lully still remains in manuscript, unpublished, unperformed, unknown. In the same way, those books which ceased to interest the Greek and Roman reading public ceased to be copied and studied, and were therefore not transmitted from one generation to another. After Vergil's *Aeneid* was issued, it was accepted at once as the great epic poem in the Latin language. It was learned at school, it was read for pleasure, it was admired and imitated. Naturally, it displaced all earlier epic poems, even the *Annals* of Vergil's greatest predecessor, Ennius. For a few generations, Ennius was respected, although little read. Then he was forgotten; his poem vanished. Nothing of it is left now, except fragments quoted by Roman scholars to illustrate oddities of archaic style—five hundred fifty lines in all, no fragment larger than a page. Only four poets of the early Roman Republic have survived entire, or almost entire: Lucretius, the philosophical missionary; Catullus, the brilliant lyricist; and the comic playwrights Plautus and Terence. All the others were neglected and even-

Three thousand years after it was buried in the tomb of an Egyptian high priest, this papyrus Book of the Dead (a sort of guidebook to the next world) was unrolled in 1960 at the British Museum. It proved to be twenty-two feet long and, except for some wear at the beginning, in good condition.

tually disappeared. No doubt some of them were trivial and others crude, but there were several masterful writers among them, such as the satirist Lucilius, and several lively works in minor genres, such as the Atellan farces, which we should dearly love to be able to read.

There was another habit of taste that tended to make books obsolete in the ancient world. This was sheer laziness. Partly to cater to lazy adult readers, and partly to create handy texts for use in schools, editors in later Greece and Rome reduced the complete works of many distinguished authors to small, neat anthologies, assimilable with little effort and easily portable. Thus, out of the eighty-odd plays by Aeschylus, the Seven Best were selected; out of more than a hundred by Sophocles, the Seven Best. These selections ousted the complete works, which fewer and fewer readers requested or even knew. So all the other plays of Aeschylus and Sophocles have vanished. With Euripides we are luckier because we also have part of one set of Complete Works. But aside from these three, we have no Greek tragedies. Many of the lost books of Greece and Rome were not destroyed: they were allowed to slip into oblivion.

There were two further hazards that the classics had to survive before they could reach the age of printing. One was a change of format, the other was a change of script. The two changes sound unimportant, but they drastically altered our intellectual history.

Suppose that all publishers decided to abandon publishing books in their present form and began to issue them only on microfilms; and suppose that we all accepted this, rearranging our homes around microfilm-readers and storage cabinets. If so, all the new books would be produced exclusively on microfilm. All important old books would be transferred to microfilm: the Bible, the encyclopedias, the scientific and technical manuals, the law books; and Shakespeare, Milton, Pope, Shelley, Keats . . . but who else?

At once the question becomes difficult. Should Butler's *Hudibras* be microfilmed? and Langland's *Piers Plowman*, which nobody reads except specialists? and Cowley's epic on King David, which nobody reads at all? A selective grid has been created. Through it must pass any book in the English language that is to reach the postmicrofilm future. The rest will be kept in storage for a while, will be forgotten, and in a few generations will fall into dust. (We have in our own lifetime seen a similar series of changes in recorded music, from the old phonograph cylinders to the flat 78 rpm discs, then to LP discs; and now tape threatens to make all discs obsolete.)

Suppose also that we were to introduce a new phonetic alphabet: all our important books would have to be transliterated into the new simplifaid spεlṃ. Within a couple of generations only a few experts and antiquarians would be able to read the older script. All the books that remained untranscribed would be neglected, difficult, remote. Soon they would sink into decay and oblivion.

Now, these two changes actually took place during the centuries after the Greek and Latin classics were composed and while they were being transmitted to us: the format and material of books changed, and then the scripts in which they were written.

In the flourishing days of Greece and Rome nearly all books were written on long narrow strips of papyrus, in parallel columns arranged from left to right. When not being read, the strip was rolled around a central rod and (although its material was thinner and its dimensions generally smaller) looked rather like the "scrolls of the law" kept in Jewish synagogues today. Although brittle, papyrus is quite a good material for books: if it does not get damp, it will remain firm and legible for a long time. The dithyramb of Timotheus can be easily read today although it was written on papyrus three hundred years before the birth of Christ. However, the specially treated leather called parchment (named for Pergamum in western Asia Minor, where it was perfected about 170 B.C.) is far more durable. Since it has a finer, smoother surface than papyrus, it will take smaller and clearer letters. And furthermore, a book with sepa-

In the Middle Ages the tedious work of copying manuscripts was often performed by monks like those at right. Opportunities for error were limitless. One example is underlined in the page above from a codex containing Trimalchio's Dinner by the Roman satirist Petronius. The copyist has written *abbas secreuit,* "the abbot isolated him"; but the phrase in the original was no doubt *ab asse creuit,* which means "he started with a nickel."

If war is the supreme destroyer of books, it also, in another sense, creates them—as happened when the sack of Rome by Alaric and the Goths in A.D. 410 inspired Saint Augustine to write The City of God. *He conceived it as a reply to those who argued that the disaster, which in effect ended classical civilization, was a retribution for abolishing pagan worship. This French miniature was painted exactly a thousand years later and shows Augustine offering his book to the pope even as the Goths are raging through the streets.*

rate pages sewn together at one edge is far easier to use than a long continuous strip which must be laboriously unrolled in order to find and read a single column of writing.

Therefore the Greeks and Romans gradually stopped using papyrus and gave up the roll format. (Actually, *volume*, which comes from the same root as *revolve*, means "a roll." The word for the flat book with pages is *codex*.) This change-over was not at first encouraged by governmental authority and took quite a long time. But the Roman lawyers liked the codex shape because it was so easy to consult. The Christians, too, who wished to read parallel passages in the four different gospel narratives and to compare the prophecies of the Old Testament with their fulfillments in the New, preferred the large book which could be opened out flat; and scribes, both pagan and Christian, found that a parchment page would take graceful script and elaborate decoration far more readily than papyrus. The eminent British papyrologist C. H. Roberts suggests that the change in format was connected with the first written versions of the life of Jesus. Saint Mark, author of the earliest gospel, wrote it in Rome in the handy format of a parchment notebook with pages. This he took to Alexandria, and there (although they continued to use the cheap local material, papyrus) the early Christians grew accustomed to having their sacred writings in the form of a flat-paged book. By A.D. 400 the roll was obsolescent, whether in papyrus or in parchment. Any book that had not been recopied into the new format could survive only by exceptional good luck. And some Greek and Roman classics now lack their beginnings because the outside of the papyrus roll, with the first few columns of writing on it, had perished before it could be transcribed. Others are only part of a once larger set. Aristotle's *Poetics* was a two-volume work, one part dealing with tragedy and the other with comedy; but the second was lost before it reached the codex form and will now never be known—unless through a fortunate find.

All Greek and Roman books were, of course, written by hand. Great changes took place in Greek and Roman script between the fourth and the eighth centuries of the Christian era. In classical times the Greeks wrote most of their important books in what we call capital letters, without much punctuation and often with no spaces between words. (The Romans, after hesitating for some time, followed them.) But, after many experiments both in the Greek world of eastern Europe, Asia Minor, and Egypt, and in the Roman west, a radical change to a script more like our own was carried through: a script in which words are separated from one another and most of the letters are unemphatic, curved, and small (hence called minuscule), while only the emphatic letters beginning sentences, lines of verse, and proper names are capitals, or majuscules.

Then and thereafter all the books written like this, "ARMAVIRVMQVECANOTROIAEQVIPRIMVSABORIS," had to be copied in the new script, with its word divisions and emphatic capitals: "*Arma uirumque cano, Troiae qui primus ab oris. . . .*"* But the work of transcription from one form of writing to another was laborious and difficult. A scribe who was accustomed to reading and writing "*Italiam fato profugus Lauinaque uenit*," sometimes made mistakes in reading and transcribing "ITALIAMFATOPROFVGVSLAVINAQVEVENIT." Therefore when a scholar today sits down to edit a Greek or Roman book, one of his most important jobs is to reconstruct the various phases of copying and recopying through which it has been transmitted and to determine just what types of error were liable to be introduced at each transition. When a sentence in a Greek or Roman author looks doubtful or senseless, one of the first devices that scholars try is to write it out INTHEOLDVNDIVIDEDCAPITALS, and then see whether the misreading of one or two letters, or a failure to separate the words correctly, led to the error.

My favorite mistake of this kind is a matter of word separation. At the vulgar millionaire's dinner party in Petronius's *Satyrica*, the guests are

---

*The Romans had no sound in their language corresponding to our *v*. They used small *u* and capital *V* for both the vowel-sound *oo* (as in *IVSTVS, iustus*) and the consonant *w* (*VIR, uir*).

discussing a friend who has just died. "Ah, he had a good life," they say, "the abbot isolated him, and he died a millionaire." There were no abbots in the days of Petronius, and anyhow the second clause is meaningless. In majuscules the phrase is ABBASSECREVIT. Divide the words differently, drop one superfluous letter, and you get *ab asse creuit*, "he started with a nickel" (see page 297).

These particular ordeals—the transference of books from one type of script to another and from one format to another—were mechanical hazards to the survival of literature. There was another, far more destructive, which depended on the will of men. This was censorship. In pagan Greece we hear very little of censorship: although the emissaries of Antipater brought Demosthenes to his death, they made no effort to destroy his speeches. The emperors of Rome were more touchy. Even the clement Augustus felt himself compelled to exile the orator Cassius Severus and burn his books, which were full of personal attacks on the Roman aristocracy and the imperial court. Labienus's history of the civil war, which treated Julius Caesar as a traitor to the Republic, was destroyed; and, rather than survive his work, the historian killed himself.

The Christians, although considered an antisocial group by the authorities, were at first not known to possess any books worth destroying. But in the last of the pagan persecutions (A.D. 303) Diocletian ordered the Scriptures to be burned. That persecution, however, soon ended; and we know of no Christian books which were irrevocably lost in it.

A generation later the Christians came to power. Soon they were destroying the books of the pagans. Because of this policy, although we possess a good deal of Christian propaganda from the early centuries, no pagan counterpropaganda is preserved intact. The great Neo-Platonic philosopher Porphyry wrote a destructive analysis of the Christian doctrine and the Christian Scriptures in fifteen volumes. It was burned by imperial order, and only a few fragments, quoted by his Christian opponents, now remain.

In the Christian church there was always a sharp division between those who thought all pagan literature vicious and dangerous and would gladly have consigned it to annihilation, and those who believed that some of it was potentially good so that it could, under proper guidance, be used for teaching and study. Christians of the first type were responsible for much wholesale abolition of the Greek and Roman classics. Christians of the second type selected most of the books we now possess, copied them, taught them in schools, and so preserved them for the age of printing.

Of the many thousands of plays enjoyed by Greeks and Romans, all were allowed to rot away except eighty-one: forty-three tragedies (thirty-three Greek and ten Roman) and thirty-eight comedies (eleven Greek and twenty-seven Roman). One more complete Greek comedy and large fragments of others have been found in the last seventy years: these were not, however, transmitted through the ages by copying, but preserved as though in a time capsule. Drama was particularly repellent to the early Christians, for many reasons. They therefore banned plays. The professional theater ceased to exist: for a thousand years men forgot the full power and meaning of drama, and the few plays that were permitted to survive were preserved mainly as models of fine Greek and Latin poetic and conversational style.

The pagan Greeks and Romans had also loved lyric poetry, which embodies or evokes song and the dance. Many of their lyric poems were loving glorifications of carnal experience: an invitation to drink ("the snow is deep outside and life is short") or rapturous desire for a beautiful body ("my eyes dazzle, a delicate flame runs through my limbs"). Others were hymns doing honor to pagan deities. Such poems were particularly hateful to devout Christians, so that the vast majority of them were allowed to perish. In Latin we have four books of songs by Horace and half a book by Catullus. In Greek almost all lyric poetry has vanished (or had vanished until the recent discoveries began): only Pindar survived, and only his Victory Odes. The rest disappeared, and even the Victory Odes came through the Dark Ages in one manuscript alone.

There was one curious way of survival for classical books, although it led through apparent destruction. For the sake of economy, scribes used to scrape or wash off the ink from pages on which a book had already been written and inscribe another book upon the cleaned surface. This could be done with papyrus, but it was both easier and more profitable with the tough surface of parchment. Usually it was a pagan book that was erased, and the Bible or a work of Christian divinity was written on the palimpsest, or cleaned-off, pages. But traces of the old writing would still remain legible underneath.

For instance: one of the best books by Cicero was his dialogue *On the State*, in which he discussed the rival claims of democracy, aristocracy, dictatorship (or monarchy), and a mixed constitution in which the powers should balance one another. He published it in 51 B.C. It was much admired and long read, but during the Dark Ages it vanished. Some medieval writers quote *On the State* as though they had actually handled a copy; but such citations are very shady evidence, for they might be secondhand or thirdhand. The great book hunters of the Renaissance were never able to discover a copy, although it was on their list of the Most Wanted Books.

However, in 1819, Angelo Mai, an expert in discovering old books beneath later books on palimpsest surface, was appointed head of the Vatican library. There he discovered a commentary on the Psalms by Saint Augustine, which had been inscribed in the northern Italian monastery of Bobbio in the uncials of the late seventh century, over a manuscript of Cicero's *On the State* inscribed in the taller capitals of an earlier era (see page 303). Cicero's words could still be read and Father Mai published them in 1822. The book was incomplete, but at least a quarter of it was there. How many forgotten libraries still contain forgotten copies of forgotten works of doctrine, beneath which there sleep great classical masterpieces?

We would know a good deal more about the Mayan culture of Yucatán if Spanish priests and missionaries had not systematically destroyed the Mayan books. Only three—or possibly four—survive. This is a page from one of them, known as the Dresden Codex. It charts with great accuracy the synodical revolutions of Venus.

If you wish information to survive for many centuries, however, cut it on stone or bake it in clay; you can even paint it, if the surface is durable and protected from weather. Do not try casting it in metal, for someone will almost certainly melt it down.

The Emperor Augustus wrote his own autobiography, listing his chief honors, benefactions, and victories. It was deposited at the Home Hearth of Rome, with the Vestal Virgins, and a version in bronze was set upon his mausoleum in Rome. Both the original and the metal transcript have vanished. But a stone-carved copy was found in 1555 on the walls of a mosque in Ankara (see page 306); since then, two more copies, fragmentary but helpful, have turned up in southern Turkey. Only through these bits of stone do we know what one of the greatest rulers in history considered his greatest achievements.

Fifteen hundred years before him the king of a little state in what is now the Turkish frontier province of Hatay, after an adventurous and successful career, composed his own life story. His name was Idri-mi, and he was king of Alalakh in his time. He possessed less taste and less money than Augustus, so he had it carved upon his own statue—not even upon an epigraphic tablet, but over his actual face and his hard-earned regal robes (see page 307). Gazing out from eyes of black inlaid stone, his effigy sat enthroned in a temple for two centuries, speaking his adventures to those who could read. Then, in 1194 B.C., his kingdom was invaded by the northern barbarians called the Peoples of the Sea. His statue was wrenched from its throne and smashed into fragments. But after the invasion had passed over, a loyal courtier of the fallen monarchy crept back and salvaged the statue of the king, and buried it with respect. And there, underground, it was discovered by Leonard Woolley in 1939, and its long-silent boasts were read, and its eyes looked out again on a changed world with the same blank arrogance as before. His name and fame were forgotten: yet the stone that carried his message remained, with an immortality for which he could scarcely have hoped.

Two hundred years after Augustus, another public benefactor, on a smaller scale, went to a stonecutter with a document to be perpetuated. He was an elderly gentleman who lived in the small Greek-speaking city of Oenoanda in Lycia. Now it is a lonely heap of ruins in Turkey; then it was prosperous, civilized, but (the old gentleman thought) not quite happy enough. He was a devoted adherent of Epicurus. Epicureanism had taught him that the gods have no interest in this troublesome little earth; that terrifying phenomena such as illness and earthquakes and comets are all explicable, not through divine malevolence, but through nature; and that the duty of man on this planet is to cultivate his garden, keep quiet, and be happy. Old Diogenes, as he was called, had had a heart attack. He determined to use some of his remaining money and energy in showing his fellow citizens and their descendants the road to happiness. So he had a huge inscription cut and set up in the central square of his little city, explaining the chief tenets of the Epicurean doctrine. Now, all the voluminous works of Epicurus himself have perished; we have nothing from his own hand except three letters and some fragments and apothegms. But the inscription set up by old Diogenes of Oenoanda, rediscovered by explorers and read by scholars in the nineteenth century, is one of the chief witnesses to an important philosophical creed that is not yet dead.

Laws and state announcements were often displayed on stone, for permanence and publicity.

This antique double exposure is a page from one of the most famous of palimpsest ("rescraped") manuscripts. During the Dark Ages it was a common practice to scrape the writing from unread books and use the valuable parchment over again. But the ghost of the old text often lingered beneath the new, waiting to be discovered by the scholars of a later age (nowadays aided by chemicals and infrared photographs). In this case part of a fourth-century manuscript of Cicero's On the State *(double columns) was found to underlie a late seventh-century copy of a work by Saint Augustine. Until the Vatican librarian Angelo Mai recovered it from these pages in 1822, the Cicero was known only in fragmentary form.*

Etenim et haec uox ascendentis est pertinens ad articulum graduum. Uerl
ita q̄ unusquisq̄ uostrum uidere inquoprofundositdequo clametaddn̄m
Clamaui deprofundisadeuertrecte. et a nonsolumsupe lucubus
uerumetaminusceripṡ belace. Nectamen illud corpusetiliplucticus in
tenclaseruntoratione ne peruenireriadaures. disdeceusinonpotuitie
defecuocemd iplaceris. penetrauitoplacis. dipisprosuspendentiad
auresdi. S̄ tamendicendumest quiadirruptisomnibus peruentadauresdi
quandoauresdi incordiprecantiserant. Ubienimdm presentem non
habetcaues. delis est uox. Uerumsalmenenospere emsiriidele
cepeseaprofundoclamemusaddm̄. Profundum enim nobisest
uitaistamortalis. quisquisetinprofundo intellexerit. Clamaiceail
suspiratdonec deprofundoeruatur. et deuiruntiradquisitidoneabis
sistisuper cherubin superomniaquite. creauti nonsolum corpora
liasedetiamspialia. donecadeum ueniatanima donecadillumtime
ueruhaecetusquidesthomo qui ehauhodiesiṗua tamqm
sinquisalerteuseagitaladetinratest et uiuenouetur et reparatur
adoquillamipraessriguando formauithominem. doneuessepotur uho
modoeasuihsuus nonest idoneus adresurrectionensuam. Semper
siperquandogrtisisriurperinuidierseperinprofundoest. Sedcum
deprofundoclamat superideprofundo. et ipsecumonnodetimperail
niolulualinisupesses. Ualdeemimprofundasunt quaecla
materdeproundo. Dicitscriptura. Peccatorcumuenerit inproin
dummalorum contemnit. Iamuidetesr qualeprofundumsi ubiconse
sistindos. Tantus quia euidenti cottidianisperatisbkeprtum aceri
bisquisdam et mol.iibusquisdaminiquitatumpreemuntur. Sidicau
illir ueniterundm̄ roget inrida quib. modissprimodiet. Sidodispli

This stylish battle scene is proof that the lavish picture book is no recent invention, for it comes from what must have been an extremely handsome copy of the Iliad produced—possibly in Constantinople—between the third and fifth centuries A.D. It is the earliest extant example of a Greek illustrated book, and in its original state it probably consisted of some 380 vellum leaves. Of these, only fifty-two separate fragments survive—and they only because a thirteenth-century collector who evidently preferred the pictures to the text cut some of them out and pasted paper over the backs. They came to rest in the Ambrosian library in Milan, where they were bound and catalogued merely as "a book of pictures." In 1819 Father Angelo Mai, the expert who discovered the Cicero palimpsest on page 303, peeled off the paper and recognized the text underneath as part of the Iliad. This plate shows the Greeks and Trojans in battle.

διηπατ.ηπ.η.Θεςαν

ΗΡΟΛΟΦΥΓΑΓΟΔΑΚΗΥΧΕΟΝΤΑ
ΟΝΕΙΜΕΝΑΙΟΥΛΛΠΟΛΕ·ϹΟΛΙ
ΤΕΛΕΙΟΤΑΤΟΝΠΠΕΤΕΗΝϹΩΝ
ΕϹϹΙΤΕΚΟϹΕΛΑΦΟΙΟΤΑΧΕΙΗϹ
ΤΕΠΙΚΑΛΛΕΪΚΑΒΒΑΛΕΝΕΒΡΟΝ
ΖΗΝΙΡΕΖΕϹΚΟΝΑΧΑΙΟΙ
ΤΑΓΕΚΑΙΟϹΗΛΥΘΟΘΝΟΡΝΙϹ
ΙΟΟΤΟΝΜΗΙϹΑΝΤΟΛΕΧΑΤΙ
ΝΑΙΑΟΝΙΙϹΑΛΟΩΝΠΕϹΕΙΝ

Many ancient kings sought immortality by committing their words to stone or metal. The inscription on the man-headed lion at right recounts the victories of the Assyrian king Ashurnasirpal II. The gold plaque below bears identical messages from Darius the Great in three languages (Babylonian, Elamite, and his own Old Persian). At bottom, the achievements of the Roman emperor Augustus are recorded on a stone temple wall in what is now Ankara, Turkey. Enthroned on the opposite page is Idri-mi, the ruler of Alalakh, who in 1400 B.C. assured his place in history by having the story of his life engraved on his own statue.

The earliest Greek legislation in existence is the code of Gortyn: it was incised on the curving stone wall of the odeum and still stands, perfectly legible, among the ruins of that city in central Crete. The names of Roman magistrates, some of them unrecorded in history books, appear on tablets of stone; so do the sums paid by the subject-allies of Athens to her imperial treasury; and so, too, the last effort of Roman bureaucratic government, the gigantic edict of Diocletian fixing the price of virtually every object of commerce throughout the Western world.

Records cut on stone or cast in metal were intended to survive as long as possible. Books passed from hand to hand and constantly recopied were deliberately kept alive. But there is a huge and steadily growing assemblage of documents that were, in the eyes of those who wrote them and used them, quite temporary. Many of them were actually thrown out as rubbish. Yet, by a combination of good luck and crazy chance, they have survived and become valuable. These are things written on ephemeral substances like papyrus and clay. The records found in Mycenaean palaces (first in Crete) and deciphered by Michael Ventris in 1952, were apparently scratched on clay tablets that were not even fired: they became permanent only when the palaces were burned down.

Some papyri have been preserved because they were deliberately buried. One of the oldest Greek literary manuscripts, containing the only known copy of a dithyrambic poem by Timotheus, was rescued in this way. It is an absurdly bad poem (although interesting to literary connoisseurs); however, someone prized it, for it was discovered in a leather pouch, laid carefully in the coffin of a dead Greek soldier buried in Egypt. And a truly magnificent copy of Book II of Homer's *Iliad*, now in the Bodleian library, was set in a coffin as a pillow beneath the head of a young woman, whose fine skull bones, small regular teeth, and black hair make us believe she was a beauty: certainly she was beloved. Other papyri—mainly letters, accounts, and official documents, though including a few treasures of literature—were found glued together or squeezed tight with water, to make cheap mummy cases molded to the shape of the corpse. (Out of one of these cases came part of the lost tragedy *Antiope*, by Euripides.) Even stranger were the finds at Tebtunis, where Bernard P. Grenfell and A. S. Hunt came on a cemetery of sacred crocodiles. One dead sacred crocodile is very like another, and the job of excavating these saurian mummies soon palled. Eventually a workman lost his temper and smashed one of them to pieces. Then it appeared that the crocodiles, too, were encased in molded papyri, and some even had rolls stuffed into their mouths "and other cavities." From such absurd hiding places do we recover the records of the past.

We have as yet no idea of the treasures that are hidden in the dry sands of Egypt and the neighboring countries. The oldest Latin papyrus ever found and the oldest text of Cicero (part of his most famous set of speeches), written down not long after his death, is now in Leipzig: it was bought from Egyptian dealers in the Fayum in 1926—and where did *they* get it? In 1945 a Gnostic library of thirteen volumes was found in Upper Egypt, containing, among other things, a Gospel in Coptic, adapted from a Christian work written in Greek, which evidently preserved some beautiful traditional words of Jesus. And an Oxford expert once told me, with affliction in his eyes, that among a pile of papyrus fragments he was classifying he had found a label bearing, in Greek, the simple words: COMPLETE PINDAR. In vain I besought him to go back to the collection and look through it again. "No," he said gloomily, "it isn't there. It must have been on the site in Egypt. But perhaps the excavator missed it when he was digging, or it had already been found and lost again, or someone stole it and sold it in Alexandria. It may turn up in twenty years. It may turn up tomorrow. It may be lying at the back of a drawer forgotten."

Last, most absurd, and yet most natural of all the hazards through which the classics had to pass was the barrier of human stupidity. When barbarism comes to outweigh culture, through foreign invasion or social revolution or deliberately nurtured sloth and ignorance, works of art are often taken to be "useless" and destroyed. In waves of materialism and in revolutions, everything old is apt to be judged obsolete. It is a barrier to progress; or it is lumber; or it is reactionary; or it is inedible and unspendable—away with it! In 1961 the commissioner of antiquities in modern Greece, Spyridon Marinatos, told a sad story of the Second World War. A farmer in the western Peloponnesus was digging a well. Twenty feet down he came upon a stone box. He smashed in its lid. Inside there was a big object "like a bundle," dark in color and crumbly in texture. He thought he saw letters written on it. He informed the police, who informed the local director of antiquities; but for some time they could not get out to the farm. It was 1944–45, and Communist squads were trying to control the roads. When at last the director was able to reach the farm, the object was gone. The farmer had thrown it on the dunghill "because it was not a treasure: it looked like dung and it fell to pieces quite soon." Others, however, had seen "many letters" on it and said that, although fragile, it held together on the dunghill for some days. Clearly it was a book roll: papyrus, or more probably parchment; clearly it was precious to the man who buried it in a stone casket; certainly it would have been precious to us. But it was of no use to the farmer, and it is gone.

And so it has always been. Boccaccio, who was a great booklover and book finder, once visited the monastery of Monte Cassino. He was particularly eager to see the library, with all its treasures of handwritten books. Very humbly he asked one of the monks for admission to it. "Walk up," said the monk, "it's open." It was. It had no door; grass was growing on the window sills; the shelves, the benches, and the books themselves were shrouded in thick dust. Some of them, he found, had lost pages or even whole quires, others had their margins cut off. Boccaccio wept. He cried tears of pity "that the work and study of so many illustrious geniuses should have fallen into the hands of scoundrels." As he left, he asked a monk how such valuable books could have been so odiously mutilated. "Well," said the monk, "some of the brothers wanted to earn a few pennies: so they took a page and scraped off the writing and made little psalters to sell to children; and from the page margins they made gospels and breviaries and sold them to women."

When a bibliophile sees good books neglected and on the road to destruction, his first impulse is to rescue them. Say not "steal." " 'Convey' the wise it call," as Pistol says in *The Merry Wives*. Some splendid books from Monte Cassino are now in Florence. If it was not Boccaccio who "conveyed" them there, it was an even more fanatical booklover, Niccolò Niccoli; or an agent of his and of the house of Medici. One of these manuscripts alone—bless the hand that saved it—is the only surviving book that contains Tacitus's account of the civil war after Nero's suicide and of the reigns of Claudius and Nero; it also has Apuleius's wonderful romance *The Metamorphoses*, sometimes called *The Golden Ass*. This magnificent codex, written in the eleventh century, now rests peacefully in the Laurentian library, above the cloister of the church of San Lorenzo. Near it is the only surviving manuscript of the first six books of another work by Tacitus, the *Annals*, found in Germany. Had these two manuscripts not been "conveyed," they might well have been cut up into amulets, and we should have lost one of the greatest historians who ever wrote of absolutism and the degeneracy of despotic power.

In 1844 a young Biblical scholar, Konstantin von Tischendorf, visited the remote monastery of Saint Catherine on Mount Sinai. There he found a great old book reduced almost to the same state as those which Boccaccio discovered in Cassino. It was a manuscript of the Bible, written in beautiful clear script between A.D. 330 and 400 and carefully corrected in or near that time. The book is now one of the chief treasures of the British Museum, which bought it from the Soviet government in 1933 for a hundred thousand pounds. But when Tischendorf first saw it, nobody had paid any attention to it for seven hundred years. In the

Some of the books rescued from medieval neglect by Renaissance scholars found their way to the Laurentian library in Florence. There, until recently, they were chained on lecterns; now they are in glass cases.

monastery, the latest intelligent markings on it, comments by readers, had been made in the twelfth century. Since then it had been brutally neglected. Fortunately, Tischendorf scented the value of this heap of waste. He copied out some of it and managed to get the monks to give him forty-three pages, which he took back to Europe and published. Fifteen years later he returned to the monastery, backed by funds from the czar of Russia. This time he obtained the remainder of the poor battered Bible, which he carried away and published. In exchange, the monks received nine thousand Russian rubles. They were disappointed. They said that Tischendorf had promised to get them a steamboat.

Stupidity; censorship; changes in format and changes in taste; war; and of course the inevitable accidents, especially flood and fire—such are the hazards to the frail life of books. How did the great classics, Greek and Roman and Hebrew and others, ever survive them?

Ultimately, they were kept alive by men who loved books and knew that books are an essential element in civilization. The biography of a single book would fill many chapters. The British Museum owns a copy of the Gospels in Latin (opposite page), together with some writings of the early Christian Fathers, that has outlived storm and fire, savagery and greed. A big book, over a foot high, with two hundred fifty-eight stout vellum pages, it was inscribed about A.D. 700 by Bishop Eadfrith in the monastery of Lindisfarne, now Holy Island, off the northern English coast. His successor, Bishop Ethelwald, bound it; and an anchorite living on the island made a jeweled case for it. In A.D. 875 the Danish pagans invaded England. The then bishop of Lindisfarne fled westward, carrying the sacred relics of Saint Cuthbert and this book. In a storm on the Irish Sea it was lost, but it was recovered at low tide as though by a miracle. For seven years it wandered; it survived more moves and invasions, and returned to its home at Lindisfarne, where it was catalogued (the simple boring work of librarians, which they think so unimportant and which is so valuable!). Next it survived the Reformation and the Protestant sack of monasteries, although it lost its jeweled case and its episcopal covers. Then, like many valuables during a revolution, it came into the possession of a government official (Robert Bowyer, Keeper of the Records in the Tower). From him it was acquired by someone who really knew what it meant: a genuine collector, Sir Robert Bruce Cotton. From him, because of a political dispute, it was confiscated by the crown. It is now in the British Museum.

The most moving of all such stories, however, and most encouraging, would be the biography of an ancient book as a work of art and thought. First we should have to describe its author and the contemporary audience whom he meant to read or hear his work. Then, some time later, the Greek or Roman scholars who accepted it as a valuable achievement and edited it (as the work of Joyce and Eliot is being edited today); and then, as the Dark Ages set in, the far-sighted optimists (pagan like Symmachus or Christian like Cassiodorus) who preserved it from obliteration; and, after them, the monks who saved it once again by recopying it, to live on for many centuries; later we should meet the fine-scented book hounds like Petrarch and Boccaccio and Poggio and Aurispa who discovered it when it was forgotten and sometimes copied it out with their own hands; until finally, after more perils than a displaced person and more sufferings than a tormented prisoner, it emerged fifteen hundred or two thousand years or twenty-five hundred years after its birth, to be copied on a miraculous machine and multiplied through the work of scholars and publishers, and—incredibly—to reach an audience who loved it as dearly as those who were present at its distant birth. Even then the life of such a book is not over. It will be read by Shakespeare. It will inspire a picture by Rembrandt, a satirical parody by Pope, and a lyric by Keats. It will be edited by Housman, distorted by Picasso, translated into music by Ravel, and remain inexhaustibly vital, immortally versatile, today and tomorrow and into a long future, as long as there are a few men and women who can read, and understand, and appreciate true greatness.

An eloquent instance of the chances and mischances that surround the survival of precious records is given by the Lindisfarne Gospels (opposite), a book inscribed about A.D. 700 at a monastery on the northeast coast of England, lost at sea, and miraculously recovered. The illuminated manuscript, a rendering of the four Gospels, carries above its Latin lines a translation in the old Northumbrian dialect, making this the earliest "English" version of them in existence. This page opens the Gospel of Saint John, reading (with its first three letters conjoined) IN PRINCIPIO ERAT VERBUM ET VERBUM ERAT APUD D[EU]M ET D[EU]S.

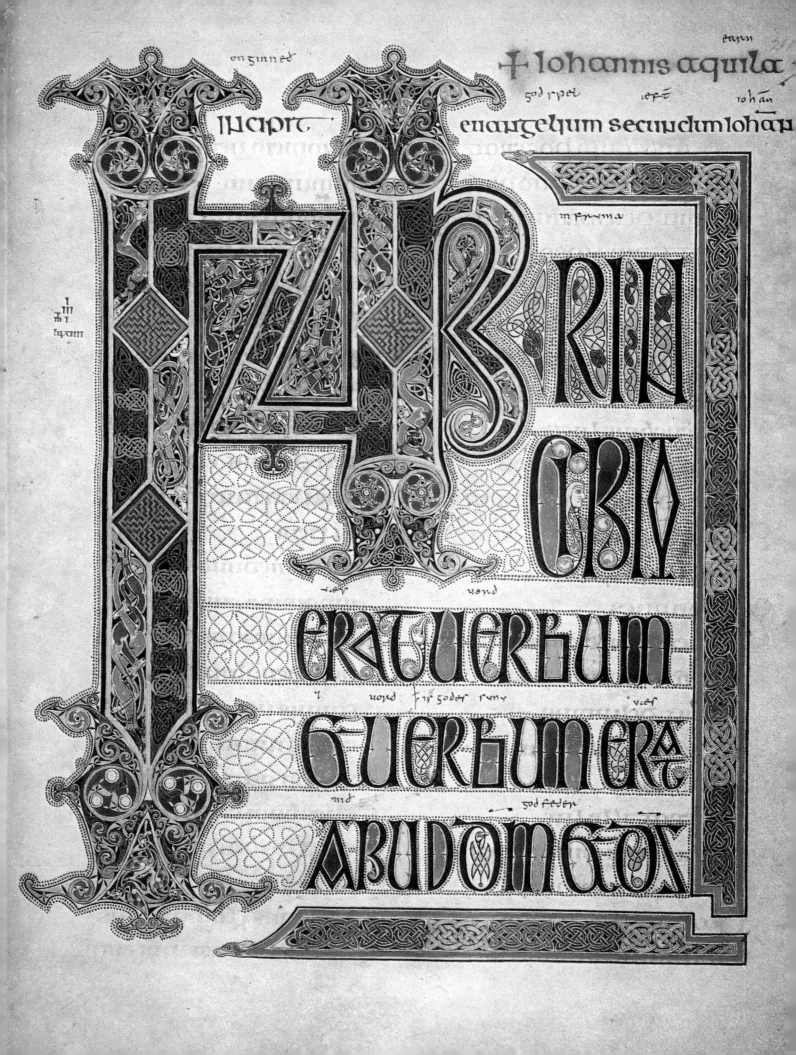

onginneð

Incipit   euangelium secundum iohan

In principa

IN
PRIN
CIPIO
ERATVERBUM
uoeð fir godes sunu   vaes
GVERBUM ERAT
god feðer
ABVDŌMA& DS

A Happy Roman Marriage

As a classical scholar, Gilbert Highet was impressed by the ingenuity with which antiquarians and archaeologists put together bits and pieces of the past to shed light on the life of ancient peoples. In this essay, originally written for his series of radio talks in the 1950's, he tells how the fragments of a Roman inscription were rediscovered and partially reassembled. When the essay was republished in HORIZON, Dr. Highet added his own contribution by suggesting some of the missing words.

The Romans wrote a great deal about passionate love between man and woman, but it was usually illicit or unhappy or stolen love. In all their thousands of verses of love poetry there are very few lines about the love of a wife for her husband or a husband for his wife. Some social historians have concluded, therefore, that there was very little real love between married couples in old Rome. To find a rebuttal you have to go not to poetry but to history, to memoirs, to biography, and even to inscriptions carved on stone.

One of the most moving of those old Roman inscriptions was put up by a husband as a memorial to his dead wife, three or four years before the birth of Jesus of Nazareth. It tells almost the entire story of their lives together—an unusually exciting story involving exile, murder, and other adventures, once at least approaching divorce, and ending, if not in happiness (because of the bereavement of one partner), at least in peace.

The adventures of the inscription itself are almost as strange as those of the couple whom it commemorates. It was put up some time between 8 B.C. and 2 B.C.; there is no date, but we can judge by the content and by the style of the letters. It was carved in fine big letters on two marble slabs about seven feet high. It had a title running along the top, in very large capitals; when new, the whole thing must have looked like two gigantic pages from a marble book. Perhaps it was attached to the front of the dead woman's tomb. Where the tomb was, no one now can tell. Doubtless it was beside one of the highroads that ran out of the city of Rome; as you walk or drive along the Appian Way today, you still see many relics of such buildings, the final homes of the Roman dead.

As Roman civilization began to decline into the Dark Ages of ignorance and barbarism, the Italians and their half-savage invaders began to break up and pillage earlier sanctuaries. The marble slabs carrying this inscription were torn off the tomb and sawn into a dozen pieces or more. Seven of these pieces survived for many centuries, and four of them are still in Rome. The two largest sections were cut down by a few inches and made into part of a coffin for one of the early Christians. In modern times, they were discovered in the catacombs; and they are now in the Villa Torlonia, where it is almost impossible to see them. Another part was carried off into a saloon and used as a gambling table; so we can tell from the lines that have been scratched on its back. This piece was found a few miles outside the city by workmen who were digging the passageway for a new sewer; it is now in the museum that was constructed out of the baths of the emperor Diocletian.

One smaller piece was built into the wall of a Cistercian abbey in Rome; there it was seen and copied several times by antiquarians during and after the Renaissance. A good thing, too, for now the abbey is gone, the wall is gone, and the inscription is gone; the copies remain, in the Vatican library. Two other pieces also survive only in copies made by equally devoted scholars. The last piece of all was discovered by Professor Arthur E. Gordon of the University of California (Berkeley campus). He has an exceptionally good memory and a fine eye for Roman lettering. He and his wife were going through a Roman museum, looking at inscriptions that no one had yet managed to place (it was the big collection in the Baths of Diocletian), when he spotted a fragment which had some words that seemed unusual to him: not the regular list of official dignities, but far more personal phrasing with touches of genuine emotion. Also, the style of the carving belonged to the "best period." So he copied it down, and when he put the words in it together with the words remaining on other fragments and copies, the sense was almost perfect.

With the existing fragments and the copies of others, we have rather more than two thirds of the original inscription, including many of the most interesting and moving passages. What we do not have, strangely enough, is the name of the man who put it up and that of his wife. On the face of one fragment (the piece with the gambling table scratches on it) there is carved, in extra large letters, *XORIS*—which, if we add the initial V, means "of my wife"; but that is all.

The inscription is in the form of a speech—a farewell speech addressed by the husband to his wife just after her death. He retells the whole story of their mutual trust and co-operation. They became engaged and were married in times as troublous as any that we have so far lived through; in fact, more grievous, inasmuch as civil war with its treachery and unnatural hate is worse than any foreign war. They were threatened before their marriage with separation and impoverishment; after it, with the banishment or death of the husband. The girl was born about 70 B.C., the man perhaps in 75. They became engaged about the year 51 or 50.

In those years Julius Caesar was just finishing the conquest of Gaul, which he had undertaken partly in order to extend the Roman Empire, but more emphatically to enrich himself and his unscrupulous supporters and to train a private army utterly loyal to himself personally, which he could use to dominate— and if necessary to invade and

This is a copy of one fragment of the inscription discussed by the author. Below, to the right of the center space, is a translation of the Latin; on the left, in italic, Dr. Highet suggests what the missing parts of each line may have been.

> XORIS
> DIA·FVGAE·MEAE·PRAESTITISTI· ORNAMENTIS
> VM·OMNE·AVRVM·MARGARITAQVE·CORPORI
> DISTI·MIHI·ET·SVBINDE·FAMILIA·NVMMIS·FRVCTIBVS
> DVERSARIORVM·CVSTODIBVS·APSENTIAM·MEAM·LOCVPLETASTI
> ITIS·QVOD·VT·CONARERE·VIRTVS·TVA·TE·HORTABATVR
> VNIBAT·CLEMENTIA·EORVM·CONTRA·QVOS·EA·PARABAS
> OX·TVA·EST·FIRMITATE·ANIMI·EMISSA
> TIS·HOMINIBVS·A·MILONE·QVOIVS·DOMVS·EMPTIONE
> EXVL·BELLI·CIVILIS· OCCASIONIBVS· INRVPTVRVM
> NDISTI·DOMVM·NOSTRAM

IN PRAISE OF MY W IFE
You provided me most generously with re sources in my exile; your jewels
you sacrificed on my behalf; you took off all your golden and pearl ornaments
and sent them to me; and constantly, with servants, cash, and produce,
skillfully evading the spies set by my enemies, you enriched my absence.
In my peril you saved my life, an endeavor in which your virtue encouraged you.
Your loyalty pro tected me by appealing to the mercy of those whom you opposed;
nevertheless your v oice was always uttered with resolution of spirit.
When a gang of desperadoes was col lected by Milo (whose house, through purchase,
I had acquired during his exile), and in the disorders of civil war tried to break in
and loot, you successfully repelled them and defe nded our home.

Tombs along the Appian Way

conquer—his native country, the hitherto free Republic of Rome. Caesar kept making demands that his opponents found impossible, because they would, if granted, have built him swiftly into an irresistible dictator. The demands were refused; they were renewed with greater vehemence; the people of Rome began to split into passionate supporters and passionate opponents of Caesar, and a civil war was evidently ready to break out.

In the first months of 49 B.C., civil war did break out. Julius invaded Italy at the head of his army. There was no force in the country capable of opposing him; so his opponents left to raise other armies in the provinces. With them went the young fiancé, to fight with the supporters of the Republic. He left the girl living quietly in the country with her parents. Their house was attacked, and both her father and mother were murdered. We are not told by whom—the inscription says simply "by a gang of criminals"—but obviously the murder must have taken place during the early disorders of Caesar's invasion, when govern-

mental authority had, for the time being, broken down. How the girl escaped we cannot tell; but she did escape, and what she did thereafter was noteworthy. As soon as order was restored, she set up an investigation of the murder of her parents; she found witnesses and collected evidence and instigated a prosecution of the criminals, and (says the inscription) she "took full vengeance on the guilty." The man who later became her husband adds that while the case was proceeding she could not live alone in the home of her dead parents because her life was not safe; she went to the house of her married sister, who had slaves and freedmen to protect her. She was a courageous and strong-willed young woman.

After this, she moved in with her fiancé's mother to wait for the outcome of the civil war. Two more dangers now appeared.

The first was that several years earlier her fiancé had bought a house from the estate of an extremist politician, Milo, who had been convicted of murder and had his goods confiscated and sold by auction

when he went into exile. Now, in the disorder of the civil war, Milo returned to Italy; a gang of his armed supporters tried to break in, take over the house, and drive the women out onto the road. The girl enlisted her servants and, perhaps with help from the neighbors, drove off the gang in complete defeat.

The second danger was that her fiancé chose the losing side in the war. He was against Julius Caesar; and Julius—although he was never so brutal as Hitler or Stalin—issued an order prohibiting his opponents (for a time at least) from returning to Italy. During the time of this order, the young man was in effect an outlaw and of course had no money. The girl sold all her jewelry, turned it into cash, and sent him the proceeds for his support. Even that had to be done through clandestine routes. There always has been an underground working against totalitarian governments, and there always will be.

Now there was a pause, while Caesar consolidated his victory. At this moment, the girl was involved in a further problem. It was a lawsuit so complicated that modern experts in Roman law can scarcely understand it. In outline, the case turned on the fact that Roman women were not considered capable of managing their own affairs. A girl who had any male blood relatives living was assumed to be the ward of the nearest of them. If she had no close male relatives, she was treated as the ward of any distant relative of the same name. For instance, if a girl called Arria were left an orphan with no uncles or cousins, anyone called Arrius could come in and take over her property and administer it for her, provided he was a distant member of the same family or clan.

This girl had been through several trials already. She faced the new one with confidence. Her murdered father had left all his property to her, to her fiancé, to her sister, and to her sister's husband. Some men bearing the name of the family now turned up and claimed that her father's will was invalid because he had made a second marriage after signing it; therefore he had died intestate; therefore the girl held all his property; and since they were members of the same family or clan, they could take it over. The girl went to court. She proved that the people who claimed to be her guardians because they bore the same name as she did, were in fact not related to her at all. She won the case.

By the time this crisis was over, Julius Caesar had conquered the forces of the Republic and had virtually become monarch of Rome. In the short interval of peace, he allowed his opponents to return home. Our young friend came back with the rest, married his girl, and settled down. But quite soon Julius was killed by lovers of the Republic and of liberty. Another civil war broke out. The husband joined the army of Brutus and Cassius; with

them he was beaten; with their supporters he was outlawed and condemned to death without trial.

By now, we know the character of the woman who was his wife. She at once set out to have her husband's sentence annulled. The empire at this time was being run by three men: Mark Antony, who was out in the East; a stupid, selfish little fellow called Lepidus, who held Italy for the moment; and Octavian, who was to become the emperor Augustus. The young wife sent her brother-in-law to intercede with Octavian for her husband's life, while she herself appealed to Lepidus. So low had the Romans sunk then that she had to lie prostrate, begging for mercy; and so harsh had the heirs of Caesar become that she was brutally pulled away, kicked, and bruised. But her brother-in-law was more successful; he got a free pardon from Octavian (who was technically equal to Lepidus but, in prestige, and therefore in fact, stronger), so that the husband was saved and could return to Italy as a free citizen or (if he had been hiding) emerge into the free air. At this point in the inscription there is a little note that reminds us of the young woman's behavior after the murder of her parents. "Through your patient endurance, the man responsible for my danger was detected and revealed; and therefore your determination proved to be his undoing."

There the story ends—or almost. The husband had been through two civil wars. Now, when he was about 33 and she about 28, they settled down like hundreds of thousands of other ordinary people, to accept the rule of Octavian and to enjoy the peace he spread over the Western world.

One more problem confronted them. This was a family problem: they were unable to have children.

(It looks as though she had suffered a miscarriage, for in the inscription he says, "We prayed for children, and our hopes expected them, but fortune turned away and ended our hopes.") She now offered to give him a divorce, so that he ocould marry a young and fertile wife; she promised that she would not only share her property with the new family (the pair had always held their property in common), but treat the children of the new marriage as though they had been her own. At this point we can almost hear the husband's voice from the stone slab. "I must confess," he cries, "that I was so distressed by your proposal that I almost lost my mind. To think that you could plan to leave me, when you, at a time when I myself was almost banished from life, remained wholeheartedly faithful!"

So the proposal was dropped, and the couple remained together, childless and aging, until the last. After forty-one years of marriage he buried her. Almost the final words on the inscription are these: "I know that you deserved everything, and yet I did not manage to give you all you deserved." He is not very eloquent, but his simple frankness is more convincing than richer periods and more complex paragraphs. We do not know his name, or hers; we do not know if any portrait of them is extant—although they may well be looking at us from one of those Roman funeral monuments which show a husband and wife, sober and thoughtful, gazing out as though from a window at the passer-by. What we do know of them is the essential: that they risked their lives and fortunes for each other; that they lived together for over forty years; and that neither found those forty years long enough to express and enjoy their love. In such men and women was the true strength of ancient Rome.

—Gilbert Highet

12: From the Tombs of China

by EDWARD H. SCHAFER

The land of China has only recently begun to yield its buried treasures. This ceramic horse, twenty-seven inches high, dates from the T'ang dynasty.

One of the most dramatic archaeological events of modern times in China was the emergence from the loam of Shensi Province, in 1974, of a host of archaic warriors, fashioned in terra cotta. This ghostly phalanx—horse, foot, and chariots—was uncovered near a great hill, the eroded remnant of the massive tumulus of a mighty autocrat of antiquity. The disinterred battalions formed part of a vast ceramic army whose duty it was to protect the eternal home of the deceased sovereign from demoniac and human intruders alike. Another great segment of this buried host was uncovered during 1976 and 1977. These handsome painted figures, mustachioed and clad in carefully reproduced plate armor, were accompanied by valuable manufactured goods: silk and linen cloth, objects of jade, bronze weapons, and the like.

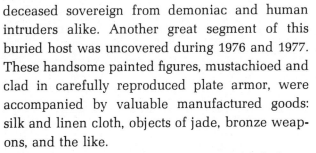

An "oracle bone" was inscribed with questions asked of the spirits. Answers were interpreted from cracks made by a hot rod.

The all-powerful monarch whose burial chamber is hidden somewhere deep under this great barrow is remembered chiefly for having fashioned a monolithic kingdom out of the chaos of contending feudal states, interlocking like the pieces of a jigsaw puzzle, which had for centuries possessed the land that is now north and central China. The buried unifier had once been the lord of the western state of Ch'in. When he had succeeded in the annexation of the lands of his rival barons, he gave the name of his own fief to the great new kingdom. The name Ch'in, it is confidently believed, survives down to our own times in the form China. The conqueror himself, dissatisfied with any such puny title as King, created for himself the magniloquent and indeed blasphemous title of Shih Huang Ti, "First of the Resplendent Thearchs," imagining that his divine line would rule forever. Today we are usually satisfied to call him merely the First Emperor.

For his holy capital Ying Cheng—such was the great man's personal name—constructed a vast city on the north banks of the Wei River. Its design was based on a cosmic model, with the palace representing the universal pole, oriented with respect to the river in the same way that the steadfast polestar—the hub and knot of the world—is placed with respect to the great Sky River, which we Westerners style the Milky Way. The name of the city was, in modern pronunciation, Hsien-yang, but its older form outlived the Ch'in "empire" for many centuries: the peoples of medieval central Asia called the Chinese capital Khumdan or Khubdan long after the thearch's sacred city had disintegrated and merged with the yellow earth of China.

Soon after his accession the divine king began the construction of his mausoleum in the fields near another sacred place. This was Mount Li, from whose bowels gushed healing hot springs, the domain of a lovely nymph said in one tradition to have been an avatar of one of the sovereign's own ancestresses, and in another, his divine mistress. Possibly she was both. In due course, after fantastic searches for supernatural aid in prolonging his life, Ying Cheng was borne away to eternal repose in the second of his microcosms, which he had himself designed. It was a subterranean version of his sacred palace, and therefore also of the universe. This was in 210 B.C. Not many years later a great Chinese historian set down a description of the burial chamber and its contents:

Singular utensils and rare and fantastic objects were transferred to be stored there, until it [the grave] was filled. He ordered artisans to make automatic crossbows with arrows, so that should anyone penetrate to a near point, these would shoot at him. He used quicksilver to make the Hundred Rivers, and the Kiang [River] and the Ho [River], and the Great Seas, and mechanisms to transport it so that it poured from one into the other. Above he had the celestial configurations set out, and below the design of the earth was fully displayed. He used the fat of were-fish [seals?] to make candles that would not be extinguished before the passage of a long period. Now [his successor, the thearch of] the Second Generation said, "It is not fitting that any in the Rear Palace [the seraglio] who failed to bear children should go forth again." And he ordered that all follow him in death, and those that died were a great multitude. When the sarcophagus had been deposited someone said that the workmen and artisans who had made the machinery and done the storage, all being informed about this, would quickly let the significance of the hoard leak out. So once the great affair was over and all was stored away, they had the central adit sealed off, and let down the gate of the outer adit, sealing in all of the workmen and artisans who had done the storage, so that not one could get out again. They planted trees and plants to give it [the tumulus] the semblance of a mountain.

Despite the uncovering of the spectacular armies of baked clay that protect the flanks of the burial mound, no one can yet be certain whether the contents of the tomb itself will finally be found unlooted and intact. As for the unfortunate builders and laborers, as well as the minor queens who had not had the good luck to bear royal princes, their bones may well be exhumed, like the bones of many hundreds of their predecessors who were sacrificed as ritual offerings and spirit-companions to so many kings of ancient China. This practice had persisted since Neolithic times but was already dying out in the third century B.C. Indeed, the historian's notion that the human sacrifices to the thearch's ghost were a due punishment for barrenness, or were necessary to protect the secrets of the construction and contents of the inner tomb, may be only a latter-day rationalization of killings whose ritual and magical purposes were no longer understood in the second century B.C. Or it may have been purposeful libeling of the great unifier, whose name was naturally abhorred by the dynasty which overthrew his only three years after his death.

The dramatic discovery of the wonders concealed in the earth around the magic mountain of Ch'in is, considered unsentimentally, only a single episode in the world-wide and ages-long exploration of richly furnished tombs, whether for the acquisition of wealth, as with professional tomb robbers, or of power, as was the case with any number of wizards and medicine men in all parts of the world, or of information to be exploited by professors or politicians, or of trophies for collectors of antiquities, as is usually the case nowadays. The Chinese, both early and late, have been no different. The looting of tombs, especially those of the high-placed and wealthy, was a commonplace occurrence from the earliest times in China, and has been much remarked on in Chinese literature. Most often this was done for material gain. But other aims were important too. In early times concoctions made by boiling the mats and pillows taken from the coffins of the dead were regarded as sovereign remedies for a variety of diseases caused by noxious effluvia and demoniac afflictions, just as *mummy*, a gum or liquid made from Egyptian mummies, was a powerful and expensive drug in medieval Europe. The bones of dead men, powdered and taken in good Chinese wine, were prescribed for a number of unpleasant ailments. These were only a few of the bewildering variety of profitable uses to which the contents of tombs might be placed.

But then as now the purposes of archaeology were as often public as they were private. Even before the beginning of the Christian era, court ritualists were much concerned to discover archaic bronze vessels and to be able to identify their sources, forms, and purposes with accuracy, in order to guarantee the orthodoxy and efficacy of the ceremonies of the state religion, continuity with the glorious past, and dynastic legitimacy. These cosmic considerations underlay in large degree the well-known interest of the Chinese in tradition and history, which led to their placing great value on such studies as philology, etymology, and archaeology, on books about personages and events of the past, as well as on the study of old names, old customs and fashions, and even old fauna and flora.

This preoccupation with antiquity had many impressive effects on the flowering of Chinese

civilization, just as the obsessive curiosity about classical antiquity led to the flowering of the European Renaissance. Taste in the arts and crafts was modulated by the admiration of such artifacts as old ink slabs. Old bricks and coins had medicinal applications but were also models of form. Ancient utensils and weapons provided tested classical archetypes and were also infused with mana, providing power and authority to their owners. Mementos of heroes and ancient kings were at the same time touchstones of fine workmanship. Indeed, by medieval times there were extensive and well-catalogued library resources for antiquarian studies. The accumulation of such precious objects as ancient swords and ritual caldrons was not easy, since severe penalties were imposed on grave robbers, but the trade flourished despite the taboo.

Moreover, the desolate sites of ancient palaces and other such romantic ruins not only provoked edifying thoughts about golden ages and the transience of glory, and inspired a great deal of sentimental poetry, but occasionally led rulers to undertake the reconstruction of the mighty mansions of their predecessors. When the ancient Wei-yang Palace of the Han emperors was partially rebuilt on its foundations in the T'ang hunting park in Ch'ang-an early in the ninth century, the chief motive again was the support of royal legitimacy and continuity. Public monuments bearing inscriptions were a source of inspiration for noble conduct, recording as they did the deeds of great men and the administrations of the past in the form of eulogies, panegyrics, law codes, or maxims; and, above all, they preserved the authentic texts of the classical books, engraved in eternal stone.

In all this devotion to the relics of the past there seems to have been little exploitation of them for determining the truth about the past. To put it differently, archaeology was hardly regarded as a means to test the reliability of written records. Some scholars now believe that by Sung times—that is, the eleventh and twelfth centuries of our era—Chinese archaeology had already developed

Ch'in Shih Huang Ti, known as the First Emperor, was buried in a tomb designed to represent the universe. On the opposite page an archaeologist measures one of the six thousand terra-cotta figures that were buried nearby to guard him through eternity.

beyond the "cabinet of curiosities" stage to a truly scientific concern for accurate dating and historical interpretation. But the Sung connoisseurs had other motivations: one was the xenophobic desire to combat the pernicious effects of foreign culture—especially those of the Buddhist religion. They hoped to purify Chinese life and thought and restore the true classical tradition. This great concern for the study of ancient artifacts died out after Sung times, however, and remained in abeyance until revived by foreigners in the twentieth century.

At the end of the nineteenth century the great nations of Europe, with vast colonies and spheres of influence established in Africa and Asia, were looking for opportunities to demonstrate the purity of their motives by rescuing—as they supposed—great works of art and technology from decadent and backward governments. As Napoleon and

Champollion had done in Egypt, so others could do in central and eastern Asia. There was one important difference. A certain glamour—of enormous publicity value—was missing from the sites of past civilizations in the Far East. In Egypt, in Troy, in the great cities of the Hellenistic and Roman empires, there were impressive ruins: colonnades, vaults, paved roads, and whole clusters of buildings, built out of enduring marble or sandstone or granite. Often the astonishing or beautiful figures of gods and heroes of the past, made of equally enduring materials, were brought to light. The same exciting opportunities prevailed in the Mexican and Mayan lands of the New World, where impressive stone monuments were visible every-

where. In China the case was very different. With the important exception of a few surviving Buddhist pagodas of the medieval period, constructed of stone ashlar or brick, and an occasional small funerary chapel, stone architecture was conspicuous by its absence. The traditional material of Chinese architecture was wood, easily subject to the ravages of fire, war, rot, insects—and simply time. In consequence, our knowledge of the buildings of early China comes chiefly from secondary sources, such as early written descriptions, representations in mural paintings in tombs, and pious Japanese wooden imitations—such as those at Nara—which have been carefully repaired and reconstructed, every post and rafter replaced by an

exact facsimile when needful through the ages.

Accordingly the best hope for the European archaeologist exploring East Asia was to uncover some normally corruptible artifact, whether of wood, cloth, leather, or paper, happily preserved in the arid reaches that stretch from the Pamir Mountains on the west to the Gobi Desert in the east. Whereas the violation of tombs within the boundaries of China could hardly be tolerated by its Manchu rulers, the explorer could reasonably hope to find traces of Chinese cultural influences under the indifferent but protective sands of central Asia, which had more than once been part of a Chinese empire but were now deserted, forgotten, and unsupervised.

The great modern pathfinder for these desolate regions was Sven Hedin, the indefatigable Swede who explored them thoroughly between 1893 and 1898, and then continued eastward through the wastes of the Gobi into north China between 1899 and 1902. He was the first to cross the Trans-Himalaya Range into Tibet and to prepare reliable maps of that mysterious land.

Close on Hedin's heels came another great discoverer—not so much a trailblazer as the first of the true archaeologists to work systematically in this region. This was Aurel Stein—or, to give him his full name, Sir Mark Aurel Stein—a Hungarian educated in archaeology and Oriental languages who spent his mature professional career working

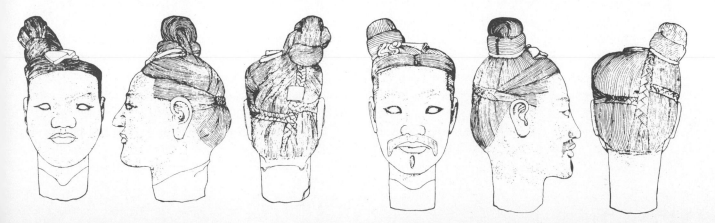

for the British in India and central Asia. It was a career studded with triumphs. His first expedition, in 1900–1901, was an exploratory survey of the region variously styled Chinese Central Asia, the Tarim Basin, Sinkiang, and most recently, the Sinkiang Uighur Autonomous Region. Probably its most apt and elegant name is the one that Stein himself gave it—Serindia, signifying that it was a place where the cultures of China (the Greco-Roman *Seres*) and India were fused. He and his patchwork crew of diggers of every race and tongue brought back a quantity of interesting manuscripts and artifacts from the buried oasis cities of the central Asian deserts. Stein's idols and precursors were the Chinese Buddhist pilgrim Hsüan-tsang (popularized in *The Tale of the Monkey*) and the confident Venetian merchant Marco Polo. Following in their footsteps on his second expedition of 1906–8, he and his tattered helpers pushed farther east through Serindia toward the remnants of the frontier defenses built against the nomads by the early Han sovereigns. Finally, in March of 1907, they reached the still inhabited but much shrunken oasis settlement of Tun-huang on the northwestern frontier of China. This ancient town had been a proud place for centuries. Its location in a broad wash of the Tang River surrounded by empty desert had made it a military and commercial hub from the beginning of Chinese history. Since the fourth century it had been a center of Buddhist influence.

That religion had been transmitted from the northwest frontier of India into Serindia and finally to the Far East, to bring century after century an everchanging mixed bag of Indo-Hellenic and Indo-Iranian cultural influences to the remote but culturally greedy cul-de-sac of China. As an important military outpost Tun-huang was held at times by Chinese garrisons against the Turks and Tibetans, at other times by the Tibetans or Turks against the Chinese. Always it was a great caravansary where travelers and merchants of every complexion exchanged tales, both fantastic and factual, of equal value to spies and to poets.

This bustling, polyglot outpost was close to the customs station long known as Jade Gate, at the Chinese terminus of the Silk Road. It got its name from the nephrite of Khotan, which had passed this way to the lapidaries of China since antiquity, as had also other precious stones, rare spices and drugs, and domestic slaves.

What Stein saw first was a canyon whose steep sides were honeycombed with caverns and grottoes, representing a thriving monastic community of medieval Buddhists (see page 326). These were known formerly as the Mo-kao Caverns but in popular parlance, even today, as the Caves of the Thousand Buddhas, after the painted and modeled images that inhabit them so plentifully. To the people for whom they were designed the paintings communicated a religious message—the truths of the Buddhist faith especially as illustrated in events in the lives of the Buddha. They are didactic, devotional, and moral. For us their value lies in the way that they illustrate medieval life in China and Serindia, since, like medieval Christian paintings, they depict the costumes and customs of contemporaries rather than the classical cultures they purport to illustrate. Today we may rejoice in unique representations of ladies' gowns and make-up, of carpenters mending roofs, men plowing with oxen, orchestras composed of flutists, harpists, and drummers, and indeed the whole gamut of medieval life in China. Here too are scenes of hosts of divine beings in hieratic postures and angelic creatures in wispy garments descending through many-colored clouds to astonish the inhabitants of our lower world.

But important as these representations are for our understanding of the complex history of art in Asia and as visions of daily life in bygone centuries, they are by no means the most significant of the revelations made by Stein at Tun-huang. The geographer found a shy Taoist priest named Wang acting as self-appointed custodian of a great archive of medieval manuscripts, most of them in the form of scrolls. All proved to date from before the beginning of the eleventh century, when the hoard had been walled up, and most of them from the T'ang dynasty. By cautious persuasion, drawing heavily on Wang's pious devotion to the memory of the great Buddhist traveler Hsüan-tsang, along with the gift of a sum of money in support of the shrine, Stein was finally permitted to make a selection of the scrolls, both written texts and painted devotional banners and embroideries. A total of twenty-four cases of manuscripts and five of paintings came to the British Museum.

The unique corpus of manuscript materials that Stein brought to light transformed the complex field of Far Eastern scholarship. It is unique because despite the enormous volume of extant Chinese literature, said to have bulked more than the collected literatures of all the remaining countries of the world at the beginning of this century, this vast heritage existed almost entirely in the form of printed books whose manuscript originals had long been lost. Now for the first time scholars had a large body of handwritten contemporary documents to work with. Most prominent among them are Buddhist materials, especially sutras copied over and over again to gain merit in the next world for the sponsors of the reproductions. But there are also unique Taoist texts; precious versions of the philosophers (e.g., the book of Lao-tzu); historical and geographical records of every sort; books of divination, astrology, and the art of physiognomizing; novels and legendary records; and music—especially tablatures for performers on the lute—with indications of choreography. The Buddhist texts are often of particular interest, being provided with exact dates and accompanied by little homely notations by the scribe that tell us much about everyday life in medieval China, the sort of things that classical Chinese literature seldom provides. Here is a typical one:

The disciple Shao-chin, Vinaya teacher of the Buddhist Church, having come to feel yearly decay and monthly distress, has sought to acquire a small stock of merit for the satisfaction of his enemies and creditors, so that being reborn as men or devas, they may receive and partake thereof, and not assume a revengeful attitude.

The austere conditions that sometimes obtained in this remote outpost of civilization are revealed in such notations as the following, written by a priest:

Copying completed . . . by the bhiksu Shen-tsung of the Southern Shrine of I-wa [Hami], a clumsy man with a pen. It is hard to obtain paper and ink.

Concern was not always reserved to human beings, especially since animals were endowed with the souls of dead humans, which might in future, if properly attended to, rise once more to the higher levels of life:

Humbly on behalf of my old plowing ox, that its soul may be reborn in the Pure Land. . . .

Among solemn academic books on medicine and magic we find such pleasant things as prescriptions for "incense for fumigating garments," "face cosmetic," and "cure for falling hair."

Moreover, quite beyond the information inscribed on these wonderful documents, we have learned much, and have yet to learn more, directly from the silks and papers that transmit this information—details about technological advances and aesthetic triumphs in medieval China. As is well known, paper was invented in China before the beginning of the Christian era and did not find its way to Europe to replace papyrus and parchment for many centuries. The earliest papers at Tun-huang are from the fifth century, but the best are somewhat later. We have beautiful golden-yellow paper from the sixth century. Yellow was considered especially appropriate for governmental communications on a high level. The Tun-huang climate has preserved a variety of other colored papers, all attractive and interesting in their own right—slate-blue, greenish-buff, pink, and so on. Moreover, the documents are inscribed with many different scripts, exotic alphabets, and syllabaries, some executed in highly specialized and individual styles.

Most startling of all to the first students of this hoard was the discovery of a printed book—the first of its kind then known. This is a xylographic version of a popular Buddhist scripture, the Diamond Sutra. It bears the Chinese date equivalent to 11 May 868. We know from Chinese history

The grottoes at Tun-huang, filled with religious images, have long been known as the Caves of the Thousand Buddhas.

At Tun-huang in 1907 Aurel Stein made these pictures of the two Chinese on whom the success of his expedition greatly depended: Wang Tao-shih (left), the jealous guardian of the Buddhist manuscript trove, and Chiang-ssŭ-yeh (right), Stein's interpreter, who helped persuade Wang to open up his hoard. Piled up below are a few of the precious scrolls, unread since the tenth century, which Stein sent back to the British Museum.

books that printing flourished after the ninth century, although it remained unknown in the Western world for many centuries more. Still another invention was revealed by the Tun-huang repository—folded books. Since the earliest times, books had been written on scrolls of silk, or on sheets of paper glued end to end as a cheap substitute. From Tun-huang we have tenth-century examples of the folded and stitched book—essentially a scroll folded accordion fashion and stitched along the edge, with great gains in compact convenience. The majority of books printed in China before Western styles were adopted there in the twentieth century were of this type. We also find examples at Tun-huang of a style that did not catch on in China as it did in the West: instead of using folded sheets as double pages, blank on the inner sides concealed by the stitching, the unstitched edges were cut free to make it possible to write on both sides. This style of book, so commonplace for us, was considered an ugly device justified only by a shortage of paper.

Despite the scintillating effects of the Tun-huang discoveries, this was by no means the last of Aurel Stein's important expeditions—incredibly long treks in weather that froze the ink in his pen. The period 1913–14 found him intensively engaged once more in Serindia, studying the faded traces of the Han frontier defenses, excavating the vanished settlements where the medieval Chinese had administered their central Asian empire. Around Turfan he found significant new evidence of Hellenistic and Iranian influences on Chinese art, especially on figured textiles, along with such exotica as petrified pastries, ladies' toilet articles, Sassanian silver coins, bits of stucco statuary, manuscripts on northern birch bark and southern palm leaves, and other such fascinating rubbish from heaps still malodorous after the passage of centuries. There were also documents in Chinese illuminating the details of the economic administration of the area, including the maintenance of pastures for war horses and other such practical matters.

Sir Mark Aurel Stein was the first of the great archaeologists who explored the remote lands of central Asia. His legendary expeditions, between 1900 and 1916, were carried out in blazing summer heat and in winter cold that froze the ink in his pen. His reward, befitting the model of a British adventurer, was to appear at Government House in Kashmir in 1912 to be made a knight commander of the Indian Empire by order of King George V.

Stein was the most renowned of the foreign archaeologists and sinologists who aroused the world's interest in ancient China. His achievements were matched in the same period by those of two brilliant Frenchmen, Edouard Chavannes and Paul Pelliot, who brought the highest standard of scholarship to the study of ancient Chinese manuscripts and artifacts. Among the Chinese themselves archaeological studies—leaving aside more or less casual antiquarianism—had been in the doldrums since the Sung period. But a renaissance was already under way. Near the end of the nineteenth century farmers working near the town of An-yang in Honan Province found fragments of old bones marked with peculiar glyphs (see page 318). These were indecipherable and might be regarded as having a supernatural origin. They were sold to druggists as dragon bones, notorious cure-alls. In 1899 the markings were identified as a kind of ancient script. But scientific excavation of the site, which was acknowledged to be that of one of the capitals of the Shang dynasty, a great Bronze Age civilization of the second millennium B.C., did not begin until 1928, when it was launched under the auspices of the Academia Sinica, with Li Chi in charge. Work continued systematically until it had to be suspended in 1937 because of the Japanese invasion. The digs, mostly in the vicinity of the village of Hsiao-t'un, yielded not only increasing numbers of inscribed bones and shells but also the foundations of ancient buildings, tombs, artifacts of stone and jade, ceramics, various bronze objects (ritual, military, and decorative), and even such elusive traces as the imprints of textiles on clay. All of these discoveries, in conjunction with the inscriptions on the bones, led to the re-creation, almost out of nothing, of a substantial picture of Shang civilization.

The inscribed bones are commonly styled oracle bones because they were inscribed with questions asked of the spirits—especially the spirits of royal ancestors—by the king, with the mediation and interpretation of a diviner. The bones were normally the shoulder bones of domestic animals or the plastrons of tortoises. The answers to ques-

tions had to be interpreted from cracks radiating from depressions where the diviner pressed a heated rod. The inscriptions, in short, represent one of the most important activities of a priest-king in his temple-palace, where he was surrounded by functionaries whose religious activities could hardly be separated from their political responsibilities. The angular script in which these colloquies were recorded represents the earliest known form of Chinese writing. They cover every subject of interest to a divine ruler: questions about sacrifice and ritual, about warfare, about ceremonial hunts, about sickness, about the weather (especially the rainfall in proper season), and about every other conceivable aspect of the affairs of a theocracy of the fourteenth and thirteenth centuries B.C.

The establishment of the communist People's Republic in 1949 brought a great surge of serious archaeological exploration, made possible by the relaxation of ancient taboos against the violation of tombs, and promoted by such ideological motives as cultivating a sense of cultural continuity, local pride, and national glory. Excavations were renewed at An-yang in 1950 and also, a few years later, at the site of an even earlier Shang capital, which succeeded to An-yang in about 1400 B.C. This yielded rich rewards for our understanding of the almost unknown culture of earliest Shang. For a while new scientific journals made the latest finds accessible to the world. But such publication came to a sudden halt in 1966 with the so-called Great Proletarian Cultural Revolution, a radical upheaval within the Mao government that sought, among other things, to break China's ideological reliance on the past. A pall of dead silence fell on the bright new archaeological scene. This silence lasted until 1971, when another ideological shift in government policy restored archaeology to favor.

Many of the significant new discoveries have come from the tombs of the great magnates and lesser royalty of the Han period. A tomb in Kansu, excavated in 1969, contained a wealth of fine bronzework, especially models of horses, horse-

This is one of the exquisite silk paintings that Stein found stuffed away in the Tun-huang vault. It shows the Bodhisattva Kuan-yin.

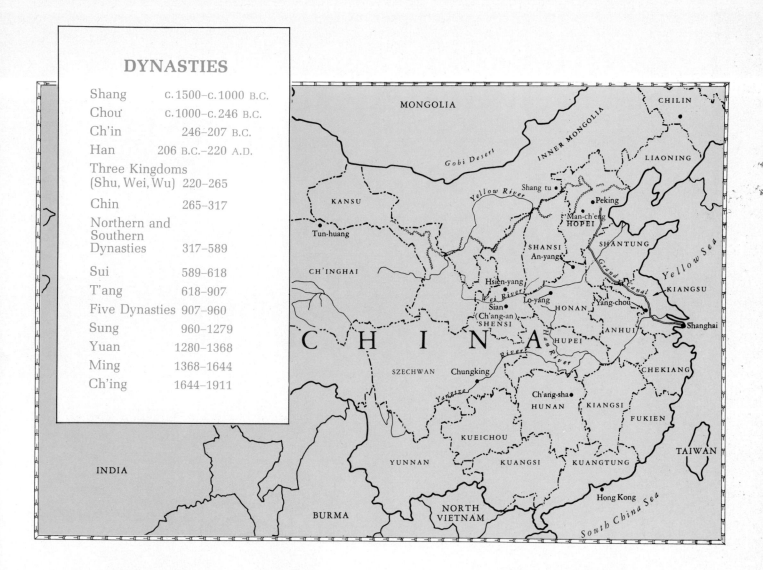

DYNASTIES

Shang	c.1500–c.1000 B.C.
Chou	c.1000–c.246 B.C.
Ch'in	246–207 B.C.
Han	206 B.C.–220 A.D.
Three Kingdoms (Shu, Wei, Wu)	220–265
Chin	265–317
Northern and Southern Dynasties	317–589
Sui	589–618
T'ang	618–907
Five Dynasties	907–960
Sung	960–1279
Yuan	1280–1368
Ming	1368–1644
Ch'ing	1644–1911

men, and carriages. One of these miniatures was the now-celebrated Flying Horse, a vigorous, spirited figure, poised on a swallow's back (see page 336). The most spectacular of these new finds were the tombs of Prince Liu Sheng and his wife, Princess Tou Wan, excavated at Man-ch'eng in Hopei Province in 1968 (see pages 337–339). The aristocratic couple had lived in the late second century B.C.—that is, during the first half of the Han period. Their bodies were splendidly arrayed in suitlike shrouds made of jade tablets linked together with gold wires and with silver-wrapped

Opposite page: In the tomb of Yuan T'u, a prince of the Chou dynasty, excavators in the late 1950's found these skeletal horses and wooden chariots. Except for the warping of their wheels, the chariots were intact after twenty-seven centuries. The map above shows archaeological sites in China.

iron wires. It is certain that these magnificent funeral garments were more than just ostentatious display to delight the inhabitants of the nether world. Jade, quite aside from its beauty, is one of the toughest of minerals, and its durability accounts in part for its important role in the Chinese immortality cult. Since the earliest times, jade amulets had been inserted into the mouths of the dead, presumably to ward off forever the evil powers that corrupt both body and soul. Other such paraphernalia of nephrite were described in books surviving from the Chou period, and many have turned up in the art and antique shops of the world. But nothing quite so elaborate and splendid as these crystalline outer skins—so to speak—had ever been known before, and they created a sensation around the world.

Even more wonderful things were soon to

This heavy bronze cooking vessel, standing fifteen inches tall, bears a moon-shaped face on each of its four sides. Both it and the mask on the opposite page date from the earliest period of Chinese bronzework, in the second millennium B.C.

come—these not from the soil of north China, in which the ancient Chinese culture was rooted, but from the once alien land of lakes, rivers, and subtropical forests south of the Yangtze River, in what is now the province of Hunan. By Han times the people who inhabited these pleasant lands, probably Thais, had been almost entirely assimilated into the intrusive Chinese culture of the north, while retaining some of their own ethnic peculiarities. The new finds were made at a place called Ma-wang-tui, near the age-old city of Ch'ang-sha, once the chief city of the state of Ch'u, until Han times a semi-independent feudal kingdom. The new discoveries consisted of the tombs of three members of an aristocratic family of the second century B.C. These are usually referred to simply by number, and are identified as follows:

Tomb 1 (excavated in 1971): the wife of Li Ts'ang; tomb constructed shortly after 168 B.C.

Tomb 2 (excavated in 1973–74): Li Ts'ang, prime minister to the last king of Ch'ang-sha (appointed 193 B.C.) and enfeoffed marquis of Tai; died 186 B.C. Soon after, this client kingdom, temporarily tolerated by the new Han empire, was obliterated.

Tomb 3 (excavated 1973-74): the son of Li Ts'ang; tomb constructed in 168 B.C.

Let us look at the most striking objects found in each of these burial chambers.

Tomb 1 yielded an extraordinary spectacle. This was the undecayed body, wrapped in twenty layers of silk, of the marchioness of Tai (see page 334). She had evidently died suddenly at about age fifty. The body, as well as some of the other objects in the grave, had been partly doused with a reddish liquid containing a mercury compound and other chemicals, which may have helped to preserve her tissues, although the hermetically sealed tomb may also have inhibited the deleterious effects both of oxygen and of bacteria. Aside from the lifelike corpse itself, the most striking object present was a banner—a kind of funeral pall—seven feet long, which covered the innermost casket. This is decorated with a picture of the lady and her attendants, surrounded by a sequence of fantastic scenes of the world of spirits.

A great batlike being hovers over the lady's portrait. Below her lies a weird underworld, populated by dragons, human-headed birds, and other bizarre creatures. Across the upper panel is a succession of dragons and fairy beings mounted on strange animals, and paired images of the sun and moon. The sun is red, and inhabited by its symbolic crow; the moon is shown as a crescent attended by its well-known inhabitants, the toad and the hare. Most attractive of all is a pretty maiden reclining on the wing of a flying dragon just below the moon. She is barelegged and clad in a plain shift. Despite her bucolic appearance, she is clearly the moon goddess Ch'ang-o on her way to her new lunar palace, where she was destined to dwell through all eternity.

Tomb 2, which had been plundered more than once in the past, contained a variety of objects, mostly fragmentary, of no great splendor or historical interest, except for the official bronze seals of the marquis, equipped with golden knobs in the shape of tortoises, and a variety of other bronze objects. Among those of especial interest to histori-

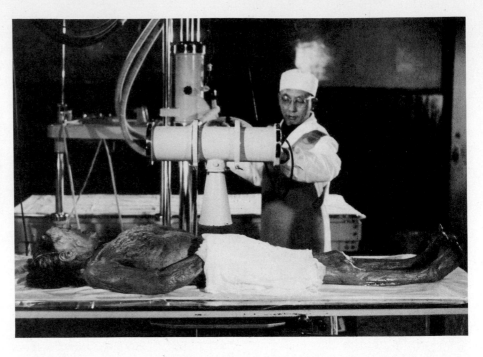

At Hunan Medical College a scientist examines the body of a great Chinese lady, the marchioness of Tai, buried more than two thousand years ago and remarkably undecayed. It was found that she had died of a heart attack an hour or so after eating melon (the seeds were still in her stomach).

ans of technology were elegantly fashioned crossbow trigger mechanisms inlaid with gold.

Tomb 3, however, yielded as rich results as had Tomb 1. To begin with, there were the bones of the young prince. A unique find was a wood-handled iron spade, evidently left behind by a workman. But the tomb offerings also provided absorbing evidence for the student of human folkways. Not counting an abundance of rich lacquer ware, weapons, musical instruments, and carved wooden figures of attendants, all analogous to finds in the other tombs, there were the actual—but somewhat mummified—remains of a noble repast of the second century B.C.: bamboo boxes containing, among other foods, venison, pork, mutton, fish, pheasant, eggs, beans, oranges, dates, pears, water chestnuts, cinnamon, and pepper. There were lengths of silk cloth in a variety of weaves—damasks, fine gauzes, and embroidered pieces. There was also a T-shaped pall or banner, similar to the one found in Tomb 1, decorated with many divine symbols and figures. It is different from the other in one important respect, namely, that instead of the divine lady Ch'ang-o, it shows the great creator pair, the goddess Nü Kua and her consort Fu Hsi, their serpentine lower bodies entwined, as they often appear in what remnants of Han religious art exist elsewhere. Three other paintings on silk were found: one, of particular interest, shows persons doing calisthenic exercises,

presumed to have a therapeutic purpose. These can be identified with techniques known only by name from early Chinese books. They are evidently elements of the age-old longevity cult, which was later completely absorbed by Taoism. Among the exercises are "directing and pulling" (yogalike exercises), and such specialized exercises as "the bear passage" and "the bird stretch."

Probably the most important objects found in this tomb, however, were written documents that open up hitherto only partially known aspects of the intellectual and cultural life of the period. Among these are treatises on medicine, especially those having to do with the prolongation of life, including diagnosis by taking the pulse, dietetics, and such typical Taoist techniques as "rejecting cereals"—the latter, regarded as peasant food, were thought to shorten life. It is interesting that although we find descriptions of the technique of cautery with moxa at critical somatic points, there is no mention of acupuncture, which, later at least, depended on the same anatomical and physiological assumptions. There are essays on the dualistic cosmology of yin and yang and on the quintuple "activity-phases," sometimes miscalled the five elements. There is a treatise on the somatology of horses. An astronomical-astrological text—two sciences not distinguished in antiquity—relies heavily on planetary motions and is provided with surprisingly accurate computations of both the sidereal and synodic periods of Saturn. There are texts on Taoist doctrine, including an early version of the Lao-tzu. Finally, of unique value, three maps done on silk in vegetable colors were found in a lacquer box. One shows the Han state of Ch'ang-sha—the fief of the deceased marquis—and some neighboring territories, with more than thirty rivers displayed accurately as to width and changes in direction. There are serpentine mountain ranges, roads, many towns and villages, and strategically placed forts. Maps of such excellent quality were not seen in China again until almost modern times.

In recent years the tombs of many elite personages of the T'ang period, whose glamorous, international culture represents the climax of the medieval civilization in China, have also been opened in the vicinity of Lo-yang, the eastern capital. One of these tombs was that of Prince Li Shou, a magnate of the seventh century. The murals are particularly pleasing for their zestful representations of all-girl orchestras, playing with animation on lutes, reed organs, harps, and zithers; their pictures of ox-drawn carts and plows, and their vivid delineations of bearded, hook-nosed foreigners, then a common sight in China, as they never were again until the Mongol conquest in the thirteenth century.

Another tomb, that of Prince Li Hsien, of a slightly later date, was excavated in 1971–72. This sepulcher had been robbed, but its mural paintings remain, especially the exuberant and vigorous scenes of royal hunts, showing mounted hunters and camels plunging through sketchy landscapes, enhanced with such exotic details as trained lynxes and hunting cheetahs (animals that supplemented hunting dogs and falcons during that period) mounted on specially built crupper saddles. Such cultural links with western Asia, although known abstractly from books of the T'ang, had never before been shown in vivid pictures to the modern world, which still tends to think of Chinese civilization as virtually self-evolved and unique. This cosmopolitan impression is much reinforced by scenes of foreign dignitaries shown being received politely, even deferentially, by Chinese officials: Koreans, fur-garbed residents of the northern steppes, balding Roman-nosed Westerners, and the like (see page 340). Among many fascinating cultural details is a picture of a miniature garden, the ancestor of the modern Japanese bonsai, carried in a tray by an attendant; no literary reference to such objects from that early period has yet been found.

Finally there is the tomb of the crown prince Li Chung-jun, who died in 701. It was uncovered in 1971. In many respects its mural paintings are like those of the others of that age, both in style and content. Particularly striking, however, are the images of the lofty watchtowers of a great city—presumably the capital itself—surmounted by roofed chambers. All are painted in vivid cinnabar red, with roof tiles of contrasting blue. Outside these courtly pylons many human figures are shown in ceremonial processions; there are some with hunting hawks, dogs, and cheetahs, but there are also aristocratic ladies with long-handled fans. Here, as elsewhere, the exotic element is prominent—for instance, the court falconers are clearly not Chinese.

One feature of most well-preserved Chinese tombs is the ceiling, usually domed, which displays a map of the sky. Most often such a ceiling shows the important constellations along the ecliptic, comparable to our twelve zodiacal asterisms but by no means the same; the twenty-eight lodgings of the moon, one of which it enters on each night of its monthly round; often other highly important combinations of stars, in particular those of the polar region, and above all the Big Dipper. The individual stars are represented as little circles, connected to other members of the same asterism by straight lines. The presence of astronomical charts in tombs had more than a merely decorative purpose. The stars were manifestations of great supernatural powers, whose glittering costumes and unearthly visages were masked from all but the most advanced adepts of Taoism. Once the adept, by dint of long study, meditation, and self-purification, had made contact with one of these astral deities, all things became possible for him, including flight through outer space and, above all, eternal life. This is why these powers, in their phenomenal aspects as glittering stars, were represented in the eternal homes of the dead. Their ultimate purpose was magical. But their interest for historians of astronomy is enormous.

During the past few decades a number of such impressive displays of the night sky have been found in tombs of many periods. One example is in a Han tomb excavated at Lo-yang in 1957. The ceiling of the central chamber shows not only the sun and the moon with their symbolic animals but also the Big Dipper; a number of the lunar stations in Scorpius, Taurus, and Aquarius; images of Orion and the Pleiades; the popular Weaver Maid (Vega), and across the Sky River (Milky Way) from her, her swain, the Ox Boy (Altair). This whole cosmic scheme is laid out on an east-west axis, with the sun placed in the east, as if rising at the entrance of the tomb.

Another recent find, also at Lo-yang but in a tomb of the Northern Wei period (fifth and sixth centuries), was made in 1974. This too shows the Weaver and the Ox Boy and the sundering Milky Way, but most prominent are the circumpolar constellations that represent the palace of the great god who rules the universe from his unwobbling pivot near Polaris.

A stellar panorama of a still later period was discovered during the excavations of 1963–65 in Turfan, in Serindia, the site of the T'ang garrison-city of Qočo. It shows the moon as white—since it was thought to be allied to pure white jade and to snow and ice—and the sun as fiery red. The solstices and equinoxes are shown at the four corners of the burial chamber. The complete lunar orbit, with all twenty-eight stations shown, is also present. (The regular presence of these features is related to the fact that classical Chinese astrology was mainly lunar rather than solar, as in the Western tradition.)

These subterranean sky charts are of unique value to students of Chinese astronomy, astrology, and astral worship for the reason that no other such charts have survived in the astronomical books of early periods. Now, by comparing charts of different periods, modern astronomers can hope to see how the configurations of the constellations have changed from age to age: for instance, the presence or absence of particular stars in tomb ceilings of different ages suggests changes in their brightness, and even the appearance and disappearance of supernovae.

Of the greatest interest for students of ancient Chinese astronomy and its religious implications is the recent discovery near Lo-yang of an actual observatory of the Later Han period. This is one of the few examples of architecture in masonry

In the central hall of a spacious tomb in Hopei (opposite page) excavators found an array of grave goods set out for Prince Liu Sheng, whose body was interred in an inner chamber, behind the low door at center. From another Han tomb, in Kansu, came the elegant, subtly imagined bronze sculpture of a flying horse (left), its hoof resting on the back of a stylized bird.

These magnificent objects were found in the graves of Prince Liu Sheng and his wife, Princess Tou Wan, an aristocratic couple of the second century B.C. On the opposite page is the body of the prince, lying in its suit of jade plates linked with gold wire. The jade provided not only a durable shroud but also mystical protection for its noble occupant. At right is a bronze servant girl holding a lamp. Below is one of four bronze leopards, with partial gilding on its body and crimson eyes.

above ground that survives from antiquity. It is the remnant of the great Ling t'ai, "Terrace of the Spirits," a type of edifice mentioned in the very earliest classical texts. This was a platform, having various accessory buildings and equipped with the most refined astronomical instruments available, from which the royal astronomers took their observations—observations of tremendous import for understanding the condition of the empire. The unseen deities hidden behind the stars gave visible tokens—in the form of color aberrations, invasions of comets and meteors, and the like—of changes in the state of the cosmos, which were inevitably echoed on earth, the lower domain of the Son of Heaven. Astronomy, in short, was a learned but inevitable part of statecraft. As the Han astronomer Chang Heng—a personage of heroic import whom we shall meet again presently—put it: the purpose of the Terrace is to study the motions of the heavenly bodies "so that we may observe the

ontological flux, and so pray for blessings or exorcise disasters." By "ontological flux" (the translation of a very technical Chinese word) the great scientist referred to the patterns of interaction of the two cosmic principles yin and yang and especially to the dire signs that made their imbalance manifest.

The Terrace proves to be one that is well known to historical literature. It was built in A.D. 59 and inaugurated with important religious sacrifices by the Han sovereign Ming Ti. It remained in use until late in the third century, well after the fall of Han. We also know that Chang Heng, who was astronomer royal during the periods A.D. 115–120 and A.D. 126–133, made his computations here—work that led to his construction of a true armillary sphere, a model of the heavens showing the apparent paths of the important heavenly bodies and essential, when used in connection with a sighting tube, to accurate measurement and prediction. The

340

sphere, built about A.D. 132, was a set of concentric rings representing celestial paths and boundaries, such as the meridian circle, horizon circle, celestial equator, and ecliptic. It was moved mechanically by water power, to co-ordinate its direction with the shifting of the constellations during the course of the night. Undoubtedly it was housed on the summit of the Terrace.

Chang Heng may be compared to an ideal figure of the Italian Renaissance, since he was equally accomplished in literature and science. In addition to his long rhapsodic descriptions of the eastern and western capitals of Han, part of his treatise on the armillary sphere, written about A.D. 125, still survives. Chang Heng's fame goes much beyond this. He was the acknowledged inventor of the seismograph; his device (which has been reconstructed from contemporary descriptions) caused bronze dragons to release balls into the mouths of expectant frogs below them in the direction of a distant earthquake. Not surprisingly, he has become a hero of the Chinese people. The memorial inscription composed for his tomb says of him: "With his arts of calculations he exhausted Heaven and Earth; in his definitive fabrications he was a match for the Fashioner of Mutations"—that is, he was a match for the great Creator Principle itself.

The archaeological discoveries that we have discussed so far have been relatively small, isolated, and private. But modern Chinese archaeologists have also undertaken more ambitious enterprises, chief among them attempts to reconstruct in drawings the great cities of the past, long since vanished and virtually forgotten. Of particular interest are the royal towns, built symmetrically around the palace, the focus of divine power in the earthly realm, and oriented according to cosmic co-ordinates. Among these vast undertakings is the attempt, now only in the preliminary stages, to retrace Hsien-yang, the capital of Ch'in Shih Huang Ti, northwest across the Wei River from that ambitious monarch's vast tumulus. Exploratory excavations have enabled the publication of drawings showing the great palace halls perched on a high artificial terrace, arranged in almost perfect Palladian symmetry. Such architectural reconstructions depend in large part on the co-ordination of the remains of the palace foundations with contemporary pictorial representations. These survive in odd places. One useful one was found on the back of a bronze mirror. It shows, for instance, that the buildings had a low horizontal profile and that their roofs sloped in straight lines, quite unlike the turned-up curves that characterize the roof design of later periods.

More extensive work has already been completed at the T'ang capital of Ch'ang-an, almost directly across the river from Hsien-yang. This gem of medieval cities had a population of about two million persons of many races and nationalities in the eighth century. There were temples for Christians, Muslims, and Zoroastrians there, and the presence of gold coins in nearby tombs demonstrates the importance of Arab merchants in the city. This brilliant metropolis disappeared in 904 when it was occupied by the traitor Chu Wen, who founded a new nation which he styled Liang. Wishing to move the symbolic center of divine power elsewhere, he had the massive walls and best buildings dismantled and all useful timbers floated down-river to Lo-yang. Ch'ang-an was gone forever.

Since the tenth century a small town has stood on the former site of its administrative center. Most new excavation has been focused on the palace enclosure, called the Great Luminous Palace, built in 662 on Dragon Head Plain north of the city proper. This work was begun by the Institute of Archaeology in 1957. By May of 1959 the entire perimeter of the palace walls had been traced, and part of the walls themselves, with several gates and the ruins of two great halls, had been rescued from the weedy rubble. As was customary in these microcosmic layouts, the palace complex was oriented according to the cardinal directions. It was about two miles along the north-south axis, and over a mile east to west. A great deal is known from historical descriptions and from contemporary poetry about the beauty and mystery of this vast complex of buildings, but until very recently relatively few of the individual buildings had been excavated—or rather, their stone foundations, since the beautifully painted and gilded wooden halls themselves had long since disappeared. One of the most successful digs, that of a ceremonial basilica, revealed an unexpected treasure: an array of great ceramic jars containing the ritual tribute of fine produce demanded from every province of the empire on New Year's day. The jars, with their shriveled contents, had been sealed with clay, stamped with the name of the province of origin, the magistrate responsible for the submission, the date, and a description of the contents.

If Ch'ang-an was the grand metropolitan city of T'ang, conjoining the mysteries of cosmic power with the secular splendor of silk and gold, Yang-chou was the commercial and pleasure city par excellence of the same age. This town, rich and beautiful, was situated at the junction of the Yangtze River with the Grand Canal, which transported rice and all the other products of the south, both staples and luxuries, to the great administrative centers of the north. It was a manufacturing center as well as a commercial hub. Among its industries were the finest metalwork, especially bronze mirrors; silks and linens and embroideries; refined sugar; excellent cabinetwork; and felt hats, which were in vogue among the young men of Ch'ang-an. It was also the center that provided every delightful recreation not only for governmental agents, who were everywhere, especially in connection with the enormous salt monopoly, but for the rising merchant class, until then more or less outside the traditional Chinese social scheme. The new businessmen enriched themselves as entrepreneurs in the distribution of tea (recently become popular), precious stones, aromatics, and drugs, and as bankers and manipulators of the gold market. In Yang-chou they could enjoy pleasures formerly restricted to the vast official bureaucracy and the powerful families of the elite: agreeable parks and gardens, endless waterways (it was said that boats outnumbered carriages in this eastern Venice), moonlight, lanterns, music—and all the enchantments offered by high-class courtesans.

This city of dreams was not destined to outlive the T'ang period. It suffered a severe shock in 760 when it was looted by the bandit T'ien Shen-kung, who murdered several thousand Arab and Persian businessmen during his occupation. But the town survived this disaster, only to be utterly destroyed in the middle of the tenth century by the armies of the new royal state of Later Chou. Poets of the Sung dynasty, which followed Chou into the supreme power soon afterward, were astonished on visiting the site of the once beautiful city. They could hardly understand the enthusiasm of the writers of T'ang for a paradise on earth that in their own time was only a "stench in their nostrils." Now at last archaeology is beginning to resurrect some of the vanished glory of this long-dead city. T'ang graves nearby have been unearthed, and since 1975 the foundations of the city itself, especially its walls, have been excavated north of the modern town. Moreover, traces of the medieval industries that were partly responsible for its wealth have begun to appear: the very kilns that produced the many-colored glazed ceramics and fine porcelain for which it was famous, as well as the furnaces of the goldsmiths and silversmiths whose work glittered in the crowded bazaars of the eighth and ninth centuries.

Much better known to the Western world, and belonging to a more recent age, is the celebrated city known to us chiefly through Coleridge as Xanadu—an exotic spelling that reflects the Chinese Shang tu, "Upper Metropolis." This was a capital of the Mongol ruler of eastern Asia, Kublai Khan, who built it in 1263. Marco Polo described it with considerable gusto, especially its fantastic gilded palace built of marble and other ornamental stones, the undoubted source of Coleridge's magical "pleasure dome." This city was both an administrative center and a commercial town, and being well situated in Inner Mongolia between running water and forested mountains, it served as the summer residence of the khans. Little remains of the great buildings—prominent among them numerous Buddhist temples—that once delighted the eyes of visitors who came from all over the world during the Pax Mongolica. Recently some beginning has been made to detect the physical remains of this romantic town. The outlines of one monastery, with glazed tiles and fragments of gilded and painted statuary that must have been among its sacred accouterments, have been discovered. Within the administrative quarter excavators have found pieces of fine porcelain and stone cannon balls—the latter symbolic of the advanced military technology that made the Mongols masters of Asia and much of eastern Europe. Eventually we may hope to attain a realistic vision or recreation of the city that Coleridge transformed into a haunted paradise by the sacred river Alph.

These pottery figures of a dancer and three female musicians probably represent entertainers who performed at court dinners.

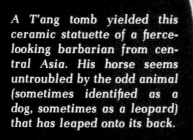

A T'ang tomb yielded this ceramic statuette of a fierce-looking barbarian from central Asia. His horse seems untroubled by the odd animal (sometimes identified as a dog, sometimes as a leopard) that has leaped onto its back.

THE AUTHORS

GEOFFREY BIBBY ("The Mysterious Celts" and "The Trail of the Vikings") is head of the Department of Oriental Antiquities at the Prehistoric Museum of Aarhus, Denmark. He is the author of *Testimony of the Spade*, *Four Thousand Years Ago*, and *Looking for Dilmun*.

LIONEL CASSON ("The Earliest Cities," "The Horse in History," and "The Scrap Paper of Egypt") is professor of classics at New York University. He is the author of *The Ancient Mariners* and *Travel in the Ancient World*, and the principal author of *Mysteries of the Past*, published by American Heritage in 1977.

ROBERT CLAIBORNE ("The Indian Discovery of America") is a science journalist, formerly associate editor of *Scientific American* and managing editor of *Medical World News*. He is the author of *Climate, Man, and History* and *God or Beast: Evolution and Human Nature*.

ALEXANDER ELIOT ("The Realm of the Mother Goddess") is an art critic and historian, and professor emeritus of Hampshire College. He is the author of *Earth Air Fire and Water*, *A Concise History of Greece*, and *Myths*.

MICHAEL GRANT ("Time Stopped at Pompeii") is a British classicist, formerly president and vice-chancellor of the University of Belfast. He has written many books, including *The World of Rome*, *Nero*, *Roman History from Coins*, and *Cities of Vesuvius*.

JOHN HEMMING ("The Lost City of the Incas") is the author of *The Conquest of the Incas* and *Red Gold: The Conquest of the Brazilian Indians*. A Canadian living in London, he was a member of the Iriri River expedition into unexplored areas of Brazil.

GILBERT HIGHET ("The Survival of Records") was Anthon Professor of the Latin Language and Literature at Columbia University. He wrote many books, including *The Classical Tradition*, *Poets in a Landscape*, *The Anatomy of Satire*, and *The Art of Teaching*.

MAGNUS MAGNUSSON ("Archaeology and the Bible") has been rector of Edinburgh University and was a founder of the BBC "Chronicle" series on history and archaeology. He is the author of *Introducing Archaeology*, *Viking Expansion Westwards*, *Hammer of the North*, and *Archaeology of the Bible*.

EDWARD H. SCHAFER ("From the Tombs of China") is Agassiz Professor of Oriental Languages and Literature at the University of California at Berkeley. He is the author of several books on Chinese history and art, including *The Golden Peaches of Samarkand*, *The Vermilion Bird*, and *The Divine Woman*.

Acknowledgments

The editors wish to thank the following individuals and institutions for their help in preparing this book: Morris Raphael Cohen Library, City College, New York—Helga Moody, Donald Petty; Jewish Institute of Religion, Emil Hirsch-Gerson Levi Library, Hebrew Union College, New York—Susan Tabor; Mercantile Library, New York; New York Public Library; New York Society Library.

The papyri translations appearing in Chapter 5 are used by permission of the following: *Oxyrhynchus Papyri*, Egypt Exploration Society (London): 112—No. 37; 113—No. 38; 114—No. 119. *Michigan Papyri*, Michigan University Press (Ann Arbor): 118—Vol. 8, No. 468; 125—Vol. 3, No. 157. A. S. Hunt and C. C. Edgar, translators, *Select Papyri*, Vols. 1 and 2, Loeb Classical Library, Harvard University Press (Cambridge, 1932, 1934): 115—Vol. 2, No. 313; 117—Vol. 1, No. 112; 118—Vol. 1, No. 149; 119—Vol. 1, No. 2; 123—Vol. 2, No. 335; 123-4—Vol. 2, No. 353; 124—Vol. 1, No. 97.

Picture Credits

Credits for illustrations from left to right are separated by semicolons; from top to bottom, by dashes.

CHAPTER ONE: 8,9—David Lees from Time-Life Picture Agency. 9—Oriental Institute, University of Chicago, courtesy Joint Expedition to Nippur. 10—British Museum. 13—Oriental Institute, University of Chicago, courtesy Joint Expedition to Nippur and *Life*. 14—George Gerster/Photo Researchers. 15 and 16—Jericho Excavation Fund. 17—Reconstruction painting by Gaynor Chapman, courtesy Thames and Hudson. 19—All, James Mellaart. 20—Both, James Mellaart. 21—Mrs. James Mellaart. 22—British Museum. 23—British Museum. 24—British Museum, Lee Boltin. 25—British Museum. 27—Baghdad Museum. 28—George Holton/Photo Researchers. 29—New York Public Library, Astor, Lenox and Tilden Foundations. 30 and 31—Both, George Holton/Photo Researchers.

CHAPTER TWO: 32,33—Leonard von Matt/Photo Researchers. 33—University of Cambridge, Department of Archaeology and Anthropology. 34—Leonard von Matt/Photo Researchers. 36—Ashmolean Museum, Oxford. 38—Archeological Museum, Heracleion. 39—Museum of Modern Art; © 1958, S.P.A.D.E.M. 40—David Lees for Time-Life Books, courtesy Whitaker Museum, Motya; University Museum, University of Pennsylvania; Victoria and Albert Museum. 41—Andreas Feininger; Alinari/Editorial Photocolor Archives. 43—British Museum. 44,45—C. M. Dixon. 46—Musée Nationale, Malta, Scala. 47—Photo Aerofilms. 49—British Museum, Michael Holford Library. 50,51—Yale University Art Gallery. 52—Reconstruction drawing by Tatiana Proskouriakoff, courtesy of the Peabody Museum, Harvard University. 53—Carl Purcell/Photo Researchers. 54—Edward Thompson, courtesy of the Peabody Museum, Harvard University. 55—All, Peabody Museum, Harvard University, photograph by Hillel Burger.

CHAPTER THREE: 56,57—Sovfoto. 57—Hermitage Museum, Leningrad, Werner Forman Archive. 58—Document of the Henri Lhote Expedition. 60 and 61—British Museum. 62—Oriental Institute, University of Chicago. 65—Peter Kaplan. 66—Museo Civico, Bologna. 67—Metropolitan Museum of Art, Gift of J. Pierpont Morgan; British Museum, C. M. Dixon. 68,69—Hermitage Museum, Leningrad, Lee Boltin. 70—Universitatsbibliothek, Heidelberg. 71—British Library, London. 74—MacQuitty International Collection—graffiti from Dura-Europos, Syria—British Museum. 76,77—Sovfoto. 78 and 79—New York Public Library, Astor, Lenox and Tilden Foundations. 80 and 81—New York Public Library, Astor, Lenox and Tilden Foundations.

CHAPTER FOUR: 82,83—Graham Finlayson/Woodfin Camp and Associates. 82—Louvre Museum, Paris. 84—Erich Lessing/Magnum. 86—From *Science Year*, The World Book Science Annual. © 1977 Field Enterprises Educational Corporation—Antonia Benedek. 88,89—Baptistery, Florence Cathedral, Scala. 90—From *The Holy Bible, with Illustrations by Gustave Doré* (London, 1866). 91—Dr. A. Mazar. 92—Oriental Institute, University of Chicago—Consulate General of Israel in New York. 93—Oriental Institute, University of Chicago. 94—From *Antiquités Judaïques*, Bibliothèque Nationale, Service Photographique—Yale University Art Gallery—C. F. Stevens's reconstruction of the Temple of Solomon drawn from specifications prepared by W. F. Albright and G. E. Wright, courtesy American Schools of Oriental Research. 96,97—George Gerster/Photo Researchers. 98—Oriental Institute, University of Chicago. 99—United Press International. 100—Courtesy Time-Life Books, Paulus Leeser. 101—Erich Lessing/Magnum (photographed from a plaster cast, courtesy of the Israel Department of Antiquities and Museums; original in the British Museum, London). 102—Rhodesian House, London. 102,103—Syndication International. 104—Don Carl Steffen/Photo Researchers. 105—National Archives of Southern Rhodesia, courtesy Thames and Hudson.

CHAPTER FIVE: 106,107—Great Ages of Man, *Ancient Egypt*, photograph by Eliot Elisofon, Time-Life Books. 106—British Museum. 108—Museo Nazionale, Naples. 110—Brian Brake/Photo Researchers; Oriental Institute, University of Chicago. 111—Giraudon. 112—Brian Brake/Photo Researchers. 113—Archives Nationales, Paris. 114—Oriental Institute, University of Chicago. 116—British Museum, courtesy Arnoldo Mondadori Editore and Kodansha Ltd., Tokyo. 121—Enzo Crea, Editions du Pont Royal, Paris. 122—Palestrina Museo Archeologico, John Ross. 124—Museum of Fine Arts, Boston. 124,125—Brian Brake/Photo Researchers. 126—British Museum. 127—Archives Photographiques, Paris.

ANTHOLOGY I: 128—University Museum, University of Pennsylvania. 131—From *Nineveh and its Remains*, Vol. 2, by Sir Henry Layard (London, 1849). 134—From *Excavations at Ur*, by Leonard Woolley (London, 1954). 136—From *Ur Excavations*, Vol. 2, by Leonard Woolley (Oxford, 1934). 138—From *La Merveilleuse Découverte de Lascaux*, by Pierre Fanlac. 140—From "Royal Mummies Found Near Thebes," by Amelia B. Edwards, *Illustrated London News*, February 4, 1882. 145—Photography by the Egyptian Expedition, Metropolitan Museum of Art.

CHAPTER SIX: 146,147—The Folio Society Ltd., courtesy the Imperial War Museum. 147—Erich Lessing/Magnum. 148—From *Pompeii and Herculaneum*, by Edwin Smith, Museo Nazionale, Naples. 151—Sopraintendenza alle Antichita della Campania, Naples. 152—Metropolitan Museum of Art, Rogers Fund, 1903. 153—Metropolitan Museum of Art. 154—Museo Nazionale, Naples, John Ross. 155—Leonard von Matt/Photo Researchers. 157 and 158—Scala, Alinari. 160,161—Anderson, Alinari, Editorial Photocolor Archives. 161—The Folio Society Ltd., courtesy Victoria and Albert Museum. 162—Both, Museo Nazionale, Naples, Anderson. 163—Giraudon. 164—Courtesy of Mrs. Chamberlayne MacDonald. 165—Museo Nazionale, Naples, Anderson. 166 and 167—Leonard von Matt/Photo Researchers. 168—Dmitri Kessel. 170,171—Leonard von Matt/Photo Researchers. 172 and 173—Leonard von Matt/Photo Researchers.

CHAPTER SEVEN: 174,175—John Bulmer/Woodfin Camp and Associates. 174—Staatliche Museen zu Berlin Antiken Sammlung. 176—British Museum. 179—Danish National Museum, Copenhagen. 181—Peabody Museum, Harvard University—Erich Lessing/Magnum. 182—Naturhistorisches Museum, Vienna. 183—British Museum—Hull Museum; British Museum. 184—Musée Borély, Marseilles, Belzeaux/Photo Researchers. 187—From *De Dis Germanis*, by Elias Schedius—Dargaud Editeur Paris by Goscinny and Uderzo; Historical and Archeological Museum of Orléans, Belzeaux/Photo Researchers. 188—Photo Furbock Graz. 189—Erich Lessing/Magnum. 190—BBC copyright photograph. 191—Digby Elliot; Digby Elliot—BBC copyright photograph. 193—Brian Seed/Black Star. 195—Scala. 196—New York Public Library, Prints Division; C. M. Dixon—Weekend Telegraph, London, Donald McCullin.

CHAPTER EIGHT: 198,199—J. Ph. Charbonnier/Photo Researchers. 199—Statens Historiska Museum, Stockholm, Ted Spiegel/Black Star. 200—National Museum of Iceland, Gestsson. 202—From *Ships and the Sea*, by Duncan Haws, © Nordbok, Sweden. 203 and 204—Universitetets Oldsaksamling, Oslo. 206 and 207—All, British Museum, Michael Holford Library. 208 and 209—Pierpont Morgan Library. 210—Ted Spiegel/Black Star; Viking Ship Museum, Roskilde, Denmark. 211—Francis and Shaw. 212—Drawn by Alan Sorrell, Crown copyright reproduced by permission of the Scottish Development Department, Edinburgh. 213—Scottish Tourist Board. 214—Ted Speigel/Black Star. 219—Antikuarisk-Topografiska Arkivei, Sweden. 220—Both, © 1977 by The New York Times Company, reprinted by permission.

CHAPTER NINE: 222,223—M. Woodbridge Williams, National Park Service. 222—Gilcrease Institute. 224—National Museums of Canada. 228—American Museum of Natural History. 230,231 and 233—National Anthropology Museum, Mexico, D.F. 234—Arizona State Museum, Helga Teiwes; Robert S. Peabody Foundation for Archeology, Andover, Mass. 235—Both, Robert S. Peabody Foundation for Archeology, Andover, Mass. 236—Both, Del Baston. 240—Donald V. Hague. 241—University of Colorado, Joe Ben Wheat. 242—Farmers' Museum, Cooperstown, N.Y. 244 and 245—New York State Historical Association.

CHAPTER TEN: 246,247—Hans Silvester/Photo Researchers. 246—Musée de l'Homme, Paris. 248—American Museum of Natural History. 250,251—Stephanie L. Marcus. 251—From the Hiram Bingham Collection © National Geographic Society. 252,253—Hans Silvester/Photo Researchers. 254—Nuestra Señora de Copacabana, Lima, José Casals. 256—From *Nueva Cronica y Bien Gubierno*, by Felipe Guaman Poma de Ayala, Royal Library, Copenhagen. 257—Loren McIntyre/Woodfin Camp and Associates. 259—© The New York Times—Loren McIntyre/Woodfin Camp and Associates. 260—Lee Boltin; Loren McIntyre/Woodfin Camp and Associates. 261—Lee Boltin; Loren McIntyre/Woodfin Camp and Associates; Lee Boltin. 262—From *Historia General del Peru, Origen y Descendencia de los Incas*, by Fray Martin de Murua, by gracious permission of His Grace the Duke of Wellington, K.G. 263—Loren McIntyre/Woodfin Camp and Associates. 264—Hans Silvester/Photo Researchers. 265—Loren McIntyre/Woodfin Camp and Associates. 266—Museo de America, Madrid, Photo Oronoz—Loren McIntyre/Woodfin Camp and Associates. 267—Drawings adapted from Poma de Ayala. 269—From *India Occidentalis*, by Theodore de Bry, New York Public Library, Astor, Lenox and Tilden Foundations—New York Historical Society, Gene Cook. 270—Drawing after Stübel and Uhle—A. Rozier. 270,271—A. Rozier.

ANTHOLOGY II: 272—From the Hiram Bingham Collection © National Geographic Society. 274—From Max Mallowan, *Twenty-Five Years of Mesopotamian Discovery* (London, 1956). 276—Drawing by Philip R. Ward, courtesy Thames and Hudson. 281—From Giulio Ferrario, *Il Costumo Antico e Moderno* (Firenze, 1823). 283—From Dr. Charles Lewis Meryon, *The Travels of Lady Hester Stanhope* (London, 1845). 285—From *Das Ischtar-Tor in Babylon*, by Robert Koldewey (Leipzig, 1918). 289—Culver Pictures.

CHAPTER ELEVEN: 290,291—Elliot Erwitt/Magnum. 291—The Ashmolean Museum, Oxford. 292—Museo Pigorini, Rome. 295—British Museum. 297—Bibliothèque Nationale, photo from Pierpont Morgan Library—Staatsbibliothek, Bremen. 298—Bibliothèque Nationale. 301—Paulus Leeser from *A Commentary on the Dresden Codex*, by J. Eric S. Thompson, memoirs of the American Philosophical Society, Vol. 93, 1972. 303—Biblioteca Apostolica Vaticana. 304,305—Scansani, Biblioteca Ambrosiana di Milano. 306—British Museum—Archaeological Museum, Tehran, Luc Joubert—Instituto Archeologico Germanico, Rome. 307—British Museum. 309—Alinari. 311—British Museum, Urs Graf Verlag, Lausanne. 315—Culver Pictures.

CHAPTER TWELVE: 316,317—Emil Schulthess/Black Star. 316—Mr. and Mrs. Ezekiel Schloss Collection. 318—East Asian Library, Columbia University. 320 and 321—Audrey Topping. 322—*China Pictorial*, November, 1975. 322,323—*Wen Wu*, November, 1975. 323—Howard Nelson. 326—James C. M. Lo—All bottom and 327—From *Sir Aurel Stein, Archaeological Explorer*, by Jeanette Mirsky, University of Chicago Press, 1977. 329—British Museum. 330—Brian Brake/Photo Researchers. 332—Erich Lessing/Magnum. 333—Academia Sinica, Taipei, courtesy James Burke, *Life*, © 1958 Time Inc. 334—Lucy Lim. 336—Robert Harding Associates. 337—Lucy Lim. 338—Marc Riboud/Magnum. 339—MacQuitty International Collection—Robert Harding Associates. 343—Three seated figures, Metropolitan Museum of Art, Rogers Fund 1923; standing figure, Museum of Fine Arts, Boston, lent by Charles B. Hoyt. 344—Robert Harding Associates.

INDEX
Numbers in boldface refer to illustrations.

Gateway of the Sun, Tiahuanaco, Bolivia, 270, **270**, 271
Gath, 91
Gaul, 176-80, 188
Gaza, 87, 92; temple of, **90**, 92
Genizah, the, Cairo, 294
Geoffrey of Monmouth, 194
George V, King of England, 327
Germani, 177
Germans, 177, 180, 185, 200, 215, 285-86, 309; 1939 invasion of Poland, 75
Gezer, 98
Gibeon, 88
Gibraltar, Strait of, 176
Gihon, Spring of, 95
Gildas, 194
Gilgamesh, epic of, 26
Giza, Egypt, 7
Glastonbury, England, 194-97; Glastonbury Tor, 196, **197**
Gnostic Library, Egypt, 308
Gobi Desert, 323
Godthàb, Greenland, 216
Goethe, Johann Wolfgang von, 160; *Italian Journey*, 160
Gokstad (farm), Oslo, Norway, 201, 205, 209; tomb (ship burial), 212, 215
Gold Rush, 7
Gordon, Arthur E., 312
Gordon, Cyrus, 49; *Ugarit and Minoan Crete*, 49
Gortyn, Crete, 307
Gospels, 310; in Latin, 310; of Saint John, 310; of Saint Mark, 299
Gotland, Sweden, 216, 219; Viking memorial stone, **219**
Graves, Robert, 42, 45; *The White Goddess*, 42
Great Plains (U.S.), 232, 237-38
Greece, 6, 43, 59, 63, 66-67, 170-73, 180, 185, 220, 281-83, 287-94, 300; empire, 322; language, 294-95; literature, 59, 63, 66-67, 293; peoples, 71-72, 186, 299, 304; religious worship, **43**
Greenland, 216-18
Grenfell, Bernard P., 109, 118, 308
Grineo, Giovanni Giacomo, 108
Guatemala, 79
Gudröd, King, 213, 215
Gudrödson, Halvdan, King, 213, 215
Gudrödson, Olav, 213, 215
Gunbjörn, 217
Gundestrup, 179
Gurna, Egypt, 139
Gustavson, Gabriel, 209

H

Hadrian, Emperor, 29, 288; Hadrian's Villa, Tivoli, Italy, 288; Hadrian's Wall, England, 191
Hagenbeck, Carl, 58
Haggard, H. Rider, 95, 105; *King Solomon's Mines*, 95, 105
Hall, James, 244
Hallstatt, Austria, 181, 183
Hamburg, Germany, 58; zoo, 58
Hamilton, Lady Emma, 159, **164**, 165
Hamilton, Sir William, 159, 165, 169
Han Dynasty, 73, 321, 324, 327-28, 331, 333, 335-41
Hannum, David, 244
Hare, Augustus, 165; *Cities of Southern Italy and Sicily*, 165
Harald II, King of England, 216
Harald Fairhair, King of Norway, 213, 215, 217
Harald Hardraade, King of Norway, 216
Hasan Dağ, **19**
Hasetshe, Syria, 275
Hastings, Battle of, 216
Hatay, Turkey, 302
Haynes, C. Vance, 231-37 *passim*, **234**
Hazor, Israel, 87-91, 98-99
Hecataeus, 176, 185
Hedeby, **199**

Hedin, Sven, 323
Helvetii, 180
Henry VIII, King of England, 196
Henry ("The Navigator"), Prince of Portugal, 6
Heraklion, Crete, 35; Archaeological Museum, 35
Herbert, Lady Evelyn Stanhope, 141-44
Herculaneum, Italy, 6, 148-61; architecture, 159; baths, 156; excavation, **161**; sculpture, **148**
Herjulfson, Bjarni, 217
Herod, King of Israel, 284
Herodotus, 64, 66-67, 71, 108, 176, 286, 293; quoted, 67
Hissarlik, Anatolia, 6
Hittites, 7, 60-64, 182
Homer, 6, 59, 63, 293; *The Iliad*, 6, 66-67, 108, 304
Homo sapiens sapiens, 7
Homosexuality, 173
Hopei Province, China, 336
Horace, 293, 301
Horsemanship: Egyptian rider, **68**; equipment, 71, 73, **74**; pony express, 67; riding, 64, 66-67; Scythian rider, **68**; training, 61; trappings, 182
Horses: breeding, 60-61; cavalry, 61, 64, 67, 75, **76**; ceramic, 316, 322, 344; *Eohippus*, 58; *Equus caballus*, 58; in Europe, 76; in farming, 75; first used with chariots, 59-60; grazing, 63, 75; in Ice Age (painting), **233**; Przhevalski's horse, 59, 64, 71; racing, 66, 67, 75; raising, 61, **70**, **71**; sculpture, 329-31, 336; as status symbol, 59; in tomb findings, 63, 331; types of, 59, 63; in warfare, 60-61, 67; wild, 58
Housman, A. E., 310
Housing, 12, 17-19. See also Building and construction.
Hrdlička, Aleš, 226, 230
Hsiao-t'un, 328
Hsien-yang, China, 318, 341
Hsuan-tsang, 324-25
Huascar, Prince of the Incas, 255
Hull, George, 242-46
Humboldt, Alexander von, 225
Hunan Medical College, Hunan Province, China, 334
Hunt, Arthur S., 109, 118, 308
Hyksos, 59-60

I

Ibit-Lim, King of Ebla, 85
Ibn-Rustah, 216
Ice Age, 41, 224, 226, 228-30, 235-39; animals, 228-29; birds, 229; climate, 228, 239; plant life, 229
Iceland, 191, 193, 200, **200**, 201, 217
Idri-mi, King of Alalakh, 302, 305
Incas, 18, 245-271; agriculture, 248, 256, **256-57**; archaeological discoveries, 248, 268; architecture, 248, 250, **250**, 258; city planning, 250, **258**; clothing, **246**, **254**, 255; decline of culture, 264; government administration, 250, 255-57, 263; human sacrifice, **259**; language (Quechua), 256; medicine (trepanning), **266**; military tactics, 255-56; religion and customs, 248, 255-59, **259**; roads and bridges, 249-50, 256-58, **264**, **265**; ruins, 248, 267-68; Spanish conquest of, 249-58 *passim*, **260**, 264; time, measurement of, 256, **259**; treasures, 255, **260**, 264; weapons, 257, **266**; women, 255, **263**
India, 7, 41, 61, 73, 81, 176; empire, 327
Indian Ocean, 29
Indians (Bolivian), 270-71; religious myths, 271
Indians (North American), 133-34, 225-43 *passim*; anthropological studies of, 226; Apaches, 238; Athapascans, 237-38; burial customs, 133-34; burial sites, 133-34; clothing, 229; description of,

225; Eskimos, 237-38; housing, 229; hunting techniques, 239-41; languages, 237; as migrant hunters, 229; migrant routes, 238; Navajo, 237; Onondaga, 243; survival of, 241
Indus River Valley, 7, 11-12
Ingstad, Helge, 218
Inishmore, Aran Islands, **174**
Inner Mongolia, 343
Iran, 26, **56**, 61, 64
Iraq, 134
Ireland, 179, 181; Irish temperament, 186; monks and monasteries, 193, 200, 294, 310
Iri River, 282
Ischia, Italy, 34
Ishmael, 87
Ishtar, 85
Isis, 45, 49, **49**
Israel, ancient kingdom of, 61, 93, 95, 98, 104; building, 95, 98-99; engineering, 88, 89, 99; fall of, 99; industry, 94, 95; northern kingdom (Israel), 91, 93, 95, 98; people, 29, 61, 91-97; religion, 84-85, 95; southern kingdom (Judah), 93, 95, 98, 99, 100; wars of conquest, 89, 91, 95; united kingdom, 93-104 *passim*
Israel Museum, Jerusalem, 98; Shrine of the Book, 98
Israelites, 93-104 *passim*; exile of, 99-100
Istanbul, Turkey, 294; Grand Seraglio, 294

J

Jacob the Patriarch, 87
Jade, 331, 339
Jade Gate, Silk Road, 324
Jadhjagha, Syria, 275
Japan, 73, 226
Jarlshof, Shetland Islands, **210**
Jebusites, 95
Jefferson, Thomas, 133; quoted, 133-34
Jehu, King of Israel, 99
Jeremiah the Prophet, 286
Jericho, 10-14, 16, **16**, 18, 21, 26, 88, **88**, 89, **96**
Jerusalem, 10, 87, 95, 98-100; destruction of, 100; King Solomon's Temple, 92-95, 100
Jesus Christ, 51, 98, 126, 308
Jews, 286, 292; monotheism, 84. *See also* Israelites.
Jezebel, Princess of Tyre, 98-99
Jezreel, Plain of, 99
Jones, Louis C., 245
Jordan, 29
Jordan River, 88; valley, 88, **88**, **89**
Joshua, 88, **88**, 89
Judaea, Wilderness of, **96-97**
Judaeans, 99
Judah (southern kingdom). See Israel.
Judaism, 95
Julianehàb, Greenland, 217
Julius Caesar, 126, 176-77, 179, 188, 294, 300, 313-15
Justin, 221

K

Kabah, Mexico, 81
Kabbala, 51
Kadesh, Syria, 60-61
Kansu Province, China, 328, 336
Kashmir, 327
Kasr River, 286
Keats, John, 296, 310
Kensington, Minnesota, 218
Kenyon, Kathleen, 10, 18, 89, 91, 93, 95
Kermanshah, Iran, 17, 132
Khasneh al Faroun ("Pharaoh's Treasury"), Jordan, 30
Khirokitia, Cyprus, **17**, 21; reconstruction of, **17**
Khorsabad, Iraq, 129